The Enjoyment of Theatre

NOTRE DAME

Communication and Theatre

W9-BMS-571

The Enjoyment of Theatre

SECOND EDITION

KENNETH M. CAMERON
PATTI P. GILLESPIE
UNIVERSITY OF MARYLAND

MACMILLAN PUBLISHING COMPANY

NEW YORK

Collier Macmillan Publishers

LONDON

Copyright © 1989 Macmillan Publishing Company, a division of Macmillan, Inc.

PRINTED IN THE UNITED STATES OF AMERICA

All rights reserved. No part of this book may be reproduced or
transmitted in any form or by any means, electronic or mechanical,
including photocopying, recording, or any information storage and
retrieval system, without permission in writing from the publisher.

Earlier edition copyright © 1980 by Macmillan Publishing Company

Macmillan Publishing Company
866 Third Avenue, New York, New York 10022

Collier Macmillan Canada, Inc.

LIBRARY OF CONGRESS CATALOGING-IN-PUBLICATION DATA

Cameron, Kenneth M.,
    The enjoyment of theatre.

    Bibliography: p.
    Includes index.
    1. Theater. I. Gillespie, Patti P. II. Title.
PN2037.C27   1989   792'.09   87-38324
ISBN 0-02-318410-8

Printing: 1 2 3 4 5 6 7 8   Year: 9 0 1 2 3 4 5 6 7

Preface to the Second Edition

We have been encouraged by response to the first edition of this book to present it again in a form we believe to be better than its first. Our revisions throughout have been based on users' responses to the first edition.

Most obvious, perhaps, is the reordering of the historical material into the chronology usually seen. The theatre history, now consolidated in one section (the final one) and chronologically arranged, is intended as a coherent unit. Using concepts that have proven successful in our theatre history text, *Western Theatre: Revolution and Revival*, we have described the theatres of the past in a simple, interesting format suitable for the introductory student.

In addition, we have added an entirely new chapter to the section, "Theatre of Other Times and Places"—that on non-Western theatre. We intend here to give the beginner the first sense of the enormous richness of the theatres of Asia and Africa, but within the context of the definition of theatre that delimits the entire book.

Many teachers told us of their enthuasiam for the first edition's introductory chapters on the nature of theatre. Those remain largely unchanged, except for the addition of comparisons between the theatre and the novel and painting, the result of requests to expand that section's usefulness in a liberal arts curriculum. As well, in response to requests from the field, we have added an entirely new chapter to this section, "How to Read a Play," and have edited "How to See a Play" to emphasize the differences between a literary and a theatrical approach.

Two new chapters round off the section on theatre makers—one that explains briefly the major settings, theatre arrangements, and funding patterns in today's theatre; another that describes practitioners of theory and criticism and that burgeoning field, dramaturgy.

Newly illustrated, more tightly arranged, and altered in response to five years' experience of the book in colleges and universities, *The Enjoyment of Theatre* will appear in its second edition as a fully integrated text for the introductory course for either majors or non-majors. It seeks to answer the difficult questions of the field, but to answer them at a level and complexity that will not discourage the beginning student.

We hope that this second edition will receive as positive a reception as the first and that it will do an even better job of introducing students to an art we love.

PPG
KMC

Contents

The Enjoyment of Theatre

Theatre and Its

Audience

Theatre As a Performing Art

Shakespeare at Stratford, Ontario . . . *Carousel* at a high school in Iowa . . . a student-written play at the American College Theatre Festival . . . *Il Trovatore* at New York's Metropolitan Opera . . . rock concerts . . . *King Lear* in a modern setting. But—an urban drunk performing before ten people? A child of nine performing for herself? An actor rehearsing on an empty stage?

Performing arts are many things, but things that have in common *performance* and *art*.

Performance involves the body and/or the voice in doing something for somebody's enjoyment.

Art is an activity that makes its product for its own ends. It is also an activity that is self-contained and artificial: it does not need to have any

5

Figure 1-1. **Performance.** Magical in their ability to astonish and delight, the performing arts bring unique experiences to their audiences. *ANERCA* by Figures of Speech Theatre. *(Photo by Rose Marasco.)*

immediate use in the world. (For example, sign painting is an application of some of the techniques of an art, painting; however, sign painting is an activity devoted almost exclusively to its usefulness—making signs—whereas painting is an art that has no *useful* product at all, although its product is often very expensive and much sought after.)

So, the performing arts are human activities that make or make up stories or movements or sounds or combinations of those things for people's enjoyment. They are highly diverse, each appealing in very different ways to different responses.

Yet what is to be prized about the performing arts is their very diversity, their variety, and their many mutual contradictions, because human beings thrive on artistic diversity. A healthy culture (like a healthy ecosystem) is one that encourages such variety; a culturally healthy individual is one who can enjoy a variety of these seemingly polarized activities—going to a movie one night, a ballet another, a baseball game on Saturday afternoon, a symphony concert on Sunday.

Because this is a book on the theatre, it will try to separate the theatre from the other performing arts. The separation is partly an artificial one, however, because one of the outstanding qualities of the theatre is the extent to which it contributes to and draws from other arts. Even for the individual theatre artist, such contributions and borrowings are valuable: actors dance and sing as well as act; they play baseball and create films, and they are often themselves members of the audience for other arts. Theatre artists—playwrights, actors, directors, designers—move from film to theatre to opera to spectacles like political events and pageants.

Because a healthy society welcomes diversity, healthy arts are themselves diverse; because artists create in diverse ways, audiences must be able to respond in diverse ways. The performing arts, it must be emphasized, are not competitors but relatives, and audiences need to learn to appreciate the entire family. Because each member of the family is complex, however, the study of any one of them takes care and time.

This is a book about one member of that family: the theatre.

Major Performing Arts and Related Activities

Enormous overlap exists among the performing arts, so much so that one of them—the theatre—has sometimes been seen as an amalgam of the others; in that view, theatre itself would be the umbrella that covers the performing arts. Although this idea fails as a definition of theatre, it is useful as a reminder that the theatre uses elements of other arts and that without them it would be a dull activity, indeed.

It is possible to include other arts *with* the word *theatre*—theatre dance, theatre music—so long as we remember that each art has its own special characteristics. We must not pretend that film, television, dance, opera, staged plays, and mime, for example, are all "theatre" in a vague and general way, or we will lose the crucial distinctions among them. The performing arts have much in common, but what they have in common does not make them identical. To talk about them and appreciate them, we must know both what they share and what they do *not* share; then, when we understand some of their similarities and their differences, we will be able to look at one of them more closely.

WHAT IS FILM?

In the movie films, he said, we only look at what is there already. Life shines on the shadow screen, as from the darkness of one's mind. It is a big business.

E. L. Doctorow, *Ragtime*

Soft music. Low lights. People taking their seats, whispering, chuckling. Popcorn. Rattle of candy papers. The music ends; the lights go to black. "Exit" signs glow. A bright image appears on a slightly concave screen: names. Images of people and places, real people, real places, their images *big*, colorful. The images move at the same rate as real people. Loud music. Voices—the people talk. The images embody a story about people. At rare times, the speed of the images slows; once, they even freeze like a still photograph. The way that these images are presented changes, sometimes giving us very close-in pictures, sometimes very distant ones. Sometimes we are presented with images of only part of what the human eye would really see—a hand, a flower, a road. Sometimes we do not even see what the human eye might look at in the same situation; the machine that makes the images is looking at something else, and that something else becomes of great importance to us. The story continues, the images flash on.

Film is a complex form of communication relying on putting things together simultaneously and sequentially.

John Harrington, *The Rhetoric of Film*

FILM:

1. Uses a projected image of events, places, and people and not the events, places, and people themselves.
2. Usually presents a story and characterization.
3. Gathers its audiences into special places ("theatres") but does not allow any interplay between the audience and the images because the images have no sensitivities of their own.
4. Can be repeated identically any number of times until the film itself breaks down—but the film can be reprinted and thus saved from any sign of deterioration whatsoever.

It was René Clair who pointed out that if two or three people were together on a stage, the dramatist must ceaselessly motivate their being there at all. But the film audience accepts mere sequence as rational. Whatever the camera turns to, the audience accepts.

Marshall McLuhan, *Understanding Media*

WHAT IS TELEVISION?

[T]he audience for American television is what may be called a mass society [that] has somewhat different values and social controls from the traditional western society. In the traditional society, the upper classes set the standards of the culture and the lower classes followed along.

David Potter, in *"The Historical Perspective"*

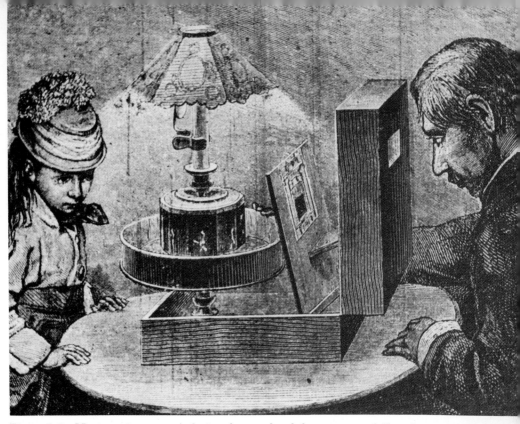

Figure 1-2. **Motion pictures.** A device that predated the camera and film, the praxinoscope allowed very small audiences to see simulated movement.

A living-room. Few lights. Sounds from the rest of the house, from the street. Somebody passing through the room to the kitchen. A screen, twenty inches or so in its long dimension; slightly distorted sound with poor treble values. Images of real people and places, the visual quality of the images rather poor in comparison with the real people and the real places, these images being made up of moving dots. Saturated colors in rather oversimple, slightly unreal values. The images of the people are playing out a story, but one of the people in the living room does not like the story and presses a switch, and another story appears. This story seems to be preferable, but it stops and other people appear and begin to talk about automobiles. Nobody in the living room seems to care much that the images are talking about automobiles, but one of the real people leaves the room and comes back with a can of beer. The images stop talking about automobiles and the other images appear and begin to act out their story again. It is a funny story, and there is loud laughter with the funny parts, as if a big audience were sitting with the people in the living room. There is an image of a living room in the story, and it looks remarkably like the living room in which the people are sitting to watch the story. In the story living room, they even have a screen of the same sort, on which other images are being shown. They are images of a news story about a real disaster of a year before.

Time was when a person went to the movies and surrendered, know-
ingly, to a few hours of fantasy, the walk from home to cinema mark-
ing the transfer from world of fact to world of fiction. Now the unreal
filters from the "tube" into the home along with the real.

Daniel Shorr, "The National Seance," in *Review* Magazine

TELEVISION:

1. Uses an image made up of dots on a cathode-ray-tube "screen"
   to create a record of events, places, and people.
2. Presents both stories with characterization and precise records of
   actual events, or "news."
3. Does not gather its audience but locates its outlets (the screens)
   in informal living spaces (living rooms, bedrooms, bars) and allows no interplay between audience and images because the images have no sensitivities of their own.
4. Can be repeated identically any number of times if recorded on
   film or tape; however, the commercial structure of the industry
   that presents television in the United States makes the frequent
   repetition of most programs unlikely.

The cool TV medium provides depth structure in art and entertain-
ment alike, and creates audience involvement in depth as well.

Marshall McLuhan, *Understanding Media*

WHAT IS OPERA?

Without music, opera is not opera.

J. Merill Knapp, *The Magic of Opera*

Figure 1-3. **Television.** Comfortable
in a living space, the audience can see
the work again and again through modern technology. *(Photo by Augustin*
Aldrete.)

A huge theatre. Elegance of decor, elegant dress on many of the audience. An entire orchestra in a pit between the audience and the stage. The lights dim; the orchestra plays—melodies, promises of what the performance to come will hold. Darkness, then stage light. A crowd in Renaissance costume, gathered before the gates of a Renaissance palace. They sing. An officer strolls among them. *He* sings. Everybody sings—nobody talks. The scene changes to a palace courtyard on a huge scale. Two women sing—glorious, soaring melodies that fill the large theatre with their voices. The audience applauds and the performance stops while the applause continues. Then the singers continue, performing a story of high passion and extreme situations—revenge, coincidence, violence. They sing in Italian, a

Figure 1-4. **Opera.** Its dominant "language," music, gives opera an extraordinary appeal. *(Photo by Augustin Aldrete.)*

language the audience does not understand. The story is printed in the program so that the audience will know what is going on, but most of them know the opera so well that they do not need the notes.

Our inner life . . . provides music with the form through which music expresses that life. Every contradiction ceases from the moment that the form and the object of the expression are identical.

Adolphe Appia, *Music and the Art of the Theatre*

OPERA:

1. Uses live performers on a real stage in artificial (i.e., made-for-the-purpose) settings.
2. Uses story and characterization.
3. Gathers its audience into theatres that allow the audience to influence the performance through their reactions.
4. Can be repeated, but with the inevitable variations natural to any human endeavor: because of the production structure of commercial opera companies worldwide, however, it is extremely rare that the same singers will repeat the same opera frequently for a long time in the same theatre, and most singers take a day or two between performances.
5. Uses an orchestra, typically located between the stage and the audience, and uses music as the dominant means of communication, both actor-to-actor and actor-to-audience.

[Opera] may be a museum piece in the contemporary world, but the true opera lover is not daunted. He is always seeking an amalgam in performance [that] will produce a miraculous result—that moment when drama, orchestra, singing, and spectacle unite to achieve what is promised by a composer and librettist of genius.

J. Merill Knapp, *The Magic of Opera*

WHAT IS DANCE?

Dancing employs rhythm in both spheres—audible and visual. It is a time-space art, and the only one.

Agnes de Mille, *The Book of the Dance*

A theatre, a stage. Low house lights. Loudspeakers for sound. Lights to black and stage lights up: an intense blue, like sky, a picket fence, a suggestion of beach or country road or moor. Two women in very long skirts. Music through the loudspeakers. The women move to the music, their movements rhythmic, stately, visually beautiful, yet not like the movement of ordinary human beings. Their movement is to ordinary human movement what the voice of the opera singer is to the speaking voice—an extension of it, virtually another kind of reality with one foot in the mundane world. The women's bodies are disciplined and trained, even athletic. Slowly, the women grow, become ten feet tall. We understand that it must be that they are carried by other dancers who are hidden by the long skirts, but our understanding does not much change the strange and wonderful effect of their height. Two men appear. They move in the same rhythmic and beautiful way as the women, but they do not increase their height. Dwarfed by the women, they dance with and around them. There is the suggestion of a story—there is interaction among the dancers, clear suggestions that they see and respond to each other. Their actions suggest familiar human events—meeting, wooing, rejecting, loving. The men collapse; perhaps they are dead. The women's height changes. They dance together in "virtual spontaneous gesture."

The primary illusion of dance is a virtual realm of Power—not actual, physically exerted power, but appearances of influence and agency created by virtual gesture.

Suzanne Langer, *Feeling and Form*

DANCE:

1. Uses live performers in a real space with artificial settings.
2. Sometimes presents stories and characters.
3. Gathers its audience into theatres and allows the audience to interact with the performance; audiences can influence the performance through their reactions.
4. Can be repeated, with the inevitable variations natural to any human endeavor.
5. Movement—both aesthetic and symbolic—is the principal means of communication, usually to musical accompaniment.

The symbol of the world, the balletic realm of forces, is the world and dancing is the human spirit's participation in it.

Suzanne Langer, *Feeling and Form*

WHAT ARE ATHLETIC EVENTS?

The battle of Waterloo was won on the playing fields of Eton.

The Duke of Wellington

A brisk October afternoon. Bright sunlight, the air cool enough for sweaters and wool jackets. An oval stadium that seats thirty thousand people; in its center, the green and grassy stretch of a football field. Food and some alcohol in the audience; color in the stands and on the field—pom-poms, pennants, young men and women in cheerleaders' uniforms, two uniformed

Figure 1-5. **Dance.** Dance has become extraordinarily popular in an age when spoken language has become suspect. *Post Cards*, by Larry Warren, performed by Maryland Dance Company, company-in-residence, Department of Dance, University of Maryland. *(Photo by Dennis Deloria.)*

marching bands. Two teams in differently colored uniforms. Four people in striped shirts on the field; one blows a whistle, and a ball is kicked from one end of the field toward the other. A player in blue catches the ball and begins to run; players in red wrestle him to the ground. The blue players gather together, then line up on each side of and behind the ball. One of them passes the ball backward. Players charge in all directions, blue and red mingling in fierce, violent contact. The audience cheers. The cheerleaders do somersaults and handsprings, and they exhort the audience to more noise. The blue players kick the ball to the red, who move it back up the field with skill and determination. The audience becomes noisier. The red cross a white line with the ball, and a larger part of the audience makes more noise than ever, tooting horns and ringing bells and shouting. Two men dressed in a horse costume canter onto the field and cavort about. The players line up again and prepare for the red team to kick the ball to the blues again.

When the One Great Scorer comes to write against your name—He marks—not that you won or lost—but how you played the game.

Grantland Rice, *Alumnus Football*

ATHLETICS:

1. Use live performers in a real performing place.
2. Use competition instead of story; have no characterization. (However, sports audiences often create near-mythic "characters" around sports heroes.)
3. Gather their audiences into prepared—and often very large—spaces and allow the audience reaction to influence the event.
4. Can never be repeated in an identical way. The rules of sports guarantee that the *form* will be repeated, but it is in the nature of games and competitions that the outcome will always be different and will always be in doubt until the very end.

Figure 1-6. **Athletics.** Carefully defined by rules, modern sports involve audiences deeply in the outcome of contests, touching some of the same areas of response as do performing arts. *(Courtesy of the University of Rochester. Chris T. Quillen photo.)*

Anyone who doesn't know how to play is illiterate. . . . Sport is where an entire life can be compressed into a few hours, where the emotions of a lifetime can be felt on an acre or two of ground, where a person can suffer and die and rise again on six miles of trails. . . . Sport is a theatre where sinner can turn saint and a common man can become an uncommon hero.

George Sheehan, in *On the Run*

WHAT IS VISUAL ART (PAINTING)?

Art is not truth; art is a lie that reveals the truth.

Pablo Picasso

The museum gallery is empty except for a bored guard. Twenty paintings are hung around it at eye level. A visitor enters and slowly circles the room, giving about thirty seconds to each painting, then returns to one painting and stands in front of it for a full minute. The visitor's eyes roam over the painting, returning several times to the same point. The visitor steps back, views the painting from farther away, then leaves.

It is actually a duty to paint the rich and magnificent aspects of nature. We are in need of gaiety and happiness, of hope and love. The more ugly, old, vicious, ill, poor I get, the more I want to take my revenge by producing a brilliant color, well arranged, resplendent.

Vincent van Gogh

PAINTING:

1. Has no performers; the work as perceived is separate from the artist.
2. Does not tell stories, but sometimes depicts moments of stories and pictures of characters; the story itself must already be known to the viewer or must be provided by an outside source.
3. Has no defined time or place for its audience, although modern museums and galleries draw audiences to certain places at certain times; the audience is limited by viewing distance and angle.
4. Is not replicable; copies are separate works in other media (print, photograph) except for rare direct copies in paint, which, once identified as copies, are treated as different from the original.
5. Color, line, and form are the primary means of communication in a form whose perception is instantaneous, or at least unordered and not bound to any real audience time; the viewer may "start" anywhere, for the work, having no linear form, has no beginning, middle, or end.

Figure 1-7. **Painting.** Its perception not restricted by time, the order of its perception not defined, painting is markedly different from performing arts. "The Annunciation" by Simone Martini.

WHAT IS LITERATURE (THE NOVEL)?

The novel is merely gossip.
Virginia Woolf

A room. A woman sits in an easy chair, one leg thrown over the chair arm, in her lap a book. She reads, once glancing ahead fifty pages and reading briefly there. A clock strikes; she jumps up, puts on a coat, and rushes out, taking the book. At the subway stop and then all the way to work, she continues reading. At the end of the day, she reads again, but has to hunt for her place. After watching television part of the evening, she returns to the book.

Make 'em laugh; make 'em cry; make 'em wait.
Charles Reade, *Recipe for a Successful Novel*

17

NOVELS:

1. Use no live performers (except when someone—rarely—reads aloud).
2. Present stories and characters.
3. Limit their audience to one per example (except when someone—rarely—reads aloud) and allow that audience to read where it likes, when it likes.
4. In their published form are already replicated; the individual reader's experience of reading is not recoverable in precisely the same way.
5. Use written language as their primary means of communication and interpose a voice or point of view between work and audience.
6. Have their own time scheme, which is independent of the time of the audience, and their own order, which the audience can violate (by looking ahead or back).

A novel is a mirror carried along a main road.

Stendhal, *Rouge et Noir*

WHAT IS THEATRE?

The theatre is the home of the Now.

A theatre. An audience, waiting, expectant in the half-light. The accents of New York mingle with those of the Midwest and the South. Many people are carefully dressed, some informally. Between audience and stage there is an orchestra pit, but there is no orchestra visible; instead, loudspeakers flank the stage opening. Darkness. Stage light. A voice, music; an authoritative man is counting a rhythm for a group of dancers. He begins to teach them a simple dance routine, then withdraws into the audience part of the theatre and directs the others through a loudspeaker. There are characterizations and a story, but the characters both talk and sing their emotions and their experiences. We learn that they are trying out for the chorus of a Broadway show. They dance. They sing. They make the audience laugh, listen, sit still with attentiveness. The sexual attractiveness of several of the women onstage is emphasized by their costumes and is part of what is sung and talked about. The language and the subject matter, by the standards of many communities, is frank, even a little shocking. But the audience responds with joyous laughter, noisy applause.

"Is this a theatre?" whispered Smike, in amazement; "I thought it was a blaze of light and finery."

"Why, so it is," replied Nicholas, hardly less surprised: "but not by day, Smike—not by day."

Charles Dickens, *Nicholas Nickleby*

Figure 1-8. **Theatre.** Theatre uses elements of many arts and technologies in affecting its audiences; its stories vary from elemental myth to contemporary news. Shakespeare's *Julius Caesar* at the University of Washington. *(Directed by Robert Hobbs.)*

THEATRE:

1. Uses live actors on a real stage with artificial settings.
2. Uses story and characterization.
3. Gathers its audiences into defined spaces and allows the audience reaction to affect the performance.
4. Can be repeated, but with the inevitable variations natural to any human endeavor.

. . . can this cockpit hold
The vasty fields of France? or may we cram
Within this Wooden O the very casques
That did affright the air at Agincourt?
. . . let us, ciphers to this great accompt,
On your imaginative forces work.

Suppose within the girdle of these walls
Are now confin'd two mighty monarchies. . . .
Think when we talk of horses that you see them
Printing their proud hoofs i' the receiving earth;
For 'tis your thoughts that now must deck our kings. . . .

William Shakespeare, *The Life of King Henry the Fifth*

SOME ASPECTS OF THEATRE

A comparison of these discussions may give the impression that there is so much overlap among these activities that only some mechanical differences separate them—that, for example, theatre is simply opera without the music, or that film is merely theatre recorded on strips of acetate, or that television is nothing but film made visible with electronic impulses. Such a view, however, is woefully inaccurate. It is not entirely false—the mechanical differences do have significance—but it does not begin to touch on other differences.

When an important element in a performing art changes, the art itself changes. That is, a composer who sets a play to music does not automatically create an opera. When, however, a story from one performing art is transferred to another—as, for example, when Victorien Sardou's play was made the basis of Puccini's opera *Tosca*—it is clear that, although the superficial elements of the versions are similar (basically the same story, the same characters, and many of the same audience-actor elements that opera and theatre share), the end products are different. *Tosca* is not simply Sardou's play sung. Its internal structure is different; its emphases are different; its audience's expectations are different. For, where the theatre audience draws its pleasure from story suspense, brilliance of language, and acting performance, the opera audience draws its principal pleasure from the glory of melody and the performance of the singers.

In fact, the differences that seem to separate dance from theatre, theatre from opera, opera from film, and so on create other and more profound differences. The *fact* of film defines the difference between movies and theatre; but the *art* of film is made possible by camera work, by quick cutting, by a juxtaposition of images that is impossible in the theatre, by a disjunction (sometimes) between sound and image that is unlikely in the theatre, and so on.

The very structure of a film script—the way the action moves forward—is vastly different from that of a play because film gives its information differently. Indeed, it is not too much to say that *the basic differences among the performing arts are founded on their differing means of communication.* Thus, it is possible to have the same story at the center of a performance in each performing art, but to have the performances themselves turn out to be markedly different because of the differences in the arts. For example, Shakespeare's *Romeo and Juliet* has been a staged play, a ballet, an opera, several films, and, in an adaptation, a Broadway musical. (See Figure 1-9.)

Figure 1-9. **Variations on a Basic Story.** *Romeo and Juliet* and *West Side Story* have the same story, but in performance they appear very different. *(Wright State University. Directed by, top, Abe J. Bassett; and, bottom, James Thorp.)*

All are significantly different, even though the Shakespearean text itself is the basis for much of the script in the film and opera versions. One of the things that happens in a case like this is that the artists themselves make decisions that select from the basic story—in this case, Shakespeare's play—those elements that will best be communicated by their art, the opera composer selecting those moments and events that are best communicated musically, the choreographer those moments and events that are best communicated in structured and pleasing movement.

Another thing that happens is that each art focuses its audience's attention in a different way. The production of Shakespeare's play may lead us to watch and listen to the actor, the richness of his or her voice, and the poetic beauty of Shakespeare's verse; the opera may lead us to listen to the music instead of watching the singer or following the dramatic development of the story; the dance may ask us to watch and to respond sympathetically with our own bodies, almost forgetting story and character, which become a pretext for the movement.

ART AND LIFE

After reading these discussions of artistic and athletic events, someone might be tempted to look at still other activities and say, "But what about rock concerts? Or the circus? Or church services? Aren't they related, too?"

Of course they are. So are many unplanned events that draw a crowd and that are then affected by that crowd—an argument between two drivers whose bumpers have locked, for example, or an impromptu street dance, or a political rally, or even a classroom with a teacher and students. Are not these in some sense theatre, too—or at least performance?

The answer, of course, is yes—but a qualified yes. In order to talk about the theatre, in order to understand the art of the theatre, we must distinguish somehow between that art and life. We must define *theatre* to give it a separate identity despite its many spillovers elsewhere.

An older definition of *theatre* included things like the separation of actors and audience, the shape and structure of the building in which theatre was done, the kinds of things that actors performed, and the aesthetics of the art. On the other hand, a radically modern definition would reject those elements and would try to include recent movements into the streets and fields ("street theatre," "guerrilla theatre"), as well as group therapy, parades, and many other activities; it might not distinguish between actors and audience; it might have difficulty identifying the things that the actors performed.

In this book, we distinguish between theatre as an artistic event and the appearance of some elements of theatre in life. For this reason, the argument between the two angry drivers is excluded from our idea of theatre—because it lacks the single characteristic that most separates the art of the theatre from theatrical events in life: *artistic self-awareness*, the intention to create art; as well, it lacks the two elements that are part of self-awareness: *preparation* and *discipline*

By *self-awareness*, we mean the performer's awareness that what is done is meant to accomplish certain ends and to have certain effects on the audience.

By *preparation*, we mean the anticipation of performing, with all the necessary training, psychological orientation, and talent.

By *discipline*, we mean the admission that performance exists for both audience and performer, and that the performer lives life so that the performance (whether by actor, playwright, director, or designer) will be at optimum level every time it is undertaken.

Artistic self-awareness does not guarantee that every performance will be good. It does try to guarantee that what is done will, in fact, be a performance and not an accident and that it will aspire to be art.

To define *performance*, then, so that it will exist within the definition of *theatre*, it should have, besides self-awareness or intention, three other elements: the *actor*, the *audience*, and the *action*.

By *actor*, we mean a performer who impersonates—that is, somebody who uses the pronoun *I* and means somebody else.

By *audience*, we mean a group of people separate from the actor who are gathered together for the specific purpose of attending the event.

By *action*, we mean an invented human development within which the actor's impersonation functions—*not an action that is told about, but one that is embodied by the actor and seen by the audience.*

The theatre, then, is an art in which performers, by impersonating, represent or embody imitations of people in a story that is shown to an audience.

The theatre is not better or worse than other performing arts because of its special nature; it has its special attributes, from which both advantages and disadvantages inevitably spring. Its greatest advantage is *immediacy*, the sense of "nowness" that arises from theatre's *showing* of human actions rather than telling about them. The theatre has been called "the home of the Now"; the person who said that meant that the theatre is a unique art because, in it, fictional events happen with convincing truthfulness even as we watch, and they happen and are gone even as a moment exists and is gone, never to be recaptured. The audience for this "home of the Now" must pay close attention because the Now will vanish; the playwright must work with great skill to make the Now so important that audiences *must* pay attention; the actors must perform brilliantly so that the Now will be arresting, vibrant, more memorable than life. Tomorrow night, the actors will perform a little differently because they are humans and not machines; tomorrow, the audience will be different, and the rich interaction between actors and audience will change.

Because of the physical presence of the actor, the theatre presents a more immediate image of human behavior than any other art. "In person" is always a selling point for live performances; "I saw her *in person!*" Or, even more magically, "I sat in the first row; I was close enough to touch her!" We are

Figure 1-10. **The Actor.** Bill Swinney as Vito in *The Realist* by Kevin O'Morrison.

human beings; we are touched, aroused, dazzled by the immediacy of other human beings. Neither the heightened intensity of portrait painting nor the close-up intensity of film can equal the impact of the live performer because we are in the theatre with those living human beings who present their stories so convincingly and entertainingly.

Perhaps, as audience members, we human beings are gossips, to put it baldly. We remain fascinated by the humanness of being human, and theatre is the art that brings us up closest to a human activity that is rivetingly like life in its immediacy but satisfyingly unlike life in its artistic separation.

The other side of the virtue of immediacy is the partial disadvantage of *nonrecoverability*. As we have seen, film and television performances can be recovered exactly as they were made; the theatrical performance cannot. When the moment is gone, it is entirely gone. We cannot play it over as we play a videotape, except in memory. Nor can we turn forward to see how a performance will come out; nor can we put the performance aside for a while and pick it up later; nor can we interrupt it (as we could, for example, a tape) and start it up again later.

Each theatrical performance is unique. The actor is quite right to sigh, "Ah, you should have seen me last night!"

"What I love," one critic wrote, "is that at any moment I may see the leading man suffer a heart attack!"

Thus, *the theatre performance proceeds at its own pace and must be followed at that pace*, and for better or for worse, *it can be neither replicated nor repeated*.

The theatre's immediacy gives it an inherent *intensity*; the theatre's very nature as an art gives it an intensity far beyond that of most of life. To say, however, that a great moment in the theatre is more highly charged than one in opera or dance is not true; it is best to say that they are different. Both dance and opera seem to offer potential for greater intensity in at least some moments of their performances. On the other hand, there is less that either dance or opera can offer that will match the illusion of a great comic or tragic scene greatly played, when it is neither movement nor music that we follow, but convincing and immediate human action.

Another aspect of theatre that can work both for and against its effectiveness is its *scenic and spatial limitation*. Film, for example, can take us anywhere and show us actual images of distant places, even on a vast scale (the Grand Canyon, the city of Hong Kong, outer space). The theatre can give us replicas of such places but can give them only on a scale appropriate to the actors working in or in front of the scene. Also, many kinds of activity are difficult or impossible to bring on the stage—aerial dogfights, elephant stampedes, and chariot races among them. Film and television can not only show such things, they can also show selective close-ups that will heighten our awareness and enjoyment of the events: speeding hooves, snorting nostrils, whirling wheels.

If the theatre tried to rival such scenes, it would have to offer compromises, as it did, for example, near the end of the nineteenth century when chariot races *were* shown onstage by putting the horses on treadmills. (See Figure 1-11.) Common sense told the audience that the treadmills were there, or else the horses would have dashed off into the wings and there would have been no race to see. Yet audiences loved the scenes, even though they were seeing a rather obvious trick—and their enjoyment emphasizes a paradox in the theatre's problems with scenic space: the very restrictions on space and locale increase the audience's enjoyment *because they know the illusion is an illusion*. Put another way, this means that *the artificial nature of theatre gives everything put on the stage a paradoxically heightened reality*. It is a curious thing, but an audience will applaud a scene in which real food is really cooked on a real stove, exactly as if they had never seen food cooking on stoves, much less been able to see such things in their own kitchens.

Thus, the spatial and scenic limitations of the theatre are a seeming disadvantage that can most potently be turned to a remarkable advantage. It is the essence of theatre that compromises, often in the form of symbolic representations, must be made: the "wooden O" must be made to hold both

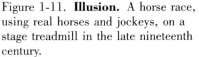

Figure 1-11. **Illusion.** A horse race, using real horses and jockeys, on a stage treadmill in the late nineteenth century.

France and England; six men must be made to represent an army; a platform must be made to represent a throne.

The real art of the theatre lies, then, not in presenting life, but in presenting heightened visions of life within the special conditions of immediacy, intensity, and symbolic representation.

Theatre and the Performing Audience

A close connection exists between an art and its society: art is either an expression of society or a response to it. The theatre is both: it directly expresses social structures and ideas, and it responds to social pressures to cause changes in itself. The expression and the response happen because of two groups: theatre artists and theatre audiences.

What Is an Audience?

An audience is people at an event.

But is it one person? Or ten? Ten thousand? Ten million?

One answer would be that the size of an audience depends on the artistic

27

medium. Ten million people could easily make up the "audience" for a television production, and many more than that have watched certain hugely successful specials; however, to have an audience for even the most successful of stage plays or musicals and number it as high as ten million, we would have to imagine filling the largest of New York theatres every night for years. An "audience" of ten or twenty million people for a film is possible, if the film is shown often enough; ten or twenty million as the "audience" for an opera or ballet would require changing the way that most ballet and opera companies work, because they do not present the same things night after night after night for years and years.

To speak of an "audience" of millions for a play or an opera or a dance performance, however, is fruitless. The millions who watch a television show or who see a film over a period of months in many different movie houses are not an "audience" in the way that the people gathered to see a single performance in a theatre are an audience. The television "audience," in fact, disintegrates into many smaller ones in living rooms and bedrooms and bars, just as the "audience" for a film disintegrates into many smaller groups who have seen it in many different places on many different occasions. In the sense that we use the word for the theatre, then, *an audience is a group drawn together by a theatrical event, at a certain time and place, that is aware of itself as a group.*

This group self-awareness is very important. The sense of belonging to the group and of contributing to its size is one of the remarkable aspects of theatre, the rich and exciting consciousness of a shared experience in which each individual's response is heightened by those sharing it and by the awareness that one's own response heightens that of others. Although television comedy often uses a "laugh track" or plays the laughter of a live audience to simulate the experience of the theatregoer, the experience simply is not the same for the individual sitting in a living room. In the theatre, the individual's laughter is buoyed up, expanded, made more joyous by other laughter, or the individual's solemn understanding of a serious play is made richer because other people are responding in the same way. Both kinds of response are tied into the idea of *permission*, the agreement common to the members of the social group—the audience—that it is all right to laugh at these events or to be solemnly moved by them. This *permission* is an extension of the very nature of theatre art: theatre as art tells its audience that what is being embodied is *not* life and that it is permissible to respond to it in sometimes unusual ways (laughing out loud, for example, at a character who is weeping in a comedy). Permission is a *social* phenomenon, carried over from the outer society into the temporary society of the audience itself.

The theatre is a social as well as an artistic experience then, and *a theatre audience is a social entity, however temporary.* Its members are drawn together by the event and by the "appetite for art" that makes them want to enjoy the event. They enter into a relationship with the event and with each other.

To join a theatre audience is to enter willingly into two remarkable rela-

Figure 2-1. **Group Self-awareness.** Even in an undefined space—here, New York's Central Park—an audience's sense of shared experience is important to its responses.

tionships, one with the artistic event on the stage and one with the other people in the audience. The audience's goal is *to share*.

A theatre audience, then, is a group drawn together by an artistic event at a certain time and place, who are aware of themselves as a group and whose goal is to share—laughter, tears, solemnity, joy, wonder.

What Determines Audience Size?

It would be difficult, it seems, for one person to be an audience. Still, royalty used to have plays performed especially for them, and "theatres royal" had special boxes for the king or queen or duke. Anyone who has gone to a movie in the early afternoon has been a member of a very small audience, and frequently we sit alone to watch television. We have to admit, therefore, that the group is not essential to the idea of audience in every medium, but *where the group is lacking, the medium will make up for the difference by saturating the viewer or by providing an artificial group* (by using a laugh track, for example, or backing much dramatic action with appropriate music), or else *the medium, lacking a group audience, will be unsatisfying.*

But how large a group is an effective audience? Twenty? Two thousand?

Two forces are at work, and they often work against each other. One is the force of the group, partly unconscious but very strong. "Groupness" needs a number of people in a confined space, or at least a *defined* space; it is no

Figure 2-2. **Audience Size.** An audience too small for its space is uncomfortable and may lose its enjoyment of the event, as in this comic early nineteenth-century engraving.

accident that theatre interiors are designed, when possible, without enormous aisles or empty spaces along the sides, because people who sit there feel "cold"; they are left out. In the same way, large theatres that sometimes host events that draw small audiences frequently have movable walls or screens to enclose the small audience—to give it a defined space in which it feels enclosed and comfortable.

A group in too big a space loses track of itself and stops behaving like an audience. It grows uneasy. It becomes self-conscious. Sometimes it becomes a mob. Schools that use their gymnasiums as theatres, for example, sometimes suffer because the huge, echoing gym space, with wide and empty gaps along the sides, encourages people to belong to a mob and not an audience.

The economics of the theatre is the force that is sometimes opposed to "groupness." It demands that the audience be big enough to pay the investors, the actors, the rent on the building, the author's royalties, the heat and light and maintenance of the space. Thus, groupness may sense that three hundred people is the right audience size; economics may demand three thousand.

Some people would say that economics is a false force and should be ignored. "An audience is people," the argument would go, "and people are more important than money." However, actors are people, too, and so are authors and maintenance persons and those who sell heat and light. A theatre ignores economics at its peril; when it does, it will have to survive with actors who do not care about being paid, authors who do not collect royalties, and so on. Such theatres certainly exist and have existed off and on for a very long time. The tension between group sense and economics has been partly responsible for the waves of "group theatres" and "little theatres" that have appeared in every age since at least the democratic revolutions at the end of the eighteenth century.

From the varying points of view of different audience members and different theatre artists, there is no perfect audience size and no perfect audience space. Most theatres are compromises in this respect, and sometimes not very good compromises, especially when theatres have become physically huge in order simply to hold more people. In those cases particularly, the little theatres and the free theatres become the conscience of the time.

Again, variety and diversity must be allowed.

Who Goes to What?

Few people are so committed to a single performing art or even to a single activity that they pursue it to the exclusion of all others. Devoted theatregoers are also members of audiences for ballet, baseball, television, and opera. Still, there are preferences among audience members, and there are tendencies toward alignments of audiences that are significant for theatre artists and theatre businesspeople.

Recent surveys give an idea of who the people are who make up America's huge audience and of what they go to see. The audience is fairly young, with the majority under forty; it has more women than men, although other figures suggest that the male-female imbalance is changing. There are very few blue-collar occupations among this audience, but a large proportion of "professional and managerial" workers. Thus, for performing arts audiences at American performances, the mainstream of middle-class society is best represented: fairly young, affluent, mixed in gender.

Overlap from one performing art to another is significant. Recently, a very successful midwestern repertory theatre had its highest overlap with audience members who attended symphony concerts, the lowest overlap with those who attended jazz concerts; the second highest overlap was with professional baseball, followed by opera, professional football, and ballet. Some of the diversity can probably be explained by the theatre's location in a city with strong professional sports teams and an excellent symphony orchestra, but the variety may be typical of the American situation, where breadth of taste typifies theatregoers. Shakespeare and baseball, Beethoven and Molière—audiences are able to love them all.

The theatre audience is a social group, but it is a group only of the moment. Just as the performance is a will-o'-the-wisp, so, too, is its audience. For all their sharing and their common experience, there is no suggestion that, by nature, the people in a theatre audience will ever come together under other circumstances.

Figure 2-3. **Audience Taste.** Audiences enjoy many kinds of activities without contradiction, especially when social lines can be crossed, as in twentieth-century America or this eighteenth-century English fair. Such fairs, with their own legal and social systems, gave people "permission" to behave differently and thus to enjoy many kinds of entertainment.

Why Do They Come?

What brings an audience into a theatre in the first place? It is easy enough to say people come to the theatre for entertainment. But *entertainment* has many meanings: some people are "entertained" by doing mathematical puzzles, others by patronizing massage parlors—and people are "entertained" at home by television, at baseball games, and at rock concerts.

Why is it that on a given night, people go to the *theatre* instead of staying home or going to a ball game or a movie or a rock concert?

Three things can be cited.

THE STIRRING OF THE IMAGINATION

All art stirs the imagination, sends it on inward journeys that, perhaps, only dreams and madness offer it otherwise. The theatre does this with enormous visual potency and tremendous immediacy; the theatre is *now*. Only contemporary film, with its intense color and its saturated, heightened sound, is a serious rival in the presentation of fictions, or "stories." The opera and the dance, too, offer other qualities: superb, soaring vocal music in one and astonishing physical athleticism and gorgeous movement in the other.

The theatre, however, has traditionally stirred its audience's imagination by giving *less* rather than *more* stimulation—not by saturating it, but by tantalizing and catalyzing it with hints. It has often put a mask on the actor's face, taking away facial mobility; it has used symbolic or suggestive scenery, or even no scenery at all, to create a richer imaginative *idea* of reality than any imitation reality could give; it has taken its stories from dreams and myth and fantasy and has thus touched levels of the mind and heart below the purely rational.

THE REVELATION OF THE FAMILIAR

Perhaps because mirrors fascinate people, visions of themselves and of their own real world have fascinated audiences. "It's so real!" is sometimes a compliment for a theatre piece. Are we entranced with our own image? Or is it that humankind is a very complex species worthy of its own deep examinings?

Reality surrounds us: Look out the window; there is reality. Watch the man next door, the woman behind the desk, the child in the playground; they are reality. Do we build special structures to house them, pay money to watch them? Hardly.

Theatregoing is a paradox. People buy tickets, travel distances, go through great difficulty to see images of themselves and their surroundings "in play," in something that is "just like life." But it is *like* life, not life itself, and it is *like* life in a very special way: compressed, focused, made magical.

Part of the magic lies in the "safety" of what happens within the playing space. What happens there is insulated from causing anything to happen in the outer world; when the play is over, it is truly over, finished, completed, and it sends nothing out into the streets except its own memory. If a man is shot onstage, he will not have to be taken to a real hospital; if a woman is widowed, she will not have to stand in a real welfare line or suffer real anguish tomorrow when she wakes up. The play is truly "play," as children's make-believe is play. So, too, with the theatre: *as art, it is harmless.*

Now, some critics of the theatre would take it to task for being harmless; they would argue that even an art should affect events in the real world.

Figure 2-4. **Imagination.** Lack of scenery, as in this traveling modern version of Shakespeare's stage, demands that the audience's imagination supply what is missing. *Romeo and Juliet* at the University of Maryland, Baltimore County. *(Directed by Sam McCready. Tim Ford photo.)*

George Bernard Shaw spoke of the play "doing its work in the world," but he was referring to the *ideas* that a play generates in the minds of its audience. The fact remains, however, that *as art* theatre is "harmless"—*and that is one of its attractions.* Many people speak of theatre as "escape," and, although the idea is a weak one to describe what really attracts an audience, "escaping the consequences" is an important element in the theatre's pull. We can watch horrifying or electrifying events; we can behave as we are not allowed to behave in life, guffawing at a human being's suffering or applauding murder—because those events are harmless.

Alvin Toffler in *Future Shock* has suggested that as existence grows more complex, individuals will need areas of comfort and calm to return to. In one sense, the theatre is such a place.

THE REVELATION OF THE EXOTIC

Here is another theatrical paradox: on the one hand, the theatre attracts people by dealing in the familiar and the comfortable; but, on the other hand, it also draws them with the new and the strange.

Thus, there is a three-way tension among three kinds of appeal to the audience: the stirring of the imagination, the satisfaction of the desire for the familiar, and the arousing of the appetite for the exotic.

The tension between the familiar and the exotic is greatly affected by the passage of time. To a considerable extent, those elements that stir the imagination persist, but *familiar* and *exotic* are rather relative terms, and it is sometimes difficult to understand which of these attractions was at work in a play from the past. What is familiar to one generation may be foreign to another; what is exotic to one may be familiar or even boring to a later generation. Science fiction is an example, for technology is always making yesterday's fantasies wrong or silly. Nevertheless, exoticism is an attraction. Before the world was thoroughly explored, foreign locales were a great draw. At the beginning of the industrial revolution, factories were popular settings. The theatre makes the exotic known to the audience—and thus, in a way, demystifies it and makes it safe.

How Does an Audience Perceive?

If an audience goes to the theatre to be imaginatively stirred through a perception of the familiar or the exotic, how does it perceive what is going on?

Three general attributes of the theatre greatly affect the way that the audience perceives a performance: convention, innovation, and style.

CONVENTION

Conventions could be called *contracts*. Conventions are shortcuts between what is meant and what is done. To the actor, a convention may be a gesture that, through continued repetition, has come to convey great meaning—a hand raised to the forehead, palm out, the eyes turned up, to indicate suffering. To a scene designer, a convention may be the placing of a scenic house so that only part of it is actually onstage, the rest of it seeming to lie outside the audience's vision at one or both sides of the stage. The onstage part that the audience sees may be a strict imitation of reality; *convention* allows the scenic designer to mean that the entire house is there, although common sense says that it is not. The very fact that both audience and actors accept the idea that there is *anywhere* offstage is a convention, instead of their insisting on the commonsense reality that *offstage* is simply a slightly dirty area in a theatre.

A convention is a contract between the audience and the theatre artists, an agreement to do things this way for the good of all. In the modern theatre, the acceptance of the idea that days or months or years pass between scenes or acts is a convention; the acceptance of taped music during dramatic action

Figure 2-5. **Recognition.** The "audience" here is made up of actors; the "theatre" is a setting, a replica of a music hall known to the real audience. Audiences flocked to see this 1900 play and the theatre they could have sat in.

is a convention; the acceptance in many theatres of actors in partial undress is a convention for total nudity.

INNOVATION

Pulling against convention is innovation. It is the introduction of new ways of giving meaning. It is novelty, "originality."

Theatre artists and audiences both demand innovation—up to a point. That point, however, is not easy to define. Many outside factors affect people's willingness to accept a convention or to demand innovation in its place.

Usually, innovation comes from the artists' side of the theatre. Audiences do not "demand" a change, at least not in the way that we are accustomed to having people demand things. Audiences, after all, do not have a real voice. Their voice is in their hands and their pocketbooks. Their "demands" may best be seen in their enthusiastic welcoming of an innovation or a change in the way a convention is used.

Technology is itself the parent of much innovation. The coming of movies

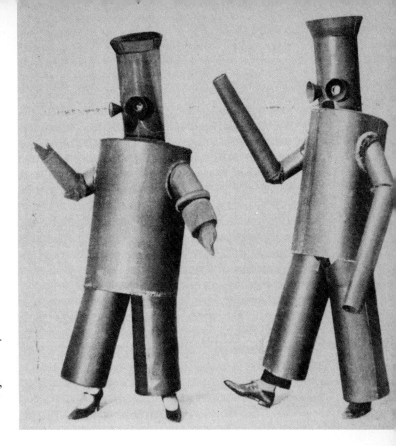

Figure 2-6. **Innovation.** New developments in technology find expression in the theatre. Here, two "machine" costumes of the Futurist movement in Italy, 1920s. *(From Huntley Carter,* The New Spirit in the European Theatre, 1914–1924. *London: Benn, 1925.)*

at the end of the nineteenth century quickly drew a large audience; what it saw was much the same thematically as what it saw in the theatre of the day, and the acting conventions were identical, but the technology was innovative. Ballet dancing on the toe—"en point"—was developed about 1825, perhaps in combination with the invention of the shoe needed to perform such a feat; it was an innovation that paralleled technology. Presumably, it was a response to a demand for greater displays of virtuosity.

Still other innovation may come from the acquisition of new information. Historically accurate costumes were possible only when historical knowledge was broadened by people working outside the theatre, and period costuming was accepted as something other than an exotic rarity only when that knowledge was disseminated through the theatre audience by historically accurate books and pictures.

STYLE

Style is the result of interaction among convention, innovation, and the life of the times. The word *style* is one of the most useful, and yet one of the most confusing, that is applied in the performing arts. Clothes are said to be "stylish"; there is a "New Orleans style" of jazz as compared with a "Chicago style"; there are "kosher-style" dill pickles. Some performers are said to have a "personal style" that distinguishes them from other performers.

Plays of the past are sometimes said to be produced in modern times in "period style," and sometimes productions are even labeled "style" productions. In the sense that we will mean it here, however, *style refers to the particular characteristics of a performance that the audience sees and hears that set it off from all other performances.*

Some characteristics that go to make up a production's style are:

HISTORICAL PERIOD.   The way people talk and move, the kind of clothes they wear, and the way their living spaces are shaped and decorated are different from period to period. Theatrical speech and movement, costumes and hairstyle, and settings reflect aspects of their historical period.

LEVEL OF ABSTRACTION.   Each group of performers in each age has its own artistic style: a mixture of inherited tradition, of meaningful convention and innovation, and of their own aesthetic sense of what is pleasing and beautiful. The style of a great mime is abstracted far from reality; the movements are themselves dancelike, beautiful, compressed. The movement and vocal attack of the traditional Comédie Française was spare and economical, with occasional outbursts of great verbal flourish; the movement and vocal attack of American actors of the 1950s was laconic and sinuous, very close to one idea of reality at one level of American society at one historical moment.

AMOUNT OF DETAIL.   In most areas of theatre, it is possible to vary the amount of information from almost none to an overwhelming amount: the actor may speak in a monotone, stand still, make no attempt to imitate life or to interpret text (little detail); or the actor may busily imitate behavior or create symbols with a thousand moves and gestures and turns of voice (much detail). The setting may be the blank wall of the theatre (little detail) or the meticulous imitation of a real place—even the real place itself (much detail). The costume may be a black leotard (little detail) or a rich silk dress covered with dollar signs sewn in brilliants (much detail).

SOCIAL CLASS.   In class-conscious societies, mannerisms of speech, clothes, and body movement, as well as personal effects, furniture, decor, and almost every other aspect of life, reflect class and money or the lack of them. A French peasant of 1670 looked, acted, and spoke very differently from Louis XIV, the French king. In the same way, a moneyed easterner of our own day sounds and dresses and moves differently from a western ranch hand. Actors playing peasants and kings show the same degree of difference, although it must be remembered that *the style of the theatre is different from the style of life.*

GIVEN CIRCUMSTANCES.   Sex, race, state of health, age, and profession create stylistic differences. A minister's sermon does not sound like a teacher's lecture; a disco dancer does not move like a golfer. A sick man neither

Figure 2-7. **Style.** Two interpretations of the middle ages from very different periods. Clear differences in style result from great differences in the amount of detail, the nature of the events chosen, and other elements.

sounds nor moves like a healthy one; men and women have noticeably different styles of dress, speech, and movement *in certain ages*.

When theatre artists choose to produce a work from the past, they have a great range of styles to choose from. In doing a French comedy of 1670, for example, they might choose to do it "authentically," that is, in as close a reconstruction as is possible of the original scenery, costumes, acting, movement, and so on. Or they might decide that, the essence of the play being comic, it is most important to make stylistic decisions in terms of such comic values as brightness, color, and symmetry. Again, they might decide to work at a level of abstraction rather different from the original, so that the costumes might have large areas of pure color without detail and the setting might be very simple and even painted like a cartoon. On the other hand, the decision might be made to change the historical period entirely in order to make the play easier for a modern audience to grasp, and so it might be put squarely into contemporary clothes and settings, and contemporary references might even be inserted into the script. In each case, consistency of style would be sought.

It should be pointed out that *historical accuracy* usually refers to social and not theatrical history. As a general rule, *revivals of past works seek to imitate the style of the life of the period and not the style of the theatre of the period.* (See Figure 2–8.) An audience will accept a copy of the styles of a period if it is convinced that the copy is a reasonably good one of the life of the times; it generally will not accept a copy of the theatrical style of a past period because conventions and theatrical styles of the past, having been supplanted by successive waves of innovation, may well look foreign or even ridiculous. A modern audience seeing a meticulous copy of the acting style, settings, and theatre costumes of 1670 might respond that the style is "not accurate." They would mean that the acting, settings, and costumes were not like the modern idea of seventeenth-century life, forgetting that life and the theatre are sometimes far from identical.

When an audience does not understand a style, it will be annoyed, for the very good reason that it cannot go beyond the style to the real business of the theatre, the stirring of the imagination, and it will give up its own imaginative participation in order to try to cope with stylistic effects. When, however, an audience has a very strong concept of a style of the past (a theatrical style, not a lifestyle) and theatre artists choose to play on that concept, the result can be "camp"—using a past style for its own sake, most often to make fun of it. Nowhere is such a "camp" approach so common as in productions of what are loosely called nineteenth-century melodramas. The curious fact is that the dramatic style being made fun of never actually existed in precisely the way that either audience or most theatre people seem to think—but no matter, it has become a style of its own, and audiences are pleased by it, for all its howling inaccuracy.

Do Audiences Have Styles?

Insofar as an audience represents an age and a social class, it, too, will show a style, probably the same style that influences the theatre. But the question does not mean "Do they have distinctive ways of moving and dressing and speaking?" because these elements are unimportant *to their role as audience.*

Figure 2-8. **Historical Period.** Modern performance usually tries to capture the feel of a historical period, not the theatrical style of that period. Molière's *Tartuffe* at the University of Missouri. *(Directed by Larry Clark.)*

It means "Do different audiences react in different ways that will affect the performance?"

The answer, of course, is yes. The social level of an audience greatly affects its response. The "gallery gods" of the nineteenth-century theatres or the audiences of the penny theatres of the same period were notorious for their raucous behavior when they were displeased, their applause when they were pleased. They were noisy, sometimes obstreperous; they interrupted plays, drowned out bad performances, and cheered their favorites to a standstill. Upper-class audiences, because of their supposed aesthetic sophistication, may put different, special demands on performers; much of the abstraction of the late-eighteenth-century French Neoclassical theatre came, for example, from its audience's insistence on a "propriety" that reflected an unreal concept of aristocratic behavior.

And the psychology of groups, as it varies from age to age, greatly affects the "style" of an audience. Our own is an age—in the theatre, opera, and dance—of restraint. Nobody throws ripe tomatoes at the performers anymore; nobody has rioted in an American theatre in decades. Our audiences for athletic events and rock concerts, on the other hand, are far more boisterous than our theatre audiences. Rock audiences sometimes weep, laugh, get high, sing, dance; at Altamont in 1968, for example, people were killed. Athletic audiences at all levels, high school to professional, sometimes come near to breaking even the bounds of law.

The factors that determine audience style are very complex. First, probably, is *group self-image*—the customs and manners of a certain group, defined by social and sometimes economic factors, as well as by gender, level of education, and the group's own sense of social place. Sometimes, an audience forms *because* it wants to assert its idea of social place—the black-tie audience at opera, for example, or the quite different, but equally self-confident, audience at Country and Western.

Of almost equal importance is *sanctity of place* and the way the audience respects it—that is, the behavior appropriate to a gilt opera house is very different from that appropriate to a drive-in movie. *Preparation for the event*

Figure 2-9. **Group Self-image.** Particularly when theatre is stratified by social class, as in this private (coterie) theatre of the late nineteenth century, an audience style emerges clearly in allowed responses, ways of dressing, and so on.

affects audience style: it is one thing to flop into a chair in pajamas to watch television and another to dress formally, travel miles, pay up to a hundred dollars a ticket, and eat a special meal before the event.

Does an Audience Work?

If audience and theatre makers interact, then it must follow that the audience itself has a responsibility in the system that we call theatre. A performance cannot be seen merely as the total product of the work done on one side of a curtain line. Nor can it properly be seen as something "given" from one kind of person (the theatre maker) to another kind of person (the audience). It is, instead, something that exists in the very complex *interaction* between them; and it follows, therefore, that the audience has a task for which it should prepare.

Ideas of "comfort" and "escape" sometimes appeal to the audience. Theatre people, however, object to audiences who want to behave passively. "They sit on their hands" is the theatre saying. But slumping into a seat and waiting to be entertained is not the proper posture of the theatre audience, because it is too limiting, both to the audience's own pleasure and to the potential of the theatre itself. "Entertain me" is like a child's "Tell me a story" in its passivity, and its end result in an audience is childish performance—the sort of mindless mush that sometimes turns up on television (where audiences are of necessity more passive) and that, regrettably, turns up in the theatre whenever the audience lets itself get complacent and lazy.

Performance is based on an unspoken agreement between artists and audience. The basic clause for the performers is "I will not hurt or offend you." The basic clause for the audience is "I will work to enjoy you."

A good audience fulfills its part of the agreement in two ways: first, by *making its imagination work* when that imagination is stirred by the performance; and second, by *remaining open* to new ways of being moved, entertained, and excited, by remaining open to having its imagination stirred in surprising ways. It does no good for Shakespeare's Chorus in *Henry V* to say,

> *Suppose within the girdle of these walls*
> *Are now confin'd two mighty monarchies. . . .*
> *Think when we talk of horses that you see them,*
> *Printing their proud hoofs i' the receiving earth;*
> *For 'tis your thoughts that now must deck our kings. . . .*

if the audience will refuse to do these things. The Chorus speaks of the audience's "imaginative forces." Forces *work*. The audience must "suppose" and "think." It is "your thoughts" that dress the actors. If the audience for such a play simply lay back in its easy chairs and said, "Ho-hum, I'm tired; entertain me," there would be no entertainment at all. Curiously, the more

Figure 2-10. **Preparation for the Performance.** This audience of "gallery gods" for the early nineteenth-century star Edmund Kean was fully prepared, knowing Kean's status and his legend, and almost certainly knowing the play, *Othello*, very well.

an audience causes its imagination to work, and the more open it forces itself to be to new imaginative stimulation, the more entertained it will be.

In addition to its imaginative responsibilities, the audience can also heighten its own pleasure through *preparation for the performance*. Its preparation falls into two categories: an *understanding of the theatre* and a *sympathy for the work*. Understanding of the theatre means a basic mastery of the how's and why's of what theatre people do, an appreciation of the arts of the performers that is distinct from the specific value of any performance. That is, it is not appropriate for an audience to say merely, "I didn't like it" or "I thought it was wonderful." Both statements say much about the speaker, little about the performance. Instead, it is the spectrum of appreciative statements that is revealing: one actor was excellent because of the understanding of the role, the way body and voice were used; the playwright created a stunning scene for two actors in Act I but didn't quite bring off a climactic speech in Act III; the set designer not only created a first-rate acting space but also created a visually beautiful treat for the audience; and so on. Through such understanding of the arts of the theatre will come greater audience pleasure; that, in turn, will contribute to an increased ability to let the imagination work.

Sympathy for the work is developed through an absorption of material available about the performance before going to see it. This means familiarizing oneself with *mediation*—reviews and advertisements, the program. It seems a picayune point, but a theatre program does give essential information about where a scene is taking place and when it is happening, and it is mere laziness if an audience does not take that information in.

Sympathy for the work means going to the theatre with a general idea of what sort of event one is going to see—so that, for example, somebody who wants to see a comedy does not leave the theatre because *Cat on a Hot Tin Roof* sounded like a funny title; or somebody who wants to introduce children to the theatre does not become enraged because *Who's Afraid of Virginia Woolf?* is not a children's play. It is fairly commonplace for someone to say, "I never read reviews or criticism; I don't want to be told how to think." But there is no reason at all why criticism should tell anybody how or what to think; it serves, instead, as a prod and a guide, leading potential audience members away from some works and toward others.

An audience cannot afford to be lazy. Its own response depends on its taking part; one can no more enjoy the theatre as a nonparticipant than one can enjoy playing tennis that way. Audience laziness leads to mindlessness, limitation of scope, and stagnation. As A. Nicholas Vardac wrote in *Stage to Screen*, "From the mid-nineteenth century to the Radio City Music Hall is a period of imaginative laziness—a laziness not on the part of the artists of the theatre, but rather on the part of their audiences. They had not come into the theatre to participate imaginatively. . . . They had come to be shown."

How To Read a Play

Seeing a play and reading a play are different experiences. They require different tools and different approaches.

Seeing the play in the theatre is the complete theatrical experience. Reading the play in a book means making the effort—and knowing how to make the effort—to understand the play as it will appear in the theatre.

Reading the play is not the same kind of activity as reading a novel or a story. The novel and the story are complete in themselves; their language fills them out completely. A play, on the other hand, is a part—a vital and important part—of a different kind of artistic experience.

The aesthetician Suzanne Langer defined certain kinds of art as having "discursive form"—form apprehended across real time, a kind of apprehension that dictates the order in which the audience perceives the work. The drama and the novel both fall into this category, which distinguishes them from painting, for example, but they are still quite different from each other. Of most importance here is the *staged* play's rigid link to the real time of the audience: it must be understood as it takes place. The novel, on the other hand, has a rigid internal time, a "pastness" that Langer called "virtual history," which is quite different from the reader's real time; and, in fact, the reader's real time can vary (when the reader puts the book down, for example) without changing the "virtual history."

Reading a play seems to put it into the aesthetic category of the novel. However, other differences of form make the play incomplete as a readable form: above all, the play text has broad areas left blank, which the reader must learn to fill in through clues that are actually clues to performance, not elements of the art of a distinct aesthetic form (as paragraphs of description, for example, are valid elements of the art of the novel). Usually, we read plays "as if" we are seeing them. (A kind of play meant only for reading is called *closet drama*; it is a special case, and in fact its form, although superficially that of plays meant to be staged, is different, generally including far more information in the speeches so as to fill in the blanks of the stageable play. Closet dramas are not usually stageable.)

Some modern theatre artists have called the playscript "not a text but a pretext" for production—that is, not a complete, self-sufficient work of art. Others have talked of the playscript as "notation" for production.

The written play seems like a contradiction: it is one part of an art form and is not self-sufficient, and yet it can be read with pleasure *as if* it were complete and self-sufficient.

The reader, then, approaches the reading of the play differently from the reading of a novel. The principal goals are *understanding the first reading of the play, analyzing the play and its parts,* and *organizing a response to the play.*

First Reading

Reading begins at the beginning—with the title, the first piece of information. The author believed it said something important about the play; therefore, it is a clue to at least one important part of the play—perhaps a central idea, perhaps a central character. A title like *Murder on the Orient Express* is very straightforward; on the other hand, a title like *Streamers* is mysterious until well into the play. (It means the death fall of a parachutist whose chute fails to open—a central image.)

Reading continues with the cast of characters, which gives information on the size of the cast and its makeup by age, sex, and so on; the characters' names and their relationships; and, sometimes, what the characters look and sound like.

The opening stage directions usually describe the setting and the play's opening moments. In the scripts of plays that have been produced, these stage directions often reflect the actual Broadway or London production; in other plays, they give the playwright's vision of the setting. Sounds may be

DOLBY'S BRITISH THEATRE.

MACBETH.

I. R. Cruikshank, Del.   White, Sculpt.

Mac. Speak if ye can :—What are you?

ACT I   SCENE 3.

Figure 3-1. **The Mind's Eye.** Learning to "see" the play while reading is important, although the result may not be like any actual performance. This is an artist's illustration of one line from *Macbeth*. Would all of us see Macbeth in kilts? The witches with sticks?

described as well. It is now possible to visualize, and perhaps to listen to, the play's opening.

However, the reader must ask some questions: *What kind of theatre is being used? What is the historical period of the play?* Can the reader carry this period into the imaginary production—in costumes and setting, for example? *What is the opening mood?* Somber or happy? Tense or relaxed? *How do characters get on and off the stage?* Is the setting inside or outdoors? Are there doors? Where? Where do the characters enter from?

Then, with the beginning as strongly visualized as possible, the reader begins to read the play, underlining and making notes on:

- What happens in the play.
- Who makes things happen and who tries to stop things from happening; also, the relative importance of the characters.
- What key words, images, and ideas run through the play (and, probably, what the relevance of the title is).

After this first careful reading, the reader is familiar with the play and has a sense of what it is about and of what happens in it, as well as of who its characters are.

The later readings of a play aim at orderly, informed analysis of the play. Analysis may result in a judgment about the play.

Figure 3-2. **Imagining the Setting.** One reason for learning about the practicalities of theatre is that it helps in visualizing settings and theatre spaces. This, for example, is the back (actor's) side of a setting for *The Merchant of Venice. (See also Figure 9-9.)*

Play Analysis

The Greek critic Aristotle (see pp. 230–231) created a theory of play analysis that others have modified. What follows is based on interpretations of Aristotle but is not strictly Aristotelian.

Aristotle said there were six parts to a play. A modern interpretation of them gives the following:

1. Plot
2. Character
3. Idea
4. Language
5. Music
6. Spectacle

This breakdown is still useful. We can go through most plays and show how every aspect—every speech, every movement, every activity—fits these categories.

In Aristotle's analysis, these six parts are closely linked and are *causes* of each other: that is, each "comes from" or "is the product of" the parts listed below it. Plot is at the top because it is most important. In the theatre, human beings follow plot and understand other things through plot. Plot is also first because it is "caused" by all the other parts, most immediately by character (characters *do* things), whereas a character is "caused" by what he or she believes and wants (idea) and by what he or she says (language), and so on.

PLOT

Plot is *the ordering of the incidents* in the play. This means that it is not only *what happens* in the play; it is also the *order* in which things are made to happen and the *reasons* why things are put in that order *by the playwright*.

KINDS OF PLOT.   We can identify two kinds of plot:

1. Causal plot (also known as *linear*, or *antecedent-consequent*, or *climactic*). The incidents of linear plot can be seen to lie along a line of causality from beginning to end. The word *climactic* is sometimes used because such plots build to a *climax*, the most exciting moment of the plot for the audience. (Note that the term refers to the response to the plot, not to the plot itself.) Causal plots are of two major types:

- Single line of development, with no subordinate lines (for example, Sophocles' *Oedipus Rex*).
- Multiple lines of development, consisting of a major line and var-

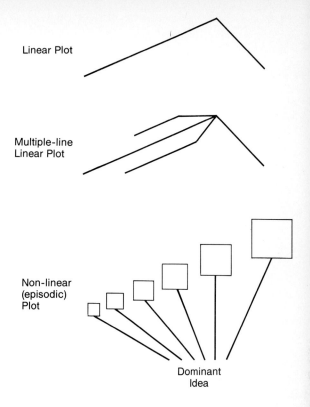

Linear Plot

Multiple-line
Linear Plot

Non-linear
(episodic)
Plot

Dominant
Idea

Figure 3-3. **Kinds of Plot.**

ious subordinate ones ("subplots") (for example, Shakespeare's *Hamlet*).

2. Episodic (also known as *contextual* or *thematic*) plot. The incidents (episodes) of episodic plot do not follow each other because of causality; rather, they are ordered by the exploration of an idea or a character. Social-problem plays have often used this kind of plot, with each scene exploring a new aspect of the social problem or enlarging the study made to that point. An extreme example is a nineteenth-century play (Georg Buechner's *Woyzzeck*) for which the author never settled on a final ordering of the scenes.

PARTS OF PLOT. Plot is itself made up of parts. Those that follow are not elements defined by Aristotle; rather, they are the parts identified by the past couple of hundred years of criticism. They are

EXPOSITION—the giving of information about past events. The greatest amount of exposition often comes at the beginning of the play, when the audience knows least about plot and character. In some plays, however, important exposition is delayed until late; in a murder mystery, for example, the most important facts about past events ("whodunit") come at the end.

ACTION—the central chain of events in the play, particularly as those events are the central character's attempt to achieve an important goal. Action and character are tightly bound to each other and are understood through each other, so that an answer to the question, "What is the play's action?" always requires inclusion of the character.

51

Successful action in a linear plot is a *whole* action; that is, it has a beginning, a middle, and an end. *Beginning* means that nothing relevant comes before (and nothing irrelevant is included); *end* means that nothing relevant is still to come. If the action is not a whole action, the play will not be understandable to its audience as a work of art.

Wholeness is fundamental. It is one of the most important aspects that distinguish art from life, which art imitates. Unlike a play, a life is not perceivable as a whole, especially while it is being lived. Our lives are diverse and complicated; we carry on several "actions," of which we perceive only dimly (and often incorrectly) the beginnings; the ends are always over our life's horizon.

People say they do not understand their lives; they are confused or they have lost control or they have identity crises. In the work of art (the play), on the other hand, wholeness allows us to understand, and so to learn. A dramatic character may be confused or out of control or in an identity crisis, but the audience sees the entirety of that situation: beginning, middle, and end.

It is important to remember that drama is able to reveal life to us *because* it is an invention and not "real life."

COMPLICATION—the opposing or entangling of the action. Often, at the beginning of the play, the action seems simple—for example, a character desires to accomplish something. It becomes complicated by obstacles, particularly by the efforts of other characters to frustrate the action, even to destroy the central character.

Most plots have many complications. Each complication changes the direction of the action as the character must deal with the complication before pursuing the original goal or must pursue that goal in terms of knowledge gained from dealing with the complication.

Two important kinds of complication are

- Caused complication, that is, complication through the agency of another character, a god, or a force.
- Accidental or coincidental complication—for example, a storm, a flood, or a chance meeting of characters.

RISING ACTION—action of increasing complication.

CRISIS—a point in the action where complication forces the character to make a decision; a turning point. Derived from the Greek for "decision," *crisis* means "decisive moment." We expect to find rising action from complication to crisis.

FALLING ACTION OR DENOUEMENT (RESOLUTION)—from the French, "the untying"—the unraveling of complication, the decline as crisis is passed and complication is resolved.

DRAMATIC STRUCTURE.   *Structure* is sometimes used as a metaphor for the internal nature of a plot, as we might talk of the structure of steel I-beams that are the skeleton of a building. To clarify, dramatic structures are

Figure 3-4. **Rising Action.** So long as complication increases, the action is said to rise; after its highest point, the dénouement ("untying," i.e., uncomplicating) or falling action takes place.

sometimes put in visual terms: linear plot is shown as a line rising from beginning to crisis, then falling rapidly. Sometimes, this structure is pictured as a sawtooth of minor rising and falling actions along the major line of rise and fall. Discussions of structure focus on the parts of plot as structural members of the whole.

PLOT AND IDEA. Plot conveys idea through our tendency to generalize from example. Plot is an example of an ordering, with their causes, of events. The choice of events and the ordering are made by the playwright to *create* the example. We may generalize, seeing that (in this playwright's view) certain causes lead to certain (good or bad) events.

CHARACTER

Dramatic character and a real human being are not the same thing. Dramatic character is an invention. The fact that a dramatic character pursues human goals, speaks human words, and embodies human responses means only that the dramatic character is part of a human artistic creation that is about life, not that it is life itself. Dramatic character is, at best, an imitation of selected aspects of humanity.

Dramatic characters have no existence before the play and no future after the play is over. They are no more than what the playwright has given us.

Dramatic characters are performed by actors to create a convincing imitation of real people.

CHARACTER AND ACTION.   Action is impossible without character; action is really *character in action*. Some people say that character *is* action, for it is very difficult to imagine a dramatic character that is inert. However, note that action is not the same as *activity*—talking, walking, gesturing.

Passive characters are very difficult to conceive, and if a character's goal is "to do nothing," the playwright has a very difficult task in making a play, for drama is active.

CHARACTER AND FUNCTION.   Because characters are inventions in a work of art, they can be seen as both imitations of human beings and as *functions* within the work. *Function*, in this case, means the dramatic task that the character performs. *Good character always has function; character without function is bad character.*

Every character can be analyzed in every scene for its function in terms of the play's parts, for example, to further the plot, to express idea, to contribute to spectacle. Reading to understand the function at each moment illuminates how the play works and how well it works.

PERCEIVING CHARACTER.   In reading the play, we perceive dramatic character in several ways:

- Through the stage directions, although some playwrights do not discuss character in the stage directions.
- Through what other characters say. However, we have to understand these other characters before we can know how to interpret what they say.
- Through what the characters themselves say about themselves, with the same problem of interpreting what they say.
- Through what the characters do—their *acts*.

Of these, the last is the most important. Therefore, the words on the pages of the playscript—the characters' speeches—must be read as *acts*. An act is something done to accomplish a goal; if we can interpret it, we can understand the goal and the reason behind the act.

We ask of every speech, "Why does the character say this in this way? What does the character mean? What is this act trying to accomplish?"

In life, we listen to other people and sometimes hear "what they are really saying"; we learn to "read between the lines." So, too, with dramatic characters. Because the play is a work of art, the words are much more compressed and *active*; they are themselves acts, as much as a kiss or a gunshot is an act.

CHARACTER AND PLOT.   Because plot is so closely linked to character (the events that are ordered are character acts or reactions), character is understood through such parts of plot as crisis. Decision reveals character; complication forces character to decision. Character is also embodied in:

- Furthering of the action. Every word said about the main action—defense of it, response to complication, acceptance or rejection of advice, statements of the moral or philosophical underpinnings of the action—reveal character. Overt nonverbal acts—fights, pauses, deceptions—are equally revealing.

Figure 3-5. **Persons and Characters.** Dramatic characters are created from the evidence of the text, although the actor's creation will be very different from the reader's. Is, then, the actor the character when offstage? Is this cast of *Sweeney Todd* the same as the characters of *Sweeney Todd*, even though this is not a scene from the musical? *(Essex Community College. Photo by Norman J. McCullough.)*

- Relations with other characters. Under the increasing pressure of the complicated action, the real nature of relationships—hate, love, friendship, dependence, forgiveness—shows more clearly.
- Progression. Change is possible in drama because it happens over time. Many serious plays and some comedies have central characters who behave and think differently at the end from the beginning; they have "learned." Some contemporary plays show neither change nor learning, however. In reading a play, it is important to look for change and then to understand why the change took place.

Learning and progression assume that later states are more enlightening (*for us*) than the earlier ones. Some critics say that "the play is understood by its ending," a great oversimplification but often a useful notion.

CHARACTER AND CONFLICT.   A hundred years ago, it was common to say that "drama is conflict." Nowadays, we are inclined to say that conflict is central to many dramas but not to all of them.

Character conflict—the opposition of another character to the central character—reveals both characters and is "dramatic" in its intensity and in its potential for complication. Conflict between opposed characters may provide an easily understandable moral or philosophical opposition (good versus evil).

Some plays contain conflicts between the central character and an impersonal force, for example, fate, the gods, or society. Frequently in these plays, the impersonal forces are personified by a humanlike character.

CONTINUING KINDS OF CHARACTER.   Critics and scholars have come to designate certain kinds of character that repeat themselves in many plays:

- Protagonist—the central figure of the main action.
- Confidant(e)—a character in whom the protagonist or another important character confides.
- Antagonist—in a play with character conflict around the main action, the one who opposes the protagonist.
- Author character or *raisonneur*—one who speaks for the author, directly giving the author's moral or philosophical ideas; usually not the protagonist.
- Foil—one who sets off another character by contrast—comic where the other is serious, stupid where intelligent, shrewd where naive.
- Sympathetic and unsympathetic characters—those created by the playwright so as either to appeal to the audience or to repel it.

IDEA

No play is without meanings. Even the lightest comedy has meaning because it imitates human action and because it expresses a time and a society. A play does not have to be full of intellectual speeches to offer meanings, and the careful reader of the play learns how to find these meanings and understand them.

Plays seldom offer single, simple meanings. The best plays offer many meanings; an attempt to reduce these to "the idea of the play" or "the theme of the play" oversimplifies the play's greatness.

The kinds of meanings fall generally into two categories: *idea*—meanings contained entirely within the play; and *extrinsic meaning*—those meanings in the society and the period of which the play is an expression. We are concerned here with idea.

IDEA AND CHARACTER.   In a good play, the play's major ideas are embodied in the character of the protagonist and the protagonist's action. If the character is positive (approved by the author, "good"), then the protagonist embodies a good. These "goods" and "bads"—the defining elements of the play's moral world—are best understood through the system of rewards and punishments in the play.

Figure 3-6. **Protagonist.** Action and character are interdependent; the character who drives the main action is called the protagonist. *(Vida Thomas in Marsha Norman's* Getting Out. *The University Company, the University of Tennessee.)*

Thus, in plays with conflict, the victor in the conflict represents a positive way of acting, a "good." The loser represents a "bad." Rewards and punishments may take other forms, like money, love, promotion, or pardon for a supposed crime.

For example, the critic Northrop Frye saw some denouements as creating a new society, different from the one at the beginning, and in his critical approach, many of the play's ideas can be understood from who is included in the new society and who is left out. Often, such society-making takes the specific form of a party, even a wedding. Analyzing the new society will reveal idea by answering questions like What kind of people qualify? What are the human qualities that cause people to be shut out?

Typically, the protagonist explains his or her own idea (ethical attitude) near a crisis; rewards and punishments come in the denouement.

IDEA AND LANGUAGE.   Some ideas, or statements of these ideas, will be found in the words of the play. Particularly important locations include:

- Important characters' speeches before and after crises. Such speeches often explore the crisis and the author's reasons for having the characters act (make decisions) as they do.
- Important characters' speeches when alone onstage or when with a confidant.
- Author characters' speeches about complications and crises.
- Speeches in the denouement that themselves tie up questions or issues raised in the play.

LANGUAGE

Because the language, like everything else in the play, has been chosen by the playwright, it, too, is an artistic expression. It is the primary carrier of meaning in the play text.

Language can be studied apart from its meaning.

As an "act" separate from the meaning of the words, the language is one of the most revealing clues to character.

Language, of itself, tells the reader the given circumstances of character (through social level of usage, vocabulary, dialect) and emotional state (through kind and amount of words and through rhythm).

The kind and use of language are important carriers of idea. Most important are:

- Key language. Careful reading often reveals words that are used again and again in important contexts. The frequent appearance of the word *death*, for example, in a play about love would suggest that the play's idea is probably not "Love conquers all."
- Key figures of speech. Critics sometimes speak of "image clusters," especially in poetic plays. Repeated images or metaphors

Figure 3-7. **Mind's Eye and Audience Eye.** The same scene from Molière's *Tartuffe*, as performed and as imagined by an artist. *(The University of South Carolina, directed by James A. Patterson. Drawing from Frederic Loliée, La Comedie Française . . . . Paris: Laveur, 1907.)*

are much more evident to the play reader than to the playgoer; they are a very subtle (sometimes unconscious) carrier of meaning. Many analysts have pointed out, for example, the many images of weeds in Shakespeare's *Hamlet;* the image cluster supports an idea about the protagonist as fighting against an evil, choking, destructive environment.

MUSIC

In musical plays, the importance of music to character, mood, and rhythm is clear. In nonmusical plays, the reader must see the language itself as embodying music. The language of drama is language for the human voice, not for the page: it is meant to be listened to. Even in prose plays, such language has rhythms and the beauty of sounds.

The difference between prose and poetry should be obvious to the reader; shifts from one poetic form to another (as in some of Shakespeare, for example) or from prose to verse must be watched for. Prose, rhythmic prose, blank verse, rhymed verse, and other musical uses of language should always be noted and questioned: Why has the playwright used these? What is the effect?

Figure 3-8. **Spectacle.** As with imagining scenery, knowing the practicalities of lighting is a considerable help. Here, very simple lighting instruments for a small studio theatre.

Primary effects of the musical use of language are mood, level of abstraction, and level of seriousness. Regular, slow rhythms create very different moods from sharp, staccato ones; verse, especially rhymed verse, is usually more abstract and, in serious plays, more serious than prose. In comedy, the rhymed couplet, although artificial, enhances the witty line by providing an extra accentuation, the rhyme.

SPECTACLE

In reading, it is important to try to visualize so as to understood spectacle. Much of spectacle in the modern theatre, to be sure, is the work of designers whose genius cannot be predicted from the page. The cues for their work are there, however, in the same text that the reader uses. The imagination must work.

Spectacle, like language, embodies idea in its use of symbols. In many ways, however, it addresses the audience at a level different from language and intellect—that is, at the level of the graphic arts. Spectacle—which, on the stage, is always working on the sense of sight—is the hardest of the six parts to understand from the text. It is necessary to imagine it as fully as possible, but the imagined spectacle of the reader will probably prove quite different from the actual spectacle of performance.

Organizing a Response

The result of a play analysis should be an organized response to the text. An organized response should be:

- Informed—that is, based on a knowledge of drama and theatre.
- Orderly—that is, consistent and well reasoned.
- Defensible—that is, capable of explanation to somebody else (in a written paper, for example).

This kind of response tries to be *objective*. This means that it is made not because of individual likes and dislikes, but because of the nature of the play and the reader's ability to understand it.

Some people try to explain their attitude toward a play by saying, "My opinion is as good as yours." The trouble with this explanation is that good, objective understanding is not a matter of opinion. Opinion is a statement of feeling. It belongs in the same category as the old line, "I don't know anything about art, but I know what I like." The trouble with not knowing anything is that it actually prevents response; all it allows is gut reaction, which is quite a different matter. Part of the enjoyment of theatre does depend on gut reaction—but only part.

One way of organizing is to determine the play's *genre*.

GENRE

Generic criticism is a major branch of dramatic criticism, and whole books have been devoted to the definition of tragedy (for example). Such definitions sometimes change under historical pressure, so that a more specific genre like Neoclassical tragedy comes into being. Here, therefore, it is possible to give only the broadest definitions of four major genres:

1. Tragedy—a work of the highest seriousness, with a serious protagonist in a serious action with serious consequences. Usually, as well, human decision is important to the idea of tragic action.

2. Comedy—a work whose issues are usually social and mundane, not concerned with ultimate (spiritual or moral) matters, with a protagonist involved in an action without deeply serious consequences. Usually, as well, human decision is limited, comic character being comic because locked into types or into intense self-interest.

3. Melodrama—a work of apparent seriousness with issues cast in terms of extremes (black and white), the actual issues being much less profound than the language suggests and often sparse in idea. "Happy endings" are

Figure 3-9. **Audience Response.** Critics do not define genre by responses (tears for tragedy, laughter for comedy), because responses are variable and unpredictable. The right kind of laughter at the right time, however, is a good test of one kind of comedy. An audience for a play in Freetown, Sierra Leone. *(Photo courtesy of Martin Banham.)*

frequent, although not inevitable. Character is much closer to comic character—locked into types and seldom driven to deep decisions. Threats to the
protagonist are often physical and play on audience sympathy.

4. Farce—a comic work whose aim is laughter, from a non-English word
meaning "to stuff," because farce is stuffed with laughter-producing elements.
The protagonist pursues a mundane, often trivial action, and the characters
are often devoid of decision or thought. Both the characters and the plots of
farce are called *mechanical,* and it is, in fact, in the working out of its
machinery that farce often finds its best laughter.

RESPONSE AND THE PARTS OF A PLAY

Analysis allows us to understand the parts of the play and how they work.
Our responses to the play should be able to determine if:

- Plot is internally consistent, interesting, and appropriate to the
  genre.
- Character is active, interesting, and consistent and has function
  throughout.
- Idea is important and is embodied in character and plot.
- Language is interesting and expressive.
- Music (including the music of language) supports and enriches the
  other parts.
- Spectacle is interesting and appropriate, and whether it supports
  or overpowers other parts.

How To See a Play

As we said at the beginning of Chapter 3, reading a play and seeing a play are different activities. They use different tools and they give different results: reading gives analytical knowledge and the aesthetic and intellectual responses possible with an incomplete artwork; seeing gives a wide range of responses, appropriate to a complete artwork but much affected by the transitory nature of the form.

Some critics and scholars have dealt only with the written play and have said that they preferred reading the play to seeing it in the theatre; however, theirs is a different activity from theatregoing and is not part of the enjoyment of theatre.

The enjoyment of theatre takes place in the theatre. Theatre is an art that exists in performance, and it is as an audience at a performance that we must approach it.

Tools for Seeing

To understand these two chapters on reading and seeing a play, it is necessary to understand that we are treating these activities as different in kind. We have treated reading a play as an analytical act—as a critical experience instead of an aesthetic one. We will now treat seeing a play as an aesthetic experience, not a critical one. This distinction is justified by the difference between the play text and the performance.

The "parts of the performance" are not the same as the parts of the play—and, in fact, the new critical dimension called *performance criticism* is still trying to define the "parts" of theatrical performance.

ARISTOTELIAN ANALYSIS AND PERFORMANCE

The analysis discussed in Chapter 3, "How To Read a Play," based on Aristotle, is appropriate to study of the play *text*. When we come to performance, however, that analysis is inadequate.

Consider the emphasis of the six parts of the play. Of the six, four—plot, character, idea, and language—belong to the text. Music and spectacle, although described in the text, belong to performance.

Yet, when we see a play in performance, plot, character, idea, and language are, in fact, submerged in a greater whole, and they do not appear to us as "parts" called *plot, character,* and so on, but as elements in that organic whole. Even more important, that organic whole has utterly different qualities: aspects of art that, by their very nature, cause us to understand qualities like character in a new way.

For example, character in performance is not written words and intellectual constructs called *decisions*. It is a very complicated creation that is mostly in the work of the actor, for whom the play text (and its six parts) is the foundation of the artistic creation, but not the artistic creation itself.

In addition, the nature of the theatre radically alters the significance of spectacle. Theatre is primarily visual. Suddenly, spectacle is primary. It is the "cause" of much of the performance. In a way that Aristotle could not have predicted, modern theatre has endowed spectacle with meaning—in light's capacity to focus attention, to create mood; in setting's and costume's capacity to give information about time, place, personality, and society; and so on.

Performance also introduces entirely new questions of art—the art of the actor above all, but the art of other theatre makers, as well. Analysis of the play text ("reading a play") raises only the question of the art of the playwright, and then considered only as the writing of text. The writing of text is a great art, but it is not the art of performance, and the formal analysis (via the parts of the play) that allows us to appreciate the text is inadequate for the appreciation of performance.

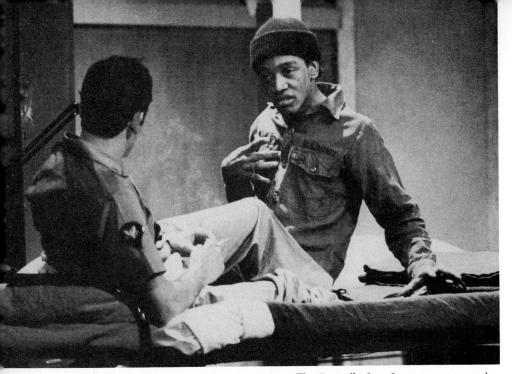

Figure 4-1. **The Play in Performance.** The "parts" of performance are not the same as the "parts" of the text. David Rabe's *Streamers. (Directed by James A. Patterson at the University of South Carolina.)*

Finally, performance is complex and *synergistic:* many elements happen simultaneously and reinforce each other. At the same time, the form of performance prevents our holding on to a moment so as to analyze it or our turning back to it. Thus, seeing a play requires our responding to many stimuli and fusing them to form a whole, moment by moment, while we quickly compare each moment (unconsciously or semiconsciously) with the moments of the performance that have already passed. One critic has called this process "electronic" to contrast it with the linear process of reading the play.

Aristotelian theory remains the bedrock of dramatic analysis. It is unrivaled for understanding the play, even the play as remembered *after* performance. However, to understand performance itself, a different (or at least a supplemental) approach is needed.

The Values of Performance

Performance acts on an audience from several directions simultaneously, so that each audience member is receiving a complicated blend of stimuli at each moment of the performance. For purposes of analysis and discussion, these stimuli can be separated into four main groupings. They are *sensory stimulation* (sight and sound); *human values* (story and character); *artistic*

Figure 4-2. **Simultaneous Values.**
One of the great moments of modern
theatre—Laurence Olivier as Oedipus.
(John Vickers, London.)

excellence; and *intellectual value.* All these stimuli can act on us *simultane-ously* and *synergistically,* meaning that in the best performances, they not only harmonize with each other but also support and enrich each other.

After World War II, the great English actor Laurence Olivier played Oedipus in Sophocles' tragedy. His performance is generally conceded to have been the greatest interpretation of that role in modern times. At the moment when Oedipus appeared, having just gouged out his eyes, the audience response was so intense that people gasped, and many of those who saw the performance still remember the moment as a high point in a lifetime of theatregoing. (See Figure 4-2.) Because the bloody effects of the eye gouging were visual, we could say that the moment was an example of intense *sensory stimulation;* however, because the horror of the moment depended on an understanding of story and character, the moment also sprang from an appreciation of the *human values* in the performance; yet again, it was

Olivier's superb performance—his *artistic excellence*—that dazzled those in the audience who appreciated the art of acting. And finally, the symbolism and meanings of the eye gouging itself were the springboard for *intellectual value* in this classic tragedy of rich meanings. All four kinds of stimuli were at work, then, and it was the four, working *together*, that made the moment.

Of the four categories of stimuli, two are inherent in *production* (sensory values and artistic excellence), and two are inherent in *text* (human values and intellectual values). This distinction lets us understand at least a few of the reasons that theatregoers see the same play many times over a lifetime without feeling bored. The text does not change (or changes very little), but other important facets change, and, because of the synergistic effect of these factors, the total impact of the performance then changes.

It is important to understand this point, for what it emphasizes is the enormous difference between *reading a play* and *participating as audience in a performance*. To read a play is to engage in an appreciation of half its potential (and then only if the reader is trained in such reading); to see the play in performance is to approach its full potential.

It will be helpful to look at each of the categories in more detail.

Production

SENSORY VALUES

Theatre comes from the Greek word meaning "seeing place." The Latin *auditorium* means "hearing place." We often speak of a performance as a "show." Thus, the vocabulary of the theatre acknowledges its remarkable visual and auditory power.

The audience relies on two senses: seeing and hearing. (Rarely, plays and movies have tried to appeal to other senses—Smell-o-vision, vibrating seats, physical contact with the performers—but the attempts are oddities.) Everything the audience understands about the performance comes through those two senses. The brain processes the information and uses it in several ways, but seeing and hearing remain the root senses of the theatre.

SPECTACLE.   Of the two senses, it is vision that is the more powerful. We believe what we see. When an actor says one thing with words but another with gestures, we believe the gesture. Our language acknowledges this power. "I see," we say when we understand something; having met a friend we say, "I saw so-and-so." Doctors "see" us; people "see" ghosts (a much more frightening experience than hearing one). "Seeing is believing."

Our eyes believe. *Spectacle*—that which is seen—rules.

So potent was spectacle in the Greek theatre that a story is told of one of Aeschylus' plays in which the chorus appeared as the Furies (avenging beings): "When, at the performance of the *Eumenides*, Aeschylus introduced the chorus in wild disorder into the orchestra, he so terrified the crowd that children died and women suffered miscarriage." *Seeing* the Furies was the shock, supported by the sense of hearing and tremendously strengthened by the play itself. Until the moment when they entered "in wild disorder," the Furies had existed as creatures of the mind's eye; suddenly, they were visible to the physical eye: they existed.

A modern audience might laugh at these very same Furies, for response to the visual changes along with all other values. Most of us, no longer sharing or even understanding the ancient Greek religious system, might find such figures interesting or quaint or even comical, but we would not have the "mind's eye" vision to prepare us for the horror of the seen. Thus, spectacle does not mean merely "what is seen" in a purely objective sense; it means "what is seen" in the context of the seer. The physical eye sees merely what is there; it is a physical system—lens, retina, optic nerve—for receiving physical stimuli. The mind, on the other hand, sees in the context of a rich and complicated mixture of symbolism, association, and meaning.

Spectacle is not merely the horrifying or the symbolic, however. It is also the beautiful and the impossible. Most of us respond strongly to the sheer visual appeal of beauty. A parade is a "show" because of its visual beauty: the colors of flags and uniforms, the arranged mass of floats and drill teams, the pleasing movement of synchronization. Football halftime shows, circus performances, laser-light shows, and the visual element of rock concerts are all great appeals to our love of visual beauty.

And perhaps of greatest importance to certain forms is the value of "seeing the impossible." Magic shows are spectacles of the impossible; so is circus trapeze work. So is much of dance, for example, the dazzling tap work of

Figure 4-3. **Sensory Values: Sight and Sound.** The musical *The King and I.* *(The University Company of the University of Tennessee.)*

Figure 4-4. **Spectacle: the Impossible.** This nineteenth-century performance included dazzling trapeze work, effective because it was live and close to the audience. *(From Stanley Appelbaum,* Advertising Woodcuts of the Nineteenth-Century Stage. *New York: Dover, 1977.)*

Broadway show dancing and the defiance of gravity that is classical ballet. We are greatly excited and moved by this "spectacle of the impossible"; through our vision, we come to understand that a certain artist is doing what we thought unlikely or undo-able. And we must *see* it "live." Notice how much weaker the value is, for example, of a magic show seen on television or a dance performance seen on film.

No wonder that our expression for going to the theatre is going "to see a show."

SOUND. Hearing is the other of the audience senses. It makes possible the beauty and excitement of the musical, emotional, rich timber of a great actor's voice. Some of the audience's richest moments in theatre have come about because of sound, often because of quite subtle sound.

Sound is not merely orchestral music or individual noises; it is the whole rich world of the ear. Perhaps it is most important in the theatre because of the actors' voices and the words they say. Voices are "orchestrated," and directors cast actors so that their voices will blend and match. There is an analogy to opera here. Each actor develops the voice to attain maximum range and flexibility. Moreover, the playwright supplies words, sentences, and overlapping lines so that voices will "sing" together, and the words and sentences and voices themselves have beauty *distinct from the meaning of the words* (an aspect of Aristotle's "music"). We are very much in the habit of listening to what actors say rather than listening to the aesthetic values of voice and language, but it is possible to do both; in opera, where the language is often not English, the reverse is true, and the meaning of the language is ignored so that one may concentrate on the glory of the voice. Actors' voices can be effective in the same way, though audiences may not appreciate them with quite the same conscious understanding. Certain actors have voices whose unusual qualities are by themselves effective—a flexible contralto; a husky, breaking voice. Other actors use their voices in surprising ways: vocal swoops, controlled tremolo, meticulous rhythm. The very sound of language, too, is part of the sensory value of the theatre, whether in obvious examples like rhyme or in more subtle poetic language.

Text

HUMAN VALUES

Drama is the imitation of human action; theatre embodies that imitation in performance. As audience, we generalize from the particular imitation to human truths. The nature of imaginative art focuses attention so that invented lives are more significant than most real ones. For many people, the memory of Hamlet is more powerful than the memory of many acquaintances.

The human values of such human imitations are many. They include *human understanding*, the increased awareness of what it is to be a human being; *emotional sympathy*, the participation through art in suffering and joy; *arousal* of pleasure, including a wide range of pleasures from the laughable to the erotic; and *psychic perception*, the observation of mythic patterns, as in dreams.

Audience response to human values comes from two principal factors: story and character. (*Not* Aristotelian plot—the ordering of incidents and the reasons for that ordering: neither order nor reasons can be perceived clearly in performance.)

STORY.   Stories are seemingly as old as human language. Some are complicated and long; some are short and simple. Stories are made up of incidents and have "coherence"; that is, each one is held together by a strong internal force. This force may be causality, but it can be chance or the oddity of the happening.

Stories serve the audience in two ways. First, they are compelling in themselves. Second, they serve as the framework for the other values of character, humor, and so on. In a sense, we understand the other values through our understanding of the story. As individuals, we tend to believe

Figure 4-5. **Story: Suspense and Surprise.** A moment of high impact in *The Foreigner. (Ohio Northern University, Ada, Ohio. Set design by Paul C. Weimer. Photo by Suzanne Heck.)*

that people are understood by their behavior; behavior, focused by art, is story.

It is possible to watch a performance for the value of story alone. Many of the action series on television, for example, offer story as their most important value.

The response to a story comes from *suspense* and *surprise*.

Suspense is the unfolding of events at the pace created by the theatre itself in an artfully crafted structure that will best ask and answer the question "And then what happened?" We must note that a question is *both* asked and answered; that is, the art of suspense lies in manipulating events and time so that the audience will understand *what* story it is to anticipate and *how* that story is progressing through time. A critic said some years ago that art is the creation and satisfaction of appetite, and the definition is not at all inaccurate for suspense, because its two parts—creation and satisfaction— catch the necessary parts of both good suspense-making and good audience response to it. We cannot have story suspense without preparation for it (creation of appetite); that is, we cannot have a haphazard succession of events and call their sequence *suspense*. Who would care if we began a play by showing John, then shifted to Mary, then to Robert, then to Jack, and so on, all evening? This would be all preparation and no story; there could be no "And then what happened?" because *then* would be meaningless. Therefore, to have story suspense that will arouse pleasurable audience response, we must have preparation, connectedness, and resolution (the answer to the question "And then what happened?").

Surprises—changes of direction, reversal, dashing of expectations—these sound like the opposite of suspense, because they suggest that instead of having the question answered, we are being sent off in a different direction or being sent all the way back to the beginning. Not so, however; effective surprise is one of the principal pleasures of story, for it puts us through a pleasing imitation of real experience, which is full of surprises and setbacks; yet the surprise of the theatre is "safe" and therefore pleasurable instead of painful, for it happens only within the contract between performers and audience.

Surprise, like other story elements, must be prepared for. There can only rarely be surprise that is outside the world that the performance creates. That is, it would be "surprising" to have a flying saucer land onstage and carry off the leading character when he got into a terrible mess in Act III, but unless the play had prepared us for flying saucers, this surprise would not truly be a surprise at all; it would be a violation of the contract. It would give us, as audience, not pleasure but annoyance.

Surprise can take several forms. There can be the surprise of the unexpected; the surprise of reversal; the surprise of the prepared-for but unpredictable, when the event (often the high point of a play) astonishes us despite the fact that we know something of the sort must happen. In *Oedipus Rex*, for example, Oedipus' blinding of himself is effective because it is so horrible and shocking. We know that he will do something almost unthinkable to himself, but we do not know what. Related to this sort of surprise is the "least likely" of several choices, a necessity in murder mystery plays. Such plays rely heavily on story for their success, and the basic question that they pose ("Who did it?") makes surprise of choice essential in the last act. Like other sorts of surprise, this will work only if the surprise is carefully prepared for—if, in fact, we can say in retrospect, "Of course! That was inevitable!" (That is, it was set up for us.)

The Aristotelian parts of plot, like plot itself, are not adequately understandable in performance. Sometimes they can be perceived after the performance is over.

CHARACTER. Representations of human beings move through the patterns we have called stories. Their behavior in those stories reveals them to us. They are not mere stick figures, mere zeros. They are *characters*.

A *character* is the representation of a human being in a theatrical performance. A character is not a living human being, nor is it ever a completely rounded imitation of a living human being (nor is a character the same as

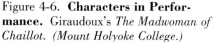

Figure 4-6. **Characters in Performance.** Giraudoux's *The Madwoman of Chaillot. (Mount Holyoke College.)*

the Aristotelian part, character.) It is a detailed representation of a human being *insofar as the audience needs to know that person in the work of art.* The aspects of character that the audience understands are often clearer than similar aspects of people in real life; we may come to know theatrical characters better than our closest relatives. Great characters become part of the common image of "what it is to be a man and woman"; they are quoted, discussed, and made examples of as few real human beings ever are.

Characters and story (like character and plot) are interlocked. We understand each through the other. Nevertheless, they remain a little independent of each other, so that we may have different characters move through the same basic story. The same sequence of events can be used in several ways. "Boy meets girl, boy loses girl, boy gets girl" was a formula for stories of the 1920s and 1930s that could be dramatized around characters as different as classical divinities and factory workers. Incidents, then, allow us to understand characters within a rough framework, but the context and the place of the incident in the story let us perceive characters more fully; when Fred hits John with a baseball bat, if we know that John was messing around with Fred's wife and that Fred has never recovered from his experiences in the Vietnam war, we can form a much better idea of the characters than we ever could from the event itself.

Responses to a character may come from several impulses: identification, subconscious reference, and association.

"Like me" is a common positive response. "It's my story" or "He could be me" are sources of pleasure or suffering. We like to see the mirror held up so that we can watch ourselves. Connected with this idea is the idea of universality of character, the character with whose theatrical experiences everyone can connect. True universality is rare, however; universal experience assumes some level of commonality in *all* humans, which is questionable outside major confrontations with ultimates: birth, death, suffering, love.

Subconscious reference is another kind of identification, but so different that it needs to be talked about separately. This is a response to something that is like us, perhaps, but that we recognize as being like us at a level below the conscious—as in our dreams or our fantasies. We watch *Hamlet* because there are aspects of Hamlet that we can identify with, true, but we watch it also because the Prince of Denmark is the main character in an action that partakes of dreams and of myth, something we fantasize about living through—or fear living through. Frankenstein's monster is not at all "like me," but he may be terrifyingly like our nightmares. Such characters are also a mirror, but not one in which we see our superficial selves; we see the selves we carry, hidden.

Historical names and famous people have their own appeal. Shakespeare's histories were, in their own day, effective character plays for this reason. The musical *1776* gained from the Bicentennial association with our own Revolution; in the nineteenth century, a semidocumentary treatment of such notorious events as real murders and trials created successful theatre. All such plays depend in part for their impact on convincing us that we are seeing "truth"—although the farther the real-life people on whom they are modeled are from us (in time and occasionally in culture), the less "truth" matters. To take advantage of the associative response, the play must choose people with whom the audience has strong ties, and it must present them in a convincing fashion (that is, by casting actors who look like the real people or by using effective makeup, and by hewing closely to known events and not violating the "facts" of history).

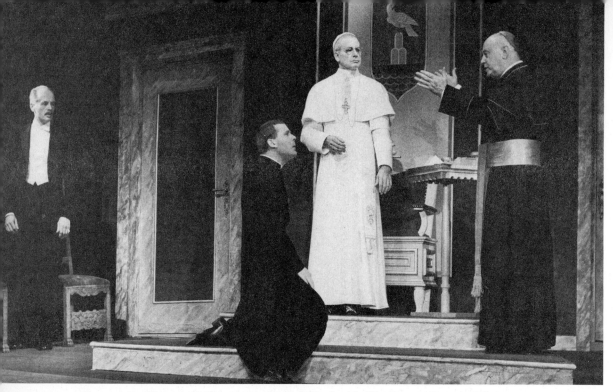

Figure 4-7. **Historical Character.** In Rolf Hochuth's *The Deputy,* historical figures involved in a papal decision during World War II are the characters. *(Produced at the Freie Volksbuhne, Berlin, directed by Erwin Piscator. Photo Ilse Buhs/Jurgen Remmler.)*

ARTISTIC EXCELLENCE

Beyond and behind the appeal of theatrical imitation, of "embodied narrative," there is an element of artistry by which all other things are given value and are heightened: the skill of the actor, the designers, the director, and others. Audience response to the actor is probably the easiest to understand and the response we most often sense. *Understanding of the art of the theatre* makes such a response possible, and that response greatly enriches all the others. A knowledgeable audience member does not applaud merely the *fact* that the actor created a brilliant character (which the indifferent audience member may confuse with the playwright's creation of character) but also applauds the *artistry* with which the actor did it. In the same way, the knowledgeable audience member is able to respond to the artistry of the director, because knowledge allows an understanding of the contribution that the director made.

This kind of response is possible when the audience member is knowledgeable and when the audience member is somewhat objective about the performance. This is not to suggest that the audience member holds back and does not participate in the performance; rather, it suggests that the perceptive audience member is able both to participate and to watch with some objectivity. "Aesthetic distance"—the separation of audience from performance through art—is set up, as if the audience member were watching the audience watch the play. Perceptions are divided between a subjective participation in the experience and an objective understanding of how the performance came about.

Above all, an appreciation of the artistic element of the theatre requires an understanding of how theatre artists work and of why they make the choices that become the performance. Why did the actor drop his voice to a whisper instead of raising it when the character was angry? Why did the costumer put her into blue instead of red? Why was only part of the house shown instead of the whole thing? The ability to perceive these choices and to understand how they were made comes from gathering knowledge about how theatre artists work, and such knowledge comes from going to the theatre, from working in the theatre, and from studying about the theatre (as in this book).

In part, an appreciation of the element of artistry comes from an awareness of potentials and possibilities—of the human voice and body; of the use of space; of light as a plastic entity; and of pictorial composition.

At its best, the theatre should make us gasp, and one of the elements at which we will gasp is the ability of the artist to transcend what we think are human limits.

INTELLECTUAL VALUES

Generally, ideas are given least thought while we sit in the theatre but are the things that we talk about most after we have left. There is a good reason for this seeming contradiction: the theatre is "the place of the now." Performance is transitory. When it is behind us, preserved only in our memories, the vividness of the sensory and artistic pleasure fades, and we are left with the intellectual content, which remains sharp and fresh because of the sharpness of our minds. Ideas, in fact, become more acute with time, if we allow ourselves to be interested in them. As well, ideas are frequently the element of theatre that reviewers and critics talk about because, being intellectual and capable of verbalization, ideas are far easier to put into words than the brilliance of an actor's gesture or the beauty of a lighting effect.

There are ideas behind or embodied in every play, to be sure, but some ideas are more interesting and more important than others. As well, some ideas are more interesting and important to certain people, less so to others.

Questions of importance and relevance are highly debatable, as anyone who has sat in on a late-night bull session knows, and more often than not, a debate about relevance and importance is really a debate about "what I like" or "what I believe." In the area of theatrical idea, however, the audience member errs by making a personal judgment. It is far better to ask, at least, why the idea was important to the theatre people who created the performances than to say unthinkingly, "That idea is not important (to me)" or "That idea is irrelevant (to me)."

The artistry of performance is best comprehended not by the intellect but by the body and the heart and the receptive self. Pure idea, which is dealt with directly by the intellect, belongs not in the theatre but in the lecture hall. Theatrical idea, which deals with the intellect through the medium of performance, belongs importantly in the theatre when it is entirely integrated into the other elements and neither manipulates them nor obscures them but speaks to the mind through them.

Too, idea is not the element that the performer cares most about. There is an old theatre adage: "If you have a message, send a telegram." Directors only rarely talk to actors about the "idea of the play"; designers do not try to express idea but try, instead, to provide good acting spaces and aesthetically pleasing spaces. A playwright may talk about "what my play means," but only rarely will director, designer, and actors work with the playwright to enhance these ideas; rather, they will work on the other values—for they know that *in performance it is those values that must succeed.*

This is not to say that ideas do not belong in the theatre. Nor does it mean that performers have contempt for ideas or that ideas are themselves an intellectual, after-the-fact invention. What it does mean is that idea is not a be-all and end-all in the theatre. In a sense, idea is the most important element in making a serious judgment about the importance of a play, but that judgment is made only if the play succeeds brilliantly with the other values. *Hamlet* is a great play both because it is a stunning experience to see *and* because it is rich in complex ideas. A less important play, effective as it may be in performance, has less complex ideas that are less central to the culture, less tantalizing on the largest scale of human concerns.

Responses of the Audience

To discuss now the internal responses of audience members to performance is to delve into an area as complex and mysterious as human psychology itself. No one can say for certain how an audience will respond; no one can say for certain how an individual in an audience is responding at any moment. Performances differ from each other; audiences differ from each other; individuals in an audience differ from each other.

Individual postures toward a performance vary from extreme involvement (identification) to extreme objectivity. At any point along this spectrum, individuals bring such vastly different psyches to the experience that two people, sitting side by side at the same performance, may have entirely different experiences and may behave outwardly in entirely different ways. Thus, any observations made about audience response are generalizations to which there must always be many exceptions.

Figure 4-8. **"The Upper Regions in Disorder."** An audience responding to an event in the house instead of one onstage.

The exterior behaviors that indicate audience response are covered in the following sections.

LAUGHTER

Laughter is the actor's reward in comedy, the actor's torment in serious drama. In general, audiences seem to laugh for two widely different reasons: because they are truly amused and because they are uneasy. The laughter of amusement is largely a response to human values—that is, to an understanding of story and character—although there is considerable intellectual involvement in our laughter at satire, for example. The laughter of amusement may range from enormous belly laughs at wit or pratfalls ("We had them rolling in the aisles!") to low chuckles of appreciation that reflect warmth and approval.

The laughter of unease can be shattering for the actor, who may find the audience laughing uproariously at completely improper moments. Such laughter springs not from amusement but from stress; it is not the laughter of an understanding of human values but the laughter of rejection of the experience represented by the performance. "Nervous laughter" is familiar in life; it has

Figure 4-9. **Mediation: Advertising.** Good audience response is prepared partly by knowledge of the work, much of which today comes from advertising.

its counterpart in the theatre. Inevitably, it means that the performance has failed (but the failure may be the fault of the audience and not of the performers).

SILENCE

"You could hear a pin drop!" The silence of rapt attention is familiar. Although we associate applause with the theatre, it is silence that is often the surest key to the effective response of an audience. Silence means attentiveness, for the body is being held still. The body at rest is not necessarily still; it shifts position, coughs, taps its fingers. A thousand people who do not make a single sound are remarkable, then. The performance has them in a very tight grip.

Such silence cannot be preserved for an entire evening. Like the pauses between movements of a symphony, when voices hum, coughs resound, and programs rattle, performances of even the most compelling sort must provide occasional release. Normally, such release points are built into the text of the play.

APPLAUSE

"Ours be your patience then, and yours our parts;/Your gentle hands lend us, and take our hearts" (Shakespeare's *All's Well That Ends Well*). The performers' request for applause—"plaudite"—dates to classical times. Clapping is still the way of signaling approval of performances of many kinds, from athletics to music to political speeches. It signals gratitude, approval, sometimes a request for more, an encore. In some instances, an audience will rise to applaud—the "standing ovation" that signals special favor.

Actors take their bows so long as applause lasts. "Milking" applause for more bows is considered bad form; contrarily, repeated bows at the curtain are the result of extended applause.

It is, perhaps, an oddity of theatrical convention that there is no audience behavior to signal positive response to serious or even tragic performance. In comedy, laughter follows comic events; in tragedy, profound silence is often the most significant response. Even at the end of many serious performances, silence will be the audience's behavior, as if even applause were too frivolous for the moment. Applause, then, is the usual sign of approval, but silence may be a sign of the deepest effect.

TEARS

People do still weep in the theatre, although the copious waterworks of years ago are seldom seen. Such shedding of tears today may be—in fact, usually is—silent; it may be only the tear in the eye, the lump in the throat. In either case, it is an outward sign of "empathy," the "believing with" an emotional moment. It is human value that stirs empathy, often at a far less than tragic level. Fictional deaths of animals and children, the parting of lovers, and similar human events can provoke tears.

We live in an age when public weeping is discouraged. Public laughter is approved; public tears are not. We still have such expressions as "having a good cry," and a certain kind of dated, highly empathetic movie is still called a "four-handkerchief picture." By and large, however, the taboo against public crying is almost too strong even for the "allowed behavior" of the darkened theatre. When we are moved, we try to hide our tears and keep our sniffles silent.

UNEASE

Audiences have several negative behaviors (most of them unconscious) that reflect negative responses to performances. The most obvious of these is *noise:* coughing, shuffling of feet, whispering, shifting positions. When a thousand or more people begin to do these things at once, the noise level can get quite high, and the actor will believe that it is deafening. All the sounds that are suppressed when an audience is attentive become noticeable the moment that the attention wanes. Coughs resound like gunshots; programs rattle like so many sails in the wind; feet scrape on the floor like coffins being dragged over a pavement. Bodies, tensed to watch and listen, are working off nervous energy. Each individual believes that he or she is being quiet, but the cumulative effect is loud—and horribly revealing.

Figure 4-10. **The Prepared, Willing Audience.** Most Broadway audiences are in the theatre because they want to be and because they understand the demands of the theatre.

More conscious negative behaviors include comments about the performance and getting up and walking out of the theatre. Rarely, nowadays, do they include catcalls, boos, remarks to the actors, or thrown objects.

Negative behaviors reflect negative responses; negative responses reflect a failure of communication between performance and audience. *Either* the performance or the audience—or *both* of them—may be responsible. Bad performances can cause negative responses, but bad audiences can have negative responses to a good performance.

What is a bad audience? It is an audience that is unable or unwilling to respond to the performance before it under the conditions of the theatre. Thus, bad audiences are of two kinds: (1) the *unprepared audience*, which does not understand the nature of theatre art and so responds to performance as it does to life; and (2) the *unwilling audience*, which refuses to accept the nature of the performance before it.

The unprepared audience is usually new, or fairly new, to the theatre. It confuses art and life. It shows inappropriate responses because the intensity of theatre acutely embarrasses it; it may laugh at scenes of suffering, love, or nobility; it may, in extreme cases, try to interrupt the performance to prevent what, in life, would be offensive behavior.

The unwilling audience can be any audience alienated from the performance by poor mediation or by personal stubbornness. Some people simply dislike musicals; others hate the circus; and so on. They should stay away from the forms they dislike; if trapped into them by accident or mistake, they show an extreme of unease. Less obvious, but far more common, are audiences who are shocked or dismayed by elements of performance—usually intellectual value, sometimes human value or sensory value—that they are unaccustomed to. These elements run a wide spectrum from nudity to religion. Again, as with the unprepared audience, there is an ignorance of the nature of art and the "harmlessness" of the theatre; in the case of the unwilling audience, however, the ignorance exists despite considerable theatre experience. The unwilling audience should know better but refuses to.

We all begin as the unprepared audience. We all have a potential for being the unwilling audience. We grow away from the first with experience and knowledge; we avoid the second with alertness to the theatre's essential nature and to the role of the audience in performance.

Today's Theatre and

Its Makers

CHAPTER

5

Making Theatre Today: The Context

Before studying the people who make theatre happen, we need to examine the contexts in which they work in the United States. In what kinds of spaces can they make their plays? Are some arrangements of actors and audiences better than others for certain sorts of plays? What kinds of producing arrangements are available, and what are their strengths and weaknesses? Finally, how can theatre productions be financed, and what are some implications of the different funding sources?

Theatre Spaces

Given the diversity of theatre groups around the country, it should not be surprising that they choose different sorts of physical spaces in which to work. With various elaborations, three basic theatre spaces now dominate: proscenium, thrust, and arena stages. In addition to these three, a few less common arrangements can be named and briefly described.

PROSCENIUM STAGES

The most popular theatre shape in Western Europe and America since the seventeenth century, proscenium theatres are marked by a proscenium arch that separates the stage and the auditorium.

The stage behind the proscenium arch is typically equipped with a rigging system, which allows scenic pieces to be "flown" (lifted out of sight above the stage floor), and a trap system, which allows objects and people to sink below the stage floor or to rise from it. Some are equipped with wagons or "slip stages" that allow scenery to be moved into place from the *wings*, the spaces on each side of the stage. In most proscenium theatres, there is an area that extends a few feet in front of the arch, an area called the *apron* or *forestage*.

The auditorium is arranged so that almost all seats face the stage. Ground level seats are *orchestra seats*. Above them are *balconies* (also called *galleries*), which may curve around at least part of the side wall. Older proscenium houses have small, separate balconies, called *boxes*, usually on the side walls of the theatre near the stage. These boxes were at one time the most prized seats in the theatre, but they are now usually avoided because of their bad angle for viewing the stage (bad *sight lines*).

THRUST STAGES

Some plays, especially those of Shakespeare and his contemporaries, were not written for production in a proscenium theatre. For this reason, several theatre companies, especially those whose repertory stresses plays from the past, have sought a variation of the theatre used in Shakespeare's day. Such groups have built theatres with thrust (or Elizabethan, or Shakespearean, or three-quarter-round) stages.

In such theatres, there is no arch separating the actors from the audience. Instead, audience members are placed on three sides of the action, usually on a raked (slanted) floor to improve sight lines, and in balconies. Actors enter the playing area from the back or through *vomitories* (passages that run through and under the audience and open near the stage itself). Because in

Theatrical Images from Other Cultures

The Western theatrical tradition, of which American theatre is a part, has been enriched by increasing knowledge of other traditions. The use of masks is important in many theatre cultures and is part of the impact of Figures of Speech Theatre's *ANERCA*. African experience and imagery inform the visual richness of Femi Osofisan's *Farewell to a Cannibal Rage* and Wole Soyinka's *The Lion and the Jewel* and find echo in Caryl Churchill's *Cloud Nine*. China's Beijing Opera and Japan's Noh theatre are ornate and beautiful, and their color and conventions have been evoked by such Western theatrical art as Bertolt Brecht's *Good Woman of Setzuan*.

C-1. Masks from (clockwise from top) Southwestern United States; Northeastern United States; Mexico; West Africa; Mexico.

C-2. *ANERCA*. Figures of Speech Theatre.

C-3. Osofisan, *Farewell to a Cannibal Rage.*

C-4. Soyinka,
The Lion and the Jewel.

C-5. Churchill, *Cloud Nine*.

C-6. Beijing Opera.

C-7. Noh Theatre.

C-8. Costume for
The Good Woman of Setzuan.

Figure 5-1. **Proscenium Theatre.** Probably the most common type today is the proscenium theatre, named for the arch that separates the stage from the audience area and noted for having all spectators watch from the same general direction.

this theatre elaborate stage machinery cannot be concealed behind a proscenium arch and because, too, of the close physical relationship between the actors and the audiences, thrust stages tend to rely on acting, costumes, and properties rather than complex scenic effects. Indeed, in such theatres, without a front curtain and a proscenium arch to mask them, all scene changes and all actors' entrances must be made in full view of the audience.

Of the many thrust theatres, perhaps the best known are those at The Festival Theatre in Stratford, Ontario, Canada, and at the Guthrie Theatre in Minneapolis, Minnesota, both of whose repertories stress revivals of masterpieces from the past.

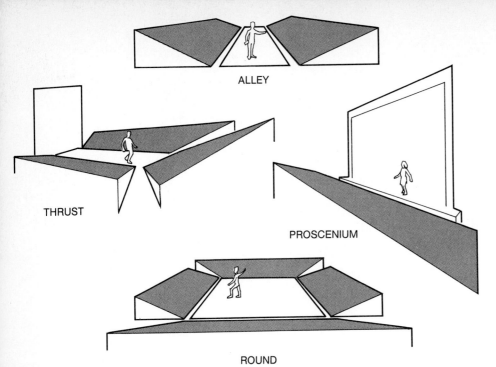

ALLEY

THRUST

PROSCENIUM

ROUND

Figure 5-2. **Common Theatre Shapes.** This diagram highlights the major differences among the major kinds of theatre. Notice especially the changing relationship between the actors and the audience.

ARENA STAGES

The audience in the arena theatre surrounds the playing area, hence its other name: *theatre in the round*. Many people prize the closeness of actors and audiences in arena staging, an intimacy especially well suited to many plays in the modern repertory. With neither a proscenium arch nor a back wall to mask movements, all property and scenic shifts and all actors' entrances must be done either in blackout or in full view of the audience. Perhaps for this reason, arena stages tend to avoid elaborate scenic effects in favor of close attention to the details of costumes, properties, and acting.

Although less common than either proscenium or thrust stages, arena stages exist throughout the country, most notably at The Arena Stage, Washington, D.C., and the original Alley Theatre, Houston, Texas.

OTHER CONFIGURATIONS

Sometimes from choice and sometimes from necessity, acting companies may take their performances to audiences instead of having audiences come to them. For such performances, a wide assortment of spatial arrangements must be found or created.

The booth stage has long been a popular solution. Here, actors erect a curtain before which they play, either on a raised platform or in a cleared

Figure 5-3. **Booth Stage.** A favorite of travelling companies, the booth stage is both flexible and inexpensive. (Anstie's Limit. *Directed by Kenneth M. Cameron.*)

area. The result is very much like the thrust stage, with the curtain serving both as a place from which to make entrances and as a background against which to perform. Because it meets the basic needs of performance and can be quickly erected and dismantled, the booth stage has long been the favorite of traveling companies.

Alley stages place the audience on two sides, with the actors performing between them, and often with scenic units at each end. In some countries, such arrangements are found in regular theatres; here, however, they are used mostly by actors who find it necessary to perform in school gymnasiums.

Finally, only the imagination limits the space in which actors perform for audiences. In the United States, we have records of theatre taking place in streets, parks, factories, and even elevators—again, an index of the great diversity of our theatre.

Producing Situations in the United States

Its center is still New York City, but American theatre now touches most cities throughout the country. Although its diversity makes classification difficult, we can divide American theatre first into *professional* and *amateur* (each with several subcategories). Because some theatres resist these categories, we have a third group: *theatres for special audiences.*

PROFESSIONAL THEATRE

BROADWAY. Say the word *theatre* to an average American, and he or she will probably think immediately of New York's Broadway. The word, in fact,

91

has several different meanings. *Broadway* is, first of all, the name of a street in New York that runs the length of Manhattan. But the word *Broadway* also designates the whole area around Times Square (Broadway and several streets adjacent to it), where most of New York's commercial theatres are located. The word was once used in various union contracts to specify a certain kind of theatre in which only union members could work, and then only for a fee or salary that met or exceeded the negotiated union minimums for that kind of theatre. And the word *Broadway* refers to a whole complex of qualities that people associate with the glamorous, glittering world of the legitimate theatre: elaborate settings, rich costumes, distinguished stars, polished performances, and sophisticated musicals and plays.

Although New Yorkers attend the Broadway theatre in large numbers, tourists also make up a sizable part of its audiences. From across the country, people flock into its theatres as part of "seeing New York." They expect to see plays written by the best-known playwrights, performed by the best actors, and designed by the best artists available, for which they are willing to pay—in the mid-1980s—about $50 a ticket (up from about $25 in the 1970s). At such prices, Broadway audiences comprise mostly the affluent: a social group that tends to be middle-class or above, white, mature, and somewhat conservative in taste and politics.

Broadway is best known for its musicals, where spectacle, rather than

Figure 5-4. **Broadway.** A Broadway theatre marquee at night announces a musical. The bright lights of the many marquees gave Broadway its other name: "The Great White Way."

intellectual value, is prized. Situation comedies somewhat like those seen on television vie with musicals for popular acceptance. The remaining repertory consists of occasional serious dramas, mysteries, biographies, and one-person shows. Because of the high costs of producing on Broadway, its theatres seldom offer untried plays; they feature instead revivals of successful plays from past Broadway seasons or recently written plays transferred from successful runs elsewhere, most often London, Off-Broadway, or the regional theatres.

Broadway's reputation today rests in large part on the high quality of its productions rather than on the literary merit of its drama. Because many theatre professionals believe that they have not established themselves until they have succeeded on Broadway, Broadway sets the standards of American acting, directing, and design. Broadway artists command among the highest salaries paid in the American theatre, and unions protect them by establishing minimum salaries and controlling working conditions. The major theatrical organizations are the Dramatists Guild (for writers), the Actors Equity Association (for performers), the Society of Stage Directors and Choreographers, United Scenic Artists (for designers), and IATSE (for technicians).

Much of Broadway's appeal, and also many of its problems, stem from money. Its costs of producing continue to climb, for several reasons. As real-estate prices in Manhattan soar, so do the costs of renting theatre space. Personnel costs rise with the demands of the unions. Costs of the goods and services needed to open a show—lumber for scenery, fabrics for costumes, advertising in newspapers and on television—have become almost prohibitive; and then, there is the money needed to keep the show running once it has opened. Costs are now so high that even a fairly modest show must run months (rather than weeks) in order to recapture its original investment, a situation that has made the *long run* a regular feature of the Broadway theatre.

Accelerating production costs have also produced the "hit-or-flop" syndrome. A play can make big money (*Godspell* returned over 20,000 percent to its investors) or it can go bust (*Hellzapoppin* lost $1.2 million for its investors). Boom or bust: "You can make a killing in the American theatre but you can't make a living there."

Another result of high costs has been to limit the potential audience for Broadway shows and to increase the power of certain New York reviewers. As ticket prices rise, the number of people able (or willing) to afford the Broadway theatre declines, as does the willingness of audiences to risk an unpleasant evening in the theatre. Audiences therefore look to a reviewer to steer them toward plays they will like and away from plays that they will not like. In so doing, audiences invest certain New York reviewers with enormous power over the fate of shows. And this audience affects the repertory in other ways as well, for producers actively seek productions to appeal to its tastes. Thus, the cycle of depending on tried-and-true plays, playwrights, and artists is reinforced. Simultaneously, opportunities for original plays, untested actors, and unknown directors are further constricted.

Broadway has tried to solve some of its money problems. For example, two low-priced ticket sources, the Times Square TKTS booth and the Lower Manhattan Theatre Center, sell tickets at half price on the day of performance for shows not sold to capacity. The computerization of ticket sales allows out-of-towners to compete with New Yorkers for good seats, and credit card payments by phone eliminate the need to write for tickets or to stand in lines to purchase them. The Theatre Development Fund, established in 1967, supports commercial productions of special artistic merit; and New York City offers incentives for the construction of new theatre buildings. The success of these efforts to make Broadway more accessible cannot yet be gauged.

Although detractors of Broadway have long deplored the grip that big business seems to have on it and have predicted its death many times, Broadway continues to be the model of much professional theatre in America. A testament to its authority in matters theatrical is that some other professional theatres, like road shows and dinner theatres, strive to imitate it.

THE ROAD.   Many communities regularly import recent Broadway hits by booking the touring theatrical companies (road shows) that each year criss-cross the country. Although such road shows originate in New York, they seldom employ the original Broadway cast; but they do use professionals. Because road companies travel with complete sets and costumes, they are usually able to offer polished performances of recent hits to audiences outside the major cities, who would otherwise be unable to see them.

DINNER THEATRES.   Throughout the United States, dinner theatres offer successful Broadway plays of past seasons as the mainstay of their repertories. The quality of such companies varies widely. Some use union personnel, and their quality tends to be higher than those that rely on pick-up personnel.

Figure 5-5. **Broadway.** Space is scarce; real estate prices soar. Advertisers use unconventional locations to promote their plays.

Figure 5-6. **Broadway Business: Problems and Solutions.** The TKTS ticket booth in New York's Times Square offers cut-rate tickets in an attempt to attract new audiences and keep shows open.

Restrictions of space and budget cause almost all dinner theatres to simplify the lavish scenery and costumes of the originals in favor of smaller casts, smaller orchestras, and fewer sets; but, like Broadway, most seek to entertain rather than to elevate or instruct their audiences. In addition to the play itself, they add the sociability of drinks and dinner, so that an evening in the theatre is a festive occasion, not unlike going out for dinner before seeing a show on Broadway.

OFF-BROADWAY. The name *Off-Broadway* derives from the location of its theatres, which lie outside the Times Square theatre district. In addition to location, Off-Broadway houses were once contractually defined by their limited capacity (no more than 299 seats) and by their lower-than-Broadway salaries (as negotiated with the major unions).

Originally, the goals of Off-Broadway differed from those of Broadway. Off-Broadway sought to serve as a showcase for new talents: untried artists could work; established artists could experiment with new techniques; new plays could find production. Off-Broadway artists hoped to remain aloof from both threats of censorship and the problems of high-risk commercialism.

Although Off-Broadway continues to offer employment to actors, directors, and playwrights (producing three or more shows for every one of Broadway's by the mid 1980s), its production costs have risen and, with them, its need

Figure 5-7. **Off-Broadway.** An extraordinarily popular musical of the Off-Broadway theatre was *Little Mary Sunshine*, shown here in a production at the University of Northern Iowa. *(Directed by D. Terry Williams.)*

to succeed at the box office. As risk has become less practical, Off-Broadway has become a rather less expensive version of Broadway, for which it now serves regularly as a tryout space. Shows that succeed Off-Broadway may move to Broadway, often with the same casts, directors, and designers, but with much larger budgets.

Even though Off-Broadway and Broadway overlap in several respects, the lower ticket prices Off-Broadway attract a more diverse audience and thus allow a somewhat more varied repertory. In addition to small musicals and situation comedies, Off-Broadway produces some serious works, even those that are potentially controversial. For about half of what it costs to see Broadway shows, Off-Broadway audiences can choose among revivals from the classical repertory, recent successes, and original plays. Some of the productions are very good; some are not. But modest risk-taking is part of attending the Off-Broadway theatre and, for those who support it, remains a major part of its attraction.

OFF-OFF-BROADWAY. As Off-Broadway moved closer to Broadway—in practice, if not in location—some artists felt the need for an alternative theatre where authors, directors, and actors could work closely together to produce plays in an artistic, rather than a commercial, environment. Thus, Off-Off-Broadway grew up in the late 1950s as a place dedicated to the process of creating art and exploring the possibilities of the theatre. It did not want to become a tryout space for Broadway or to succumb to Broadway's or Off-Broadway's commercialism.

Productions feature imaginative, but seldom elaborate, sets and costumes. Although the casts and designers in such spaces are not necessarily union members and are seldom paid even their expenses, they continue to work, exploring the limits of a vision that is often socially, politically, or artistically alien to current American values. Lower ticket prices encourage attendance by people priced out of the Broadway theatre, and the excitement caused by unknown plays and artists draws adventurous patrons to coffeehouses, lofts, cellars, churches, and small theatres tucked away all over Manhattan and even some of the other New York City boroughs, where they watch artists perform plays that stimulate them.

Although sometimes amateurish and often controversial, the offerings of Off-Off-Broadway provide a genuine alternative to the commercialism of both Broadway and Off-Broadway. Off-Off-Broadway remains the focus of much of the truly experimental and political theatre in America.

REGIONAL THEATRES.   The vitality of regional professional theatres is one of the most heartening developments in the American theatre. In more than fifty major cities throughout the United States and Canada, more than sixty professional theatres bring art to their audiences. Unlike the commercial Broadway theatre, these groups are usually organized as not-for-profit enterprises and so can be more adventurous with play selection, production style, and personnel decisions. They contribute to theatre throughout America by diversifying and enriching its repertory, developing new audiences, training and revitalizing theatrical artists, and providing employment opportunities. Perhaps for this reason, regional theatres have been called "the conscience of the American theatre."

Regional theatres offer five major benefits:

1. *A forum where new plays and classics can coexist and provide an alternative to the comedies and musicals that are now the mainstays of Broadway.* Some, like the Guthrie Theatre in Minneapolis, have earned reputations through the excellence of their classical revivals. Others, like the Dallas Theatre Center and the Actors Theatre of Louisville, have been especially successful in sponsoring new plays. Such theatres have reversed the tradition of plays' beginning in New York and then trickling down slowly to the rest of the country. Much new drama now appears first around the country, where it is nurtured and tested. The best of it moves beyond its local area and throughout the country, often ending in New York.

2. *A source of new audiences for live theatre.* The art of theatre suffers without knowledgeable audiences, because theatre artists become complacent, accepting the ordinary or the mediocre rather than demanding the excellent. With the growth of regional professional companies, audiences across the country have come to appreciate live theatre as an art form and a cultural resource.

3. *A training ground and an energizing center for theatrical artists.* Colleges and universities begin the training of many young artists; the professional regional companies serve to introduce young artists to the profession, allowing

them to work intensively with experienced artists. Today, many of our best talents in acting, directing, and designing begin their careers at one of these regional companies—and some elect to stay there throughout their careers.

4. *An important opportunity for the seasoned professional.* Commercial theatre can dull an artist's creativity and vitality because its repertory is restricted and because its productions, when successful, can run for months or years, a numbing experience for an artist. Moreover, the commercial theatre seldom offers those roles from the classical repertory that stretch the actor's craft. For these reasons, the best actors are often anxious to spend time with a resident theatre, where they can play a wide variety of roles from many of history's best plays. The exchanges between the regional and the New York theatres seem to be raising the standards of the whole profession.

5. *More jobs.* In New York City, job opportunities are dismal. There are at least five times as many professionals as there are jobs. Regional theatres offer an alternative to New York. For several years, more professional actors have been working outside than inside New York; and designers, few of whom

Figure 5-8. **Regional Theatre.** Among regional theatres noted for reviving classical works is the theatre at Stratford, Canada, whose renowned 1955 production of *Oedipus Rex* is shown here. *(Courtesy of the Stratford Shakespearean Festival, Stratford, Ontario, Canada.)*

get more than *one* show per season in New York, are now shuttling back and forth across the country, providing scenery, lighting, and costumes for professional productions.

The network of regional professional companies is large and growing. Both in quantity and quality, they are a major force in the American theatre. They may be, when taken together, what so many critics and scholars have long sought: America's National Theatre.

AMATEUR THEATRE

Amateur theatre is theatre performed and produced by people who do not earn their living in the theatre. The two major kinds of amateur theatres in America are educational theatres and community theatres.

EDUCATIONAL THEATRES.   Theatre existed in American colleges and universities even before there were professional theatres here. Theatre and drama were at first extracurricular, performed at special events like commencements. They were later included within the curriculum of departments like classics or English. Drama and theatre became college subjects in their own right only early in this century, when George Pierce Baker (1866–1935) instituted classes in playwriting (and later play production) at Radcliffe College (1903), Harvard (1913), and Yale (1925). By 1914, Carnegie Institute of Technology was offering the first theatre degree. Shortly after World War II, most colleges and universities organized departments of drama (often in combination with speech) and offered, in addition to coursework, both undergraduate and graduate degrees.

Although differing in principal emphases, the functions of educational theatres now closely parallel those of the regional professional companies: training future artists, developing new audiences, expanding the theatrical repertory, and providing jobs.

Obviously, the major goal of academic programs is the education and training of students. With the demise of the resident stock companies, training in acting, directing, playwriting, design, and technical production has been largely assumed by the academic institutions. Although many persons complain of the limitations placed on such training because of the basically conservative, even stultifying atmosphere of many academic organizations, the fact remains that most training for the profession now takes place in this world. Although each program is unique, the general pattern of instruction involves some combination of formal classroom work and public performances of selected plays.

The number of educational theatre programs alone is sufficient to render their influence strong. Whereas America now boasts more than sixty professional regional companies, it supports more than two thousand theatre programs in colleges and universities. In small cities without resident professional companies, theatre productions at the college are the best for miles around, and in smaller towns, such productions may be the citizen's only

Figure 5-9. **Educational Theatre.** Harvard University's production of *Oedipus Rex* in the 1880s, performed in the original Greek as a part of the classical education of the students.

opportunity to view live performances. Through introductory classes and small touring companies, college and university theatres introduce thousands of students at all levels of education to a variety of plays. For many students, these are the first brush with live theatre. Thus, the role of educational theatre in building new audiences can scarcely be overestimated.

Happily, because education is a primary goal, such theatres usually display a strong commitment to a wide range of plays and production styles. Alongside standard musicals, comedies, and domestic dramas, collegiate seasons are likely to include significant works from the past and experimental works for the future. Consequently, audiences for university theatre productions often enjoy far richer fare than would normally be possible in community or dinner theatres.

Too, the number of people required to maintain theatre in an academic setting has given the employment potential of the profession a healthy boost. At the college and university level alone, more than ten thousand productions are mounted each year and more than four thousand teachers are employed. When the growing number of high school drama classes, elementary programs in creative drama, and producing groups devoted to children's theatre are considered, it becomes clear that the academic complex is a major source of jobs. Indeed, educational theatre, considered at all levels, is probably the largest employer of theatre artists and scholars in the United States at the present time.

COMMUNITY THEATRES.   Community theatres exist throughout the country. Cities with one or two regional professional companies may have a dozen community theatres. In towns with neither professional nor educational theatre (except, perhaps, the annual high-school play), a community group may produce plays in a school, a church, or a civic auditorium, providing entertainment and recreation for both participants and audiences.

Community theatres vary enormously. Some pay none of their participants, drawing directors, actors, and office personnel from volunteers in the community; others pay a skeleton staff—a technical director, box-office manager, and an artistic director—who work for a governing board of community

Figure 5-10. **Educational Theatre.** More than two thousand college and university theatre programs across the United States now offer productions. Here, *The Secret Lives of Mildred Wilde* at Arkansas State University.

Figure 5-11. **Community Theatre.**
An early rehearsal of San Antonio Little Theatre's production of Tennessee Williams's *Cat on a Hot Tin Roof.*

volunteers. Almost no community theatres pay their actors or stage crew except under very special circumstances.

In communities without professional companies, community theatres fill the important role of introducing new audiences to the theatre and of keeping live theatre a part of the cultural life of a community. Where professional companies do exist, community theatres serve important recreational needs of people for whom participation in theatre is a greater pleasure than sitting in an audience. In their constant search for volunteers to help with production, such theatres regularly introduce many new people—especially young people—to the world of the theatre. Community theatres are, in fact, the first theatre experience for many people who later enter the profession. Finally, the relatively modest ticket prices of most community theatres bring into their theatres many who might not at first pay the price of a regional professional company. Some of these newcomers will become lifelong supporters, not only of their local community theatre but also of the regional professional companies and, when in New York, of its commercial theatres.

THEATRES FOR SPECIAL AUDIENCES

Some theatres cannot be categorized according to our earlier scheme, for they have both professional and amateur companies. Such theatres define themselves not by their financial structure but by the specific audiences that they aim to serve.

Figure 5-12. **Children's Theatre.** Imaginative masks, rich costumes, and exciting action appeal to young audiences in *The Honorable Urashima Taro. (Produced by the Department of Drama at The University of Texas at Austin.)*

CHILDREN'S THEATRE. Among the most long-lasting of such groups are the children's theatres. Whether an established professional company, a university program, or an amateur group composed of community volunteers, whether using adult or child actors, a children's theatre aims to produce plays with special appeal to young audiences in order to instill in such audiences a love of the theatre.

The repertory usually consists of plays specially written for youth, using stories and issues of interest to that age group. Their range is great—from imaginative retellings of popular fairy stories, myths, and legends to sensitive treatments of contemporary social problems like drugs and divorce. Production styles vary, but most avoid domestic realism in favor of less literal presentations. With relatively modest ticket prices (adults often get in at reduced rates when accompanied by a child) and an unusually high commitment to their audiences, children's theatres introduce many young people to the art of the theatre and, from this large group, recruit some as lifelong supporters of all kinds of theatre.

POLITICAL THEATRES. In another kind of theatre for special audiences, the goals are openly political: black theatre, Chicano theatre, feminist (or women's) theatre, and gay theatre. These groups note (correctly) that theatre through the ages has been controlled by middle- or upper-class white males. Although their individual aims vary, they share common assumptions:

- That the interests of middle-class white males are not their own.
- That group awareness can be heightened by art. They seek, therefore, a theatre that can display their group's experiences and explore its problems.

Figure 5-13. **Political Theatre.** Both black and women's theatres sprang up during the 1960s and 1970s to promote social change. *For Colored Girls Who Have Considered Suicide/When the Rainbow is Enuf*, in rehearsal, at the University of South Carolina. *(Directed by Bette Howard.)*

These theatres serve their audiences in very different ways. Some favor intense political statements; others avoid polemical works altogether. Many urge a continued separation of their theatres from those of the mainstream; others work to integrate their own art and artists into the commercial theatre as quickly as possible. Some of the theatres produce works with high production values and traditional dramatic texts; others disregard accepted production values and work largely through improvisation. Some seek modest social change; others advocate revolution. Some have budgets of hundreds of thousands of dollars; others have no budgets at all. Some charge audiences to attend; others perform in the streets and parks—wherever people congregate—and charge nothing.

Whatever their techniques, these theatres for special audiences strive to offer an alternative to the traditional theatre, which they believe has either demeaned them or ignored them.

Theatre Funding

From its beginnings, American theatre has been organized as a profit-making business: businesspeople invest money in a theatre company or a production and hope to recover their investment, with interest, from box-office receipts. This same pattern persists today on Broadway and Off-Broadway, though now the stakes are higher and the sale of film, television, and video rights joins the box office as a likely source of revenue. Dinner theatres adapt this basic pattern by adding income from the sale of food and drink; community theatres, by relying on volunteers for donations of time, money, and goods.

Educational theatres are subsidized. Although the out-of-pocket costs of their productions must often be defrayed by the sale of tickets and program advertisements, the salaries of the faculty (who usually direct, design, manage, and mount the productions) are almost always paid by the university. Because the students who act and crew the productions are seldom paid, the majority of the labor costs associated with producing plays is charged to the university, not to the production. This substantial subsidy allows such theatres to be somewhat adventurous in their selection of plays.

With an occasional exception, government funding for theatre in this country has been conspicuously absent. Thus, one of the most closely watched developments of recent years was the establishment in 1965 of the National Endowment for the Arts (NEA), whose purpose was to encourage the development of the arts throughout the country. It did so in two major ways: by establishing state arts councils as coordinating and funding units and by subsidizing some existing performance groups. To receive grants, theatres must be organized as not-for-profit theatres, a radical departure from the Broadway model.

The precedent set by the NEA may help account, as well, for a new phenomenon: cities and counties, through their parks and recreation departments, are supporting theatre as a form of recreation, for citizens who seek an alternative to their well-established programs in sports and crafts. Through both advice and money, recreation departments strive to improve the work of local community theatres, which they view as an important civic resource for the participants and their audiences.

Some people are encouraged that new patterns of funding may be emerging in America, patterns that will make it possible to produce theatre freed from the hit-or-flop syndrome, from the drudgery of the long run, and from an unemployment rate of more than 90 percent among Actors Equity members.

The Playwright

"Good playwrights begin as bad poets," a writer (not himself a good play-wright) is alleged to have said. What he meant was that playwrights show much of the poet's concern with language but finally lack the poet's control of it. Many literary people (by whom we mean poets, novelists, book critics, literary and academic historians, and so on) consider it a bad thing that playwrights "start out as bad poets"—that they do not enshrine the word above all else. In fact, to see this quality as "bad" is to overlook what the playwright's task is all about.

Wright means "maker." As a wheelwright used to be a maker of wheels and a shipwright used to be a maker of ships, so the playwright is a "maker of plays"—not a *writer* of plays. At least, not basically and primarily.

The playwright is a writer because writing—the setting down of a set of symbols—is the best way we have to describe certain kinds of events. It is partly an accident that what the playwright does looks like what the poet does and like what the novelist does—setting down words on paper. If playwrights had a set of symbols like mathematical notation or musical notation, we might be less tempted to think of them as literary artists (i.e., people who started out as "bad poets"), for nobody thinks of mathematicians or composers as literary artists gone wrong. In addition to the use of language to describe dramatic action, of course, the playwright also deals in the language of the characters, and because they speak with the same words in which poems and books are written, the playwright "writes" dialogue for them, and so is a "writer."

It is a common misconception that any writer who writes good conversation "ought to write a play." Novelists and short-story writers often write excellent conversation in their works. Is this talent a clue to their potential to write plays? Not really. The connection between fictional conversation and stage dialogue is a very thin one, more one of accidental resemblance than of real substance. The novelist's conversation is praised for its truth to life, for example; so is the playwright's sometimes—but the playwright's dialogue is a much more terse, loaded, *active* thing than the novelist's, because it has to serve the needs of the stage and not of the page, and those needs are different, involving character motivation, density of information, and rhythm.

To say categorically that playwrights are not "writers" would be foolish. To say that they are not literary artists would be silly. Playwrights join novelists and poets in various academies of arts and letters; their works are studied in literature courses; literary scholars write books about them. They are not, however, *primarily* literary artists; they are primarily artists of the theatre who leave a literary record (the play) of their work behind. In trying to remember this distinction, we should keep in mind a critic's observation that "Molière saved French comedy from literature"—that the theatre artist triumphed over the purely literary artist.

This is not to say that writing plays somehow disables one from writing other things. On the contrary, some poets and novelists have been excellent playwrights. However, relatively few people have been artistically successful with other forms as well as the play. Usually, then, the playwright is an artist related to literary artists but separable from them—by the nature of the thing created, by the nature of the materials, and probably by temperament and impulse. What the playwright shares with all artists is the need to create: art is a way of knowing oneself and the world, of expressing ideas and feelings about oneself and the world.

Why a Playwright?

Why somebody becomes a playwright instead of a novelist or a poet is something of a mystery. There is a germ of truth in the idea that playwrights often start out to be something else. But then, many theatre people start out as something else—directors as actors or stage managers, agents as designers or actors. Perhaps there is a difference in that so often playwrights start out to be something quite outside the theatre. It has often been observed that

Figure 6-1. **The Playwright and the Play.** Left, the seventeenth-century playwright Molière; right, an early twentieth-century performance of his *Monsieur de Pourceaugnac.* *(Right photo from* Le Théâtre.)

much of the vitality of new movements in theatre comes from the entry into it of people from entirely outside the theatre who then write a play or plays. The germ of the mystery is why they decide to write that play.

The answer lies in the nature of the playwright's craft: creating replicas of human action rather than records of it (novels) or responses to it (poems).

Outside the mainstream, the theatre has been very tolerant of forms, length of plays, and styles radically different from those in vogue in the mainstream; that is, what would be "bad plays" by mainstream definition may be welcome outside the mainstream. In fact, a case can be made for saying that the newcomer's strength lies in ignorance; lacking knowledge of the "rules" of mainstream playwriting, the newcomer writes in a seemingly new and refreshing way. The first plays of playwrights as widely different as Molière and Edward Albee illustrate this "strength of ignorance," and it is no accident that in both cases the early plays were very short, for the newcomer is unwittingly innovative when creating what is there to be created and then stopping, without regard for the so-called full-length entertainment of mainstream practice. It is when, then, a newcomer has an idea for what we have called a "replica of human action," however slight and however short, that a playwright is in the making. When the newcomer is brought by luck or design into contact with a theatre and theatre people, plays get written.

It is not an accident that new playwrights often appear in bunches. Whether they are the University Wits of the Elizabethan period or the Off-Off-Broadway playwrights of the early 1960s, they are drawn to playwriting by the same theatrical conditions at the same time—in the case of the University Wits, the explosion of theatrical interest in Oxford and London; in the case of the Off-Off-Broadway playwrights, the explosion of theatrical excitement in the cafés of New York City.

Other factors are, of course, important. A dying or dead theatre rarely attracts new playwrights; a vital one does—and, paradoxically, a vital commercial one attracts them both to itself and to its avant-garde opposite. Money is often an important factor, as is social status. It is sometimes argued, for example, that the English theatre did not attract would-be playwrights in the eighteenth century because the licensing laws made the craft financially unattractive, and many turned to the novel instead. When, on the other hand, a theatre offers large financial rewards, as the American theatre did from the 1920s to the 1950s, many new writers are drawn to it.

But only rarely does somebody sit, like a cartoon character, with a light bulb overhead and the words "Aha, I'll be a playwright!" coming out of the mouth in a balloon. Most often, there are early tries at other kinds of creativity, a sense that something needs to be got out of the self and into a form, but that form is unclear until the often accidental connection with the theatre comes about and the first play takes shape.

Training and the Craft

Playwrights are neither born nor made; they happen. Unlike actors and directors, they do not, as a rule, go through structured periods of formal training to perfect their art. To be sure, there are playwriting programs in American universities, but their record of producing playwrights who write plays of recognized quality is not comparable with the impressive records in acting, direction, and design. Courses in playwriting often familiarize theatre students with the problems of the playwright and give an enriching new slant on other areas of theatre work; advanced degrees in playwriting are frequently combined with scholarly work in such a way that playwriting becomes an adjunct of critical study. Playwriting as an academic discipline, however, suffers from the same problems as creative writing in general, and when it seems to produce results it is because the same factors are at work: teachers who are themselves artists and who teach as much by example as by precept; constant encouragement of creativity itself, so that the student is surrounded by other writers and playwrights; and strong professional links with agents, producers, and publishers, so that entry into the mainstream is greatly eased.

This is not to say that playwriting can be neither learned nor taught.

Certain supposed "rules" can always be taught. And when a theatrical style remains in vogue for a long period, playwrights can be "taught" the hallmarks of that style, meaning really that they can be taught how to imitate the plays that have already succeeded in that style. Thus, in the realistic theatre, would-be playwrights could be taught to put exposition into the mouths of characters who had a reason for explaining things; they could be taught to prepare for the third-act resolution by planting information about it in Act I; they could be taught that taxi drivers and duchesses do not speak in the same way; and so on. Insofar, then, as playwriting is a craft, such teaching was and still can be effective. Its limitations lie in the difference between the craft and the art of writing for the theatre and between the imitation of an existing style and the innovation of a new one (the newcomer's "gift of ignorance").

As well, when imitation of an existing style has been wanted, playwrights have frequently come from within the theatre. They are "people of the theatre" who are "theatre-wise." What is really meant is that they have familiarity with a particular style. Thus, the actor Dion Boucicault could become a playwright when he wanted a vehicle for himself in the mode of the day. (See Figure 6-2.)

When imitation of an existing style has not been the principal object, however, playwrights have often come from totally unexpected directions, and their practice of the craft has been radically different (and has been much pounded by critics; indeed, the work of such newcomers is most often called "not really a play" by reviewers, which is often a way of saying that the work in question is not an imitation of the dominant style). Most often, when newcomers have a very strong impulse to say something in the theatre, however, they do not take kindly to an imitation of the existing style, because styles that have dominated for a long time become increasingly drained of their potential for saying something new. Consequently, we sometimes find newcomers doing really remarkable things—flying in the face of established practice, writing "nonplays," being viewed with derision by mainstream professional and critic alike.

In our own time, this separation has been spectacularly true of both black and feminist playwrights. Both groups have been deeply committed to a view that by its very nature has rejected some aspects of mainstream practice, and both groups have been made up of people who feel personally rejected and who, more often than not, *are* rejected by the mainstream. The black plays of the 1960s, therefore, were called "crude," "naive," and so on, just as were the feminist plays of the 1970s. Both groups of playwrights found audiences, however—obviously an essential for any new playwright—and their successes with those audiences, being noted by the mainstream, caused some of the playwrights to be adopted or coopted into the mainstream. As a result, what had been "crude" and "naive" and "not a play" became "experimental" and "new." In such a way are some playwrights' careers shaped; others find success by careful adherence to tradition and established form.

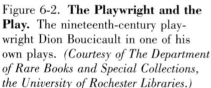

Figure 6-2. **The Playwright and the Play.** The nineteenth-century playwright Dion Boucicault in one of his own plays. *(Courtesy of The Department of Rare Books and Special Collections, the University of Rochester Libraries.)*

Playwright and Audience

"The drama's laws/The drama's patrons give," Samuel Johnson wrote in the eighteenth century. The remark illustrates the uneasy relationship between the playwright and the audience, for, to the playwright, the audience is a fickle monster that can make the artist either rich and loved or humiliated and poor. Between playwright and audience exists a relationship that is often ambivalent in the extreme.

Johnson's remark should remind us, too, that the playwright and the critic not only take a quite different view of the "laws" of the drama but also are frequently indifferent to each other. Not all critics, to be sure, set about to define the "laws" of the drama, but many do; yet while they are doing so, the playwrights are listening not to them but to themselves or to the audience.

Figure 6-3. **The Playwright and the Play.** Left, the nineteenth-century innovator Henrik Ibsen; right, his *Ghosts.* *(Ibsen photo from* Le Théâtre. Ghosts *at Western Carolina University.)*

In fact, innovative playwrights frequently work apart from or even in opposition to the "laws" of the moment, and what they write is written according to a set of "laws" that are yet to be discovered. Thus, it is a mistake to think that playwrights pursue their craft by listening to critics. Very few do. Probably they often should, but most do not. Many playwrights would insist that they do not because they are themselves the makers of the drama's laws. In fact, they are not. They are artists, who neither make rules nor observe them; they make windows, as it were, through which the landscape of dramatic law can be glimpsed.

The relationship between playwright and audience is rather different. Audiences do not care for the laws of drama either. They care for their own responses. They are, however, often conservative and cautious. When they go to a theatre, they want to get their money's worth, and they seldom want to be lectured at, shocked, frightened, or bored. They do not want to suffer either heart attacks or fits of yawning. As a result, they look with enthusiasm on any novelty that is an imitation of what they are familiar with.

This attitude leaves many playwrights in a quandary. They are all right if they are content to do hackwork—but few are, and even those who are successful hacks dream of one day having an artistic hit. Consequently, the majority of playwrights find themselves caught between their own urge to create and their audience's demand that they imitate what has already been done.

The new playwright may at first write plays that attract only a small audience, but the playwright will be encouraged if even a small audience is supportive, finding that it responds to the newness of the work. After a small initial success, the playwright may move toward the mainstream; an audience may be moving toward the playwright at the same time, both being the product of historical change. Sometimes, audiences accept new language, new ideas, and new forms with a speed that is startling. If the moment is not right, however, the playwright may not find an audience, may not even find production, and then will stop writing.

Once established, the American playwright enjoys one or more years of acceptance and then, more often than not, begins to lose the audience. Yesterday's innovator becomes tomorrow's has-been. Rare is the contemporary playwright who is a lifelong success, even a lifelong presence in the theatre; most reach a plateau and then seem to imitate themselves or to decline. One American playwright estimated that an Off-Broadway or Broadway career lasts ten years.

A few playwrights, however, hold their audiences and grow with them. They are the masters of their theatres—playwrights of lasting and secure power.

The Playwright's Compromise

In the realistic theatre, playwrights have had to strike a balance between their own impulse to expand meaning and the stage's impulse to limit meaning to the same role that it plays in life. For earlier playwrights, language was a primary means of theatrical communication, and realistic plays about upper-class life could be heavily verbal because the people they were about were (or so it was believed) articulate and literate. However, as the theatre focused more on inarticulate protagonists in a democratized theatre, verbalism became a less useful tool and playwrights found themselves trying to find a compromise between their own impulse to "say" things and their characters' inability to say much of anything.

This example illustrates the kind of compromise that playwrights have always made. In the early nineteenth century, it was a compromise with the pyrotechnical needs of Romantic acting and the needs of Romantic scenery; for Molière, it was a compromise with the moral and literary proprieties of a rigid society; for Euripides, it was a compromise with tradition and established, even ritualized, form. No playwright escapes the awareness that there must be a compromise between the creative impulse and the conditions of the theatre of the time.

The theatre has two characteristics that do not belong to other arts (except, perhaps, film—whose compromises are often even more severe). First, it is an art in which the need to provide a frame for the arts of acting and design must be met; and second, it is a public art, subject to both a legal and a social censorship that the novel, the poem, and the essay do not know. Satisfying the first of these requirements—providing a structure for actor and designer—is not a compromise but a basic quality in writing plays. Satisfying the second—whether it is meeting the stylistic demands of realism or the moralistic demands of censorship—requires a compromise that playwrights make only with reluctance.

The Playwright in the Real World

Plays begin as a great variety of things: a story overheard, a chance remark, a note jotted down on a slip of paper. There are as many beginnings of plays, probably, as there are playwrights: some begin with an idea, some with a character, some with a situation, some with a story. And from that beginning, different playwrights take widely different tracks: some write detailed outlines, some write none: some write hundreds of pages of dialogue, some put down on paper no more than will appear in the finished play. One way or another, however, the play is written—over a period of days, months, or even years—and then its real life begins, for a play on paper is only a long step toward a theatre performance, holding the promise of life instead of life itself.

GETTING THE PLAY PRODUCED

In recent years, the number of theatres in which new plays can be produced in the United States and Canada has increased noticeably. Many plays now begin their lives in regional theatres; in addition, organizations like the National Playwright's Conference of the O'Neill Theatre Center give first productions to a wide spectrum of scripts, many of which are later produced elsewhere. New York, however, and most especially Broadway, remains the goal of most playwrights. There are two reasons: money and status. Broadway royalties are far higher than anywhere else, and Broadway production is subject to the best reviewing and is the most prestigious.

Plays are not produced at any of these theatres by accident. Nor are many new plays that attract widespread attention (except at an institution like the O'Neill Center) scripts that come out of nowhere. Most are submitted to regional theatres or Broadway or Off-Broadway producers by agents. Far less often, a play may reach a producer by way of an actor or a director. In any case, the playwright's first high hurdle is finding that first production, whatever the medium used to reach a producing organization.

THE PLAYWRIGHT AND THE THEATRE

Producers have readers who read scripts and make comments. When a script is accepted for production, it already has an accompanying list of such comments as well as the producer's own views; added to these will be the

Figure 6-4. **New Plays in America.** Universities and regional theatres now give first performances of many new American plays. Here, Frank Manley's *Two Masters*. *(Emory University. Directed by James Flannery. The play was the 1985 winner of the Great American Play Contest at the Actors Theatre, Louisville.)*

ideas of the director when one is chosen. Each principal actor will add ideas, and each of these people—producer, director, actors—may have still other ideas that have come from friends, wives, lovers, and relatives. The playwright having a first play done is tempted to try to please everybody. By the time several plays have been done, however, the playwright may be downright rude about suggestions coming from any source at all. Between these two extremes lies the kernel of the playwright's work during the production period: accepting ideas for changes that are wisely based in the unique circumstances of the production. Perhaps regrettably, in the modern American theatre the director is assumed to have considerable critical skill and to be an expert in everything from dramatic structure to dialogue. Changes in a script, however, are rarely simple; as the Broadway playwright William Gibson said some years ago, altering a play is like taking bricks out of a wall: for every one that is taken out, half a dozen others have to be put back. At times, the playwright wonders what it was about the play that ever caused people to want to do it, because they have asked for so many changes that nothing seems to be left of the original. Confronted with this situation, the playwright may throw a temper tantrum, go home, or say, as more than one successful Broadway playwright has, "Do it as it is!"

Figure 6-5. **The Playwright's Living.** Before copyright and regular royalties, playwrights earned some money from performances dedicated to them as "benefits"—as in the case of this eighteenth-century ticket.

THE ECONOMICS OF PLAYWRITING

A few playwrights do make livings, especially as the number of regional theatres has multiplied, but the hit-or-flop life of Broadway still prevails; the playwright can still make only a killing, rarely a living. Standard Broadway contracts, under the aegis of the Dramatists Guild, give the playwright a percentage of the theatre's weekly gross, a percentage that climbs as the gross climbs past certain plateaus. On a hit, these figures can be impressive— well over five thousand dollars a week. On a modest success, they can be a thousand a week or less. On a flop, nothing. Considering that few playwrights have a successful play every year, we can easily see that the income from even a hit must be spread over several years, and after an agent's commission and professional expenses and taxes are taken out, the prorated remainder may be less than many upper-level businesspeople take home. There are, of course, the significant additional income of film and television sales—and perhaps most importantly, there is the secondary income of amateur and stock production.

Amateur rights are handled mostly by two organizations, the Dramatists Play Service and Samuel French, Incorporated. They collect royalties on productions by amateurs (community, school, and university theatres) for the life of the play's copyright—since the Copyright Law of 1977, the author's life plus fifty years. Although the royalty on a single performance of a play is small, the collective royalty per year on a play that is popular with the nation's several thousand community and college theatres can be large, and even plays that fail on Broadway can become staples of amateur theatre and go on providing income for decades.

Yet, with all this, relatively few people make a living as playwrights. It is a difficult craft that requires special talent, and it is made far more difficult by the conditions under which plays must find production.

The Actor

The actor stands at the center of the theatre. The actor is its linchpin, its keystone; without him or her, there is nothing—an empty building, a hollow space. Directors cannot direct nor designers design without actors; the playwright can create only works to be read like novels.

The actor alone can make theatre without the help of other artists. The plays that the actor invents may not be very good, it is true, and they may even be merely stories told well (as in oral cultures, when the storyteller is an actor-narrator.) The actor can make costumes, can build a theatre, and can provide at least crude scenery for it. At a level of development that can be identified in several periods, we see just such an actor and just such a primitive theatre: the plays improvised or crudely crafted, the costumes emblematic of the craft of acting rather than of a character (as a circus clown's is, for example), the stage a platform with a curtain behind it instead of elaborate scenery. Out of such an actor-intensive theatre may occasionally grow an even more developed one, such as the *commedia dell'arte* of Renaissance Italy (see p. 280). More often, however, such an actors' theatre changes in the direction of the theatre that we know, adding playwright, designer, and director. No matter how far this theatre develops, however, it remains the descendant of that primal theatre—actor-centered.

We often identify the greatness of certain ages in the theatre with the names of plays and playwrights, when in fact what we are doing is identifying great ages not of theatre but of drama. Plays survive and are easier to recapture than that ephemeral now, the actor's performance. The existence of great plays from fifty-century B.C. Greece, Elizabethan England, or seventeenth-century France should not cause us to forget that these were also great ages of acting. It is no accident that Sophocles, Shakespeare, and Molière were actors as well as dramatists.

We cannot have great plays without actors, but we can have great acting without plays.

The Paradox of the Actor

The French theorist Denis Diderot (1713–1784) used the expression "the paradox of the actor" as the title for an essay on acting, in which he tried to capture what seems to be an essential contradiction in the art: in order to appear natural, the actor must be artificial.

This contradiction takes several forms, whose language and whose specifics change from age to age; nevertheless the paradox remains at the center of most thinking about the art.

NATURAL VERSUS ARTIFICIAL

One of the things to be learned from a study of the history of acting is that almost every change in acting for the mainstream theatre has been seen as an improvement of the "natural" or the "real." Partly, changes in philosophy are at work, for the idea of "natural" and "real" human behavior is one of the root concerns of philosophy. When an age's idea of "what it is to be human" changes, the manner of depicting human beings on the stage changes as well, and what is typical of the older concept is viewed as outdated and "nonhuman"—that is, artificial.

However, there is a distinction to be made as well between the idea of what humanity is and the idea of what humans might or should be. Certain ages and certain forms of theatre have prized an idea of humanity that was sometimes rigidly defined in its behaviors; such an idea of humanity sets up many "proprieties"—rules based on the ideal—that must be observed. On the stage, elegance of diction, grace of movement, and limitation of gesture may become almost moral issues, and we find such extremes of stage propriety as the "rule" that the left hand must never be used for an important gesture. Such a strictly limited kind of acting will seem highly "artificial" to anybody who believes that the stage must imitate life explicitly, and what will seem

Figure 7-1. **The Actor.** Masks have been used in many cultures, and they have
come to symbolize the theatre; they suggest the primary importance of the actor.

"natural" will then be a kind of acting that does not stay within the proprieties.
Much of the conflict between French and English acting in the eighteenth
century and between Neoclassical and Romantic acting in the early nineteenth
century arose from precisely this difference. The "artificial" actor in such a
dispute would see the greatest allegiance to the rules of the theatre, based
on an ideal and not on a literal concept of "what it is to be human"; the
"natural" actor would see the greatest allegiance as being to life—or to an
interpretation of life. Neither idea is better than the other, although bitter
battles have been fought over their differences.

TECHNIQUE VERSUS INSPIRATION

Our own age is one whose theatrical heritage is primarily a "natural" one, at
least in the realistic theatre. Modern American actors sometimes speak
disparagingly of an actor who is "technical," meaning one who builds character out of careful, conscious use of body and voice—meticulously rehearsed
inflections, carefully chosen poses and gestures, and so on. Their belief is
that "technical" actors work mechanically and so fail to bring imagination
and life to their work. The technical actor is seen as "full of tricks." Again,
there is a strong belief that "technique" is somehow an enemy of the convincing, the lifelike, the believable.

At the far extreme from the technical actor is the "inspirational" one, whose work, although carefully rehearsed, is not assembled from external behaviors but is created through application of mental and emotional techniques that supposedly work to reach the actor's emotional and mental center and then somehow push outward into onstage movement and vocalization. In theory, the character created by the inspirational actor will be more "real," more "natural" because it does not rise from conscious intellectual work but from the inner sources that also give rise to music and poetry. To the inspirational actor, the approach is fresh and the creation original and not stereotyped.

INNER AND OUTER

Technical and inspirational acting have their direct counterparts in "outer" and "inner" acting. As one actor put it some years ago, "I like to build my house first—then I start to live in it." She meant that she liked to create the "outer" part of the role; then, comfortable with that—voice, posture, costume, gesture—she could move inward toward emotional intensity and conviction, believably "living in" the shell she had created.

Other actors work from the inside out. All of their early work will be devoted to mental, emotional, and spiritual exploration. Only when that work is completed do they feel that an outer structure can be built. In the cases of both the "inner" and the "outer" actor, truth to the character is being sought, and the difference is really a difference of emphasis and of sequence. The "inner-outer" distinction is not quite the same as the "technical-inspirational" one; the "technical" actor's work begins and ends with externals, whereas the "outer" actor's work finally leads inward, and the "inner" actor's work leads toward externals in a way that the "inspirational" actor's does not. Inspiration supposedly gives rise to externals through a nonintellectual leap, and, as Diderot suggested, those externals can vary from performance to performance and may supply only an occasional "sublime moment."

BEING AND PRETENDING

To reach emotional truth, it might be said, the actor must *be* the character; on the contrary, another point of view insists, the actor must always stand aloof from the character and *pretend*. Here is precisely the paradox that Diderot observed. If an actor were really to be the character, how would he or she control onstage behavior? What would keep the actor from becoming inaudible at times? What would keep the actor, as Othello, from actually killing the actor who plays Desdemona? What would cause the actor to modulate the voice, control the tempo of a performance, listen to other actors? And, contrarily, if the actor always pretends, what will he or she be but a lifeless imitation of humanity, a puppet, a windup toy? How will the actor keep the speeches from sounding like empty nonsense? How will gestures be anything but graceful hand-waving?

Figure 7-2. **"Truth."** These four great actors represent widely different ideas of natural and artificial acting, yet all have been highly praised. Left to right, Charles Macklin (eighteenth century); Rachel (nineteenth century); Charlotte Cushman (nineteenth century); Albert Finney (twentieth century). *(Photo of Albert Finney courtesy of the British Tourist Authority.)*

Because the actor is at the center of the theatre, this paradox is the paradox of the theatre itself: in order to be convincing, one must lie. The actor both "is" *and* "pretends," exploiting both inner and outer, both technique and inspiration. It is never enough for the *actor* to be satisfied that a sigh or a smile is perfectly truthful; the sigh or smile must also have the carrying power and the communicative value to be perfectly truthful *to the audience.*

The two halves of the paradox of the actor are always in tension. Their relative strengths vary from actor to actor and from age to age. It is only rarely that a really good actor will be found at either extreme.

The Actor and the Role

It should now be clear that actors do not create real human beings, on the one hand, nor do they somehow transform themselves and erase their own personalities utterly. Instead they engage in a creative act whose end product is a *construct*, that is, an entity made by human agency for a particular purpose. Both the actor and the audience must be very careful to remember that the creation *is* a construct and not a full-fleshed, living human being, for all that actors and audiences may speak of the construct by its name, just

Figure 7-3. **The Paradox of Acting.**
What the Butler Saw is a nonrealistic
play in which the actors must be convincing yet must exercise careful control. *(Directed by Walter Rhodes at
Wright State University.)*

as if it were a real person named Hamlet. The construct remains an invention,
and one actor's construct may be quite different from another's construct of
the same name—Laurence Olivier's from Stacey Keach's Hamlet, for example. In the literary sense, character is a construct that represents human
personality and that expresses itself through *action*. In the sense of the word
used by Aristotle, the effectiveness of a character depends on how well it fits
into the narrative whole and affects plot. This idea has an important impli-
cation for the actor: we define character on the basis of the function within
the artistic whole and *not merely on the basis of how well it imitates a human
being.* Therefore, a dramatic construct may be a convincing imitation of a
human being in its superficial attributes—it may talk like one and may have
preferences in clothes and food and entertainment like one—and yet it may
be a "bad" character in that it makes no important contribution to the artistic
whole and the action. An actor who concentrates on mannerisms of the
character and fails to grasp the character's function as contributor to the

action will fail and will be guilty of what the Russian actor and theorist Stanislavski called "tendencies."

For the actor, *character* means something like "the imitation of a human being as it expresses itself through the words and the decisions created by the author, *in relation to the other characters in the play and their decisions and words.*" The actor's character exists on the stage (only) and has no life off the stage; the actor's character exists in an artificial time scheme that is quite different from the time scheme of real life. It is helpful for the actor to figure out where the character is coming from when it walks on the stage, what it has been doing, and so on, but such analysis has to be limited strictly to conclusions relevant to onstage action and onstage time or it will lead to sideshows and tendencies, or even to the creation of a play that the author never wrote (and one that, regrettably for the audience, takes place offstage).

The actor is a person; the character is a construct. In order for the character to *seem* to be a person during the two or three hours of performance, the actor must use parts of his or her own real self, observations of other people, and sheer invention and imagination.

THE WHOLE ACTOR

In approaching character, actors bring three aspects of themselves to the task. We can identify these three parts of the actor's creative self as:

1. *The actor's consciousness.* Several components of successful acting are conscious. Primary among these are *concentration, selectivity,* and *analysis.* Without concentration, the actor might at times dissolve into neurotic collapse, haunted by personal problems that would destroy the work. What can be noted about successful actors is the astonishing degree of concentration that they bring to their task. "The show must go on" is a cliché, but it does describe the good actor's tenacious ability to continue when the physical or emotional self is hurt or threatened.

Selectivity is the ability to discriminate among possible solutions to an acting problem. (The process is more or less conscious in different actors.) Choices may be as simple as between two qualities of voice for a word or line or as complex as identification of a memory, among many memories, from which an emotion springs. Often, there is no one correct answer in such a selection; there is one that may work best for a particular actor in trying to illuminate a certain moment of a performance. It is because of this selectivity that actors so often experiment, trying, rejecting, and trying again with different voices, gestures, and rhythms. To an outsider, an actor's process in creating a character often seems slow, repetitive, and aimless. Even in their conscious work, however, actors do not proceed as scientists might proceed, and often they are still trying to frame a creative question while already searching for the answer, because the conscious process is so highly complex. The guidance of the director is of enormous importance here, of course, and the same outside observer who wondered why the actor seemed to work so slowly might also wonder why the director asked the actor so many questions; the answer is that the director is trying to help the actor to frame questions and to select the best answers to them.

Analysis is the element of the actor's consciousness that deals with the reading of the dramatic text on its first level—breaking it into units and understanding its complex inner relationships. The analytic element is exercised throughout the the prerehearsal, rehearsal, and performance periods by actors who are determined to perfect their understanding and interpretation of the script and of their characters.

2. *The actor's instrument.* By the *instrument* we mean the entire physical self that the actor uses in playing a character; it is conveniently separated into body and voice. Whereas the audience does not see or hear the work of the consciousness or the imagination directly, it always sees and hears the instrument, for the instrument is the medium through which the others express themselves.

The "external" or "artificial" or "technical" actor might appear, at first glance, to be the one who makes the most conscious use of the instrument. However, this association of the instrument with the externals of acting is at least partly an appearance and not a reality. The properly trained actor of any method will make the maximum use of body and voice, because without

Figure 7-4. **Concentration.** Good acting demands intense concentration on the tasks of acting to achieve truthfulness and life. *The Beaux' Stratagem* at the University of Wyoming. *(Directed by Gladys Crane, designed by John Galbraith, costumes by Michael Chetterbock.)*

Figure 7-5. **The Instrument.** The nineteenth-century American actor Ira Aldridge had a superb voice and an expressive body, both essential to good acting.

them the consciousness and the imagination are strangled. What the bad actor of any method will do, however, is use *learned* instrumentation—"tricks," clichés, personal mannerisms—rather than instrumentation that springs from creative understanding of the character and the play.

The instrument is given to the actor. What is given can be developed, and good teaching can do wonderful things to improve voices and the use of bodies; the fact remains that the size and shape of bones, the delicate tuning of vocal mechanisms, and the size and shape of the body are in large part given at birth. "Talent" does not consist of having a beautiful face or a beautiful voice, or even of having a body and voice that are flexible and expressive without training. Insofar as "talent" applies to the instrument, it consists of making maximum use of what is given and of recognizing its strengths and its limitations.

3. *The actor's imagination.* Within the actor's mental and emotional self lies the wellspring of creativity; the imagination. It is the force that impels all creativity, working often in images rather than in rational discourse, surfacing into the consciousness unpredictably, frequently working while the rest of the organism sleeps. In all fields, including science, great and original

ideas and creations have come while the conscious mind rested or actually slept: "I woke up with the problem solved," or "It came to me in a dream," has been a common story for millennia. Sometimes the imagination works while the conscious mind is "at rest" because of a condition other than sleep; the disassociation used in marathon running, for example, has given rise to the solutions to problems, and other such irrational "leaps" have come through Yoga and other meditative disciplines.

Contemporary psychology and physiology now suggest that the "lateral hemispheric specialization" of the brain may play a large part in what we call the actor's imagination. Recent findings indicate that the right and left halves of the normal brain have separate but interconnected functions, the left dealing with logic and language, and the right with image, metaphor, pictures, and music. Early training "teaches" the brain to mute the signals coming into the consciousness from the right half (probably because language and logic are vitally important to European and American culture); it may be this muting that causes us to see the imagination as irrational, mysterious, and hidden. The muted or "hidden" quality is also the reason for the many exercises used in actor training and rehearsal to penetrate years of habit in order to help the actor to work directly with the imagination. It is as if, in early life, we learned to erect shields around the imagination—the work of the right half of the brain—and to lower those shields only in sleep and altered states of consciousness; then, as adults, we must learn new techniques to penetrate them or to lower them for creative work.

Imagination is the key that opens the door to memory, itself a rich source of the actor's understanding and playing of character. Imagination is also the function that processes nonrational data (from such sources as the text, the creative work of other actors and the director, the setting and costumes) and that gives back new understanding of play and character. It is the function that gives the actor an understanding of stage space and the body's relation to it. It is the source of whatever is new, particular, and magical in performance, for it is unique to the individual actor, and its nonrational "leaps" are like the working of magic. Yet, because it comes from a part of the brain that does not process data rationally, it is held suspect by purely rational people; in an age that considers itself rational, imagination in acting is suspect and is made to give way to the more understandable, visible process of analysis. Conversely, when a society permits extensive inner searching and is familiar with such searching through its own religion and thought, an acting that relies perhaps excessively on the imagination may result, and such acting may, like the workings of the right half of the brain, lack the logical, communicable links to the external world that make most performances understandable to the audience. The result in such a case might be a performance that could be called "novel" or "original" but that is beyond comprehension.

The successful actor, then, effectively uses consciousness, imagination, and instrument in balance. The conscious mind analyzes the playscript and the "conditions of performance" and translates that information into a form usable by both the instrument and the imagination. Even as they work, however, the consciousness continues to analyze and to shape and change its findings; at the same time, the decisions and findings of the imagination are communicated directly, along with the decisions of the consciousness, to the instrument. The complexity of the process is virtually beyond description—and, in fact, it is not adequately understood by either scientists or artists. Perhaps it is enough for our purposes to suggest that if we seek to define the word *talent* in acting, we do so by looking at this three-way, continuing, constantly changing interchange. Talent, we may be able to say, is the ability of the consciousness to inspire in the imagination a set of actions and sounds that the instrument can express to an audience as theatrical character, excitingly and brilliantly.

ACTING AND PERFORMING

A full-fledged talent for acting cannot be thought of merely as an ability to entertain well in public—to clown at parties or to tell jokes superbly. The latter are parts of a talent for *performing*—that is, for reaching and delighting an audience without regard to character or theatrical action. As we have already tried to suggest, there is more to acting than this. A good actor, of course, is also a good performer; a good performer, however, may not be a very good actor.

Some kinds of theatre or the related arts put a higher premium on performing than on acting; circus high-wire work, for example, requires great performers and has no use for actors. Musical comedy, on the other hand, requires both acting and performing, but the ability to "sell" a song requires performing of a high level. Because performers must often play themselves, strong performers who act theatrical roles sometimes have difficulty, or they so overpower the dramatic character that it is obscured. In star-oriented theatres, productions are sometimes thrown out of balance by the casting of famous performers who are so habituated to playing themselves that they cannot or will not break out of that pattern.

Performing must not be confused with external or artificial acting, which may seem like performing because of its planned and deliberate gestures, and its sometimes exaggerated vocal effects. External acting, however, focuses on communicating an idea of character in theatrical action; performing focuses on communicating the performer.

The performer plays *to* the audience; the actor plays the character *for* the audience.

The Personality of the Actor

The personality of men and women who act has been a source of fascination for centuries. The actor has long been seen as a special sort of person; even before the Romantic interest in odd and exotic individuals, actors were studied because of their ability to interpret human psychology and because

Figure 7-6. **Performing.** The performer affects the audience without dramatic character or dramatic text. Acting and performing overlap but are far from the same.

of their apparent ability to balance both halves of the "paradox of the actor." Too, a number of traditions came to surround the acting profession, and if they were not always accurate, they came to seem accurate as actors themselves believed in them: "all actors have to be crazy"; "all actors are immoral"; "the theatre attracts misfits and oddballs"; "actors like to show off"; and so on. Such ideas are no better than gossip until they are proved by objective standards, and for every immoral actor and show-off, there is an opposite to disprove the stereotype. Nonetheless, some of these old ideas persist.

Because of a lack of hard data and the persistence of stereotypes, we cannot describe accurately the "personality of the actor." We might note the following, however:

The actor's profession puts him or her outside the mainstream of most lives, because actors work odd hours, work at a very high level of energy and concentration, and live a life of extreme professional and financial peril.

Part of the actor's reward is applause and other forms of audience approval, and a personality geared toward applause may be an insecure one; yet, to face tryout after tryout, opening after opening, show after show takes stamina and a courage unknown to men and women in secure careers.

The actor's personal relationships are easily threatened by unusual hours, job insecurity, and the need to be able to move geographically on short notice.

Because theirs is a high-stress life, actors are as subject to the allure of drugs and alcohol as the rest of the population, and perhaps more so.

The ability and desire to act, like all creative work, is "different," and the committed actor may be judged an outsider by the rest of society.

Thus, although we cannot draw a profile of a typical actor, we can point

Figure 7-7. **The Actor's Life.** *Le Roman Comique* was an early novel about actors and their atypical life style.

Figure 7-8. **Teaching the Actor.** Earlier acting styles depended partly on standardized gesture, which actors learned through imitation.

out some qualities that frequently occur. What must be clearly understood, however, is that the qualities that make a good actor—creativity, concentration, determination, stamina, access to the imagination, playfulness, the ability to cope with rejection, nonrational thinking, and detailed emotional memory—should be kept separate from qualities that may appear because of the *profession* of acting and its stresses; in other words, the nature of the profession in our society may bring out behavior that is not typical of the art of acting but of our society's use of it. Thus, the "personality of the actor" has to be a composite of those qualities that make up talent and those qualities that appear in response to the environment in which talent is used.

Actor Training

Although there are supposedly actors who are "born," and although there have been young children who were talented actors, it is a fact of theatrical life that all actors must train long and hard and must refresh that training throughout their careers.

Actor training does not refer to a specific kind of study or to a set period of time. Acting is taught in hundreds of colleges and universities, for example, and degrees in acting are granted by many of them, but the chronological length of such programs and the granting of degrees does not mean that the actors are through training when the degrees are given. In the final analysis, every actor's training is special to him or her, and its length will be different from the training periods of other actors.

There are a number of actor-training systems. The most influential in the United States and Canada are those based on the ideas of Konstantin Stanislavski. Other systems have very different foundations, such as the psychological theory of transactional analysis or the theory of games and improvisations. Different as these are, they are helpful in varying degrees to different actors. *No one system is best for everybody.* The important thing about these systems is that they organize the work of the actor's consciousness, instrument, and imagination. Without a workable system, the would-be actor makes progress only randomly, repeating mistakes and often making bad habits worse. With a workable system, the actor finds the way out of this self-destructive cycle. A good system trains all three parts of the actor.

PRELIMINARY TRAINING

There was a time when would-be actors "came up" through a provincial and repertory system, moving from small roles in minor companies to larger roles and more important theatres. They learned by imitation and they learned by taking hints from experienced actors. Nowadays, most professional actors have had formal training, either in a college or in one or more private studios. Each such institution uses a system, but most of them require some kind of preliminary training. Many young actors have trouble recognizing this preliminary work as part of acting, although it is essential. (In a college, such work usually comes in the freshman year.) Without it, most actors would not succeed. Partly, it is a process of *un*learning mistaken notions and bad habits, and partly it is a process of training mind and body to adapt to the conditions of the theatre instead of the conditions of life (by learning, for example, that behavior that is considered ridiculous in life is sometimes essential in rehearsal and performance.)

It is usually thought to be unwise for beginning actors to go directly into the rehearsal and performance of plays or parts of plays—so-called scene work. Instead they are given preliminary training in the following areas:

RELAXATION.   Surprisingly, many people who want to learn to act are so tense that they are quite literally unable to act; that is, muscle tension inhibits or totally prohibits any creative use of the instrument. Physical tension causes sudden, random, or pathological movement (shaking, trembling) and dangerous misuse of the vocal mechanism. Tense actors may think of themselves as *in*tense and not tense; without training, they have no way of telling the difference. They see themselves as "really into" a role, when the teacher or the audience sees nervous, confusing, and uncontrolled movement.

Relaxation exercises cover a broad range from disciplines as different as modern dance and Yoga. All are intended to cause the consciousness to let go of the body, to return it to its natural state of receptiveness and awareness, and to make the body itself supple and loose.

CONTACT OR AWARENESS.   The relaxed body, freed from the tyranny of tension, becomes aware of itself and its environment. The consciousness no longer hurries it along toward some rigid goal; it has time, as it were, to stop and enjoy the scenery (including its own internal scenery). The coming and going of the breath, the comfortable positions of the body in standing, sitting, kneeling, and lying, the sense of the nearness and farness of objects and people—these things and many more can be explored. Sensory awareness is raised, and exercises are given that can be repeated (throughout the actor's life, if necessary) to maintain or renew that awareness.

Contact with others can also be taught so that the beginning actor learns to relate to other people, to help them, and to accept the help that they offer. The accepting of such help is, perhaps surprisingly, very difficult for many beginners, probably because not asking for or accepting help is a habit brought in from life. Most of us are taught to be "self-reliant" and "independent," and our society prizes these qualities. However, the *self*-reliant actor is a menace. *Taking* and *giving* are the bases of good performance.

CENTERING.   Many disciplines, among them Eastern meditative religions and some schools of modern dance, emphasize exercises that focus on a bodily center—that is, a core of balance and physical alignment, a place from which all movement and energy seem to spring. This idea of a center concerns both the body (balance, weight, and placement) and the voice (breathing and sound making). In Yoga, the abdomen below the diaphragm is such a center; in the dance of Martha Graham, the center is slightly above the pelvis.

Centering leads the beginning actor away from the mistaken idea that the physical self is located in the head and the face, that the voice is located in the mouth and the throat, and that the physical relationship to the rest of the world is located, through gravity, in the feet; rather, the actor finds the center somewhere near the crossing point of an X of arms and legs—a center of gravity, a center of balance, a center of diaphragmatic breathing.

PLAY.   Dramas are "plays"; actors are "players." Yet beginners are often anything but playful. A terrible intensity and a terrible seriousness rule the work. To counter this tendency, much of early training is spent reteaching people how to play, in the sense both of teaching them to play games and of teaching them to approach the creative act joyously. Because children often have this sense of playful theatricality in their own pastimes ("Let's pretend"), many theatre games are versions of children's games or of adult "parlor" games that are noncompetitive fun.

Figure 7-9. **Contact.** Taking and giving are essential attributes of good acting. Alice Childress's *Wedding Band. (The University of Maryland. Directed by Harry Elam.)*

TRAINING THE INSTRUMENT

"Stage movement" and "voice production for the stage" sound like titles of academic courses. They suggest that the subject matter can be learned and that then, like familiarity with Shakespeare's plays or a knowledge of the calculus, they can be forgotten or assimilated. In actuality, the training of the instrument is a lifelong process.

Both body and voice use complicated sets of muscles put into action by the brain, sometimes consciously, sometimes unconsciously and habitually (for example, few of us have to remember to breathe). The actor has to be made aware of the muscles being used, has to improve the condition of the muscles, has to unlearn or relearn or learn a pattern of use of those muscles, has to repeat such patterns so often that they become habits, has to learn precisely what muscular actions will produce what results (sounds or movements), has to learn what combinations of commands and muscular sets will provide new, unusual, and effective sounds or movements. As well, the actor has to learn the "proper" application of certain kinds of voice (singing) and movement (fencing and dancing).

BODY AND MOVEMENT. The actor's body need not be heavily muscled, but it should be flexible, strong, and responsive. The actor does not train as an athlete does (one set of muscles would be developed at the expense of

135

Figure 7-10. **Movement.** Actors learn both specific skills like fencing (top photo) and the physical control that allows both the slumped, inward posture and the expansive gesture in the bottom photo. (Above, *The Rivals* at DePauw University; below, *The Cracker Factory*, adapted from the Joyce Burditt novel, produced by Anstie's Limit. Both productions directed by Kenneth M. Cameron.)

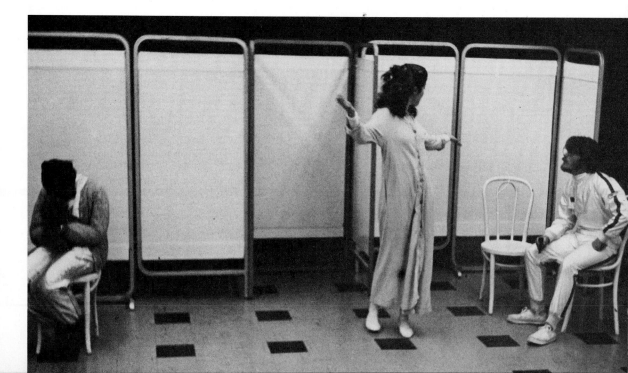

others); instead, the goal is *resistance to fatigue, quick responsiveness,* and *adaptive ability* (that is, the ability to imitate other kinds of posture and movement or to adapt movement to, for example, aged posture and movement or the posture and movement of a body much heavier). The actor also learns the following:

1. *Body language and nonverbal communication.* We all express our emotional states and our basic psychic orientations through *body language.* The actor learns to "move" the physical center to match that of the character. The actor also learns how all of us communicate without words, through such simple gestures as the waving of a hand ("hello" or "come here" or "no thank you") to complex "statements" of posture and gesture that say things completely different from the words that pass our lips. Such training takes two forms: study of the subject (much of it still in the fields of psychology and anthropology) and application to the actor's body.

2. *Rhythmic movement.* Ballroom dancing, simple modern dance, disco dancing, and the like have the double advantage of being enjoyable and of helping the actor to move to an external rhythm.

3. *Period movement and use of properties.* Historically accurate, and theatrically effective, use of fans, canes, swords, shawls—the list is endless.

4. *Movement in costume.* Theatrically effective movement and gesture in wigs, capes, hoop-skirts, boots—again, the list is a long one.

5. *Movement onstage.* Traditional interior settings do not have walls that meet at the same angles as rooms, and so stage furniture in such settings is rarely angled as real furniture is. As a result, "crosses" (movements from one point onstage to another) take unreal routes. On the proscenium stage, actors must learn to "curve" crosses so that they end up on a line parallel to the curtain line with another actor (in this way, neither winds up speaking upstage into an acoustical well). On thrust and arena stages, the actor learns to play to all of the audience, to adapt posture and movement so that each section of the audience is treated fairly. Too, there are ways of bending, sitting, and standing that are appropriate to the stage in that they are not awkward or comical, although training in these "correct" ways of doing things is becoming more appropriate to training in period movement.

VOICE PRODUCTION. The human voice is a product of controlled muscular work and chamber resonance (head and chest). Its shaping and control are not simple. Nonetheless, we make sounds and shape them all the time—only to find that our everyday sounds are inadequate for the theatre because they cannot be heard, they cannot be understood, and they are unpleasant. Unlearning and relearning are necessary for most actors.

The human voice is produced when air is forced over the *vocal folds* or *cords,* causing them to vibrate and to set a column of air vibrating, producing sound. This sound induces vibrations in cavities in the head and in *bones* in the head and chest. The sound is shaped in the throat and mouth, primarily with the jaws and tongue and is further shaped into the sounds we call words by initiation of sound; interruption of sound by the interaction of lips, tongue,

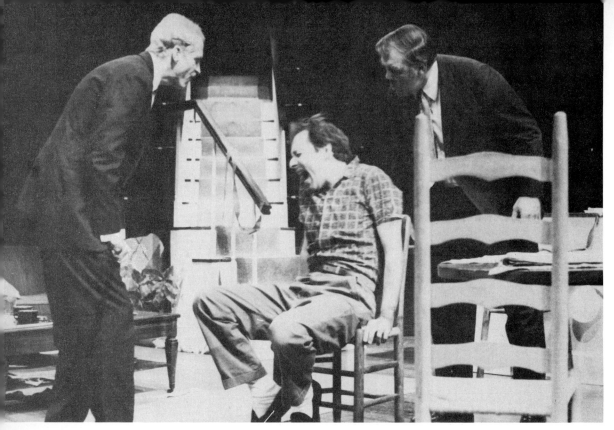

Figure 7-11. **Voice.** When seemingly out of control, as in screaming, the actor's voice most needs control. Harold Pinter's *The Birthday Party. (The University of South Carolina. Directed by Richard Jennings.)*

and teeth; and placement of sound through action of the lower jaw and of the tongue.

The actor trains the vocal mechanism for maximum control of *every word that is uttered*, as well as for the production of sounds that are not words.

Other voice and voice-production training covers:

1. *Breath control.* The principal source of the pressure that pushes air over the vocal folds is the *diaphragm*, a large muscle curved up under the lungs. When it flattens (downward), air is pulled in; when it releases (upward), air is pushed out. Lesser muscles along the ribs and upper chest are not so important to proper breathing; many untrained people, however, are "chest breathers" whose diaphragms are little used. Chest breathing, without effective use of the diaphragm, limits capacity and control and, under the stress of making loud and extended sounds in a theatre, often tenses muscles and transmits that tension into the throat. *Diaphragmatic breathing* is as essential for the actor as for the singer, giving increased capacity and maximum control.

2. *Throat relaxation.* Tightness in the throat and the lower jaw is a source of common and severe voice problems. Muscular tightness there "chokes" the sound, restricting the vocal folds and closing up the resonating chambers. The actor learns to produce enormous volumes of sound without ever allowing the muscular effort in voice production to affect throat and jaw.

3. *Tongue and lip dexterity.* "Lazy tongue" is a common ailment; it produces slurred consonants and sloppy speech. Tongue twisters and other exercises tone the muscles and force actors to listen to the sounds they make.

4. *Sound placement.* Like singers, actors learn to "aim" sound at different resonating elements in their heads. Sounds may be more or less nasalized; they may make more or less use of deep "chest resonance."

5. *Correction of habits and defects.* Few actors come to training without such vocal defects as adenoids (which cause denasalized sound), poor dental structure (lateral lisp), vocal nodes (hoarseness of voice). Some problems are the result of habit or acculturation, such as nasality, regional accents, and lazy tongue.

6. *Dialects.* The idea of a "stage speech" that is radically different from "standard English" is disappearing, and the day of the actor who talks like an English aristocrat is past. Nonetheless, accurate knowledge of how different ethnic and regional groups speak is essential. In learning the specific characteristics of each variety of speech, the actor will probably make use of the *phonetic alphabet*, a system for recording sounds rather than spellings.

TRAINING THE IMAGINATION

The word *training* may be inaccurate. Actors go through a process in a training atmosphere and are *encouraged* to discover their imaginations. Whether or not the imagination itself can be "trained" remains open to question, and many psychological data suggest that what we have called *imagination* is a capacity of the brain and the mental-emotional self that is always at work but that rarely surfaces. Still, if one can teach the rational brain mathematics, perhaps one can teach the nonrational brain imagination. Most certainly, one can try to encourage the nonrational brain to speak up and make itself heard.

CREATIVE EXERCISE.   In the belief that all people have imaginations and that all are "creative" (as children are creative), teachers devise exercises to free actors from both embarrassment and inhibition. Writing down dreams as a regular part of daily preparation can help many, especially those who insist that they "never dream" or "dream nothing interesting." The very fact of causing themselves to remember and write down dreams leads to an acceptance of the idea of dreaming and hence to a greater willingness to "listen to" their dreams, which demonstrate imaginative elements—images, metaphors, and puns. Dreams are often playful in their structure and their language, and they have both content and form that our rational minds would never think of.

Childhood memory can be turned to good account in the same way. An exercise in memory becomes an exercise in imagination as the actor finds how much detail the mind is capable of holding and of using.

Other exercises in sensitivity or creativity use group participation in building a story or a moment. Each actor in turn builds on the story. Student

Figure 7-12. **Imagination.** Acting often requires the creation of that which the actor cannot know from life, as in this interpretation of Hamlet's encounter with the ghost of his father.

actors have earlier gone through work in relaxation and contact, so that they will have got rid of any fear of participation.

IMAGE EXERCISES. The creative mind probably works, at least a good deal of the time, in images rather than in words (although many words are themselves images). Image exercises encourage the actor to grasp the mental pictures that the brain offers. For example, simple character-creation around pictures, objects, or sounds can be beneficial. An actor is given an object and told to perform a related character for the group: a knife is set out; the actor bends forward, walks with difficulty, the body held to protect its center greedily. From "knife," the actor went to "sharp," sharp in business, a miser, then added the element of "a cutting wind."

VISUALIZATION. Group exercises build a scene, each member contributing details and working to *see* the scene. Such an exercise is useful in touching the actor's sense of creativity, in sharpening concentration and sense of detail, and in preparing for those times in rehearsal and performance when the actor must "see" for the audience:

HORATIO: *But look, the morn in russet mantel clad*
Walks o'er the dew of yon high eastward hill.

Hamlet

140

SENSE MEMORY.   Like group storytelling, individual recounting of the "picture" around a memory encourages a sense of detail and of visual memory. As many senses as possible are incorporated. Such memories need not come from childhood; they may come from the day before, even moments before. The purpose is to cause actors to capture a sensory moment in all its fullness and, through both remembering it *and* recounting it, to cause them to be able to create such sensory reality around moments that come not from memory but from the theatre.

IMPROVISATION.   No single word and no single tool has been more used and misused in the last several decades than *improvisation*. Improvisation—the creation of quasi-theatrical characters or scenes or plays without the "givens" of drama—has been used to create theatre (without a playwright), to enlighten an actor about a character (the so-called *étude*, or improvisation based on material in a dramatic script), to structure theatre games, and to teach many aspects of acting. As a tool for training the imagination, it is an application of the techniques already mastered. In a sense, it is the basis of some of the other techniques; having an actor create a character around an image is such a use of improvisation. It can be used to apply the imagination, to stimulate it, or to supply raw materials not within the actor's experience. (That is, an improvisation focused on a frightening event may help the actor who has never experienced fear.)

In order to work, improvisation is kept simple and is carefully focused by the instructor. Improvisations can quickly develop along unwanted lines,

Figure 7-13. **Improvisation.** Actors can create theatre through controlled improvisation, which requires rehearsal and may use a director and playwright. *(Anstie's Limit in* The Funniest Joke in the World. *Directed and scripted by Kenneth M. Cameron.)*

especially with actors who want to "tell stories" (create theatrically interesting situations); when that happens, there are often so many processes going on that student actors do not understand what they are doing. For the purposes of the imagination, it may be enough to create, for example, a scene of the sort discussed under "Visualization" and then to have the group improvise their participation in the scene—feeling the air, wading into the water, and setting up a picnic on the beach. To do more risks complete loss of the imagined setting and a departure into other areas altogether.

TRAINING THE CONSCIOUSNESS

Certain areas of the actor's conscious work can be taught through example and through guided participation in production work. These include discipline, concentration, theatrical analysis, observation, and script analysis.

DISCIPLINE. Actors are taught to be *prompt, alert,* and *ready to work*—to get enough sleep, to avoid alcohol and drugs when working, and to come in a frame of mind and a set of clothes that will permit maximum work. Actors *prepare:* they do bring the script and a pencil; they have done whatever homework on the play has been requested. Actors are *constructive*, not destructive: they do not make comments about other actors, do not break out of character while another actor is working, and do not indicate in any way that another actor's experiment with a character is wrong or comical or foolish. Actors are *respectful:* they talk to the director about problems, not to other actors or the costume designer or the playwright.

CONCENTRATION. The habit of concentration comes from work. In many cases, student actors whose acquaintance with mental work has been limited to the classroom will have difficulty at first with the level of concentration that is needed. Not only the length of time but also the depth of the concentration that is required may seem unreasonable. Yet, it is only through remarkable efforts of concentration that progress is made. An actor who cannot attain such concentration may need to return to exercises in relaxation and contact to find out what is distracting the mind. Where a severe problem continues to exist, there may be a psychological difficulty that a nontheatrical expert will be needed to resolve.

THEATRICAL ANALYSIS. It should be a goal of actors' training to make them aware of their place in the theatre in each production. This does not mean merely that actors must understand their roles; it means that actors must grasp how they relate to the entire complex of the performance, including:

1. *Spatial understanding*, which includes an awareness of each setting in which the actor appears, its shapes and proportions, as well as an understanding of the relationship of the setting to the size and shape of the theatre

Figure 7-14. **Space.** The actor must understand and use both the space on the stage and the space in which the audience sits.

and its audience. To reach this goal, actors in many theatre training programs are required to study design, lighting, and costume and to work on productions in nonacting jobs.

2. *Research resources*, for which the best preparation is usually a study of the history of the theatre. Knowledge becomes a resource, and formal study in this discipline will include a working knowledge of resources in the field.

3. *Dramatic appreciation*, for which the best preparation is usually a study of dramatic literature and a broad reading in the field. Every actor should be expected to know the classics of each period.

OBSERVATION.   As distinct from imagination and visualization, *observation* is a conscious perceiving and recording of sensory data. For the actor's purpose, it is limited mostly to the seen and the heard. Observation can be taught through a variety of devices that require attention to detail, such as talking through or writing highly detailed descriptions of objects (a specific chair, a dead fish). It can be encouraged by requiring the keeping of a notebook with daily or weekly entries of sounds and sights (people). The goal is to cause actors to build a "library" of people on which they can draw in building character.

143

SCRIPT ANALYSIS.   The dramatic script is the foundation of the actor's work. *Imagination* and *instrument* are the means through which the script is embodied. Training in script analysis has three principal goals:

1. *An understanding of the entire drama.* On the first reading, the actor will be making judgments and sorting out impressions. Trained in the theatre, the actor will read the script as a "notation" for a performance: the potential for production will be grasped, at least in general. Likes and dislikes (sometimes vague ones) will form. An awareness of the play's *totality* will take shape. Of particular importance to the actor on first reading will be the *style* of the play, its main *impact* on its audience, and its overall *shape*. Under style, the actor will understand the degree of abstraction of the script; the kind of language, whether poetic or mundane; and the historical period. The *impact* will be comic or serious and will be expressed most importantly through language or action, through idea or spectacle. The *shape* will describe the play's gross structure and its overall rhythms, whether it builds slowly or quickly to crises, whether it relaxes gradually from them or drops abruptly. This first contact with the totality of the play will also indicate what demands it will put on its actors—the size of the cast, special requirements of their instruments, the size of the major roles, and the relative degree of intensity of the emotions to be embodied.

Figure 7-15. **Character Creation.** Joseph Jefferson's Rip van Winkle was created over many years and was performed by him so often that he became identified with the role.

Figure 7-16. **Stock Character.** The "comic man" was a type in many nineteenth-century plays. He has disappeared, but other stock characters can be seen today. Stock character, having its essentials already defined, does not require careful script analysis and so suits a system where the actor performs different scripts constantly (as in television soap opera, for example).

2. *An understanding of the place of the character in the whole drama.* The actor is trained to resist one question—*What makes my character stand out?*—and to ask another one instead—*How does my character contribute to the whole?*

Dramatic action means change; when a character is offstage, changes are taking place, and when the character returns, those changes must be noted. The actor balances two lines of development: the character's and the play's.

3. *An understanding of the details that make up the character.* A deeper understanding of the play and the character's part in it emerges from repeated readings, as does a detailed sense of just what the character is. The actor keeps a notebook in which ideas about the character are written down, as well as all those things in the script that indicate the nature of the character. These include those things discussed under "Character" in "How To Read a Play," especially action and decision, with character traits as they appear in the stage directions, the character's own speeches, and the speeches of others. All must be evaluated in terms of the production and should be discussed with the director and the other actors. For example, one character says of another that she shows "facial contortions" and her voice goes up "two octaves." The actor playing the character described must know whether these things are true (that is, whether the other character's description is accurate) and then work out when and where to use these traits.

It is essential for actors, as for all theatre makers, to look at the play in terms of its theatricality, that is, its artistic, sensory, intellectual, and human values. Such a breakdown gives them a grasp of the play's entirety and of its theatrical potential. It should not, however, dictate character. Grasping a play's idea, for example, must never suggest to the actor the reason for the character's existence, nor should the actor worry about how to "play the idea," or, worse yet, how to *be* the idea. The actor who says something like "In this play, I represent goodness" simply has not done the proper homework. Except in pure allegory, characters do not represent abstract ideas; they represent persons (who may embody or apply certain ideas).

In the same way, script analysis should help the actor to avoid moral value judgments. Characters in a play are not "good" or "bad" *to themselves*. Few real persons say, "I am a villain." The actor does not, then, play a villain; the actor plays the representation of a person whose actions may be judged, after the fact, as villainous—by others.

Put most simply, training in script analysis is training *to read*. It is training to understand what is *on the page*—not what might have been put on the page but was not, and not what the actor might prefer to find on the page. Script analysis deals with a very limited amount of information and tries to squeeze every drop from it; it neither invents nor guesses. Most of all, it requires that the actor read *every* word and understand it in clear detail; from that clarity and that detail will come an objective understanding of the script that can be returned to again and again when acting problems arise.

THE AMERICAN STANISLAVSKI SYSTEM

The specific details gained from analysis are usually applied to modern realistic acting, which continues to dominate the work of most American actors. Basically, these are ideas originated or articulated by Konstantin Stanislavski, modified by the American Method and subsequent theories.

The actor is trained to analyze character for:

1. *Given circumstances.* These are the undeniable "givens" that the actor must accept: age, sex, state of health, social status, educational level, and so on. Often they are contained within the script, either in stage directions or in dialogue; sometimes they must be deduced or even invented. (How old is Hamlet? Was he a good scholar at the university? Is he physically strong or weak?)

2. *Motivation.* Realistic theatre believes in a world of connectedness and cause. All human actions in such a world are caused or motivated. To play a character in such a world, the actor looks for the motivation behind each action.

Some teachers have their students make notebooks for each character with a column in which a motivation can be noted after each line or each gesture. It is important that the student actor understand that, in this system, *all* behavior is motivated—every word, every movement, every inflection. *All action results from choice.*

Figure 7-17. **Individual Objectives.** Analysis of the scene shows that various characters are pursuing—quite correctly—very different objectives and therefore have different responses. (Woyzeck *at Murray State University.*)

3. *Objective.* Like motivation, the objective is part of a system of causality. It is the goal toward which an action strives. Motivation leads to action; action tries to lead to objective.

4. *Superobjective.* "Life goal" might be an equivalent of the superobjective if a dramatic character were a real person. The superobjective includes all objectives pursued by a character and excludes all improperly defined objectives. For example, we might say that Hamlet's superobjective is "to set the world right again"; his objective in the first scene with his father's ghost might be "to listen to this creature from Hell and put it to rest" (thus setting the world right by quieting the ghosts in it). In this case, the objective and the superobjective agree. If, however, the superobjective was defined as "to take my father's place in the world," and the objective in the ghost scene was defined as "to listen to the ghost out of love for my father," there would be a severe problem, and the two would have to be brought into sympathy. By defining the superobjective, the actor is able to check on the validity of all the character's objectives.

Both the objective and the superobjective must be active. We have expressed them here as infinitives—"to set," "to listen"—but the actor does better to express them in active terms beginning with "I want," so that their strength and vitality are clearly visible.

Figure 7-18. **The Star.** Stars are often treated differently from other actors—so long as their box-office appeal lasts. The nineteenth-century star Sarah Bernhardt. (*From* Le Théâtre.)

5. *Through line.* If motivations and objectives are seen as beads, they can be strung on a through line that runs consistently through the character's entire presence in the play. The through line (sometimes called the *spine*) may also be seen as the line that runs through all objectives toward the superobjective. The actor learns to recognize that something is wrong when a motivated action does not fit on the through line. Such an action was what Stanislavski called a "tendency." It leads to poor acting because it takes the character away from the pursuit of correct objectives and into vagueness and contradiction, which an audience finds confusing and finally annoying. Much of what we call bad acting is, in fact, the playing of tendencies rather than the playing of a strong through line.

Audition, Rehearsal, and Performance

Actor training goes on long after actors begin to take an active part in performance. Most actors continue to work on their instruments throughout their careers, and many return to professional workshops to refresh and sharpen their inner work. After the initial period of actor training, however—college, sometimes graduate school, an independent studio or teacher—the actor begins to look for roles and, having found one, begins the work of building and performing a character. Each step in the process has its special conditions, and for the professional actor, these steps will be repeated over and over throughout his or her life.

AUDITION

Most actors get roles through auditions ("tryouts"). Stars are the exception; sometimes productions are built around them. (See Figure 7-18.)

Most auditions are done for the director of the production. Usually, the stage manager is there as well, along with someone representing the producer, if there is one. Somebody is there, as well, to read with the actor if a scene with another character is being read. (Usually, the stage manager does this.)

The most important things an actor can show in an audition are basic abilities and the capacity to work creatively with the director and other actors. One of the director's problems in auditions is to try to sort out the creative actors from the "radio actors"—those who have the knack of reading well on sight but who lack the ability to improve much beyond that reading. Thus, cleverness in a first reading is not necessarily an advantage for the actor. What may count more is the capacity to work creatively and interpersonally.

Unfortunately, auditions cannot always be a good indicator of how well an actor will perform, and they can have heartbreaking results. Imperfect as they are, however, auditions will remain one of the most important elements of casting until a more objective, less flawed device is invented.

REHEARSAL

The actor will undoubtedly arrive at the first rehearsal with many questions. One of the functions of rehearsal is to answer those questions and to turn the answers into an exciting performance.

Actors often work very slowly in rehearsal. An outsider coming into a rehearsal after, let us say, two weeks of work might well be dismayed by the apparent lack of progress. Actors may still be reading some lines in flat voices, and, except for bursts of excitement, the play may seem dull and lifeless. This situation is, in part, intentional, however. Many actors "hold back" until they are sure that things are right. They do not want to waste energy on a temporary solution to a character problem. Temporary solutions have a way of taking on a life of their own: other actors become accustomed to hearing certain lines delivered in certain ways and to seeing certain movements and gestures; they begin to adapt their own characters to them. The actors begin to commit themselves to a pattern. To avoid this, many find it productive to withhold commitment for a good part of the rehearsal period.

The actor experiments. Some of this experimenting is done away from the rehearsals; homework takes up a lot of the actor's time. Much of it takes place in rehearsals. Again and again, an actor will say, "May I try something?" Or the director will say, "Try it my way." *Try* is the important word—

Figure 7-19. **The Product of Rehearsal: Performance.** Jean-Paul Sartre's *The Flies* at South Carolina State College. *(Directed by H. D. Flowers, II.)*

experiment, test. The good actor has to be willing to try things that may seem wrong, absurd, or embarrassing.

Most important, the rehearsal period is a time for building with other actors. Actors use the word *give* a lot: "You're not giving me enough to react to," or "Will it help you if I give you more to play against?" Such giving (and taking) symbolizes the group creation of most performance.

At some point during rehearsals, the creative and lucky actor may have a "breakthrough." This is the moment when the character snaps into focus. Motivations and actions that have been talked about and worked on for weeks may suddenly become clear and coherent. The breakthrough may be partly a psychological trick, but its reality for the actor is very important: the creative imagination has made the necessary connections and has given usable instructions to the instrument. The character is formed.

The rehearsal period, then, is not merely a time of learning lines and repeating movement. It is a time of creative problem-solving, one in which the solving of one problem often results in the discovery of a new one. It is a time that requires give and take, patience, physical stamina, and determination. It frays nerves and wearies bodies. The intensity of the work may cause personal problems. Nonetheless, many professional actors love rehearsal more than performance because of its creativity.

PERFORMANCE

Society has an overblown image of "opening night" and "being in the spotlight" that makes the first performance unnaturally stressful. The fantasy of instant stardom, rave reviews, the actor's name in lights, and standing ovations makes performances still more stressful. Few actors, in fact, achieve stardom or standing ovations, and it is a sad mistake for any actor to think that such things are the only reward for performing.

Performance causes emotional and physical changes in the actor that are associated with stress. Some change, of course, is helpful; it gets the actor "up" so that energy is at a peak, ready for the concentrated expenditure that rehearsal has made possible. Too much stress, however, cripples the actor. "Stage fright" and psychosomatic voice loss are very real problems for some. Ideally, good training and effective rehearsal will have turned the actor away from the root cause of stress (dependence on outside approval of the performance); where this does not happen, the actor may have to return to relaxation work or find outside therapeutic help.

Opening nights raise energy levels because of stress and excitement. As a result, second nights are often disspirited and dull, because when the tension of opening is removed and the energy has been expended, a feeling of dullness, even of depression, often results. The wise actor expects this pattern. Again, preparation is a help—complete understanding of the role

Figure 7-20. **Nonrealistic Performance.** Not all performance follows Stanislavskian lines: some, like this "Blue Blouse" troupe in the 1920s, emphasizes a didactic point. (*From* Theatre Arts.)

and the total performance, creative rehearsal work, open lines between consciousness and imagination. Before the second and subsequent performances, the prepared actor reviews all character work, goes over notes, reaffirms motivations and objectives. The good actor does not say, "Well, we got through the opening; the rest will take care of itself."

Once in performance in an extended run, actors continue to be aware of a three-pronged responsibility: to themselves, to the other actors, and to the audience. Those responsibilities cannot end with the reading of the reviews.

In developing his system of acting, Stanislavski was interested both in actor training and in the problems of performance. His work cannot be viewed as merely a study of how the actor prepares; rather, it is also a prescription for the continuing refreshment of the performing actor. His system allows the actor to create what has been called the "illusion of the first time" again and again. Put most simply, this means that the actor is able to capture the freshness and immediacy of the "first time" (both for the character and for the audience) by going back each time to the mental and emotional roots of the truthfulness of the performance—a process that is possible only if that performance is grounded in truth to begin with.

Continued performance for the trained actor, then, is not merely a matter of repeating rehearsed sounds and gestures night after night; it is a matter of returning to internally satisfying truths (motivations and objectives) and satisfyingly effective externalizations of them. Such a system may not be perfect, but it is far better than the repeated performance that grows tired and dull with repetition and that leaves the actor disliking both the performance and the audience because of boredom.

Audience response to performance sometimes suggests where a performance is effective or poor, and the actor works at correcting errors as the performance period continues. Thus the creation of a character must seem completed by opening night, and yet it is never truly finished.

What Is Good Acting?

Recognizing the art of the actor depends, first, on the ability to separate the actor from the role. An attractive or well-written role can obscure the actor's lack of imagination; a poorly written role can hide the actor's excellence; an unsympathetic role can make the actor seem unsympathetic. By learning to read and see plays, we learn to distinguish the character from the actor, then to see what kind of material the actor had to cope with. For example:

- Was the character fully realized by the playwright? Or did it have internal contradictions? Or large blanks?
- Was the character rewarding to perform, or was it "thankless"? Was it merely a function, or was it a character? Did it have progression, or was it unchanging? Varied or monotonous?

Figure 7-21. **Good Acting.** John Gielgud as Julius Caesar. *(Courtesy of the British Tourist Authority.)*

Answers to such questions tell us how difficult the actor's job was. Once we understand that, we can begin to talk about what the actor did and how well the job was done.

Good acting fulfills the technical requirements of the theatre:

- The voice is clear and interesting; every word is understandable.
- Movements are complete and definite; any incompleteness or clumsiness is of the character, not the actor.

Good acting is believable—within the style.

Good acting overcomes the inherent difficulties of the role and capitalizes on the strengths of the role. It does not call attention to the actor; it creates the character fully within the context of the entire performance.

Good acting has detail and "texture" (variety and human truth), but it is not merely a collection of details; it has what one artist calls a "center," another a "through line"—a common bond tying all details together and making the whole greater than the sum of its parts.

Good acting has the capacity to surprise. Its truth is recognizable, but it goes beyond imitation to revelation.

Good acting, then, has technical proficiency, truth, a through line, and creativity; bad acting calls attention to itself, lacks technical control, dissolves into mere details because of its lack of a through line, and never surprises with its creation.

153

The Director

There have always been theatre people who exercised a strong, central influence on productions, but in the sense that the word has been used for the last hundred years, *directing* is a phenomenon of the nineteenth and twentieth centuries.

If we look at the period when this practice began and flourished, we may be able to deduce what its importance is and why it appeared at that time; that is, we may be able to deduce something about directing by recognizing that it appeared when illusionistic detail became important in the theatre and when industrialism was important in Western society. The era of the director is also the era of the pictorial illusionist and of the industrial manager, and we may deduce that directing is concerned with illusionism and picture making, and with management and organization, in a way or ways that had not concerned the theatre before.

Directing, like any artistic practice, has changed since its beginnings. Directing may continue to change, but we cannot say with any certainty in what direction; what we can say is that a hundred years after their first important appearance, directors are the dominant figures in theatrical production.

A few theatres now function without directors, most notably those organized around cooperative or communal principles (see p. 364). With those exceptions, however, theatres at every level now have directors: in high schools and colleges, it is the director who organizes and oversees all productions; in many community theatres, it is the director who oversees the selection and mounting of plays; and in the professional theatre, in Europe as in North America, it is the director whose stamp goes most clearly on every production.

In essence, the director now does things that either were done by several people before the modern period or were not done at all. Put more briefly, it may be said that what the director does is to *unify*. Thus, if a single difference could be noted between a modern and an older performance, all question of styles aside, it would be this binding of all the elements of performance into a unity—a unity of meaning in the interpretation, of visual effect in the designs and staging. Because of our way of looking at things, we tend to see this unity as desirable and even inevitable, and we would find the *pluralism* (multiplicity of effects) of an older performance confusing or even comical. A theatregoer in another age, however, would accept pluralism as quite natural to the theatre and might find modern directorial unity puzzling, or even oversimple and boring.

The Function of the Director

The director unifies within two main categories, *interpretation* and *presentation*. By *interpretation*, we mean not only the analysis of the dramatic text but also the evaluation of the nature of the audience and the assessment of the abilities and potentials of the other theatre artists. By *presentation*, we mean the whole process of embodying the interpretation in the form that will be most effective for the audience. The director, then, is the crucial person who stands between the theatre's potential and the audience's enjoyment; the director is the person who is most responsible for realizing that potential.

Before the appearance of the director, interpretation was done by the other theatre artists themselves: the dramatic text by the playwright, the roles by the actors, the scenes and spectacle by a painter or machinist. Presentation was done by actors and technicians who were organized by a manager or a theatre owner, but without that artistic unity that we now almost take for granted; that is, there was always somebody to "put the show together," but in the eras before the director appeared, that someone was a merchant or a religious or civic leader (as in classical Greece or medieval Europe), and the goal was not aesthetic unity but efficiency. Of course, there were people in those earlier eras who selected plays, cast the actors, rehearsed them, and made sure that everything was ready by opening night (or day); however, those jobs were often parceled out among several people, and none of them was profoundly concerned with making the finished product all of a piece.

In doing the jobs that formerly may have been done by many people, as well as in doing a job that had only rarely been done before—unifying the performance—the modern director must be effective in more than one area. Of primary importance are skills in *organization, human relations*, and *decision making*. Organization includes the director's ability to put ideas into order and to combine them with the ideas of other people, as well as the ability to order rehearsals, schedules, and budgets; human relations includes both the ability to inspire other artists and the ability to work directly with people of quite different kinds, imposing the director's own wishes only when absolutely necessary and working creatively with other people on group solutions to complicated problems; and decision making requires the clear-headedness to define problems and to see the conditions under which they must be solved (including limitations of budget, time, available talent, and so on), as well as the self-knowledge that will allow the director to make decisions (or to postpone certain decisions), often under stressful conditions. To put these skills to the greatest effective use, the director needs *stamina* and *concentration* as well as artistic talent.

In some theatre organizations, of course, some of the director's jobs are done by another person, especially in the professional theatre. Many aspects of production will be handled by a production stage manager. Business matters will fall to a business manager or producer, and artistic matters will belong to the director; however, as one moves away from the high-powered organization of Broadway, more and more responsibilities fall into the director's

Figure 8-1. **The Directed Production.** *The Miracle*, directed by Max Reinhardt, one of the most influential of modern directors. His total control of all aspects of production—including lighting—was a model for many authoritarian directors. (*From* Theatre Arts.)

Figure 8-2. **The Undirected Production.** Directing is a nineteenth-century art; before it, leading actors took center stage and held it.

lap, until, in many community, school, and university theatres, it is safe to assume that the director is aware of and actively engaged in every aspect of production.

The following, then, comprise the director's functions and responsibilities (some of which may be delegated to others in some situations): the *artistic* functions of (1) script selection or approval (including work with the playwright on an original script); (2) script interpretation; (3) design approval and coordination (sets, lighting, sound, and costumes); (4) actor coaching; and (5) staging (including pictorial creation, orchestration of voices, stage movement, and performance rhythm), as well as the *managerial* functions of (1) production coordination and planning; (2) casting; (3) rehearsal scheduling and conduct; (4) performance coordination, including timing; and (5) liaison among management, actors, and designers.

Play Selection

Directors in community, school, and university theatres most often select the plays they direct; in the professional theatre, they at least approve the scripts (if they are staff directors) or find themselves "matched" to a new play by a producer. Never, if at all possible, does a director take on a play he or she

Figure 8-3. **Directorial Functions.** In educational theatre, the director has both managerial and artistic functions. Shaw's *Caesar and Cleopatra. (The University of Missouri. Directed by Larry D. Clark.)*

does not like. The demands are too great, the depth of involvement too extreme; the dislike would ruin the production.

Directors choose to do plays because the plays excite them; idea and spectacle are probably the most common elements to prompt directorial interest. Ego certainly enters in, as does the desire to exercise artistry. However, if theatrical elements conflict, directors sometimes find that they have made a bad choice; that is, they may love the idea of the play but may not know how to make the music of the language exciting or how to compensate for a lack of spectacle. As directors gain self-knowledge through experience, they learn what they do well or badly, and they learn to make wise script choices. Most important, perhaps, is the acquired knowledge of learning to study the script in great depth—not to be led astray by enthusiasm for a single element, only to find to one's sorrow later that serious problems were overlooked.

With the script chosen, the director begins to translate that early enthusiasm into the stuff of performance. To do so, the director needs a "springboard," a taking-off place from which to make a creative leap. The terms *concept* and *directorial image* are also used, but *concept* implies rational thought, and *image* implies picture making, and the director's process at this stage may be neither rational nor pictorial. Certainly, very few directors *begin* their creative work with a reasoned, easily stated idea, and those who are drawn to a script because of (for example) its music or because of the opportunity it gives to display the artistry of an actor will probably not *begin* with images. On the contrary, what many directors begin with is a seemingly random, sometimes conflicting medley of ideas, impressions, and half-formed thoughts whose rational connections may still be hidden. It is then the director's task—and the exercise of a special talent—to sort all these out and to find their connections and to see which can be given theatrical life and which cannot. Thus, much of the director's early work is not the definition and application of a "concept," but the establishment of a jumping-off place, the sorting out of raw materials from a whirlwind of impressions.

Seldom—perhaps never, except in the most perfunctory sort of work—is the springboard merely "to do the play." A director who sets out merely "to do the play" is like the actor who sets out to learn the lines and not bump into the furniture—going through the motions without ever confronting the real task. This is as true of a classic play as of the most avant-garde script. It might seem that classic plays would be an exception because, supposedly, so much is known about them and so many other productions can be drawn on—the director would simply stage the play's established greatness. Such

Figure 8-4. **Expanded Directorial Function.** Some directors develop works from nondramatic materials, as in this scene from Poe's *The Fall of the House of Usher.* (University of Maryland, Baltimore County. Directed by Sam McCready.)

an approach is a guarantee of dullness, at best. A play will not be exciting in performance simply because other audiences have found other productions of it exciting; it must be made exciting all over again every time it is staged.

A good director takes nothing for granted—least of all the presence of the audience. Everything that is tried will be measured against an idea of how the anticipated audience will react—with the qualification that every director knows that mere reaction is not in itself a good thing; the *proper* reaction is what is wanted.

In early readings, the director usually has both positive and negative thoughts about the play and its audience impact. Two lists could be made, one of strengths and one of weaknesses. These two lists *taken together* would show how the director's ideas were forming. It is important to remember that weaknesses as well as strengths are included. Just as artists in any form are inspired by obstacles, so the director is inspired by script problems (as, for example, the poet finds inspiration in the problem of rhyme).

Let us suppose that the director is considering a realistic nineteenth-century play. The play is a classic of its kind and so has established merit; on the other hand, it is also old enough to seem dated to a modern audience in language and some plot devices. Thus, after early readings, the director could list some strengths and weaknesses:

Plus	*Minus*
Strong subject matter	Creaky structure—melodramatic
Excellent central character	Dated language
Great third-act climax	Some "serious" stuff now funny
Good potential for probing Victorian attitudes	Soliloquies, set speeches very hard to make convincing today

To the director who is excited by the play and is setting out to do it, these two columns might better be titled "Potentials" and "Challenges." From the realization of the one and the solution of the other will come the director's best work.

THE DIRECTOR AND THE PLAY: TEXT OR PRETEXT?

The play is chosen; the first identification of strengths and weaknesses is made. The work of interpretation begins. It is an open-ended process, and, like the actor's, it never really finishes; it merely stops. A director who does more than one production of the same play may create quite a different production the second time: the process of interpretation has gone on and has changed as the director and the world have changed.

But a serious question arises: What is the director's responsibility to the dramatic text? Is it the director's job to put the play on the stage with utmost fidelity, or is it the director's job to create a theatrical event to which the script is merely a contributing part? Can the director cut lines or scenes, transpose scenes, alter characters? Can the director "improve" the play, or must it be treated as a sacred object?

Directors vary widely in the way they answer such questions. Their views range from veneration of the text to near indifference; the play is seen as a holy object on the one hand and as a merely useful artifact on the other.

THE WORSHIPFUL DIRECTOR'S APPROACH.   "The play is the only permanent art object in performance; it is a work of art in its own right, to be treated with respect and love. Because it has stood the test of time, it has intrinsic value. By examining it, we can know its creator's intentions—what meanings the playwright meant to convey, what experiences the audience was meant to have, what theatrical values were being celebrated. The playwright is a literary artist and a thinker, and the playwright's work is the foundation of theatrical art. It is the director's job to mount the playwright's work as faithfully and correctly as is humanly possible.

"Historical research and literary criticism are useful tools for the director; they illuminate the classic play. Quirky modern interpretations are suspect, however: to show Hamlet as a homosexual in love with Rosencrantz and/or Guildenstern would be absurd and wrong because we know that such a relationship would never have been included in the tragic view that Shakespeare held.

"The director's job is not primarily to create theatre; it is to cause the play

Figure 8-5. **The Worshipful Director.** A "faithful" production of Shakespeare's *Julius Caesar* from the turn of the century. (Compare with Figures 8-6 and 8-9.)

to create theatre. The difference is crucial. The director says quite properly, 'I must allow the play to speak for itself and not get in the way.' To do otherwise is to betray the play, and I will not do it *even if the 'betrayal' is great theatre.*"

The worshipful director views the opposite approach with something like horror; at best, such productions cause regret. What the worshipful director knows of Peter Brook's *Midsummer Night's Dream* or Grotowski's *The Constant Prince* (modern productions of classics that drastically altered the originals) causes offense and grief. Most often, a single word is used by the worshipful director to describe such productions: *wrong*. Because they are not faithful to their classic originals, they are *wrong*.

THE HERETICAL DIRECTOR'S APPROACH.   "*Interpreting the text* means *making a theatrical entity of it for an audience.* Not making *the* theatrical entity of it, and not 'finding its meaning' or 'doing it correctly.' There is no single interpretation of a play that is 'correct.' There are only interpretations that are right for a given set of performers under a given set of conditions for a given audience.

"How, then, can a director judge the rightness of the production? The director does not, any more than a painter judges the rightness of a painting. The director's final criterion is the satisfaction of an overall goal: Is it good theatre?

"It is foolish to think that the director's task is to stage the play according to some other standard. Fidelity to some 'authorized' or time-honored view of the play is not, simply in and of itself, a good thing. It is foolish to say that the director did the play 'wrong' unless what the director did was to make bad or dull theatre. The director has to be faithful to a vision, not to tradition or academic scholarship or propriety; only when that vision fails can the director be said to be wrong.

"Does this mean, then, that the director has no responsibility to the 'meaning' of the play? Yes, in the sense that the director's responsibility is to the meaning of the performance, of which the play is only a part. Are we, then, to have homosexual Hamlets? Yes, if such extreme interpretations are necessary to make the plays into effective theatre and if they are entirely consistent within their productions. Are we, then, to have productions of classics that are directly opposite to their creators' intentions? Yes, because it is finally impossible to know what somebody else's intentions were and because an intention that was dynamite in 1600 may be as dull as dishwater in 1990; and anyway, theatre people have always altered classics to suit themselves: *Macbeth* was turned into an 'opera' in 1670, and *King Lear* had a happy ending in the eighteenth century."

The extremes of the heretical director's views can lead to results that many people find offensive or meaningless; on the other hand, those views can also lead to innovative and truly exciting productions. Generally both sorts take a risk: the heretical director takes the chance of being ridiculous, the worshipful director of being vapid. At their best, however, both can create productions that thrill audiences, the one with revelations of familiar material, the other with a brilliant rendition of the strong points of the classic.

Script Interpretation

No matter what the orientation toward the text, the director must now work to analyze it: take it apart, reduce it to its smallest components, "understand" it. (To *understand* does not mean to "turn the script into a rational description of itself"; it means, rather, to make the director's consciousness capable of staging it.) The job of interpretation has many aspects, which are often explored simultaneously, both before and during rehearsals.

TONE AND AUDIENCE IMPACT

Funny/serious, cheerful/sad, light/heavy—the possibilities are many and must be identified for each act, each scene, and each line, as well as for the entire play. The director looks both for the play's effects—funny lines,

Figure 8-6. **The Heretical Director.** A modern interpretation of the same scene in *Julius Caesar* as Figure 8-5. *(The University of Washington. Directed by Robert Hobbs.)*

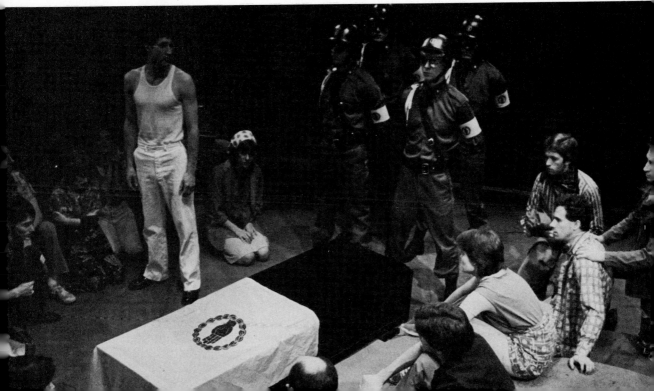

frightening moments, spectacular events—and opportunities to exercise invention. Neither laughter nor powerful emotion necessarily belongs unchangeably to parts of many scripts, especially when realistic acting and the concept of *subtext* (action implied but not stated in the text) are applied; the director will spend a good deal of time deciding what to do. Even when the proper tone is found for the play, the lines alone will not deliver that tone to an audience. Laugh lines must be carefully set up and "pointed," with both business (small activities performed by actors) and timing; moments that have a wonderful potential for powerful emotion can easily be lost without careful, intense study and work by the director.

Of particular interest in this aspect of interpretation is *mood*—the emotional "feel" that determines tempo and pictorial composition—and *key*—(as in "high key" and "low key"), the degree to which effects are played against each other or against a norm for contrast. High-key scenes may even go to *chiaroscuro* ("light/dark") effects that use the darkest darks and the lightest lights, as in dramatic painting; such a technique is of great value in setting the mood for a play like *Dracula*.

RELATIVE IMPORTANCE OF ELEMENTS

Modern directors try to work carefully with all elements of theatre. The director must study the play to find which elements are most important and which can be used most creatively to serve the play. Spectacle (including lighting, costume, the pictures created by the actors' movement, and scenery) and sound (including music, sound effects, and language) are often elements that the director can manipulate and can bring to the play as "extras" that the playwright has not included. Character, idea, and story, on the other hand, are usually integral to the script itself, although subject to considerable interpretation and "bending" by director and actors. Many directors annotate their scripts in great detail for these three elements, some marking every line of dialogue for its contribution to character, idea, or story. Such annotations give the director both an overall sense of the play's thrust and specific instances of that thrust at work.

This area of interpretation is critical. An element misunderstood at this stage can mean a moment lost in performance, or even an important thread through the whole play; to miss a major emphasis can mean a failed production. For example, a play that depends heavily on the beauty and intricacy of its language (sound) will usually suffer if directed to emphasize story or character, with the language overlooked or ignored (a not infrequent problem in productions of Shakespeare's plays); a play of character, if directed for its story, often has incomprehensible spots and long stretches where "nothing seems to happen." Thus, the director must not only pick the element or elements that can be given theatrical life, but *must also pick the element or elements that the script gives theatrical life*. This means knowing *which* element(s) is most important; *where* in the play each has its heights and depths; and *how* the director will give theatrical excitement to each.

Figure 8-7. **Selection of Elements.** The masks, the sand floor, and the costumes exploit the element of spectacle. Euripides' *Hecuba*. *(Emory University. Directed by James Flannery.)*

ACTION AND PROGRESSION

Performance is active and most plays have progressive actions; that is, they occur through time (audience time and their own time), and they must at least seem to increase in intensity as time passes (as, that is, the audience is led from preparation through complication to crisis and resolution). There is a trap here for every director, however, in that it is the very nature of audience perception to need greater stimulation as time passes—a familiar enough situation to all of us, who can become bored after a time with something that entertained us at the beginning. Thus, it is part of the director's problem to counter the apparent drop in intensity that occurs as time passes by using every device possible to *increase* intensity, that is, to support theatrically the progressive intensity of the script. When it enjoys a performance, an audience's responses may be compared to a parabola: they start at a low point, rise higher and higher as time passes, and usually fall off after the climax. The director wisely structures the performance to serve this perceptual structure (or another equally satisfying one.) *The director cannot allow a performance to become static*, or it will seem to fall off rather than to remain still.

It is not enough, then, to find the important elements and to know where the script emphasizes them. The director must now find how each element grows in interest as the performance progresses. The word *progression* must be used again and again: What is this character's progression? What is the progression of the story? Is there progression in the spectacle?

If the progression is missed, the audience will become confused or bored. They may say things like "It went downhill," or "It got dull after the first act," or "It went nowhere." Theatre people seeing such a performance often say that "They played the last act first," which is a way of saying that the climactic points of the important elements were so much in the director's mind that the entire play was directed to emphasize them, and the progression was thus destroyed.

The reverse of the question "What is the progression?" is "What can I save for the climax?" In other words, how can the director emphasize the highest point of the performance (usually toward the end, coincident with the story's climax) by contrast or by saving effects for that moment? Preparation and contrast are important; equally important is *saving* something—the final high pitch of emotion, the most exciting tempo, the loveliest visual effect.

ENVIRONMENT

As the actor determines "given circumstances," so the director determines environment: place, time of day, historical period. Much is given in the script, although if it is given only in the stage directions, the director may choose to ignore it. Some directors cross out the stage directions before ever reading them, believing that they were written either for some other director's production (e.g., for Broadway) or for readability for armchair theatregoers. Classic plays often have no stage directions at all.

It has become common directorial practice to change the period of classic plays. Shakespeare's *Troilus and Cressida*, for example, has been done in the costumes and accents of the American Civil War. The play is about the Trojan War, but the director may have wanted to stay away from classical Greek costumes and settings because of what they say to the modern mind or may have wanted to stay away from Shakespearean costume and setting because they say something quite different (and something that might seem more comic than anything else). Setting the play in the American Civil War, then, not only had the advantage of novelty, it also identified the play with a conflict real to Americans and yet slightly distant, one that is viewed both romantically and cynically (applicable to a play that is both romantic and cynical), and it had the added advantage of separating the often confusing warriors of the opposing sides by their Americanized accents (northern and southern).

Questions of tone, mood, and key influence the director's thinking about environment. There are excellent reasons for putting a murder mystery in a country house on a stormy night, just as there are excellent reasons for putting a brittle comedy in a bright, handsome city apartment. It is not only

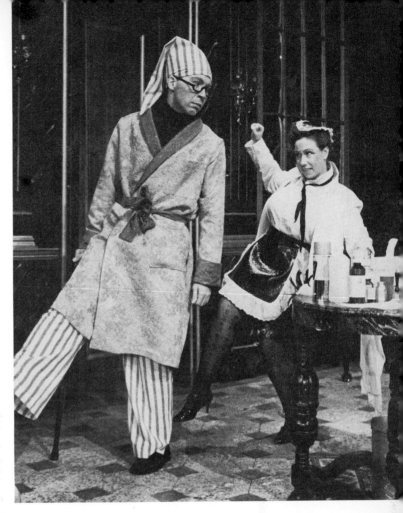

Figure 8-8. **Changed Historical Period.** What has the director gained by updating Molière's seventeenth-century *Imaginary Invalid? (Montclair State College. Directed by Ramon Delgado.)*

the rightness of the environment for the characters that the director thinks of (i.e., if they are rich they should have a rich environment, if Russians they should have something Russian, and so on) but the rightness for the indefinable subtleties of mood: the laziness of a warm day, the tension of an electric storm, the depressing gloom of an ancient palace.

IDEA

As we have already pointed out, idea is the element of theatre that gets the most attention after the audience has left the theatre and the least while it is enjoying the performance. Paradoxically, idea is an important criterion in play selection, many directors being committed to plays because of enthusiasm for their subject or approach. Idea may continue to influence their interpretation and their work; however, they are careful *not* to direct the play so that it is "about the idea." The other elements will usually determine the shape of the production, and idea will inhere in all of them but be blatant in none. Even an impassioned "idea" speech at the most thrilling moment of

167

the play must spring from action and character and must exist *because* of action and character. If it exists because the playwright or the director wants to make a statement, it will leap out of the performance, and the performance will suffer.

Idea, in fact, does not inhere in individual speeches or in literal statements that can be neatly extracted from the play. The very word *idea* describes not a single, literal statement but a body of matter that we call *meanings*. It is woven into the texture of the performance, embodied in the actors' creation of their roles and the director's creation of mood, among other things. The director does not spell out the meanings for the audience; where meanings excite the director, they become something to be embedded in the entire performance.

Design Oversight and Inspiration

After beginning the work of interpretation, and well before rehearsals begin, the director meets with the several designers. When feasible, this process may actually begin months before rehearsals, but the practicality of production in many theatres means sometimes that it comes within short weeks or even days of casting. Communication with the designers is best started early. Many directors have approval of the hiring of designers and so can begin almost as soon as they agree to direct.

Depending on the theatre itself, the director and the designers (sometimes

Figure 8-9. **Direction and Design.** The director solved the problem of having actors sit between the focus of the scene and the audience by having his designer sink those actors below stage level. Compare the same scene from *Julius Caesar*, Figures 8-5 and 8-6. *(Designed by Lucien Jusseaume; director unknown. From* Le Théâtre.*)*

with producer, playwright, stage manager, technical director, costumer, and so on) hold *production meetings* weeks or months before the actors are cast. These meetings have three principal goals: *artistic coordination*, so that direction and designs are in harmony; *managerial efficiency*, to coordinate budgets, schedules, and personnel assignments; and *communication*, to encourage the complete exchange of creative ideas.

Within this framework, the director works on the following areas:

DESIGN MOOD AND MEANING

The director is rarely a designer but knows the practical needs and the aesthetic values of both play and production. Communicating feelings and ideas about play and production to designers is an important directorial skill, especially when it is done without insisting on restrictions. The designers will have made their own interpretations of the play, which will sometimes be different from the director's. Bringing them all into a single focus is the director's task.

The director has to be careful at this stage not to be so rigid or so narrow as to cause the designers to make a single statement over and over. Unity *and* variety (or variety within unity) must be stimulated, and the potential for progression must always be inspired in the designs.

The visual potency of lighting, set, and costume is a very important determinant of mood. The director must be clear about the interpretation and must be sure that the designers share that vision. Inconsistency here will lead to a severe weakening of the performance.

GROUND PLAN

The ground plan is a "map" of the playing area for a scene, with doors, furniture, walls, and so on indicated to scale. In a realistic interior, the director may almost design the entire acting space simply by setting down directorial needs in detail. The number and location of entrances, the number and location of seating elements, the number and location of objects that will motivate behavior and movement (for example, stoves and refrigerators, fireplaces, closets, and bookcases) are important to the way many directors think about realistic plays and may be determined by such directors even before they meet with their designers. Some directors even give their set designer a ground plan, complete except for minute matters of dimension. Others may remain open until the designer has created a ground plan around a more general statement of needs.

In the nonrealistic play, or sometimes in the realistic play with exterior scenes, directors may have less rigorous requirements. Still, for variety, mood, and emphasis, the director will probably specify differences in level, separation of playing areas, the location of seating elements, and so on. An effect created by the director may strictly require certain things: one director's production of *Macbeth*, for example, had the witches shift magically from a ledge far above the stage to stage level (two sets of actors were used to play the witches); here, obviously, the designer had to provide precisely the levels demanded by the director.

As well, other design elements may be suggested or required by the director; for example, the size and shape of the space where a crowd is used, or where a sense of the isolation of a single figure is wanted, or where a feeling of cramped oppression is sought.

Once ground plans are established, they become the basis for all staging. Drawn to scale, they can be used with scale cutouts of furniture and actors to plan movement and picturization. They are also the basis for the three-dimensional model of each setting that the designer usually provides, and they are also useful to the director in planning the staging.

COSTUMES, LIGHTS, AND SOUND

As with the ground plan, so with the other design areas: both the practical and the aesthetic must be considered. The kind and amount of movement wanted by the director influences costume design; the costume designer's work influences movement (as when, for example, the tight corset of the late nineteenth century or the very broad skirts of the eighteenth century are used). So, too, with colors: bright pastels may be suitable for a comedy; dull colors and heavy fabrics under gloomy light may match a serious interpretation. Practical considerations influence other decisions: certain areas will have to be brightly lighted so that the action can be seen; certain actors will

Figure 8-10. **Design for Good Direction.** Direction and design come together to produce good acting spaces, convincing environments, and interesting and communicative pictures. Molnar's *The Guardsman.* (*University of Arizona. Directed and designed by Robert C. Burroughs. Costumes by Peggy Kellner.*)

have to be in strong colors or outstanding costumes so that they will gain focus. Lighting colors must be carefully coordinated with the colors of sets and costumes so that lights do not wash out or change other colors; the location of lighting instruments has to be coordinated with the location of set pieces and rigging to avoid casting shadows or creating physical interference.

As the production meetings continue and rehearsals near, these and many other matters will have been considered: budget, shifting of scenery, time for costume changes, location of offstage storage space. As decisions are made final, each designer provides the director with a detailed plan in the most appropriate form: color renderings and fabric swatches for costumes; ground plans, scale drawings, renderings, and models for sets; light plots with gel colors for lights. The sound designer (where one exists) may work with an annotated script and lists of sound materials (music, sound effects). These renderings, plans, and other materials represent the culmination of the designers' work with the director: detailed, readable plans for a total production, all in harmony with each other and with the director's interpretation of the text.

Actor Coaching

Most modern directors involve themselves closely in their actors' creation of their roles. It is a very rare director who does not. The influence of Stanislavski, in particular, has led to a collaboration between actor and director that has developed, in some cases, into a great dependency on the director, a dependency that is sometimes fostered by the teacher-student relationship at universities where acting is taught. Just as there are now playwrights who expect to have their plays "fixed" by the director (a relationship that grew primarily from the Broadway playwright-director collaborations of the twentieth century), so there are actors who expect to have their interpretations "fixed" or even given to them whole by their directors. Particularly in educational and community theatres, great trust is put in the director by the actors, and many interpretations are virtually handed down entire from director to actor.

When the actor-director relationship works as a productive collaboration, however, the director functions as a coach who advises, inspires, and encourages the actor. Significantly, the director works in such a relationship with questions rather than with statements ("Why do you think the character says it just that way?" instead of "What the character means is . . ."). The director will have mastered the actor's vocabulary and, using it, can ask those questions that the actor may not yet be able to phrase. The director is the sounding board and the artistic conscience of the actor—mentor and interpreter, bringing to the actor's work another dimension, another voice, another view of the whole play and all the characters.

THE DIRECTOR-ACTOR RELATIONSHIP

The director and the actor have had to learn to need each other, for there is no reason to suppose that early directors were warmly welcomed by actors, who, until then, had been independent. There is still much in the relationship to make it difficult for both. The actor is worried about one role, the director about the entire performance; the actor works from a narrow slice through the play, the director from the whole thing; the actor risks everything in front of an audience, the director does not; the actor naturally resents commands, the director sometimes has to give them. Add to these differences the natural indifference or apathy of people brought into a working situation by professional accident rather than affinity, plus the stressful atmosphere of rehearsals, and the relationship can be strained.

Perhaps surprisingly, then, most directors and actors work quite well together. Credit for much of this goes to the director's human skills, although some of it must go to the patience and determination of the actor. The most potent factor may be, in the end, the knowledge that both are engaged in a creative enterprise whose success benefits both.

The director-actor relationship takes several forms:

THE DIRECTOR AS PARENT.   "Do it my way because I say so." The authoritarian director gets results early and keeps control of the production. He or she risks alienating or stifling the creative actor and often lectures at considerable length and takes the role of a professor with students.

Figure 8-11. **The Director as Director.** Variety and convincingness were created over weeks of rehearsal by a multifaceted, creative director. Molière's *The Miser. (The University of Maryland. Directed by Walt Witcover.)*

THE DIRECTOR AS GURU.   "If you do it my way, it will demonstrate our spiritual sympathies." A product of the 1960s, the guru is as much spiritual cult leader as stage director. The vision is a vision of existence, not merely of performance, and the actors are acolytes and members of a spiritual community. Brilliant work sometimes comes from devoted followers—innovative, revealing, revolutionary. The uncommitted may find it puzzling or silly.

THE DIRECTOR AS THERAPIST.   "Trust me; tell me your problems." In the psychologically oriented theatre of the 1940s and 1950s, the director-therapist functioned well. This director is still effective with actors trained in that tradition, especially when the actor's self and the character are made to dovetail. The director-therapist is somewhat of a mystery, if not a nosy busybody, however, to actors who work in another way.

THE DIRECTOR AS SEDUCER.   "You're wonderful; we're going to do great things together." Sexual seduction is not really a directorial technique, although it is not unheard of; rather, emotional attachment and even dependency are the object. This approach often succeeds in binding the actors to the director with great affection and loyalty. The difficulty lies in the lack of correspondence between affection and creative work, in the loss of perspective through noncritical, "global" attitudes on both sides.

THE DIRECTOR AS VICTIM.   "Do I have to do *everything?*" The director-victim suffers a lot. The weight of the production, the stress of rehearsals, the emotional demands of each scene seem draining. This director pleads, begs, cajoles, often gets remarkable results from sympathetic actors, and succeeds in touching their own emotional selves but suffers from a loss of authority.

THE DIRECTOR AS PLAYGROUND DIRECTOR.   "Let's have *fun* with this show!" Buoyant and youthful, the playground director tries to make everything fun, funny, cute, or touching. Much of theatre is work, however, and many plays have other qualities. This kind of director is good with children and probably an inspiration to beginners and amateurs but is too one-sided for serious actors.

THE DIRECTOR AS GREEN THUMB.   "I think we have something growing here." Totally organic, this director puts little or nothing down on paper, seldom seems to prepare, and always waits for things "to develop." Such directors, if inexperienced, have been known to ask when the actors were going to start to move around. With gifted and experienced actors, the director-gardener can build a profoundly creative situation, but the method—or lack of it—causes frustration and anger in many actors.

THE DIRECTOR AS LUMP.   "Be better." He or she mostly sits there, a lump in the rehearsal hall, occasionally complaining to the stage manager. Directions are so vague that the actors despair: "Sort of drift to the left a little way" or "Kind of give him a love–hate look." The actors, forced to shift for themselves, may either work it out or quit.

THE DIRECTOR AS DIRECTOR.   This director is an amalgam of all the above—occasionally authoritarian, sometimes seductive, organic when prepared solutions do not work, fun-loving when there is genuine fun in a scene or a situation. The complete director is multifaceted, even many-faced, all things to all people and all plays. What the good director tries to avoid is being limited, because a strictly limited approach inevitably antagonizes at least some of the actors.

Actors depend on their director. Therefore, the more precise and sure the director can be, the better. Precision and sureness come from *preparation*, and so the basis of the most productive actor-director relationships is the director's own work in advance of rehearsals.

THE DIRECTOR AND THE CHARACTERS

Many directors are themselves actors and/or acting teachers. They understand actors' approaches and vocabularies. Only rarely do they try to impose a new system on their actors, and then only if they are gurus or director-teachers. Thus, their work on character will be adapted to the system used by the actor playing the role.

Basically, the director does the same character homework as the actor, keeping a notebook, with pages or columns for each character. The director focuses, however, not on the objectives and motivations of a single character (except when working with the actor playing that character) but on shifting patterns of objectives that conflict, part, run parallel, and conflict again. It is not merely that the director maintains an overview of the terrain that the actors travel; it is that the director finds the heart of the play in the coexistence and conflict of character lines.

Too, the director is profoundly concerned with the "outside" of the performance. The director is a master communicator, interested almost obsessively in *things that signal to the audience*. This is the art of external signals, both visual and auditory. The actor devotes time and energy to the inner reasons for giving signals; the director works on those inner reasons only to help the actor, saving creative energy for the signals themselves.

As the director plans the schedule, attention is given to how each actor will build character. Some actors make great progress early, but one or two may never do so. Still, the director knows that by a certain date, "inner" work must be well under way. By some later date, the director must let go and "sit farther back," working more externally and more comprehensively. The closer the date of the first performance, the less attention the director will be able to give to detailed actor-coaching, which is only one aspect of the modern director's total job.

Staging

"Blocking," "staging," or "traffic direction," as some people wryly call it, is one of the director's inescapable responsibilities. No matter how much the actors and even the director are devoted to inner truth and to characterization, the time must come when the director must shape the actors' moves and timing and must give careful attention to *picturization* and *composition* and to *movement*. It is in the very nature of theatre that the visual details of the stage have significance, and the director must make that significance jibe with interpretation.

Significance is the crux of the matter. We live in a world where movement and visual arrangement signify: they give signals. In the realistic theatre, the same things signify that do in life; in the nonrealistic theatre, these things can be kept from signifying or can be made to signify differently only with careful control and effort.

Figure 8-12. **Visual Significance.** Physical interaction, placement, and gesture are parts of the director's communicative language. Osborn's *The Vinegar Tree*. *(The Clarence Brown Theatre Company at the University of Tennessee.)*

Before the appearance of the director, audiences seemingly found less significance in stage movement, gesture, and picture—or, more accurately, they found a *theatrical* significance in them: the star took center stage, facing front, with other actors flanking and balancing; a hero's movement pattern and posture were heroic; the heroine moved so as to show herself off and to divide or punctuate her speeches. Modern staging, with its meticulous attention to visual symbolism (picturization), beauty (composition), and movement was probably not seen before the nineteenth century except in special cases.

Much of what is taught about directing today is devoted to these matters. By and large, what is taught has been established by tradition and extended by popular theory, little of it having been tested objectively. Much of the theory of picturization—especially the supposed "meanings" of various stage areas—derives from the traditional use of the proscenium stage and probably has less relevance to thrust and arena staging. Indeed, as realistic plays exert less influence on the theatre, and as new theories of theatre evolve, many of these traditional theories of directing will probably fade.

MOVEMENT

As actors are aware of and exploit "body language," so the director is aware of and uses "movement language." Stage movement is more abundant than real-life movement; in a real situation, people often sit for a very long time to talk, for example, whereas on a stage characters in the same situation will be seen to stand, walk, change chairs, and move a good deal. Partly, this abundance of movement results from the physical distance of the audience— small movements of eyes and facial muscles do not carry the length of a theatre; and, partly, it results from the director's need for variety, for punctuation of action and lines, for the symbolic values of movement itself, and for the changing symbolic values of picturization.

Stage movement is based partly on the received wisdom of the movement implied by statements like "Face up to it," "She turned her back on it," "He rose to the occasion." Too, it serves to get characters into positions with which we have similar associations—"at the center of things," "way off in the blue," "out in left field."

The director is concerned with *direction, speed,* and *amount* of movement. Direction reveals both motivation and human interaction; speed shows strength of desire or strength of involvement (impassioned haste, for example, or ambling indifference); amount is perhaps most useful for contrast (a character making a very long movement after several short ones or in contrast with the small moves of several other characters).

Movement also *punctuates* the lines. It introduces speech: the character moves, catches our attention, stops and speaks. It breaks up speech: the character speaks, moves, speaks again, or moves while speaking and breaks the lines with turns or about-faces. (Pacing is frequently used for this reason. In life, we associate pacing with thought, and so a pacing character may

Figure 8-13. **Pictorialism.** This is pictorialism with a vengeance. Many of the vices of over-direction can be seen; they were, perhaps, typical of the early days of the professional director. *(Compare with Figures 8-5 and 8-15, from the same era.)*

seem thoughtful, but the turns are carefully timed by the director to mark changes in the speech itself.)

Movement *patterns* have a symbolic value much like that of individual movements and can be derived from the same figures of speech: "twisting him around her finger," "winding her in," "going in circles," "following like sheep," "on patrol," and many others suggest patterns for characters or groups. They are used, of course, to underscore a pattern already perceived in the play or the scene.

PICTORIALISM

Pictorialism—the exploitation of the stage's potential for displaying pictures—is not entirely limited to the proscenium theatre but has its greatest use there. From the late nineteenth century through the middle of the twentieth, the proscenium was seen literally as a picture frame, and the audience sat in locations that allowed it to look through the frame at its contents. With the advent of thrust and round stages, however, this "framing" became impossible, and audiences were located on three or all four sides of the stage, so that each segment of the audience saw quite a different picture. Thus, only certain aspects of pictorialism have universal application, and of these the most important by far is picturization.

Of considerably less importance, except on the proscenium stage, is the

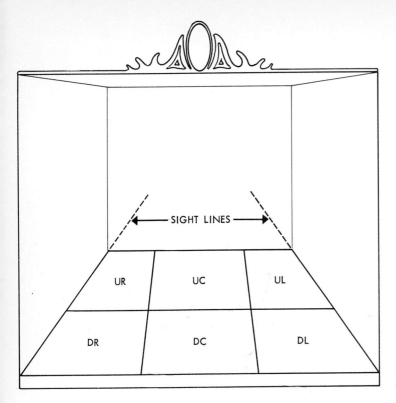

Figure 8-14. **Proscenium Stage Areas.**

symbolic value of *stage areas.* These areas (on the proscenium stage) are Down Center, Right, and Left (*Down* meaning toward the audience, *Right* meaning to the actor's right and thus the audience's left) and Up Center, Right, and Left. Down Center is unquestionably the most important (or "strongest") area, followed by Down Right and Down Left. Traditional wisdom has it that Down Right is more important than Down Left and that it has a "warmth" that Down Left lacks. The Upper areas are weaker, and Up Left is supposed to be the "coldest." The real value of identifying the stage areas is in creating *variety* and *identification,* variety because it is tedious if the audience has to watch scene after scene played in the same area, and identification because the association of an area with a character or a feeling is an important tool for conveying emotional meaning to the audience. And, unquestionably, the matter of "strength" does have some importance, if only because common sense tells us that the downstage areas are stronger because we can see the actors more clearly there—and, as a result, we want to play our most important (but not all) scenes there.

PICTURIZATION. Puns and traditional sayings give us a clue to how picturization works—and also suggest to us how the mind of the director works as it creates visual images of the sort that communicate to us in dreams. "Caught in the middle," "one up on him," and "odd man out" all suggest strong pictorial arrangements of actors. When a director combines them with area identification, for example, they become richer and more complex. The additional use of symbolic properties or set pieces—a fireplace, associated with the idea of home ("hearth and family"), for example—gives still greater force to the picture. Thus, a character who "moves in" on the hearth of a setting while also moving physically between a husband and wife ("coming between them") and sitting in the husband's armchair ("taking his place") has told the audience a complicated story without saying a word.

Sometimes, as in Shakespeare's *Richard II* (Act III, Scene iii), the playwright's own symbolism creates a rich texture of both picture and movement.

["King Richard appeareth on the walls" (First Quarto); "Enter on the walls" (First Folio)]:

NORTH: *My lord, in the base court he doth attend*
        To speak with you; may it please you to come down?
RICHARD: *Down, down I come, like glist'ring Phaeton . . . ,*
        Wanting the manage of unruly jades.
        Is this the base court? Base court, where kings grow base

[Richard comes down to stage level; the usurper Bolingbroke kneels to him, as is evident from omitted material]

BOLINGBROKE: *Stand all apart,*
        And show fair duty to his Majesty.
["He kneels downe." First Quarto.]
        My gracious lord.
RICHARD: *Fair cousin, you debase your princely knee*
        To make the base earth proud with kissing it. . . .
        Up, cousin, up; your heart is up, I know,
        Thus high at least, although your knee be low.

The scene begins with Richard "on high" while his enemies are in the "base court" at stage level. (A base court was a part of a castle, but *base* means "common" or "unworthy," as well as "low" in both the physical and the social sense.) Richard says he will come "down, like glist'ring Phaeton," that is, like the young man who drove the chariot of the sun too near the earth because he could not control the horses that pulled it ("wanting the manage of unruly jades"). But the audience already knows (from earlier reference) that the sun is Richard's emblem, and the director has probably made sure that it is visible on Richard's costume and may even be suggested by the shape of his crown, so the sun is being *debased*, brought down, even as Richard physically moves down to stage level. There, the usurper tells everyone else to "stand apart," that is, to give them room, but the word *stand* may be ironic and the director may use it to make an ironic picture, because they should kneel to the king. Bolingbroke himself does kneel (stage direction, First Quarto), but the gesture is a mockery, as Richard notes, "You debase your princely knee/To make the base earth proud. . . ./Up, cousin, up . . . ," reminding the audience that Richard himself was, only moments ago, "up" on the higher level. And Richard goes on: touching his crown (a traditional bit of business), he says, "Up, cousin, up/Thus high at least. . . ." That is, he will raise himself high enough in the presence of his king (though he should be kneeling) to seize the crown.

Thus, in a quick sequence of moves and gestures, the symbolic flow of the scene is given to the audience. With a scene of this richness and detail, the director need only follow its lead; few modern scenes are this explicitly symbolic, however, and directors usually have to create their own picturization to match the interpretation.

FOCUS.   A stage is a visually busy place, with many things to look at; therefore, the audience's eyes must be directed to the important point at each moment. A number of devices achieve *focus: framing* (in a doorway, between other actors, and so on); *isolating* (one character against a crowd, one character on a higher or lower level); *elevating* (standing while others sit, or the reverse, or getting on a higher level); *enlarging* (with costume, properties, or the mass of a piece of furniture); *illuminating* (in a pool of light or with a brighter costume); and *indicating* (putting the focal character at the intersection of "pointers"—pointing arms, swords, eyes, and so on).

Focus is largely a mechanical matter, but it is an important one that affects both movement and picturization.

COMPOSITION AND BALANCE.   Most stage pictures are rather well *composed,* or good to look at, but directors are often careful to study the production with an eye to improving the aesthetic quality of the scenes. What is *not* wanted is easier to say than what is: straight lines, lines parallel to the stage front, evenly spaced figures like ducks in a shooting gallery, and so on. *Balance* is also sought so that the stage does not seem heavy with characters on one side, light on the other. Composition is, finally, an irrational matter and a highly subjective one; directors who concern themselves with it in depth learn much from the other visual arts, especially traditional painting.

MOOD.   Mood is established most readily with lighting and sound and with the behavior of the characters. However, certain visual effects of character arrangement contribute, as well: horizontals, perhaps, for a quiet, resigned scene; looming verticals and skewed lines for a suspense melodrama. Mood values are as subjective and irrational as those of composition, however, and as hard to describe. In reality, what the director remains watchful for are clashes of mood, where movement and picturization conflict with other mood establishers.

DIRECTORIAL RHYTHM

Rhythm is repetition at regular intervals. The elements of rhythm in the theatre are those things that regularly mark the passage of time: scenes, movements, speeches, words. For the director, rhythm includes *tempo* and *timing*, as well as one aspect of *progression*. The director is concerned, then,

Figure 8-15. **Focus.** Can there be any doubt that the visual focus is at stage center, where Caesar is about to be murdered? How many focal devices have been used?

not only with the interpretation of character and the visual signals of inter-pretation but also with *the rate(s) at which things happen.*

We have seen that speed of movement is important to movement meaning. Now we may say that it is also important to intensity and rhythm. We associate quickness with urgency, slowness with relaxation; change in speed is most important of all. We may compare this phenomenon with the beating of a heart: once the normal heartbeat (base rhythm) is established, any change becomes significant. The director establishes the base rhythm with the open-ing scenes of the play and then creates variations on it, and the shortening of the time (cues) between moves, between lines, and between entrances and exits becomes a rhythmic acceleration that gives the audience the same feeling of increased intensity as would a quickening of the pulse.

Pace is the professional's term for "tempo," but it is not a matter of mechanical tempo. Much of what is meant by *pace* is, in fact, emotional intensity and energy, and the director who tries to create a feeling of intensity by telling the actors to "pick up the pace" or "move it along" will probably succeed only in getting the actors to speak so fast that they cannot be understood. Tempo has to grow naturally out of understanding and rehearsal of a scene, not out of a decision to force things along. Indeed, the scornful dismissal of such an attempt as "forcing the pace" and "pumping it up" suggests how futile it is.

Timing is complicated and difficult, something felt rather than thought out. *Comic timing* is the delivery of the laugh-getter—a line or a piece of busi-ness—after exactly the right preparation and at just that moment when it will

Figure 8-16. **Focus, Picturization, and Balance.** How have these things been achieved? Synge's *The Playboy of the Western World. (The University of Arizona. Directed by Robert C. Burroughs.)*

most satisfy the tension created by a pause before it; it also describes the actor's awareness of the timing that has produced previous laughs and of how each builds on those before. The timing of serious plays is rather different and depends far more on the setting of (usually) slow rhythms from which either a quickening tempo will increase tension or a slowing will enhance a feeling of ponderousness or doom. For example, at the end of *Hamlet*, Fortinbras has the following speech (Act V, Scene ii):

> *Let four captains*
> *Bear Hamlet, like a soldier to the stage;*
> *For he was likely, had he been put on,*
> *To have prov'd most royally; and, for his passage,*
> *The soldier's music and the rights of war*
> *Speak loudly for him.*
> *Take up the bodies: such a sight as this*
> *Becomes the field, but here shows much amiss.*
> *Go, bid th' soldiers shoot.*
>
> *(A dead march. Exeunt, bearing off the bodies;*
> *after which a peal of ordnance is shot off.)*

This follows an active scene of dueling, argument, and violence, and a short, less active scene of Hamlet's and Horatio's final words to each other, with the arrivals of ambassadors and Fortinbras. Fortinbras' speech is jumpy and uneven, effective because it *lacks* regular rhythm, but it finally settles down into the firm, regular rhymed couplet, "Take up the bodies . . ." that sets the final rhythm of the play. The rest could be timed on a metronome, taking the base rate (the pulse) from the couplet. *Go* is a long sound, followed (in one director's view) by a pause of two beats. The words that remain have but a single stress among them, on *shoot*. After this one-beat word, there is another pause of as long as three beats (in the major rhythm of which *Go* and *shoot* are major units). Then, the drum ("a dead march") starts its slow beating on the same tempo; a measured number of beats later comes the cannon sound ("a peal of ordnance"); another measured number of beats later, the lights begin to dim or the curtain to close, still on units of the original rhythm.

This control of a scene may seem unnecessarily rigid, and controlled rhythm of this kind works only when it is carefully planned and rehearsed because there is no such thing as a timing that is "almost rhythmic." The rhythm is either exact or it is nonexistent, and it is in stage effects like the drum and the cannon that the director can most carefully control it. (It is partly because of the need for control of such effects, in fact, that the director came into being.)

The Director As Manager

Although we have separated the artistic from the managerial functions of the director so that we could talk about them, no clear line exists between the two. A strong element of the manager is needed in the execution of all artistic decisions, and managerial abilities are always needed in the director's work with people. Directors have to be both artists and managers in almost all of their work, and they are unique among professionals precisely because of this unusual combination of traits: on the one hand, the often solitary consciousness of the artist, and on the other, the gregarious organizational intellect of the manager. Within the same person, then, the artist proposes and the manager disposes, sometimes at widely different times and sometimes simultaneously.

Insofar as the director-as-manager can be separated, however, he or she will work in the following areas:

PRODUCTION PREPARATION AND COORDINATION

In a Broadway production, many managerial functions are performed by the producer or the producer's office; in community and school theatres, the director performs most or all of them: *scheduling, budgeting, personnel selection, research,* and some aspects of *public relations* all fall to the director's lot. Scheduling includes the overall flow of production work from inception to performance, including production meetings, rehearsals, and the coordination of design and technical schedules, at least for purposes of information (including costume fittings for actors, clearing of the stage for construction work, and so on). These schedules are kept by the director or the stage manager on some easily read form like an oversized calendar.

Budgets are rarely initiated by a director, who does not hold the purse strings of the theatre, but the director must be able to keep a staff budget and to understand and honor costume, setting, and other budgets. In many college and university theatres, the director functions as producer and has budget control over the design areas (that is, the production money is budgeted as a single figure, which can be carved up as the director wishes).

Personnel selection (not including that of the actors) covers the director's own staff, most particularly the stage manager and assistants. In many situations, it will extend to the choreographer and the music director, with whom the director must work closely; it may include selection or at least approval of designers.

Research is carried out by a director on virtually any aspect of the production. Designers do their own research, to be sure, but such matters as the actors' accents, social mores, manners and mannerisms, the traditions surrounding the staging of a classic, the historical conventions associated with it, critical comments on it, and the work of other actors and directors in other productions of it concern many directors. It is not their aim to steal ideas from other productions; rather, it is their aim to learn from them, to honor traditions, and to build on what has been done before. This is particularly true in the staging of something like the operettas of Gilbert and Sullivan, for example, where audiences are familiar with the work and the traditions of performance are strong. In some theatres, directors have the help of a dramaturg in this task.

Public relations is not usually a directorial responsibility, but as a matter of taste and even of self-protection, the director often wants at least advisory approval of graphic and written material. Staging publicity photos, providing historical material from research, and appearing on interview shows to publicize the production are only a few of the things that a director may do.

CASTING

"Style is casting," the late director Alan Schneider said some years ago. The remark underlines the enormous importance of casting to the director; its success or failure indelibly stamps the production.

The producer or director puts out a *casting call* and schedules *auditions* or *tryouts*. In New York, much casting is done through agents and private contacts. In university and community theatres, almost the opposite situation holds true, because maximum participation is wanted and closed or private auditions are frowned on. In repertory theatres, of course, where the company are under contract, the director must work rather differently to make the company and the plays mesh, and casting and play selection have a good deal of influence on each other.

The director's conduct of a casting session is a trial of tact, patience, and

Western Dramatic Masterpieces Today

Today's productions of great plays take many approaches, from alteration of the text to stylistic innovation in physical production. Euripides' *Electra* is produced on a stage very different from that of ancient Greece, while Sophocles' *Antigone* has been transformed into a feminist piece by Martha Boesing in *Antigone, Too*. Shakespeare's *The Taming of the Shrew* has become the basis for a musical comedy, *Kiss Me Kate*, and John Gay's *The Beggar's Opera* has been altered by Bertolt Brecht and Kurt Weill to become *The Threepenny Opera*. Molière's comedies have been produced in period and in modern styles. The lightness of eighteenth-century comedies like Oliver Goldsmith's *She Stoops to Conquer* and Carlo Goldoni's *La Locandiera* have been captured in costume and setting. Oscar Wilde's *The Importance of Being Earnest* has been given a "soft sculpture" setting of foam rubber and quilted fabric, and Anton Chekhov's *The Cherry Orchard* has been staged in a highly selective, non-realistic setting.

C-9. Euripides. *Electra.*

C-10. Sophocles/Martha Boesing. *Antigone Too.*

C-11. Shakespeare/Cole Porter, Sam and Bella Spewack. *Kiss Me Kate.*

C-12. Brecht/Weill. *The Threepenny Opera.*

C-13. Molière. *The Imaginary Invalid.*

C-14. Molière/Frank Dunlop and Jim Dale. *Scapino.*

C-15. Costume design for
Goldsmith, *She Stoops to Conquer.*

C-16. Goldoni,
La Locandiera.

C-17. Wilde.
*The Importance of
Being Earnest.*

C-18. Chekhov.
The Cherry Orchard.

Figure 8-17. **Casting.** "Style is casting"—the right actors for the right vision of the play. Molière's *Tartuffe* at Western Carolina University. *(Directed by James B. Wood.)*

humanity. Auditions exist for the director, but would-be actors often believe that the sessions exist for them, and directors disabuse them of this error as gently as possible. Both good and bad actors try out, including good actors who are wrong for the play and poor actors who may have a quality that somehow seems right. The director wants to hear and see each one but wants to see and hear only enough of each one to know what each can do. Directors learn to make sound preliminary judgments on the basis of less than a minute's audition. It remains the director's task, however, to be considerate, positive, and polite. The goal is to relax tense actors, to help rid them of nerves that obscure talent by strangling good voices and tensing flexible bodies.

The director or an assistant keeps notes on each aspirant, often in the form of a checklist with headings for physical characteristics, voice, and so on. "Type" may also be indicated—the range of given circumstances that the individual's voice and body would suggest in the realistic theatre. Abilities and outstanding characteristics are noted in enough detail so that the notes themselves will both recall the individual to mind and serve as a basis for later judgment.

In a tryout, the director is looking not for a finished performance but for a display of potential. Script readings, performance of prepared materials, and improvisation and theatre games may be used. Aspirants may be asked to work singly or together or with a stage manager. Some will be called back one or more times because the director feels that they have more potential than was shown the first time or because more information is needed; and, as a final decision nears, the director will want to compare the "finalists" very carefully.

The actual selection of a cast is complicated and, finally, irrational. It is partly a creative act—the creation of the artistic unit that will bring life to the play. Feelings and hunches are important; so, unfortunately, are personal prejudices. Above all, the director wants to be sure, for replacing an actor after rehearsals have started severely upsets the creative process.

When the cast is chosen, the director posts the cast list. In some situations, the director will notify actors personally or will have them notified through agents. Each person who tried out but was not cast should have been thanked. If the whole process has been conducted well, there will be inevitable disappointment among those not cast, but no sense of bitterness or injustice.

REHEARSALS

Every director has a rehearsal pattern, and every pattern has to be adaptable to the special needs of each cast and each play. In general, however, a structure like the following is used:

FIRST REHEARSAL. The cast gathers, a trifle nervous and unsure. Many are strangers to each other. The director plays the role of host—making introductions, breaking the ice, moving these individuals toward cohesion. (Even when the playwright sits in, it is the director who is the "host.") The play will probably be discussed at some length, the director explaining general ideas and the overall direction; the designers may be asked to show and discuss models and sketches. Certain practical matters are got out of the way by the director or the stage manager (the signing of necessary forms, the resolving of individual schedule conflicts, and so on).

Then the play is read, either by the entire cast or by the director or the playwright. Some directors interrupt this first reading often, even on every line, to explain and define; others like to proceed without interruption so that the actors may hear each other. Either way, once the books are open and the lines are read, the rehearsal period is truly under way.

REHEARSAL BY UNITS. Rehearsing entire acts is often not the way to do detailed work, and so the acts are further broken down into *French scenes* (between the entrance and exit of a major character) or *scenes* (between curtains or blackouts), and then further into *beats* or *units* (between the initiation and end of an objective). These short elements are numbered in such a way that, for example, all the appearances of a major character can be called by listing a series of numbers, for example, 12, 13, 15, 17, meaning scenes 2, 3, 5, and 7 of the first act. By scheduling detailed rehearsals this way, the director often avoids keeping actors waiting. Or this same number system can be used to call scenes that need extra rehearsal.

As a very general pattern, it can be said that many directors move from the general rehearsal of early readings into increasingly detailed rehearsals of smaller and smaller units, and then into rehearsals of much longer sections when the units are put back together.

RUN-THROUGHS. A *run-through* is a rehearsal of an entire act or an entire play; it gives the director (and the actors) insight into the large movements

Figure 8-18. **Early Rehearsal.** The rehearsal space is far from elegant; the actors carry scripts; the properties are substitutes. *(Anstie's Limit.)*

and progressions of the play. After run-throughs, the director will probably return to rehearsal of certain small units, but, as performance nears, more and more run-throughs are held.

TECHNICAL AND DRESS REHEARSALS. As production coordinator, the director cannot forget the integration of lights, costumes, sound, and scenery into the performance. *Technical rehearsals* are devoted to any or all of these elements, normally done with the actors but sometimes without them (when "cue-to-cue" or "dry-run" technical rehearsals are held). In either case, the stage manager usually takes over the management of the script and the cues in preparation for running the show during performance; the director makes the decisions affecting the look and sound of the production and conveys them to the stage manager.

    Dress rehearsals incorporate costumes into the other technical elements, and final dress rehearsals are virtually performances in all but their lack of an audience. Nothing is now left to chance: actors must be in place for every entrance well in advance of their cues; properties must be in place, with none of the rehearsal substitutes now tolerated; costumes must seem as natural to the actors as their own clothes (achieved by giving them, weeks earlier, rehearsal costumes of cheap materials); every scene shift and light cue must be smooth, timed as the director wants it.

    And then, for the director, it is over. To be sure, polishing rehearsals may be called even after opening night, or full rehearsals if the play is a new one that has gone into *previews* (full performances with audiences in advance of the official opening) and needs fixing; but, as a rule, when the play opens, it belongs to the actors and the stage manager, and the director is a vestige

Figure 8-19. **Directorial Selectivity.** Not pictorialism, but a careful selection of details has resulted in a radically different production. Chekhov's *The Seagull*. *(The University of Iowa. Directed by Jan Skotnicki.)*

of another era in its life. The director may continue to check the production regularly, even for months or years if it is a Broadway success, but in effect, after opening night, the director is a fifth wheel. Until the next play, of course.

More than one director has compared directing to being a parent, the child being the production. The director rears it from birth to maturity and then pushes it out into the world. It is a paradox of the craft—as it is, perhaps, of parenting—that the proof of one's success is the loss of one's function.

What Is Good Directing?

To understand directing, we must be able to assess what the director has brought to the play and what the play presented to the director as strengths and weaknesses. Our evaluation of the direction will then depend on answers to questions like:

- How well did the director analyze and interpret the script?
- How well did the director solve the problems presented?

It is important to separate the *production* being studied from the *play* being studied. The production is not necessarily bad because it fails to stage the "playwright's intentions"; nor is it necessarily good because it either stages the "playwright's intentions" precisely or turns them upside down. As we have seen, different kinds of directors take different approaches; we must try to understand the approach and then evaluate it for what it is.

Good directing is seen in an internally consistent, exciting production. It deals with the play's problems and exploits the play's strengths in the terms of the director's approach.

Good directing shows most of all in the work of the actors. If the actors are good and are working in a theatrically compelling whole, the director has laid a good foundation. If the actors have not been unified, if they seem to hang in space when not speaking, if they perform mechanically, if they lack motivation at any point, if they do not perform with each other, they have been poorly directed.

Good directing has technical polish—smooth cues, precise timing, and a perfect blending of all elements—that radiates "authority", the artists' confidence in their work.

Good directing creates compelling pictures and movement, but only when they expand the work of actors and playwright, never when they contradict—and never when they exist for their own sake.

Good directing gives the performance tempo without giving it mechanical speed; there is no sense of too-fast or too-slow, but the organic tempo of a living entity.

Good directing combines all elements into a whole; there is no sense of

Figure 8-20. **Good Directing.** The performance is lively, convincing, compelling, the pictures neither overstated nor self-conscious, the tempo organic. Hugh Leonard's *A Life. (Wright State University. Directed by Richard D. Meyer.)*

good ideas left over or of things unfinished. Everything belongs; everything is carried to its proper full development; nothing is overdone.

The good director, then, understands the play and takes a consistent approach to it, bringing the actors to life in a complete production; the bad director does not fully understand the play, often failing to ask detailed questions; does not coach the actors or coaches them only incompletely, or directs them mechanically in postures and positions and movements dictated by a mechanical notion of picturization and composition; achieves not tempo but clockwork timing; and leaves ideas undeveloped and elements unassimilated.

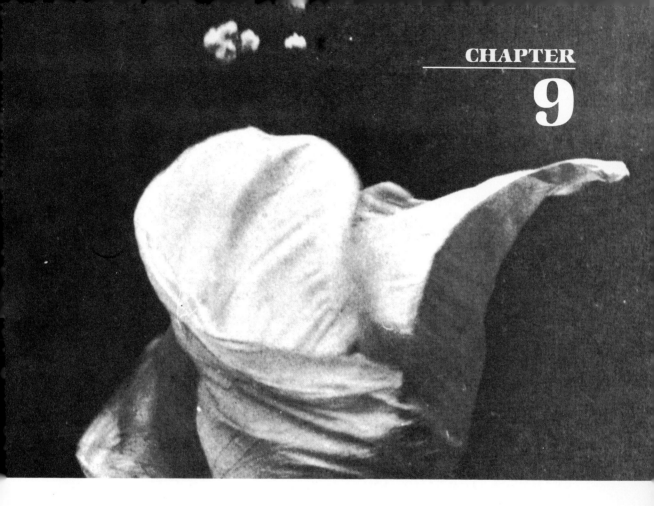

The Design Team: Scenery, Lighting, and Costumes

The Design Team

Sitting in the modern theatre, we sometimes take the presence of scenery so much for granted that it is easy to forget that theatre does not have its roots in either spectacular effects or localizing settings. We have become acculturated to the presence of physical environments that so closely suit the mood and meanings of each play that we may lose sight of the fact that the theatre for a very long period used little more than the architectural details of the theater building itself as environment, and that for centuries after that it was satisfied with stock settings that could do for many plays: a room in a palace,

191

a garden, a forest. We live in a period of magnificent settings and superb designers; however, stage design has not always been considered fundamental to theatre or its performance.

Much the same thing is true of costume designers, although it seems likely that their art (extended to include the making of masks) is a very, very old one, whereas sound designers are so recent an innovation that most theatregoers over forty are still surprised to see them listed in the program. Creators of lighting effects may be said to go back to the Renaissance, but it is probably more helpful to think of the art of stage lighting as coming into its own when a controllable means of illumination was invented: gaslight (about 1830).

Actors, directors, and playwrights work with life as their material. Theatre designers, however, work with the *environment* of human life, and their materials are the materials of our world: light and shadow, fabric and color, wood and canvas, plastic and metal and paint. Because their materials are of this kind, the designers are far more vulnerable to shifts in technology than are actors, playwrights, or directors. In fact, advances in technology inevitably change the way in which theatre designers practice their art, and, in the case of both light and sound, technology virtually created the arts. Thus, theatre designers stand in both the world of the artist and the world of the artisan or the mechanic, and they usually must be expert in both.

What Is Theatre Design?

Because the designers derive their materials and their subjects from the real world, their art is the creation of worlds on the stage. These worlds are sometimes imitations of the real world, sometimes not; in either case, they use familiar materials, but often in unfamiliar ways. The scenic and costume designers know that their products will be seen under colored light and so will look quite different on the stage from the way they look in sunlight; the lighting designer knows that the audience must see the actors, no matter what the demands of mood, color, and emphasis, and that the surfaces being lit are quite different from the things they imitate; the sound designer may be asked to create sounds that never existed in life or to amplify and distort real sounds to match the needs of a bizarre world.

The world that the designers create is the world of the play, which is not at all the same thing as a literal copy of the real world. Each designer goes about his or her task differently in creating that world, but they all share a common goal: to create an environment within which the actors can create convincing life. This goal means that the designers must work as a team and that they must work in concert with the director so that a compatible world is created by all of them.

This environment begins with the play. Contemporary design is tied inescapably to the dramatic text. The world that it creates has its roots deep

Figure 9-1. **The Work of the Designers.** Realistic theatre paradoxically requires meticulous design to produce a convincing illusion on the stage. William Inge's *Picnic. (The University of Arizona. Designed by Gary English; costumes designed by Peggy Kellner; directed by Robert C. Burroughs.)*

within that text—*not* merely in the stage directions, but in the lives of the characters.

Several factors, all to be found in the play, govern how the designers create their world.

TONE AND MOOD

Designers pay close attention to the differences between comedy and tragedy, but these two categories are simply not enough. Every play is its own category and must be approached through the range of tones that it contains: light-heartedness in several early scenes and great seriousness in a last act; both the romantic quality of a protagonist and the fragility of another major character, both funny gags and the real sadness of a central character's dilemma. *And* they must express these subtleties in the settings, costumes, lights, and sounds that are required by the scripts.

LEVEL OF ABSTRACTION

The designers are faced with a very wide spectrum of possibilities, from literal realism to fantasy to almost pure abstraction. At one extreme, for example, could be the setting for an American tragedy, where the decision might be made to create a literal replica of a house in New England down to the last detail of the patterns in the wallpaper. At the other extreme might be one of the "space stage" settings of the 1920s—abstract constructions of stairs, ramps, and levels. In costuming, we might find real clothes, purchased from actual stores and dyed to look sweaty and dirty; at the other extreme,

Figure 9-2. **Communicative Design.** Designer David W. Weiss's sketch for the setting of *Scapino* at the University of Virginia. How has the sense of "city" been achieved? A hint of comedy? An idea of social level?

we might find the costumes of some modern dancers, which use elastic fabric, extensions of limbs, and various kinds of padding to change completely the outline of the human body.

In part, the decision about how abstract the designs will be comes from the designers' and director's interpretation of the script; in part, it comes from a decision about how much the abstraction or literalism of the play itself will be emphasized. In a realistic play, for example, the decision to create literal settings and costumes is not an inevitable one; with equal justification, the designers might decide to create a mere suggestion of a house. In the same way, the designers of a play of Shakespeare's may decide that an abstract setting is inappropriate and may go to quite literal, realistic settings.

HISTORICAL PERIOD

The shifting of classical plays from one period to another has become common. Designers are confronted constantly with plays that do not have contemporary settings, costumes, and sound. The look and the "feel" of other periods become important aspects of design, then (and even the lighting designer is affected by historical period, when, for example, ideas about the direction and quantity of light and the quality of shadow come from paintings and engravings of the period). In setting and costume, some of the implications of historical period are obvious; the kinds of problems that they raise are most often handled by careful research by the designers. Sound, too, may be affected if period music is used or if certain kinds of sounds are called for—footsteps, for example, echoing from the stone walls of an old corridor instead of from modern materials; or the sound of a trumpet flourish; or the sound of Hamlet's "peal of ordnance."

Historical period contains a trap for the designers in the perceptions and knowledge of the audience: the designers must consider not only what things looked like in the period but what the audience *thinks* they looked like. What we know of the 1920s, for example, is conditioned by what we have seen in cartoons, old movies, and magazines—but did all women really bob their hair, and did all men really wear knickers and high collars? In the Elizabethan period, were all houses made of plaster-and-timber fronts, and did all men wear puffed-out breeches and hose? Did warriors in the tenth century wear plate armor? Or, to reverse the calendar, will all people in the distant future wear tight-fitting clothes of unisex design?

And there is still another trap; contemporary fashion. Audiences are greatly influenced by their own ideas of beauty. As a result, a hairstyle that is supposed to be of 1600 and that was designed in 1930 will often look more like a 1930 hairstyle than a 1600 one; or to take a familiar example from the movies, cowboys' hats in the movies of the 1940s looked far more like 1940s ideas of what was becoming to men than they ever looked like the actual headgear of westerners of the frontier period.

So designers must think of several things at once when confronted with historical period. It is not enough to go to a book and copy literally what is there.

Figure 9-3. **Historical Period.** Shakespeare's *Love's Labor's Lost* has been moved from the sixteenth century to a later one. What has been gained? *(Wright State University. Scenery by Joseph P. Tilford, lighting by Norman L. Frith III, costumes by D. Bartlett Blair.)*

Figure 9-4. **Social Level.** Properties, costumes, and setting communicate abundant details about the play's social circumstances. Preston Jones's *The Last Meeting of the Knights of the White Magnolia. (Murray State University. Designed by Bill Peeler. Photo by Hal Rice.)*

GEOGRAPHICAL PLACE

Like historical period, geography greatly influences design, unless the decision is made to abandon it altogether (that is, to be abstract instead of literal). The whitewashed houses of the Greek islands are different in color, texture, and scale from the adobes of Mexico or the balconied houses of New Orleans; the traditional clothes of Scotland, Morocco, and Scandinavia are distinct; the light in Alaska and Texas is very different. Sound and light are quite different outdoors from in. Even at considerable levels of abstraction, differences in geography inform some design definitions.

SOCIOECONOMIC CIRCUMSTANCES

The clothes and house and furniture of a Roman emperor were different from those of a servant; the same elements have certain special characteristics for the characters in an American play like *The Last Meeting of the Knights of the White Magnolia.* (See Figure 9-4.) As with the other considerations, a decision may be made to ignore such matters, but a *decision must be made.* The matter itself cannot be ignored. And the more realistic the level, the more important these considerations become.

Historical period greatly complicates social and economic matters. As with other historical elements, audiences may have general or inaccurate ideas about what constituted the look of wealth or position or power or poverty in a distant era. What, for example, did a wealthy merchant wear in the seventeenth century that a noble did not? What furniture did the noble own that the merchant did not? What separated serf from artisan in the Middle Ages?

AESTHETIC EFFECT

Put most simply, every designer hopes that the designs will have beauty. That beauty is a variable should be clear—the romantic loveliness of a magic forest cannot be compared with a construction of gleaming metal bars and white plastic plates—but that every designer aims at a goal of aesthetic pleasure seems true. Intentional ugliness may occasionally be aimed at, but even then we are tempted to say that the result is beautiful *because* its ugliness is artfully arrived at.

Composition and balance enter into aesthetic consideration, just as they enter into the considerations of the director. Teamwork is again essential, as setting, costumes, and lights are inevitably seen by the audience as a whole. Thus, unity is also an aesthetic aim, one achieved through a constant sharing of ideas by all the designers.

The Designers at Work

Although many of their decisions are reached in concert (at production meetings), the designers do most of their work in solitude or with the technicians who execute their designs—the scene designer with builders and painters, the costume designer with cutters and sewers, and so on. At this distinct stage of their work, each specializes and proceeds separately.

THE SCENE DESIGNER

It is the scene designer's job to create a performing space for the actors and a physical environment for the play's action. The result is the setting, which normally has the added function of supplying the audience with clues about the play's locale.

Other important questions are the *number of settings* (Can the entire play be played in one set, or must different sets be designed and changed for each scene, or can some sort of *unit set* serve for all scenes?); the *shape and size of the stage* (Will the audience surround it or look at it through a proscenium arch? If it is small, how can it be kept from seeming cramped? Will the actors play within the setting or in front of it?); the *sight lines* of the theatre (What peculiarities of the theatre's architecture demand that the settings be built in special shapes so that every member of the audience can see?); the *means of shifting the scenery* (Is there overhead *rigging* so that scenery can be "flown," or is there an elevator stage or a turntable stage for bringing new settings in mechanically?); the *materials from which the scenery will be built* (Is it better to use traditional *flats* of wood and canvas, or will built-up details of wood or plastic be better, or will such special materials as poured polyurethane foam or corrugated cardboard or metal pipe be better?); any *special effects* that make special scenic demands (Are there vast outdoor scenes in a proscenium theatre that require large painted *drops*, or will such unusual events in the play as earthquakes, explosions, and so on require special solutions?); any decision to imitate *historical scenery* that creates special requirements (That is, if a seventeenth-century play is to be done with Italianate scenery, what will the effects be?); and the demands of *budget* and *schedule*.

All of these matters may influence the designer before pencil is ever put to paper, although preliminary doodles and sketches may attempt to catch the "feel" of the play long before any practical matters are dealt with. These early impressions will spring from early readings of the play, and they will eventually be incorporated in some form into the *rendering* of the settings that the designer gives the director. Together, they will have worked out the ground plan of each setting, and the ground plan will form the basis of both renderings and three-dimensional models. If the renderings are acceptable, the designer will proceed to elevations and scale drawings of all scenic pieces, and these, with all instructions for building and painting, will go the production's *technical director*, the man or woman in charge of executing the scenic designs.

In addition, the scene designer is normally in charge of the design or selection of all *properties*, the things used by the actors that are not part of the scenery (furniture, flags, hangings, and so on), as well as such "hand props" as swords, cigarette cases, guns, and letters. Where such things must be designed, as in a period play, the designer creates, and the technical staff executes; where they are acquired from outside sources, the designer haunts stores and antique shops and pores over catalogs of all sorts. In plays done with minimal scenery, as in arena staging, the properties take on added importance, and their design and selection are carried out with great care.

THE COSTUME DESIGNER

The costume designer clothes both the character and the actor, creating dress in which the character is "right" and the actor is both physically comfortable and artistically pleased. This double responsibility makes the costumer's a difficult job. It is never enough to sew up something that copies a historically accurate garment; that garment must be made for a character, and it must be made for an actor. The actor must be able to move and speak and should also feel led or pushed by the costume to a closer affinity with the character and the world of the play. Generally, actors want costumes to be becoming to them personally, and costumers need tact in dealing with people who feel that their legs or their noses or their bosoms are not being flattered.

In designing for the character, the costumer must keep firmly in mind the *given circumstances* of the character, such as age, sex, state of health, and social class, as well as the focal importance of the character in key scenes (Should it form part of a crowd or stand out?), and most important of all, those elements of character that would express themselves through clothes.

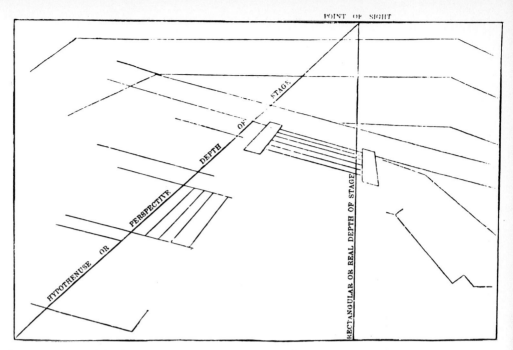

GROUND PLAN OF STAGE, PALMER'S THEATRE, NEW YORK.

Figure 9-5. **Ground Plan and Setting.** Above, the designer's plan for a setting, below, for *Othello*, 1893. An illusion of great depth was an important goal.

Is the character cheerful or somber? Simple or complex? Showy or timid? Majestic or mousy?

Other important matters are *silhouette* (the mass and outline of the costume as worn); *the costume in motion* (Does it have potential for swirl or billow or drape or curve as it moves? Does it change with movement? Will it encourage, even inspire, the actor to move more dynamically? What aspects of it—fringe, a scarf, coattails, a cape, a shawl—can be added or augmented to enhance motion?); *fabric texture and draping* (Does the play suggest the roughness of burlap and canvas or the smoothness of silk? What is wanted—fabrics that will drape in beautiful folds, like velour, silk, or jersey, or fabrics that will hang straight and heavily?); *fabric pattern* (all-over, small, repeated patterns as opposed to very large designs on the fabric, or none at all); *enhancement or suppression of body lines* (the pelvic V of the Elizabethan waist, or the pushed-up bosom of the French Empire, the pronounced sexuality of the medieval codpiece, or the body-disguising toga; and, for the individual actor, are there individual characteristics like narrow shoulders, skinny calves, or long necks that must be disguised by padding or by control of costume?); and, where necessary, *special effects* (such as animal or bird costumes or fantasy creatures).

In addition, the costumer must consult with both scene and lighting designer to make sure that the costumes will look as they are designed to look under stage light and against the settings. Practical considerations like budget and deadlines are, of course, always important.

The costumer's designs are usually presented as color renderings, normally with swatches of the actual materials to be used attached and with detailed notations indicated for the *costume shop supervisor* (see color C-8). From these, patterns are made, where needed; the costumer selects the fabrics and usually oversees their cutting and the construction of the costumes themselves. Most theatre companies of any size keep a stock of costumes from which some pieces can be pulled for certain productions, thus saving time and money. Costume support areas of any size usually include, besides the stock, fitting rooms, cutting tables, sewing machines and sewing spaces, and tubs for washing and dyeing.

THE LIGHTING DESIGNER

When stages were lit by candles, attempts to control the light were very crude and seldom very successful. In those days, the lighting designer's work was largely confined to special effects, such as fire. With the introduction of a controllable light source, however, and with the demand in the nineteenth century for more and more realistic imitations of phenomena like sunrise and moonlight, the designer's task became far more challenging and the creation far richer. Very shortly, the possibilities of stage lighting expanded enormously from simple imitation of natural effects, and lighting became a design element as important and as potent as scenery itself.

The possible uses of theatre light are enormous. Through manipulation of intensity and direction, for example, a designer can change the apparent

Figure 9-6. **Nonrealistic Costume.**
By Pablo Picasso, early twentieth century. *(From Huntley Carter,* The New Spirit in the European Theatre, 1914–1924. *London: Benn, 1925.)*

shape of an onstage object. Through manipulation of intensity and color, the lighting designer can influence the audience's sense of mood and tone. Through manipulation of direction and color, the designer can create a world utterly unlike the one in which the audience lives, with light coming from fantastic angles and falling in colors never seen in nature.

Modern equipment has made theatre lighting more flexible than early designers ever dreamed. Small, easily aimed *instruments* (lighting units) and complex electronic controls, sometimes with computerized memories, have made possible a subtlety in stage lighting that was unknown even thirty years ago.

The lighting designer works with three fundamentals: *color, direction,* and *intensity* of light. These are partly interdependent because of the nature of the light source, usually an incandescent filament. *Color* is changed physically by the placement of a transparent colored medium (usually called a *gel*) in the beam of light; this is not usually changed during a performance. *Direction* is a function of the location of the lighting instruments, of which there may be hundreds in a contemporary production. Each instrument is plugged into an electric circuit either individually or with a few others to illuminate the same scene. The location of instruments is rarely changed during performance, and so designers are limited by the number of instruments and the number of electrical circuits available to them. Light *intensity* is controlled by changes in the electrical current supplied to the instrument; this process is called *dimming* and is done by manipulating the levers on dimmers, of which several different kinds are in use. All have the same goal of changing the amount of light coming from the instrument from zero to full intensity, with the capability of stopping at any point in between.

The lighting designer's plan is called a *light plot*. It shows the location and direction of each instrument, as well as what kind of instrument is to be set at each location—usually either a *floodlight* (soft-edged and wide-beamed) or a *spotlight* (hard-edged and narrow-beamed). The locations chosen are over and around the playing area, so that light falls on the actors and the acting space at an angle, both vertically and horizontally. (Light that falls straight down or comes in parallel to the stage floor gives very unusual effects, although both have their uses.) In addition, such subsidiary instruments as *light borders* or *strip lights* (rows of simple lights without lenses, suspended overhead for general illumination), *footlights* (at floor level along the front of many proscenium stages), and *follow spots* (very powerful spotlights that swivel so that their bright beam can constantly illuminate a moving performer) are sometimes used.

The lighting designer is usually responsible for projected scenery or projected shadows, clouds, and similar effects.

The lighting designer has the special responsibility of making everyone else's work accessible to the audience. Light determines what the audience will see. Light creates depth, for one thing, and it can make an actor's eyes seem to sink into deep sockets or vanish in a bland, flat mask. Light gives or takes color, and it can make costume colors glow with vibrancy or fade into dirty gray. Light is selective, and it can show the audience precisely what is to be seen or it can obscure all manner of things.

In making the other artists' work accessible to the audience, the lighting designer has to consider all three elements: intensity, direction, and color. There are no hard-and-fast rules here; rather, there is need for a manipulation and an experimentation that is like putting colored paint on canvas. Although much of the lighting designer's work is done in production meetings and at the drawing board, much more of it is done in *technical rehearsals*, when, with the director, the designer experiments with colors and intensities and, frequently, makes decisions to change the locations and the plugging of instruments. Because of this experimental work that comes very late in the production period (often only days before opening), the lighting designer's work is crammed into a short time, and he or she works then at great intensity.

THE SOUND DESIGNER

Sound became a theatre art with good stereo equipment and related amplification, blending, and tuning equipment. To be sure, sound was used in theatres before that time, and as long ago as Shakespeare's Globe, someone had to be responsible for rolling the cannonballs that simulated thunder, but a sound that could be shaped dimensionally and controlled in pure, correct

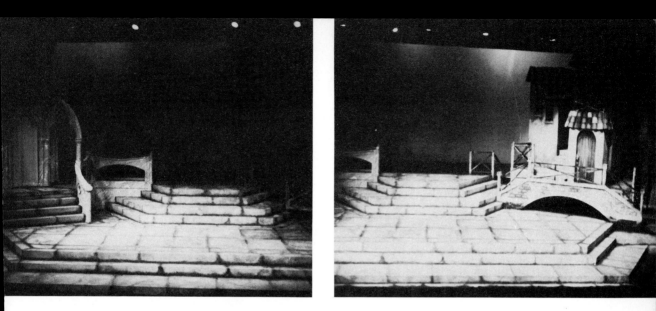

Figure 9-7. **Lighting Design.** The same setting for Shakespeare's *Merchant of Venice*, lighted differently to create two different locales: left, "Belmont"; right, "Venice." Below, the designer's light plot for the production. *(Trinity University, San Antonio. Setting and lighting design by Steven L. Gilliam.)*

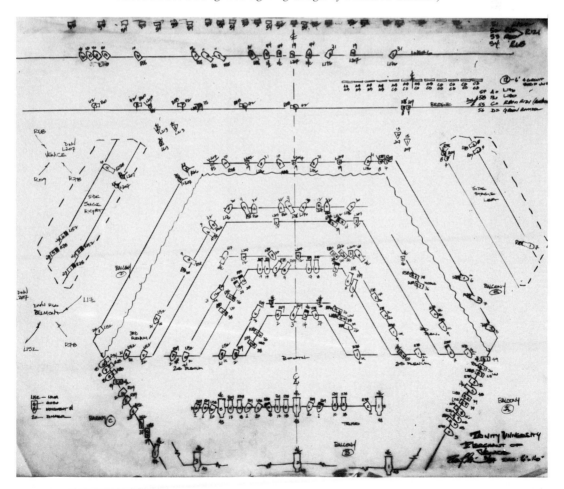

Figure 9.8. **Good Design.** Three historically influential works: above left, costume renderings by Leon Bakst, 1911; below, set rendering by Nicholas Roerich, 1909; above right, costume by Loie Fuller, 1900. *(From Le Théâtre.)*

tones was not possible until very recently. To the regret of many, the sound designer's job has been expanded in many theatres to the "miking" of performers, so that today many actors are heard through speakers rather than directly. As good as modern equipment is, it is not yet good enough to imitate in range, vibrancy, and direction the natural voice of the actor. It has proved a benefit, however, to actors who lack sufficient voice to be heard in large theatres.

As equipment becomes still more sophisticated and as expertise increases, the work of the sound designer may become as important and creative as that of the lighting designer. Limited at present to concepts of "sound effects" and "background music," the sound designer will one day be able to wrap the audience in sound as the lighting designer wraps the stage in light, and to play as flexibly with sound as the other plays with light. Rock concerts and sound-and-light shows are already pointing the way.

What Is Good Design?

Good design is good art. It is created in terms of the production, however, and it is created within the context of other artists' decisions. Knowing what is the product of a designer and what of a director can often be difficult, however, and, especially in our director-dominated theatre, assessing each designer's work is sometimes difficult.

Good design, above all, serves the actor—giving the actor good spaces in which to act, clothing the actor, illuminating the actor.

Good design serves the production. It does not necessarily serve the "playwright's intentions"; interpretation may have greatly changed this production from those intentions. Obvious changes may have been made—in historical period, geographical location, social class—along with less obvious ones (genre, mood, style); the play may even have become the framework, in this production, for an idea the very opposite of the "intention." In serving the production, good design meshes with other elements and does not call attention to itself.

Good design, where possible, is dynamic, not static: it has the capacity to change as the performance progresses. Such change is clearest in costumes and lighting, less so in scenery, where the number of sets is limited. A set that makes a powerful statement right off the bat and never goes beyond it for the entire performance may be a bad set.

Good design is not redundant. It does not merely "state the theme." It has its own complexity.

Good design has detail and texture (variety within the whole): light is not merely a bland wash of light; a costume is not merely a wide stretch of draped and sewn fabric; a setting is not a mere painted surface.

Good design has technical finish. Designers must design within the technical limitations of their theatres, so that everything the audience sees is technically well done. Often, designers oversee the technical work or approve it; nothing second-rate should pass their eyes.

Good design is daring: it tries new technologies, avoids old solutions, and chances failure.

The good designer, then, is one who creates effective works of visual art that serve the actor, that are right for the performance, that are richly textured and dynamic, and that can be perfectly finished by the technical capabilities of the theatre. The bad designer is one who ignores the actor; who creates ugly or uninteresting things; who designs for a predetermined idea of the play, not for this production; who creates statically; who ignores the capabilities of the technical facilities and allows shoddy work to go on the stage.

The Mediators

Mediation surrounds the theatre, preparing the audience for the performance. Mediation informs, educates, and sometimes entertains. Although mediation includes the work of professionals connected with the theatre itself (public relations copywriters and graphics people, for example), it also includes men and women who may work at several removes from the theatre—who may even, in fact, have no direct connection with the theatre at all.

These people are not theatre artists. Their interest in the theatre is intellectual rather than artistic. Their influence can be great, although it can vary enormously from situation to situation. Their writings can be important evidence of theatrical history. These are people concerned with theatre theory and criticism, dramaturgy, and theatre reviewing.

The Theorist

A theory is an intellectual construct that seeks to define and explain a phenomenon. In the theatre, we have two kinds of theory:

- Dramatic theory, which deals with plays (Aristotle's theory of tragedy, for example).
- Performance theory, which deals with performance, and which has, as yet, no workable, effective example.

A theory must meet three requirements:

1. It must be systematic (i.e., reasoned and orderly).
2. It must cover all cases.
3. It must agree with the evidence.

In the strictest sense, no comprehensive theory of drama or performance exists. However, Aristotle's theory of tragedy is usually accepted as a comprehensive theory of at least Greek tragedy, and sometimes of other kinds of drama, as well.

The lack of a comprehensive theory of performance is caused by the temporary nature of the evidence (the performance) and a failure to agree, as yet, on precisely what the evidence is; by the enormous difficulties in

Figure 10-1. **Performance Theory.** Theorists seek to define and categorize, among other things. They have so far not formulated a consistent theory of performance. *Where, Now, When, Now?*, created by Don Redlich for Improvisations Unlimited, dance-company-in-residence, Department of Dance, the University of Maryland. *(Charles Anderson photo.)*

creating a systematic theory of performance; and by the bewildering number of cases that must be covered. (Shall we include dance theatre? ritual performance? improvisation?) Performance theory is further complicated by the need to include the audience in the notion of performance.

Theorists seek to answer questions like: What is theatre? and What is drama? They may seek to answer questions of genre: What is tragedy? What is comedy? Their answers may be limited to historically defined answers (Neoclassical tragedy) or political ones (social-realist drama).

Theorists mediate theatre most powerfully through education. Major theories are complex; they form the basis of university-level courses ("Aristotle on Tragedy," "Plato on Drama," "Suzanne Langer's Aesthetic of Drama"). They then filter into the general consciousness through the work of other mediators and artists—not always in a form that the theorists themselves would recognize.

The creation of theory is an activity of major importance. Its goal is self-justifying, and it often has nothing to do with affecting the art of the theatre. At its best, it is a branch of philosophy.

The Critic

Criticism is the application of theory, but the line between criticism and theory is not a clear one. Many theorists are also critics, and many critics make theoretical statements; they may not themselves be theorists because their theoretical work is not comprehensive or systematic.

Like theory, criticism has two branches: dramatic criticism and performance criticism.

Dramatic criticism is most practiced in universities. Teaching dramatic literature is sometimes a kind of dramatic criticism. Many scholarly articles are examples of dramatic criticism, although the theories on which they are based may, in fact, not be theories of drama so much as theories of literature (e.g., new criticism, phenomenology, semiotics). The criticism of Shakespeare, for example, is a major academic industry with many theoretical branches.

Specific assumptions often underlie dramatic criticism and explain the critic's analyses. These may be political (Marxist criticism) or social (feminist criticism). The critic may choose to deal only with formal criticism (matters of form, structure, and so on) or only with content criticism (matters of idea, metaphor, and so on), although the two converge.

Because we have no adequate performance theory, we have no adequate performance criticism; nonetheless, we have many performance critics—men and women who are trying to at least describe performances seriously. At this stage, most performance criticism is purely descriptive and seeks to record the complex impacts of the many discrete moments of performance. Performance specialists are working hard to create theories of performance, but they have the difficulties we have already noted in even talking about

Figure 10-2. **"Spirits of the British Drama."** When kinds of performance compete belligerently, critics may take sides, and criticism may be influenced by this competition. *(Courtesy of the Astor, Lenox and Tilden Foundation of the New York Public Library.)*

performance systematically. (For example, the vocabulary of dramatic criticism is not adequate: the concept of dramatic action does not suffice for the actor-playing-character-in-costume-making-decision at a moment that is only one of thousands of moments. And what is a moment?)

A further difficulty in performance criticism is the intervention of the critic: the act of criticism appears to change what is going on in the performance.

Criticism, whether of drama or performance, is a highly serious intellectual undertaking. Its need for reflection militates against deadlines and pressure. Probably as a result, most of the best modern critics have had academic connections and have published their work as books. A few critics have been theatre artists.

The Dramaturg

Long a recognized figure in European theatres, the dramaturg has only recently appeared in America. The dramaturg is a specialist in dramatic literature and dramatic and theatrical history. Dramaturgs now have places on the staffs of resident theatre companies; their functions include:

Figure 10-3. **Reviewers and Theatregoers.** The reviewer can be the theatregoer's best consumer advisor; quotations from reviews—used as advertising—can draw theatregoers. Brooks Atkinson, after whom this Broadway theatre was named, was one of New York's most respected reviewers.

- Assisting in the selection of plays.
- Reading and evaluating new plays.
- Providing historical and literary background to directors, designers, and actors.
- Providing program notes.
- Assisting directors, sometimes by advising on the production.
- Working on plays—adapting, restructuring, translating.

A dramaturg is not a theatre artist but may be called on to act as one, particularly as a playwright. The historical and theoretical knowledge needed, however, and the knowledge of dramatic literature, suggest that university-level education is necessary. In fact, some American universities now offer graduate degrees in dramaturgy.

The dramaturg's mediation shows most obviously in program notes but may be present in public relations materials and in aspects of the production itself and the selection of plays.

The Reviewer

Reviewers are men and women who see plays and then write about them. Their orientation is toward consumer protection; that is, presenting themselves at best as an "ideal audience," they recommend or warn against performances on the basis of a taste shared with their readership.

Reviewers are seldom critics. They do not rely consistently on theory; they rarely pretend to objectivity. They lack the time to reflect on what they have seen, their work usually appearing in a daily or weekly publication. Often, their format is so limited (one minute on radio or television) that little can be said at all.

Reviewers are reviewers of both drama and performance. They do not attempt to tell readers or listeners what performance is or how it works, but they do tell them whether or not performance is likable within certain limits.

Some reviewers have theatrical backgrounds or education. Some do not. Experienced reviewers have trained themselves to recognize their own responses and to turn them into interesting, often witty prose, one of the functions of reviewing being to entertain.

Reviewers develop degrees of power within their communities, the New York reviewers supposedly having life-or-death power over Broadway productions. Their mediation extends beyond the review itself when quotations from the reviews are included in theatrical advertising. Because of this practice, some reviewers come to write quotable reviews, eager, perhaps, to see their names on theatre marquees with those of the actors. When this point is reached, the reviewer, although still a mediator, has crossed over from reviewing into public relations. In this way, a few reviewers become media stars in their own right.

Theatre of Other

PART III

Times and Places

The Present and the Past

Because the theatre of the present is not merely a theatre of today's plays and today's techniques but is also a theatre of plays and techniques from many periods, the alert and responsive audience member will be knowledgeable about the theatre's past and its present. The prepared audience studies the past to enrich the present. It studies, too, to understand what the forces of change are and how they work and to see that audiences and artists of every age have been much like us, subject to the same pressures, glad of the same pleasures.

It is tempting, perhaps, to think of a theatre of the past as filled with people who were somehow different from us—more polite or stuffier or older or stupider or less sophisticated—but as a study of the theatre's history will show, they were not all that different. They laughed and wept, applauded and hissed, got bored by bad performances and gave standing ovations to great ones. To understand this fact—that the theatre is a great force and that its audience is a great, vital constant—is to understand why the theatre is an art that stands at the center of human concerns.

The Uncertain Origins of Western Theatre and Drama

The issues surrounding the origins of Western theatre have been raised again and again and have never been satisfactorily resolved. As the evidence we have does not permit clear answers to such questions, a number of theories have been suggested.

Everyone agrees that theatrical and dramatic elements exist in life and therefore in all societies. The question is why, when, and by what means such elements were transformed into activities whose primary aim was artistic (as distinct from religious or instructional).

Some scholars have proposed that Western drama developed from storytelling. Telling and hearing stories, according to this theory, are pleasurable and natural; so too is the tendency of a narrator to elaborate parts of the telling by impersonating the various characters, using appropriate voice and movement. From here, it seems merely a short step to having several people become involved in the telling of a story; and from this, it is thought, drama and theatre arose.

214

Other theorists suggest that movement rather than speech was at the core of the drama. By imitating the physical behavior of animals and humans, and by donning appropriate skins or garments, a dancer first impersonated them and later embroidered this performance with sounds and words. The single dancer was joined by others who likewise impersonated and garbed themselves, and a form of theatre was born, it is supposed.

A few scholars have sought the form of drama in the judicial system of Athens. Alluding to the many instances in which debates and arguments occur in the plays and to the instances in which judgments are required, such theorists have sought the beginnings of Greek drama in the courtrooms of its early societies.

Probably the most fashionable, but not necessarily the most correct, view of the origin of theatre is the so-called ritual theory. A ritual is an activity that is repeated to gain a specific and predictable outcome. Religious rituals have developed in all primitive cultures as a means of affecting events, propitiating gods, transmitting information, educating the young, and so on. The ritual theory of drama proposes that from primitive religious rituals, in particular those connected with fertility and the spirits of the seasonal cycle, dramas evolved. Although few respectable scholars still accept the idea that drama "evolved" in some organic, necessary way from religious ceremonies, most acknowledge that ritual probably influenced the emerging theatrical forms.

Two statements by Aristotle, too, bear on the question of the drama's origin. He claimed, in Chapter 4 of the Poetics, *that "tragedy was produced by the authors of the dithyramb, and comedy from [the authors] of the phallic songs." Dithyrambs were choral odes; phallic songs were fertility rites whose precise nature is not known. Although tantalizing, Aristotle's account does little to clarify for what reasons or in what manner the authors shifted from dithyramb to tragedy or from phallic song to comedy. He also observed that "imitation is natural to men from childhood and in this they differ from the other animals . . . and then everybody takes pleasure in imitation." Because Aristotle was writing closer to the event than any of those advocating other theories, his account deserves consideration; still, it should be remembered that Aristotle was himself writing more than two hundred years after the event he was describing.*

Finally, some scholars view the appearance of tragedy and comedy as a supreme creative act of an unidentified artist (perhaps Thespis, perhaps Aeschylus, perhaps another). Arguing that art neither evolves like a biological organism nor happens by chance, such scholars look for the birth of drama in a revolutionary discovery made by a human being, an artist: that the synthesis of many elements already established in the Athenian society (dance, music, storytelling) would produce a more sublime work of art—and thus drama was born.

In its essence, the argument over the origin of theatre is an argument over the most important element of theatre. To the anthropologist who looks at mimings or impersonations as different as the Mandan Buffalo Dance, the Iroquois False Face Society, and the Egyptian "Passion Play," the essence of theatre is ritual, and the ritual theory will be favored. To the critic who finds the bedrock of drama in conflict, mythmaking or legal battle will seem the most like dramatic action, and the storytelling or the judicial theory will be favored. To the artist who looks at world theatre and sees a form rich in human meaning and almost indescribable in complexity, only a nonrational leap will explain its beginnings.

In fact, we do not know how theatre began. And finally, it is not so important for us to know its beginnings as to theorize and to argue about them, for in that thinking and that argument we preserve our sense of the extraordinary richness of a great art that will not allow itself to be reduced to simple explanations.

CHAPTER 11

Façade Stages: Greece and Rome

The first phase of theatrical and dramatic history of which we know began in the sixth century B.C. and ended around A.D. 500, a period of about one thousand years. Despite important differences, the theatres of Greece and Rome shared important traits:

1. *A façade stage*, where actors performed in front of a neutral background.
2. *A relationship with religion*, in which plays were presented as a part of larger, religious celebrations.
3. *A sense of occasion*, because performances were offered only on special occasions and never often enough to be taken for granted.
4. *A noncommercial environment*, in which wealthy citizens or the state itself bore the costs as part of the obligations of citizenship.

217

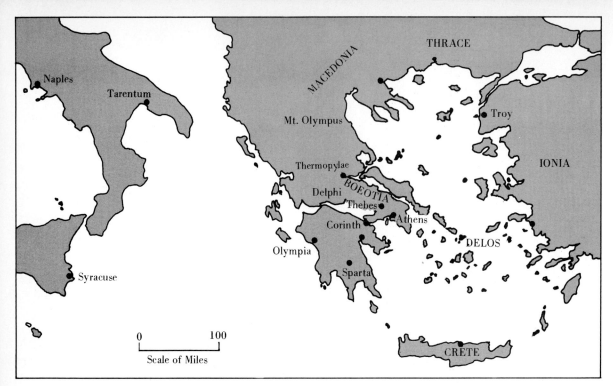

Figure 11-1. **Map of the Greek World.** Athens, the leading city-state during the age of Greek drama, had colonies as far away as Syracuse and Tarentum (in present-day Italy).

The Greek Period

BACKGROUND

Although civilizations had existed in Greek lands for thousands of years, the civilization that produced the first recorded theatre and drama dated from about the eighth century B.C. By the fifth century B.C., the society had developed a sophisticated system of government and culture. The basic governing unit was the city-state, or *polis*, which consisted of a town and its surrounding lands. Many were important (e.g., Corinth, Sparta, Thebes), but Athens emerged during the fifth century as the cultural and artistic leader of Greece. The Athenians established the world's first democracy (508 B.C.) and provided a model for the participation of citizens in the decisions and policies of government, achieving a level of participation unequaled except perhaps by the New England town meetings.

Under Pericles (c. 460–430 B.C.), Athens soared to new heights in art, architecture, and drama and headed an empire in the eastern Mediterranean, providing protection and trade outlets for other city-states in exchange for payments and other forms of tribute. Athens developed a drama that is still acknowledged as superb; buildings like the Parthenon and the Theatre of Dionysus were major achievements; and the arts in general achieved a status seldom rivaled since.

A defeat in the Peloponnesian War (404 B.C.) ended Athenian supremacy among the city-states, and an invasion of Greece by Alexander the Great (336 B.C.) changed the political and social configuration of the whole peninsula. By the time the Roman Empire encroached on the area in the second and first centuries B.C., little of the former glory of Athens remained.

Greek theatre and drama lasted for over a thousand years. Records of organized theatrical activity date from the sixth century B.C. and continue well into the Christian era. The unquestionable impact of the audiences of its day can be explained, at least in part, by four qualities that characterized this very vital theatre:

1. Greek theatre was closely associated with Greek religion.
2. Greek theatre was performed only on special occasions.
3. Greek theatre was a competitive venture.
4. Greek drama was choral.

GREEK THEATRE AND GREEK RELIGION.   Whatever the theatre's origin, Greek theatre was closely associated with Greek religion, which, unlike Judeo-Christianity, had many gods: Zeus, the king of the gods; Hera, his wife; Athena, goddess of wisdom; and so on. Private worship was interwoven into the daily lives of the people, but public worship occurred at festivals dedicated to a particular god. The festivals might last several days, and each *polis* had several festivals each year. In and around Athens, there were four festivals every year devoted to Dionysus, god of wine and fertility. At three of these festivals (the Great, or City, Dionysia; the Rural Dionysia; and the Lenaia), dramas were regularly performed as a part of the festivities.

For at least two hundred years after the first surviving records, all drama in Greece seems to have been performed only at Athens and only at religious festivals devoted to the god Dionysus.

The close association of Greek religion and Greek theatre is further shown by the presence of an altar within the playing area and, later, by places of honor in the theatres for the priests of Dionysus. Although the intimate connections between religion and theatre had been loosened by the end of the fourth century B.C., their relationship persisted: when an actor's union was formed in the third century B.C., it took the name "Artists of Dionysus" and drew its officers from the ranks of Dionysian priests.

THE OCCASIONAL NATURE OF THE THEATRE.   The fact that a festival is religious does not make it solemn; Mardi Gras and Halloween are, after all, religious festivals. Indeed, the fact that drama was performed at religious festivals in Greece seems not to have inhibited its joy or power. Experience suggests that annual celebrations often result in a more festive atmosphere and a more exuberant audience than regular affairs, simply because the event is relatively rare and therefore special. Because Greek drama was performed at festivals, it was performed only on special occasions, several times a year rather than several times a week. In trying to capture the effect of the festival arrangement, it might be well to compare it with celebrating a birthday or attending Mardi Gras, rather than with attending a play or a movie.

THE COMPETITIVE SIDE OF THEATRE.   To add to the excitement of the event, dramatic works in the festivals were competitive, with dramatists competing among themselves for awards in writing and actors competing for prizes in performing. The audience was interested not only in hearing the individual plays but also in learning who had won the various contests. Greek theatre, then, probably had some of the elements of a long-standing football rivalry, as well as those elements associated with drama and theatre.

THE CHORAL DRAMA OF GREECE.   In addition to actors, Greek drama required a chorus, a group of men who dressed alike, who were masked alike, and who moved and spoke together most of the time. The chorus often figured prominently in the working out of the play's action, and its importance to the total theatrical experience can scarcely be overemphasized; indeed, it has been theorized that *choral* song was the beginning of Greek theatre.

The presence of the chorus in the performing area throughout the performance provided considerable spectacle, its costumes, songs, and dances adding to the visual experience of the production. Because the chorus danced

Figure 11-2. **Greek Chorus.** This contemporary revival of *Medea* at the University of South Carolina shows Medea and a chorus of women (which, in Athens, would all have been played by men). *(Directed by James A. Patterson.)*

as it spoke, chanted, and sang, its rhythms indicated changing moods and shifting fortunes. By focusing attention on certain characters and events and avoiding others, by supporting some actions and denouncing others, the chorus provided a point of view, serving often as an ideal spectator. The chorus established the ethical system operating in the play and indicated the moral universe of the characters. Finally, and perhaps most important of all, the chorus—like an actor—participated often and directly in the action of the play, providing information and making discoveries and decisions.

Whether in comedy or tragedy, the chorus was an invariable fact of the performance and influenced a number of practices. Although estimates of its size are questionable, the traditional view is that in tragedy, the number of men in the chorus was first fifty, then twelve, and then, with Sophocles, fifteen, where it remained throughout the Classical Age; in comedy, the chorus numbered twenty-four.

EFFECT OF THE CHORUS ON DRAMA AND THEATRE.   Because the chorus usually came into the performing space soon after the play opened and remained there until the end, its presence had to be considered both in the physical layout of the theatre and by the authors of the drama; the chorus required a space large enough to move about in; and the presence of the chorus had to be justified and their loyalties made clear when secrets were shared. Because the vocal and visual power of the chorus was great (the contribution of each chorus member was, after all, multiplied by fifteen or twenty-four), the actors adjusted their style so as not to be overwhelmed by the impact of the chorus.

THE STUDY OF GREEK THEATRE AND DRAMA

Beyond the facts that Greek drama and theatre were closely associated with religion, were performed on specific occasions, and were competitive and choral, little else is certain. Evidence is scanty and often contradictory. Most of what is known comes from five kinds of sources: the extant plays; scattered dramatic records of the period; commentaries such as those of Aristotle and others; the archaeological remains of theatre buildings; and certain pieces of visual art, most notably vase paintings. Ironically, most of the extant plays date from the fifth century B.C., but most of the other evidence dates from the fourth century and later. The result is that for the period in which we know most about the theatre *buildings,* we know least about the *plays;* and for the years for which we have plays to study, we know very little about the buildings in which they were done or the techniques used to produce them.

Unfortunately, some have "solved" this problem by grouping all of the evidence together and speaking of the Greek theatre as though its practices remained invariable throughout its thousand-year history. But Greek theatre changed as markedly during its existence as the modern theatre has changed in a thousand years (since c. A.D. 990). And so it is necessary to identify which period of the Greek theatre is meant when considering production practices.

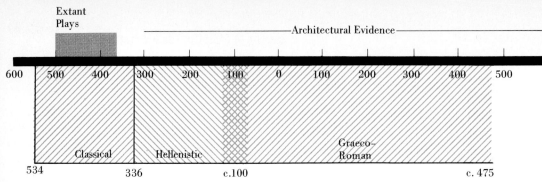

Figure 11-3. **Time Line.** Although Greek theatre lasted for about one thousand years, we have Greek plays from a period of less than two hundred years; and, for the period of the plays, we have almost no architectural evidence to help us understand the theatre buildings.

To simplify matters, we divide the Greek theatre into three major periods: the Classical, the Hellenistic, and the Graeco-Roman. Because most of the extant dramas date from the Classical Age, its practices will be described first and in greatest detail.

THE CLASSICAL PERIOD (c. 534–336 B.C.)

THE THEATRE.   The Theatre of Dionysus, Athens' first important theatre, was situated on a hillside, with a circular playing area as its base and the audience seated on the slope looking down. The first documented production occurred there in 534 B.C., and the winner of the contest was Thespis, who both wrote and acted in the winning tragedy. For a time, the playing area *(orchestra)*, the audience area, and the corridors separating the two may have been the only parts of this theatre.

By 458 B.C., however, a scene house (the *skene*) had been erected adjacent to the orchestra. Although its exact appearance remains a matter of conjecture, it probably had two or three doors and was used first as a place for the actors to change costumes and masks, later becoming a background for the play's action, representing variously a palace, a temple, a home, or even a cave. *If* a raised stage was present (scholarly opinion is divided on this point), it probably ran the length of the scene house and was low enough to allow easy access from the orchestra, thus permitting the necessary mingling of actors and chorus. So long as the scene house was built of wood, it was temporary and may well have been remodeled often; once built in stone, the scene house must be considered permanent and inflexible. Thus, Greek theatre early adopted a *façade stage*, a convention in which actors perform in front of a neutral façade, with the audience facing or arcing to three sides.

THE AUDIENCE.   That the theatre was out-of-doors meant, of course, that the audience, numbering perhaps as many as fourteen thousand, was subject to the caprices of the weather. Being outside also meant that the audience was as visible as the performers, an attribute shared by modern football

Figure 11-4. **Early Theatre of Dionysus.** An imaginative reconstruction of the early theatre, where audiences, seated on the hillside, presumably looked down on a circular performance space overlooking a temple.

games but not by modern theatres. Laws passed in Greece making violence in the theatre punishable by death suggest that theatrical audiences of the time were sometimes unruly.

PRODUCTION PRACTICES.   The basic setting, at least after 458 B.C., was the scene house. Whether or not its appearance was altered in an attempt to suggest changes in locale is not known. Something resembling modern-day flats existed, but their exact use is unclear. Two machines were used for special effects: an *eccyclema* and a *mechane*. The *eccyclema* was a movable platform capable of being rolled or rotated out of a door in the scene house, typically to reveal the bodies of characters presumably slain indoors. The *mechane* was a cranelike machine that allowed objects and people to be "flown" into the acting area. So often did the playwright Euripides fly in gods to bring his plays to a suitable conclusion that the Latin expression *deus ex machina* ("god from the machine") now refers to any obviously contrived ending in dramatic literature. Various properties were used in productions. Tragedies called for altars, tombs, biers, chariots, staffs, and so on; comedies often required domestic furniture. *Periaktoi*, scenic units with three faces mounted on a central pivot, may have been available during the Classical Age, but their use can be documented only for a later period.

COSTUMES AND MASKS.   Costumes and masks helped to differentiate one character from another and often provided clues about the characters wearing them. For example, in some plays, references can be found to characters

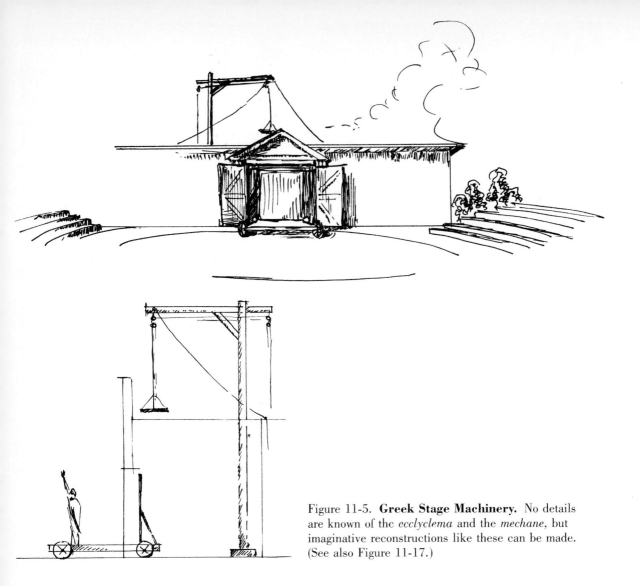

Figure 11-5. **Greek Stage Machinery.** No details are known of the *ecclyclema* and the *mechane*, but imaginative reconstructions like these can be made. (See also Figure 11-17.)

who are dressed in the manner of Greeks and others who are dressed as foreigners. Black was a color often worn by characters in mourning; and in a comedy, a god was dressed in yellow to make a point about his effeminacy. Although some historians have argued for a standard tragic costume, it seems more likely that costumes were a variation on the garments worn by contemporary Athenians; in the case of tragedy, probably like the elegant garments of the upper classes, and, in the case of comedy, more like the clothes of the lower and middle classes, but made laughable by having them ill-fitting, too tight, and too short. To the costume of many male characters in comedy was attached a very large phallus, intended probably as much for comic effect as for a reminder of the drama's associations with fertility and the god Dionysus.

Masks were worn by all performers (except possibly the flute player). The masks were full and carried on them hairstyles and beards as well as appropriate facial expressions. During the Classical Age, the masks, headdresses, and footwear were not exaggerated (the high boots and large-mouthed tragic masks often seen in books belong to a later period). Whereas the masks and costumes of the actors served primarily to distinguish one character from another, those of the chorus members stressed the *groupness* of the chorus by all looking alike.

ACTING.   Acting, like playwriting, was a competitive activity during the Classical Age, and rules governed its practice. For example, apparently no more than three *speaking* actors were allowed in the tragedies and five in the comedies, although any number of extras might be used. Because the leading actor, or *protagonist*, was the only one competing for the prize, he was assigned to the playwright by lot, so that chance rather than politics decided who got the best roles. The second actor and the third actor were probably chosen by the playwright and the protagonist in consultation. With only three actors, doubling of roles was required, for the plays themselves often had eight or more characters. If the protagonist had an exceedingly demanding role, like the title role in *Oedipus Rex*, he might play only one character, but the second and third actors were expected to play two or more secondary roles. Doubling, the use of masks, and the use of only male actors suggest that the style of Greek acting was more formal then realistic; this means that, although the acting was true and believable *in its own terms*, its resemblance to real life was of considerably less importance than its fidelity to the dramatic action. Given the size of the audience, the physical arrangement of the theatre, and the style of acting, it should be no surprise that vocal power and agility were the actor's most prized assets.

PLAYS.   Of the thousands of plays written during the thousand years of Greek theatre, only forty-six survive. Most of these date from the Classical Age and can be attributed to four authors: Aeschylus (seven), Sophocles (seven), Euripides (eighteen), and Aristophanes (eleven).

THESPIS. The semilegendary Thespis supposedly wrote tragedies using only one actor and a chorus. Although none of Thespis' works survived, they probably were based on the intensification of a single event rather than the development of a story, because stories require changes to occur. With only one actor and a chorus, the opportunity to introduce new information into a scene (and thus, to introduce *change* into a situation) was severely limited. The continual disappearance of either the actor or the chorus to fetch new information would obviously have been awkward and was thus necessarily curtailed.

AESCHYLUS. Aeschylus probably introduced a second actor, thereby permitting change to occur within the play. Although a second actor would also allow conflict between two characters, Aeschylus still tended to depict a solitary hero, one isolated and facing a cosmic horror brought about by forces beyond his control. With such a grand tragic conception, Aeschylus required great scope, and so he often wrote *trilogies*, three plays on a single subject

Figure 11-6. **Greek Tragedy.** An eighteenth- and a nineteenth-century actor as Sophocles' *Oedipus Rex*. Compare with productions at Stratford and Harvard (Figures 5-8 and 5-9) and London (Figure 4-2).

that were intended for performance on the same day. One of his trilogies, the *Oresteia* (comprising the *Agamemnon*, the *Choëphoroe*, and the *Eumenides*) has survived intact along with the single plays *The Persians*, *Seven Against Thebes*, *The Suppliants*, and *Prometheus Bound*. All display characteristics for which Aeschylus is admired: heroic and austere characters, simple but powerful plots, lofty yet sturdy diction. His general tone is well summarized by an ancient commentator: "While one finds many different types of artistic treatment in Aeschylus, one looks in vain for those sentiments that draw tears."

SOPHOCLES. Sophocles (496–406 B.C.) was credited with adding the third actor (Aeschylus also used three actors in his late plays) and with changing practices in scenic painting and costuming. Less interested than Aeschylus in portraying solitary heroes confronting the universal order, Sophocles wrote plays that explored the place of humans within an established order. The tragedy of Sophocles' heroes typically erupts from decisions made and actions taken based on imperfect knowledge or conflicting claims. Various aspects of the hero's character combine with unusual circumstances to bring about a disaster caused not by wickedness or foolishness but merely by humanness. For Sophocles, to be human was to be potentially a hero of tragedy.

The role of the chorus in Sophocles' plays remained important but not so central as in Aeschylus'. Conversely, the individual characters in Sophocles tend to be more complex, to display more individual traits, and to make more decisions: the result is that in Sophoclean tragedy, the actors, not the chorus, control the rhythm of the plays. Unlike Aeschylus, Sophocles did not need a trilogy to contain his tragedies; his plays stood alone. Of the more than one hundred attributed to him, seven have survived: *Ajax, Antigone, Oedipus Rex, Philoctetes, Electra, Trachiniae,* and *Oedipus at Colonnus.* Of these, *Oedipus Rex* is recognized by most critics as among the finest tragedies ever written.

EURIPIDES. Euripides (480–406 B.C.) was never very popular during his lifetime but came to be highly regarded after his death. Growing up at a time when Athens was embarking on policies of imperialism and expansionism that many patriots found repugnant, Euripides became a pacifist and a political gadfly. Although the populace viewed him with considerable distrust, the intellectual elite apparently admired him. It is reported, for example, that Socrates, one of the wisest men of the age, came to the theatre only to see the tragedies of Euripides and that Sophocles dressed his chorus in black on learning of the death of Euripides.

In comparison with the plays of Aeschylus and Sophocles, those of Euripides are less exalted and more realistic. His characters seem less grand and more human; their problems are less cosmic and more mundane. Euripides tended to examine human relationships and to question the wisdom of social actions: the purpose of war, the status of women, the reasons for human cruelty.

In keeping with Euripides' changed outlook came changes in dramatic technique. Replacing the philosophical probings common in the plays of Aeschylus and Sophocles, Euripides substituted rapid reversals, intrigues, chase scenes, and romantic and sentimental incidents of the sort later associated with the plays called *melodramas.* (Euripides is said by some to be the father of melodrama.) He further reduced the role of the chorus, until sometimes it was little more than an interruption of the play's action. As the role of the chorus declined and the subjects became more personal, the language became less poetic and more conversational. Many of the changes that Euripides introduced into Greek tragedy, although denounced in his own time, became standard dramatic practice during the Hellenistic Age.

COMEDY. Comedy was introduced into the Great Dionysia in 486 B.C., some fifty years after tragedy. It seems never to have been comfortable there, perhaps because the festival was an international showcase for Athenian culture and thus often visited by foreign dignitaries. The real home of comedy was the winter festival, the Lenaia, where a contest for comedy was established in 442 B.C. At both festivals, an entire day was set aside for competition among the comic playwrights, five of whom competed.

Of the twelve extant Greek comedies, all but one are by Aristophanes (c. 448–c. 380 B.C.); therefore, information about comedy during the Classical Age necessarily comes from these plays. It is possible, of course, that Aristophanes was atypical, and so the conclusions drawn from his works may be incorrect.

During the Classical Age, comedy was highly political and was filled with references to contemporary people and events. Although no two extant comedies are exactly alike, they bear similarities and suggest a highly formal structure that can be summarized briefly.

Figure 11-7. **Greek Old Comedy.** Aristophanes' "old comedy" *The Birds*, as performed by students at Cambridge University at the turn of this century.

Greek "old comedy" was in two parts divided by a section during which, typically, the chorus or the choral leader broke the dramatic illusion and addressed the audience directly.

The first portion of the play generally consisted of a prologue, during which the outrageous assumption on which the comedy was based was set forth. Following the entrance of the chorus, there was a debate about whether or not the basic assumption, or "happy idea," should be adopted. The first part of the comedy ended with the decision to put the "happy idea" into practice.

The second portion consisted simply of a number of episodes and choral songs showing the "happy idea" at work. The comedies ended happily on a note of feasting and merriment. Although all of Aristophanes' comedies follow this pattern more or less, no one of them corresponds in every detail.

Near the end of the Classical Age, when Sparta defeated Athens in war, some sort of censorship was apparently imposed, and so comedy became less political. Aristophanes' later plays refrain from the numerous topical references and often vitriolic attacks that mark his earlier comedies. The change has been noted by a number of scholars, and so the early comedy is called *old comedy*, and the less political, later works are called *middle comedy*.

CONTEST RULES. During the Classical Age, plays were produced in Athens by the city-state in cooperation with selected wealthy citizens. At the Great Dionysia, three tragic writers competed each year for the prize. To compete, each submitted three tragedies and one satyr play (a short comic piece that followed the tragedies and occasionally burlesqued them). One day was set aside for the work of each tragic author; therefore, each year there were nine tragedies and three satyr plays presented at the Great Dionysia. At the Lenaia, only four tragedies competed each year, each by a different playwright. At both festivals, five comic playwrights competed for a prize, and a single day was set aside for this competition.

How the competitors were selected is unknown, but, once chosen, each author was matched with a wealthy citizen-sponsor, who was then responsible for meeting the costs incurred by the chorus. The city-state provided the theatre in which the plays were performed and the prizes that were awarded to the winners.

THE HELLENISTIC AGE (c. 336–c. 100 B.C.)

Historians mark the beginning of the Hellenistic Age with the conquests of Alexander the Great. The system of city-states was replaced with a more centralized form of government, and the seat of power shifted away from Athens. Theatres began to be built outside Athens and throughout the eastern Mediterranean. Productions came to be seen in many cities and on numerous occasions, military and social as well as religious. Indeed, in general, the civic and religious nature of the theatre eroded as its professional standing increased. Actors, for example, were no longer merely citizens; they became

Figure 11-8. **Hellenistic Theatre.** Architectural remains of the theatre at Epidauros, Greece. Like the earlier Classical theatres, Hellenistic theatres retained the full orchestra circle.

professionals who organized along with other performers into the Artists of Dionysus, an agency that oversaw contracts between the actors and the cities wishing to hire them. The citizen-sponsors turned over their financial responsibilities to the state.

Theatres were built of stone during this period, and so archaeological evidence remains. The primary features of the Hellenistic theatre included a two-storied scene house, to which was attached a very long and narrow and high stage. Usually, the stage could be reached by steps or ramps affixed to each end, but in some theatres the only access was apparently through the scene house. The orchestra circle remained essentially unchanged, but its use during this period is uncertain. Was the chorus there and the actors on stage? Or were they both one place or the other? Or did it depend on the play?

Tragedy appears to have declined in popularity during the Hellenistic Age. Those tragedies written seem to show the influence of Euripides' innovations, including the reduced importance of the chorus and the increased importance of sensational and melodramatic scenes. Satyr plays disappeared altogether.

Comedy, on the other hand, remained very popular. Its strong political flavor now gone, *new comedy*, as it came to be called, portrayed domestic situations of the Athenian middle classes; featured love, finances, and family relationships; and often included intrigues involving long-lost children and recognition scenes. The highly formal structure of old comedy disappeared, leaving behind only a series of episodes and choral songs, with the chorus often quite incidental to the action of the play. Because Greek new comedy greatly influenced the development of Roman comedy, its qualities assume an importance beyond that accorded Hellenistic tragedy. One example of new comedy, Menander's *The Grumbler* (c. 300 B.C.), survived.

ARISTOTLE.   During the Hellenistic Age, too, the world's first and probably most influential dramatic theorist appeared. In his *Poetics* (335 B.C.), Aristotle provided a theoretical definition of the form tragedy (Aristotle defined neither comedy nor mixed forms in *The Poetics*). He proposed that "tragedy . . . is an imitation of an action that is serious, complete, and of a certain magnitude . . . in the form of action, not narrative . . . producing pity and fear and the catharsis of such emotions." The meaning of the definition has been endlessly debated, especially the phrase about catharsis, which some scholars believe refers to the response of audiences (though elsewhere Aristotle said he did not intend to talk about audiences), and other scholars think refers to emotions embedded within the episodes of the play itself.

He then defined and discussed the six parts of a play (plot, character, idea, language, music, and spectacle). Of the six parts, plot was the most important to Aristotle. He therefore discussed it in the most detail, considering its wholeness (having a beginning, a middle, and an end, connected by causality); its unity (so that if any part is removed, the whole is disturbed); its materials (suffering, discovery, and reversal); and its form (complication and dénouement).

Figure 11-9. **Hellenistic Theatre.** An imaginative reconstruction of a Hellenistic theatre, showing a raised stage and scenic units that may have been in use during this period.

He then considered the remaining parts of the play in turn. Along the way he argued that the best tragic protagonist is one who causes his own downfall through some great tragic error (*hamartia*), that the play's language should be both clear and interesting, and that spectacle is the business of the stage machinist rather than the poet.

Because *The Poetics* is so cryptic and its translation so difficult, its meaning has been hotly debated for two thousand years. Certainly, it remains the base from which most discussions of dramatic theory must proceed, through either acceptance or rejection of its primary tenets.

THE GRAECO-ROMAN AGE (c. 100 B.C.–A.D. 500)

By about 100 B.C., the expanding Roman Empire was exerting pressure on Greece. Trends begun in the Hellenistic Age continued but were altered to bring them more in line with Roman ideals and practices. For example, Roman theatres were built in Greek lands, and Hellenistic theatres were remodeled to resemble Roman theatres more closely (we call these remodeled Hellenistic theatres *Graeco-Roman*). Although some records show that theatre in Greek lands persisted throughout this period, the center of influence clearly shifted to Rome around the time of Christ, and so attention to Greek theatre declined and was replaced by interest in Roman practices.

231

Figure 11-10. **Graeco-Roman Theatre.** Architectural remains of the theatre at Leptis Magnis. Such theatres were Hellenistic theatres remodelled to conform more closely to Roman ideals of beauty. Note especially the changed orchestra. *(Photograph courtesy of Mert Hatfield.)*

The Roman Period

BACKGROUND

Rome was unparalleled among great Western civilizations simply because it remained intact so long. From a small prehistoric settlement, it grew to become the center of a far-flung empire that touched Asia and Africa as well as Britain and western Europe.

The city, although founded in the eighth century B.C., did not control the Italian peninsula until the third century B.C. By that time, Rome had developed a republican form of government, the leaders of which were noted for their economy, discipline, loyalty, and rhetorical prowess. In technology and military matters, moreover, Rome had no contemporary equal. By the first century B.C., its territory was vast and included much of western Europe as well as many of the lands once within the sphere of Greek influence. Whenever Romans made contact with another culture, they freely borrowed its arts, religion, technology—anything that seemed useful. Roman culture, then, in many ways, was an amalgam of attitudes and practices drawn from other lands but always adapted to the particular needs and interests of Rome and Romans.

In 27 B.C., the republican form of government was abandoned in favor of an imperial form; that is, power once vested in many representatives now resided in the person of the emperor. By that time, too, the energies of the government were becoming increasingly directed at maintaining control of

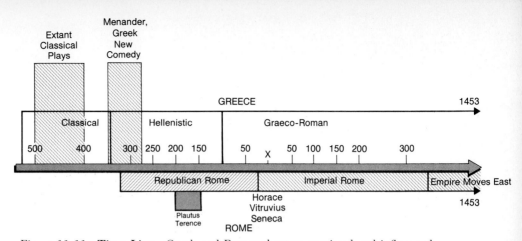

Figure 11-11. **Time Line.** Greek and Roman theatres coexisted and influenced each other for about eight hundred years. In Rome, as in Greece, the periods for which we have plays do not correlate well with the periods for which we have information about the theatre buildings.

the conquered territories, which were both numerous and distant. That the Western Empire lasted until the sixth century A.D. is a tribute to the administrative and technological sophistication of the Romans. Internal struggles and attacks from the north led to the collapse of Rome by the sixth century. Although the Eastern Empire, centered at Constantinople, continued until 1453, Rome's influence was no longer a significant factor in the political life of Europe after about A.D. 500.

For convenience, the Roman theatrical era is divided into two parts: the Republic (364 B.C.–27 B.C.) and the Empire (27 B.C.–c. A.D. 500). The extant dramas come from the period of the Republic; the stone theatres (and so archaeological evidence about stage spaces), from the period of the Empire. Therefore, in Rome as in Greece, the period of the plays and the period of archaeological evidence do not correspond well.

SOURCES FOR THE ROMAN THEATRE

GREEK.   The first record of Roman drama comes from 240 B.C., when Livius Andronicus, a Greek, was brought to Rome, where he produced a single play at the *Ludi Romani* (the Roman Games). Greek influence on Roman drama was strong; but two other sources predated it and accounted for major differences between Greek and Roman practice: The Etruscan and the Oscan.

ETRUSCAN.   Roman theatre, unlike the Greek, had from the outset an atmosphere in which a variety of entertainments competed for the attention of the audience. Chariot racing, boxing, wrestling, gladiatorial combats, and rope dancing occurred simultaneously with dramatic performances at the games. This carnival arrangement apparently came to Rome with the first recorded theatrical performance in Rome (364 B.C.), when Tarquin the Great,

233

234 THEATRE OF OTHER TIMES AND PLACES

an Etruscan, established the *Ludi Romani.* The Etruscans also probably introduced the stadium seating later used in the Roman theatres and encouraged an extensive use of music within Roman plays.

OSCAN. During the fourth century B.C., the Oscans (from an area slightly to the south of Rome) introduced a kind of short, improvised play that used a wide range of stock characters whose costumes and masks remained the same from play to play. Called the *Atellan farce,* this Oscan importation probably influenced the direction that Roman comedy took and may even have served as the basis for the *commedia dell'arte* (see pp. 279–281).

By the time Rome came into contact with Greece in the third century B.C., some of its theatrical traditions were already set and Greece was well into its Hellenistic period.

PRODUCTION ARRANGEMENTS

Theatre in Rome took place at *ludi,* or games, most of which were state religious celebrations devoted to the worship of any of Rome's several gods; occasionally, *ludi* were staged in celebration of birthdays, funerals, military victories, and political rallies. *Ludi* were managed by a civic or religious magistrate who received a government grant to cover the expenses of the festivals, whose complexities he was expected to oversee. Typically, among his other duties, the magistrate contacted the heads of several acting troupes and established fees for the performances. This fixed fee, paid by the state, might be augmented either by the magistrate himself (as the success of a festival reflected well on him) or by a bonus that the state awarded whenever public acclaim was unusually vocal. This bonus apparently resulted in some people's being paid to applaud wildly the work of certain troupes and in government officials' being bribed to notice such responses.

Drama in Rome was free and open to everyone. Apparently, it was quite popular, for the number of performances of plays steadily increased, from only one in 240 B.C. to more than one hundred during the third century A.D. Typically, several troupes participated at each festival, and on the days set aside for performances, plays were presented continuously, without intermissions.

PLAYS

TRAGEDY Although no tragedies survived from the Republic, titles and fragments indicate that they resembled Hellenistic Greek tragedy: sensational and melodramatic elements took precedence over philosophical inquiry, and the role of the chorus was peripheral rather than central to the development of the action. Depending on the subject matter and the costumes worn by the actors, Roman tragedy was divided into two types: (1) those written about Greeks, in which the actors dressed as noble Greeks, and (2) those written about Romans, in which actors were dressed as upper-class Roman citizens.

Figure 11-12. **Roman Tragedy.** Probably a statuette of a Roman actor from Imperial Rome. Notice the exaggerated mask, the high headdress, and the platformed footwear, none of which were used in the Greek Classical period.

Seneca. From the Empire, ten tragedies are extant, nine by Seneca (c. 5 B.C.–A.D. 65). None was intended for production in a public theatre. The importance of Seneca's tragedies rests neither on their literary excellence nor on their position among contemporary Roman audiences but on their monumental effect on Renaissance writers, who discovered, translated, and copied them (probably because they were both linguistically and physically more accessible than the earlier Greek tragedies).

Seneca's plays display characteristics assumed to be typical of Greek Hellenistic tragedy. His chorus is not well integrated into the action, and so his (usually four) choral odes (songs) serve to divide the plays into five parts. His protagonists are often driven by a single dominant passion that causes their downfall; his minor characters often include messengers, confidants, and ghosts. The language of his plays emphasizes rhetorical and stylistic figures, including extended descriptive and declamatory passages, pithy statements about the human condition (*sententiae*), and elaborately balanced exchanges of dialogue. Many of his plays feature spectacular scenes of violence and gore. Although it is now customary to scoff at the plays of Seneca, their influence on the subsequent development of tragedy in Italy, France, England, and even Germany has been incalculable.

COMEDY. Comedy, like tragedy, was divided into that written about the Greek middle class and that written about Romans. Although many titles, names, and fragments remain, only twenty-seven comedies survived, all from two authors: Plautus and Terence. Both wrote during the first century B.C., and both wrote about the Athenian middle class. Both drew heavily from

Figure 11-13. **Masks.** These drawings of a variety of masks seem to show a range of both comic and tragic masks.

Greek "new comedies" for their materials and stories, and neither used a chorus. Despite these obvious similarities, however, the plays of Plautus and Terence are very different from one another and suggest a considerable range within Roman comedy.

PLAUTUS. Plautus (254–184 B.C.) made a good deal of money as an actor-manager before turning to playwriting at about forty. He become a prolific and popular author. Of the more than one hundred works credited to him, twenty-one have survived, doubtless a tribute to the esteem in which he was held.

Plautus's sense of humor was always evident. The three names by which he was officially known (Titus Maccus Plautus) translate roughly as "big, splay-footed clown," perhaps a reference to his acting the role of the clown in Atellan farces. Probably his experiences as an actor working to entertain a fickle public accounted for the *theatrical* (as opposed to literary) qualities of his comedies. Plautine comedies are noted for their loosely linked episodes, which are filled with visual gags, verbal wordplay, and characters who are ludicrous in appearance as well as behavior. Never one to pass up an opportunity for a laugh, Plautus often broke the dramatic illusion, addressed his audience directly, and incorporated references to contemporary Rome in his comedies about the Athenian middle class. Among his many plays, *The Braggart Warrior*, *The Menaechmi*, *Pot of Gold*, and *Amphitryon* have provided material for Shakespeare, Molière, and others.

TERENCE. Terence (d. 159 B.C.) was less boisterous than Plautus. His use of language, for example, was so careful and elegant that his plays were used in schools throughout the Middle Ages as models of Latin eloquence. His plots, although based on those of the Greek Menander and his contemporaries, often combined two or more of the Greek comedies into a single, highly complicated dramatic action. He avoided the episodic quality of Plautus's plots in favor of more carefully contrived actions that proceeded by means of seeming cause and effect; his characters, too, appeared more normal and human, and thus more sympathetic. The result was, of course, comedies that were more elegant and refined but less robust and free, more thoughtful but less fun than Plautus's.

Finally, Terence's use of the prologue was unusual. Unlike Plautus, whose prologues contained exposition, preparation, and summary, Terence used his to argue matters of dramatic theory, to encourage audiences to behave politely, and to defend himself from the attacks of drama critics. In a prologue that is as revealing of republican audiences as of Terence's prologues, the playwright explained, "*Hecyra* is the name of this play. When it was represented for the first time, an unusual disaster and calamity interrupted it, so that it could not be witnessed throughout or estimated; so much had the populace, carried away with admiration, devoted their attention to some rope dancing."

Although comedy had always been more popular than tragedy in Rome, even *its* popularity waned within fifty years of Terence's death, its favor usurped first by the Atellan farce and later by *mime* and *pantomime*.

THEORY: HORACE. About the time that regular tragedy and comedy were disappearing from public theatres, Horace (65–8 B.C.) wrote his *Ars Poetica*, a work that exerted even more influence on the Renaissance than Aristotle's *Poetics* (on which it was loosely based). *Ars Poetica* is concerned with the standards and procedures to be followed in writing poetry, with special references to comedy and tragedy. Unlike Aristotle's work, which is a philosophical inquiry into the nature of the form *tragedy*, Horace's is a practical guidebook intended for people wanting to write. As such, it is considerably more prescriptive than Aristotle's work about such matters as the unities, the separation of the genres, and the appropriate arrangement of language. In many ways an "unmethodical miscellany" of rules, *Ars Poetica* seems to have captured the views current among theorists of the day but far afield from contemporary practice in the popular theatre of Rome; therefore, Horace's importance rests on his appeal to the erudite dramatists of the Renaissance and Neoclassical theatre, who used his work as a guide for constructing their orderly and decorous works.

NONLITERARY DRAMA. Despite the theories of Horace and men like him, drama and theatre during the Empire became increasingly nonliterary. The

Figure 11-14. **Roman Entertainments of the Empire.** Competing with mime and pantomime for public favor were large sea battles, staged in specially constructed spaces. Condemned criminals often participated, and thousands might die in a single battle, watched and applauded by the assembled audience, visible at the top of this imaginative reconstruction.

two most popular forms, pantomime and mime, depended on spectacle and not language and thus can scarcely be appreciated at a distance of two thousand years.

PANTOMIME. A pantomime was a solo dance that told a story by means of movement alone. Accompanied by an orchestra and a chorus, the dancer generally enacted a serious story taken from history or mythology. Because the dancer never spoke, pantomime masks were built with closed mouths. Although pantomime for a time took the place of tragedy as a serious entertainment popular with the audience, soon it too was overwhelmed by the growing popularity of mime.

MIME. Paralleling the rise of Christianity, the rise of mime caused several changes in Roman theatre. First, from its earliest days, mime included women among its performers, the only theatrical entertainment in Greece or Rome to do so. Second, performers in the mime did not generally wear masks, and so their personal appearance was both noticeable and important. Indeed, mime performers were often successful because of their looks: the very handsome or beautiful and the extraordinarily grotesque or ugly had the best chance of success, for they could more readily appeal to the audience as sympathetic or comic characters. Some mime actresses set fashions in clothes and behavior (one married an emperor), and many actors were the Roman equivalent of movie stars and matinee idols. Mimes could be either funny or serious, simple or spectacular, but whatever their form, they usually dealt with some aspect of daily living.

Mime was both Rome's most popular and its most notorious theatrical entertainment during the Empire. Because some mimes presented violence and sex *literally* as a part of the performance and because many of the works scoffed at Christian beliefs and Church practices, Christian writers and clerics called often and loudly, if unsuccessfully, for outlawing the theatre in Rome. Even though the artistic merit of mime was low and its performances were often offensive to the growing Christian community, mime continued to thrive for as long as the Empire survived.

It is well to remember that Roman drama and theatre were forced to compete with other forms of entertainment for public support. Perhaps many of the excesses of the mime can be explained, if not excused, by the enormous popularity of imperial athletic activities like chariot racing, gladiatorial contests, wild animal fights, and staged sea battles, where violence and death were both accepted and applauded. Although such activities were generally performed in specially constructed buildings like amphitheatres (e.g., the Colosseum) and circuses (e.g., the Circus Maximus), occasionally a theatre would be temporarily converted and appropriated for such events, serving again to bolster the arguments of those advocating theatre's abolition.

PRODUCTION PRACTICES

The first *permanent stone theatre* was not built in Rome until 55 B.C., very near the end of the Republic. Almost immediately, construction began on other theatres, until, by the end of Roman influence, more than one hundred theatres existed around the Roman Empire. Because they bore similarities to each other, a brief survey of their typical features can be provided.

THEATRE BUILDINGS.   Like Greek theatres, Roman theatres were façade stages; that is, actors performed *in front of* a neutral background. Unlike Greek theatres, Roman theatres were typically built on level ground, and the seating was built up, stadium style. At the rear of the Roman auditorium was a wide, covered aisle, whose roof joined that of the scene house to form a single architectural unit. The orchestra remained, but, unlike that in Greece, was a half circle, whose diameter was marked by the front of a stage raised to a height of about five feet and extended to a depth of up to forty feet. The stage was very long (100–300 feet) and was enclosed at each end by side wings jutting out from the scene house. At the back of the stage was the scene house, whose elaborate façade was decorated with numerous statues, porticoes, columns, and so on. Perhaps to protect this elaborate structure from the weather or perhaps to improve acoustics, a roof extended from the top of the scene house over part of the stage. The corridors between the scene house and the audience area were covered and used as audience exits.

Architectural evidence suggests that in the Roman theatre, a front curtain may have been used. Its introduction may well have been Rome's most significant contribution to theatre, as its use had implications for the kinds of plays written as well as the kinds of scenic displays possible.

Accounts suggest that Roman theatres could seat between 10,000 and 15,000 patrons and that considerable care was taken to ensure their comfort. Aisles were apparently wide and numerous, permitting easy comings and goings. An awning was used as protection against the sun, and at least in one theatre, a primitive air-conditioning system was contrived that used fans and ice brought down from nearby mountains. Important people could have reserved seats in the orchestra or in the special boxes atop the audience exits.

Most historians assume, perhaps incorrectly, that Roman theatres of the Republic were similar to those of the Empire, but, as evidence is limited and often perplexing, the appearance of the earlier wooden theatres remains a mystery.

MASKS AND COSTUMES.   Roman masks, costumes, and scenic practices resembled those of Hellenistic Greece. Roman masks for tragedy and comedy were full and exaggerated, with high headdresses and large mouths; the costumes resembled either Roman or Hellenistic fashions, depending on the kind of comedy or tragedy being done. As in Greece, all actors in the Roman theatre wore masks except for the mime performers. Clearly, as the popularity of mime increased, the use of masks on the Roman stage declined.

SETTINGS.   The basic setting in the Roman theatre was apparently the scene house itself. For comedies, its several doors represented entrances to

Figure 11-15. **Roman Entertainments of the Empire.** Horse races, chariot races, and shows were held in *circuses* like the one shown in this imaginative reconstruction.

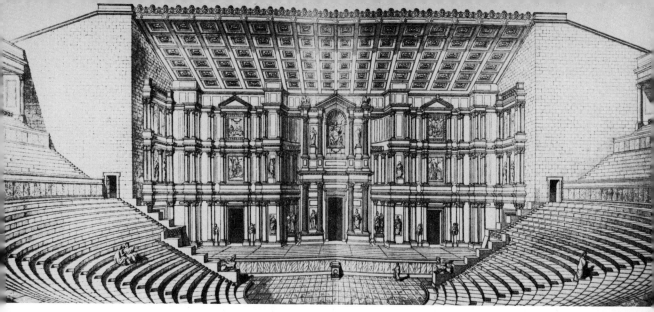

Figure 11-16. Roman Theatres. Stone theatres in Rome (and perhaps the wooden theatres that predated them) had elaborate facades, side wings, and semi-circular orchestras. Shown here, an imaginative reconstruction.

separate homes; for tragedies, its doors were entrances to various parts of a palace or a temple. The stage itself represented either a street running in front of dwellings (in comedy) or a gathering place before a temple or a palace (in tragedy). *Periaktoi* were used to suggest changes of place. According to one ancient commentator, they were located near the ends of the stage and could be rotated to reveal one of three scenes: a tragic scene (e.g., columns and statues), a comic scene (e.g., balconies and windows), or a satyric scene (trees, caves, and "other rustic objects"). Because the *periaktoi* could not possibly have hidden the façade of the scene house, they probably served simply to inform the audience of location, not to portray the place in a realistic way. Oddly, the mime used a back curtain that hung against the façade of the scene house; the size of this curtain increased during the Empire at about the same time that the elaborate stone theatres were being built. The seemingly contradictory trends are a mystery.

Also tantalizing are contemporary accounts of wondrous special effects. How they were achieved is unclear, but for one event there were reportedly "sliding cliffs and a miraculous moving wood," and for another, a fountain of wine springing from a mountain top just before the mountain sank into a chasm and out of sight. In what certainly must be hyperbole, Pliny, an ancient commentator, recounted yet another marvel:

> [*There were*] *two large wooden theatres built close together; each was nicely poised, turning on a pivot. Before noon, a spectacle of games was performed in each, with the theatres back to back so that the noise in each would not interfere with the other's performance. Then, suddenly, toward the latter part of the day, the two theatres would swing around to face each other with their corners interlocking, and, with their outer frames removed, they would form an amphitheatre in which gladiatorial combats were presented.*

241

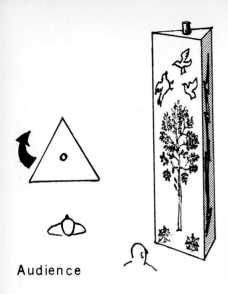

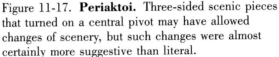

Audience

Figure 11-17. **Periaktoi.** Three-sided scenic pieces that turned on a central pivot may have allowed changes of scenery, but such changes were almost certainly more suggestive than literal.

VITRUVIUS. Just as Horace influenced Renaissance dramatic theory and Seneca Renaissance tragedy, the Roman architect Vitruvius influenced the nature of Renaissance theatres. He published a ten-volume work detailing Roman architectural practices, including ways to build both theatres and scenery. He described the theatre, the scene house, and three types of scenes: tragic, comic, and satyric. Because his work was not illustrated, Renaissance artists interpreted his instructions in light of their own artistic conventions. Although (mis)interpreted, Vitruvius's work influenced both theatrical and scenic design of the Renaissance.

DECLINE AND FALL

A series of barbarian invasions first dissipated and finally destroyed the power of Rome. The "fall of Rome" managed to accomplish what the opposition of the Christian Church could not: the end of formal and organized theatrical activity in Western Roman lands, an event usually dated from about the middle of the sixth century A.D.

For many years, it was fashionable to dismiss Roman theatre as inartistic and unworthy of serious study, but clearly it was a vital theatre and one enormously popular with its audiences. With the collapse of Rome, its theatre disappeared, only to be reborn, not in the period immediately following, but in the more distant Renaissance, whose scholars studied Roman theories and plays, imitated them, and thus ensured a Roman legacy to the theatrical world.

Emblem and Simultaneity: Middle Ages and Golden Ages

The second phase of theatrical and dramatic history began in the tenth century and ended about 1650 (one hundred years earlier in Italy). Despite important differences, the theatres of the Middle Ages and those of the Golden Ages of England and Spain shared important traits:

1. A staging convention of *simultaneous settings,* where several widely separated locations could be presented simultaneously to the audience.
2. The sharing of meaning through *emblems,* shorthand embodiments of richer content (a flag standing for a country, a crown for a king).
3. *Complicated plays* with numerous characters, many lines of action, and elastic time and place.

The Middle Ages

BACKGROUND

Although civilization in the East was flourishing, that in the West was in a state of increasing confusion after the fourth century A.D. From then until the eighth century, western Europe experienced political disarray, out of which emerged a different kind of Europe, one based on new nations and diverse languages and traditions.

With the collapse of Rome in the sixth century, various forces that had before served to unify Europe weakened or disintegrated. The Roman system of roads and waterways fell into disrepair, and transportation and communication became at first troubled and at last almost impossible. Laws were ignored and order broke down, replaced by the rule of force: bands of pirates and brigands grew wealthy and influential enough to challenge kings. Without the support of a government, the monetary system failed, and barter, with all of its cumbersome trappings, was the basis of trade.

Into the power vacuum created by Rome's defeat came a variety of competitive interests, each sparring for political and economic clout. The Church

Figure 12-1. **Emblem and Simultaneity.** On stage simultaneously at Valenciennes, France, in 1547 were structures representing heaven (far left) and hell (far right) with several other structures in between. Just as the huge mouth is an emblem of hell, the jail to its immediate left is an emblem of limbo. Are other emblems recognizable?

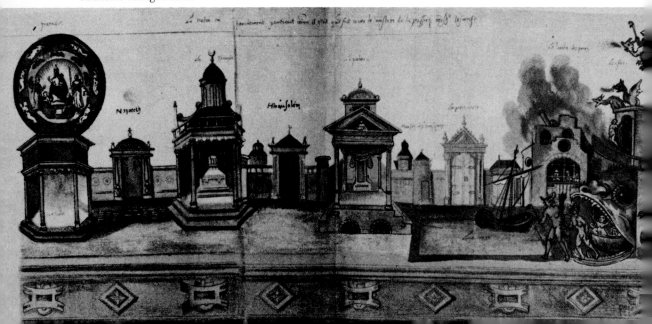

exerted increasing influence, especially after the tenth century, in part because its hierarchy ensured an orderly governance, and in part because its influence in the daily lives of people gave it a substantial base. The other prevailing social organization was feudal, whose primary social unit was the manor. On the manor, each serf owed absolute allegiance to the lord, who, in turn, owed allegiance to more powerful lords, and so on. Similarly, in the Church, the priests ranked below the bishops, who ranked below the archbishops; at the top was the bishop of Rome, the pope, who spoke with authority on Church matters. Both power hierarchies were essentially pyramidal, with one (male) person at the top, relatively few (male) persons immediately under him, and so on until, at the base of each pyramid, were the peasants, that great mass of people who tilled the land and provided all those above them with the necessities and amenities of life. The two pyramids interlocked when Church leaders were drawn from the noble classes; the peasants provided goods and services for both Church lords and secular lords.

The series of crusades after the twelfth century against the Muslims and other forces served to encourage trade and the opening of new sea routes. This, in turn, encouraged the development of towns, a movement well under way by the eleventh century. These towns and the merchants and tradesmen in them existed outside the feudal structure and gradually undermined it. As tradesmen organized themselves into guilds (trade brotherhoods), they were able to confront the feudal lords and eventually to challenge them successfully. With the rise of towns and the weakening of feudalism, nations began to take shape, and kings emerged to govern them. By the fourteenth century, the domination of the Church was under attack, and its monopoly on matters of faith was being eroded.

With the decline of feudalism and the authority of the Church, and with the emergence of towns and a sense of nationhood, the era ended.

MEDIEVAL DRAMA

For many years, historians believed that no theatre or drama outlived the collapse of the Roman Empire in the sixth century, but it is now certain that, after the empire divided into two parts, plays continued to be performed in the Eastern Empire around Byzantium, and that, even in the West, remnants of the professional performers traveled about Italy, France, and Germany, plying their trade and eking out a living. Scattered references to *mimi*, *histriones*, and *ioculatores* (all words used to describe actors) surfaced periodically in medieval accounts, but the degree to which such performers engaged in actual plays, as distinct from variety entertainments like juggling, tumbling, dancing, and rope tricks, is not known. Clearly, if traditional dramas were performed between the sixth and the tenth centuries, their scale was much reduced and they no longer enjoyed the support of those two most powerful social organizations of the time, the Church and the State.

However, in the tenth century, a woman (a nun), Hroswitha of Gandersheim, wrote comedies in imitation of Terence's; but we do not know if the

Figure 12-2. **Mimi, Histriones, and Ioculatores.** Scattered references to such performers appear in even early medieval records. Some believe that these performers, along with the popular court *fools*, were descendants of the still earlier Roman actors and entertainers.

plays were staged. Hroswitha is important on at least two counts: as the first known post-Roman playwright, and as proof of intellectual continuity from Rome.

Usually, the revival of institutionalized drama is dated somewhere between 925 and 975 and is credited to practices within the Church itself. Once reintroduced, theatre quickly established its place in the religious and civic life of the West and became once again a vital and vigorous expression of that society.

For purposes of convenience, theatre and drama during the Middle Ages can be divided into two traditions: that performed inside the church and that performed outside. Drama in the church was a part of the standard worship service, or liturgy. It was called *liturgical drama*, or *Latin music drama*.

LATIN MUSIC DRAMA. Liturgical dramas were done in monastic and cathedral churches and were acted by clergy, choirboys, monks, and occasionally traveling scholars and schoolboys. All actors were men, except in female convents. As a part of the church service, liturgical plays were given in Latin (the language of the Church) and were sung or chanted rather than spoken. Their subject matter was almost always drawn from the Bible. The stories most often dramatized were those involving events surrounding Christmas and Easter. Initially, the audiences for such works were probably monks and others living in monasteries, but once cathedral churches became common (during the thirteenth century), laypeople were the principal audiences for the plays.

PLAYS. During the ninth and tenth centuries, the Church had become increasingly self-aware and had begun to decorate and elaborate various of its practices; the music, calendar, vestments, art, architecture, and liturgy all changed in the direction of greater embellishment. Although the reasons for the emergence of Latin music drama are not entirely clear, probably its development proceeded as a part of this general movement.

Central to the drama was a particular sort of liturgical embellishment known as a *trope*, a name given to any interpolation into an existing text. A Continental European Easter trope dating from 925 was sung by the choir antiphonally and began, "Quem quaeritis in sepulchro, o christocole." Translated into English, the piece reads, in its entirety:

> *Whom seek ye in the tomb, O Christians?*
> *Jesus of Nazareth, the crucified, O heavenly beings.*
> *He is not here, he is risen as he foretold;*
> *Go and announce that he is risen from the tomb.*

By 975, someone had taken this choir song and turned it into a small drama, complete with stage directions. Directions for this new drama first appeared in the *Regularis Concordia*, a monastic guidebook written by Ethelwold, Bishop of Winchester, England, who described in detail how this part of the Easter service was to be performed:

> *While the third lesson is being read, four of the brethren shall vest, one of whom, wearing an alb as though for some different purpose, shall enter and go stealthily to the place of the "sepulchre" and sit there quietly, holding a palm in his hand. Then, while the third response is being sung, the other three brethren, vested in copes and holding thuribles in their hands, shall enter in their turn and go to the place of the "sepulchred," step by step, as though searching for something. Now these things are done in imitation of the angel seated on the tomb and of the women coming with perfumes to anoint the body of Jesus. When, therefore, he that is seated shall see these three draw nigh, wandering about as it were and seeking something, he shall begin to sing softly and sweetly,* Quem quaeritis.

> *Translated by Thomas Symons*

From this modest beginning, Latin music drama blossomed into many plays of varying lengths and varying degrees of complexity. The biblical stories most often dramatized dealt with the visit of the three Marys to the tomb, the travel of the Magi, Herod's wrath, and the Slaughter of the Innocents, but other plays depicted such diverse stories as the life of the Virgin Mary, the raising of Lazarus, and Daniel in the lion's den. Almost all were serious, but at the Feast of Fools and the Feast of the Boy Bishops, the usual dignity was abandoned, and in its place was substituted considerable tomfoolery, as this French account makes clear:

> *The deacons and subdeacons took pleasure in eating puddings and sauces on the altar, before the nose of the celebrant priest; they played*

cards and dice; they placed in the thurible some pieces of old shoes to make a terrible odor. After the mass, . . . they processed through the streets in carts full of dung, which they took pleasure in throwing on the populace crowded around them. They stopped and struck indecent postures and made lascivious gestures.

Translated by George Bryan

STAGING. The staging of Latin music drama was highly conventionalized and rested on two sorts of scenic spaces:

- The *mansion*, a small scenic structure, which served to locate a particular place.
- The *platea*, a neutral, generalized playing area.

The principal conventions of this theatre were that

- Widely separated places could be presented simultaneously in full view of the audience.
- Actors first established the specific location by reference to the appropriate mansion and were then free to move about the platea.

In complex plays, many mansions would be arranged around a generalized playing space. For the mansions, existing church architecture was often used and was supplemented whenever necessary. For example, the choir loft might

Figure 12-3. **Mansion and Platea.** This diagram shows two of several possible arrangements for the small scenic structures and the generalized playing spaces for Latin music dramas performed in churches.

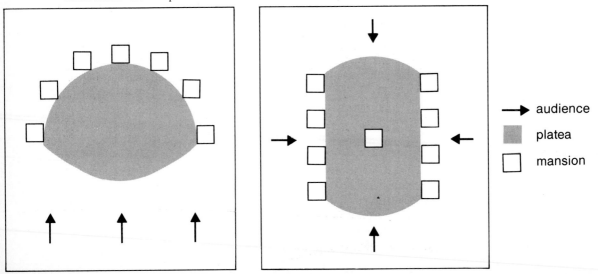

represent heaven or other high places; the crypt, hell or other low places; and the altar, the tomb of Christ. For more elaborate plays, special mansions were constructed, some small but others large enough for several persons to be hidden inside by means of curtains.

An important part of the scenic display in the church depended on *machinery* capable of flying objects and actors in and out of the playing area: angels and doves flew about, Christ rose to heaven, and the three kings followed a moving star that led them to the stable of the Christ child and there stopped to mark the spot.

Costumes for the Latin music drama were ordinarily church vestments to which *signifying elements* had been added: keys for Saint Peter, wings for angels, hoods for women, wallets and staffs for travelers. Occasionally, clerics playing kings or prophets might be garbed in ornate, nonclerical costumes, but these were exceptions.

DRAMA OUTDOORS.   Plays continued to be performed in many churches into the sixteenth century, but, by 1200, a different tradition was developing as well: some religious plays were being given outdoors. Records of such productions are scant until about 1350, when relatively abundant accounts begin to describe a civic and religious theatre of magnificent proportions throughout most of western Europe. The new tradition differed from the old in several important ways:

- The plays outdoors were spoken in the vernacular, rather than being chanted or sung in Latin.
- Laymen, rather than priests and clerics, served as actors.
- The stories and themes, no longer limited to liturgical sources, became more far-ranging.
- The performances tended to cluster in the spring and summer months, especially around the new Feast of Corpus Christi, rather than spreading throughout the church year, as before.

Of these changes, the most significant change was the shift from a universal language (Latin) to the various national tongues (e.g., English, French, and German), for with this shift came an end to an international drama and the beginning of several national dramas, a trend important to the future of theatre.

Why drama developed outside the churches has been endlessly debated. Some argue that abuses in the church buildings, like those at the Feast of Fools, caused the Church to force the drama outdoors. Others argue, rather, that the appearance of drama outdoors merely reflected the changing needs of the plays and their audiences rather than any Church-enforced banishment.

Dramas outside the churches were supported in various ways. Sometimes entire towns oversaw productions; sometimes special committees were formed and charged with the task. Most often, however, labor and religious organizations (called *guilds* and *confraternities*) assumed the financial and artistic responsibility for finding and rewarding actors, providing scenery and prop-

Figure 12-4. **Hellmouth.** Both inside and outside the church, the most elaborate mansions were those representing heaven and hell. Shown here is a rather typical hellmouth from the Low Countries, complete with special effects of fire and smoke.

erties, and establishing and enforcing regulations. If a guild was weak or poor, it might combine with others to meet its obligations. Plays were often assigned to guilds on the basis of their members' particular skills; for example, plays depicting the Last Supper were given to bakers' guilds, those of the Three Kings to goldsmiths', of Noah's Ark to shipbuilders' and fishermen's. Once assigned, plays usually remained with the same guild(s) year after year.

Roles in the plays were open to all male members of the community (in France, occasionally a woman might perform) and were generally performed without compensation. As in any primarily amateur operation, the quality of the performances varied considerably, and it was probably in an attempt to upgrade the general level of acting that many cities hired "property players" to take the leading roles and to instruct the less talented in improving their performances. Although these few actors were paid, they were not looked down on as socially undesirable, as were professional actors in secular plays.

The enormous complexity of some medieval dramas caused some people to be hired to oversee the production and to serve as the medieval counterpart of the modern producer. Although the responsibilities differed with the particular circumstances, the tasks of one medieval producer in France included:

1. Overseeing the building of a stage and the use of the scenery and machines.
2. Overseeing the building and painting of scenery and the construction of seating for the audience.
3. Checking all deliveries to ensure accuracy.
4. Disciplining the actors.
5. Acting in the plays whenever necessary.
6. Addressing audiences at the beginning of the play and at each intermission, giving a summary of what had happened and promising greater marvels to come.

Because mechanical reproduction and printing were unavailable, a single copy of the script, with its various directions for production, was hand-written and retained from year to year. This master copy, called a *register*, was held by a designated party, often the producing organization or church. Obviously, if any political group could secure the register, they could prevent further production, as indeed occasionally happened by the late sixteenth century, when religious dramas were being censored and then banned.

Because special effects in the dramas were so extraordinary, some men, called *masters of secrets*, became specialists in their construction and workings, which included:

- Flying: angels flew about; Lucifer raised Christ; souls rose from limbo into heaven on Doomsday; devils and fire-spitting monsters sallied forth from hell and back again; cotton-covered platforms, resembling clouds (*glories*), bore choruses of heavenly beings aloft.
- Traps: appearances, disappearances, and substitutions, as when Lot's wife was turned into a pillar of salt, and tigers were transformed into sheep.
- Artistic control of fire: hell belched smoke and flames (in 1496 at Seurre, an actor playing Satan was severely burned when his costume caught fire), and buildings ignited on cue.

The scale of these effects can perhaps be suggested by the following account of a French production:

The spectacle lasted twenty-five days, and on each day we saw strange and wonderful things. The machines of the Paradise and Hell were absolutely prodigious and could be taken by the populace for magic. For we saw Truth, the angels, and other characters descend from very high, sometimes visibly, sometimes invisibly, appearing suddenly. Lucifer was raised from Hell on a dragon without our being

Figure 12-5. **Dragons and Devils.** The "Norwich Dragon" was a property piece with a movable mouth and wings, carried in a procession through the city streets. Devil costumes, like dragon properties, were among the most elaborate in the medieval theatre.

able to see how. The rod of Moses, dry and sterile, suddenly put forth flowers and fruits. Devils carried the souls of Herod and Judas through the air. Devils were exorcised, people with dropsy and other invalids were cured, all in an admirable way. Here Jesus Christ was carried up by the Devil who scaled a wall forty feet high. There He became invisible. Finally, He was transfigured on Mount Tabor. We saw water changed into wine so mysteriously that we could not believe it, and more than a hundred persons wanted to taste this wine. The five breads and the two fish seemed to be multiplied and were distributed to more than a thousand spectators, and yet there were more than twelve baskets left. The fig tree, cursed by Our Lord, appeared to dry up, its leaves withering in an instant. The eclipse, the earthquake, the splitting of the rocks and the other miracles at the death of Our Lord were shown with new marvels.

Chronicler of Valenciennes

STAGING. The conventions of staging resembled those used in the churches: mansions and platea remained the spatial elements, and simultaneous display of several locations continued. But within this general pattern, two rather different traditions developed:

- Fixed staging, mostly on the Continent (excepting Spain and parts of England).
- Movable staging, mostly in Spain and parts of England.

In fixed staging, mansions (or *scaffolds*) were set up, usually outdoors, in whatever spaces were available (e.g., courtyards of noble houses, town squares, the remains of Roman amphitheatres). Depending on the space, the mansions were arranged in circles, straight lines, or rectangles, and the platea and the audience area were established accordingly. Although the individual arrangements varied, heaven and hell (ordinarily the most ornate mansions) were customarily set at opposite poles.

In movable staging, *pageants* (pageant wagons) allowed the audience to scatter along a processional route while the plays were brought to them and performed in sequence, much like a homecoming parade with floats. Each play, then, was performed several times. A common pattern was for the first play (Creation) to be presented at dawn at the first station; when it moved to the second station to perform, the second play (the Fall of Man) was presented at the first station. For most of the day, several plays were performing at once. The word *pageant* is important in a discussion of movable staging because it was used to describe the play itself, the spectacle of the plays in performance, and also the vehicle on which the presentation was staged.

The appearance of pageant wagons has been much discussed, but as available evidence is scant, few firm conclusions are possible. Only one English description, dating from slightly before 1600, has survived, and its reliability is suspect:

> *Every company had his pagiant, or parte, which pagiants weare a high scafolde with two rowmes, a higher and a lower, upon four wheeles. In the lower they apparelled themselves, and in the higher rowme they played, beinge all open on the tope, that all behoulders mighte heare and see them. The places where they played them was in every streete.*

Archdeacon Robert Rogers

An obvious problem with the description, and one of the reasons its accuracy has been questioned, is that the wagons as described would need to be more than twelve feet tall to allow for the wheels and the two levels, yet narrow enough to be pulled by horses through the medieval streets. The resulting structure would be highly unstable and perhaps unable to turn corners as required in its trek from station to station.

PLAYS. Regardless of the conventions of staging, the same sorts of plays were done in all countries. The plays remained decidedly religious, if not always scriptural. In general, they dealt with:

- Events in the life of Christ or stories from the Old Testament (plays often called *mysteries*).
- The lives of saints, both historical and legendary (called *miracles*).
- Didactic allegories frequently portraying the human struggle for salvation (the *moralities*).

Although the plays differed in subject matter and form, they shared several characteristics. First, they aimed to teach or to reinforce belief in Church doctrine. Second, they were formulated as melodramas or divine comedies; that is, the ethical system of the play was clear, and good was rewarded, evil punished. Third, the driving force for the action was God and His plan rather than the decisions or actions of the dramatic agents. To a modern reader, the plays often appear episodic, with their actions unmotivated, their sequences of time and place inexplicable, and their mixture of the comic and the serious unnerving.

In fact, their traits expressed well the medieval view. The plays presented the lure and strength of sin, the power and compassion of God, and the

Figure 12-6. **Pageant Wagons.** In movable staging, wagons, whose exact appearance we do not know, carried plays to the audience, which was scattered along a processional route. Shown here is one artist's imaginative reconstruction of such a wagon.

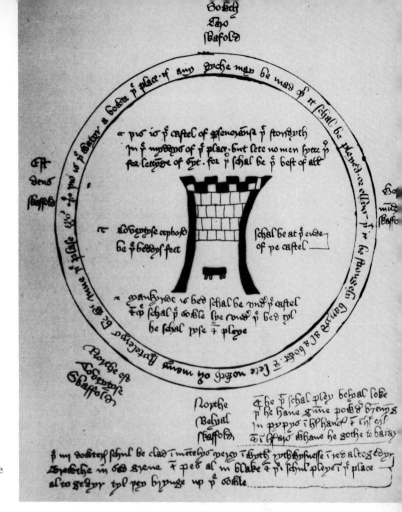

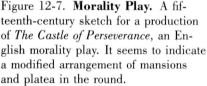

Figure 12-7. **Morality Play.** A fifteenth-century sketch for a production of *The Castle of Perseverance*, an English morality play. It seems to indicate a modified arrangement of mansions and platea in the round.

punishment awaiting the unrepentant sinner. They called for all people to repent, to confess, and to atone for their sins.

Because history was God's great lesson to humankind, the most vivid drama that could contain His plan was nothing less than the entirety of human history, from Creation to Doomsday. Any combination of events, any juxtaposition of characters, and any elasticity of time or place that would illuminate God's plan and make it more accessible and compelling was suitable drama. The great dramas of the fifteenth and sixteenth century that showed this history are called *cycles*, or *cosmic dramas*.

SECULAR THEATRE. At the same time that these great religious plays were at their zenith, another tradition moved tentatively toward maturity.

Records of secular plays exist from about the time that religious dramas appeared outside the churches. By the fourteenth century, some secular entertainments were seen at, for example, banquets and tournaments. In fifteenth-century schools and universities, *Latin comedies* and *tragedies* were being studied, copied, translated, and emulated. For less crudite tastes,

255

medieval farces poked fun, with impish delight, at all manner of domestic tribulations, particularly infidelity and cuckoldry. Some morality plays developed within the secular tradition, their allegories based on classical gods and heroes rather than Christian virtues and vices. Moralities also became involved in the battles of the Reformation: anti-Catholic moralities costumed devils as Catholic prelates and Christ figures as Protestant ministers; anti-Protestant moralities did just the reverse.

At court and in the homes of the very wealthy, plays were given at tournaments (perhaps in an attempt to make these war games less lethal) and on holidays, particularly Christmas and Mardi Gras, when entertainments called *mummings* and *disguisings* were popular. By the late fifteenth century, almost any interruption within an activity—for example, between the courses of a formal banquet—was an excuse to perform a short dramatic entertainment, the *interlude*. But the most spectacular of the court entertainments was the *masque*, in which allegorical compliments to the guests of honor were framed by intricate dances involving the courtiers themselves.

Towns, too, staged street pageants and royal entries for a variety of special occasions. As a part of these events, plays were embedded within the elaborate processions designed to mark the event and were given for the entertainment and instruction of the dignitaries.

Secular plays, unlike the religious dramas, were sometimes performed by professional actors, some of whom were attached to noble houses as servants by the fourteenth century. When they were not needed to entertain there, they could enrich themselves by performing throughout the surrounding countryside. Such actors were viewed as social undesirables. Because they performed most often in interludes and moralities, these forms came to be associated with the rise of the professional actor.

DECLINE AND FALL

By the sixteenth century, the Catholic Church, already weakened by internal conflicts, looked on while a series of rival factions splintered away from Roman domination. To complicate matters, the religious Reformation quickly became embroiled in various dynastic squabbles. Because each side of a controversy often cast its position and arguments in dramatic form, the religious theatre served as one focus for the religious and dynastic struggles of the period and added to the problems of rulers striving to maintain civic tranquillity. In country after country, therefore, religious plays were outlawed (in Paris in 1548, in England in 1558, and by the Council of Trent in 1545–1563).

The results were profound. The religious and occasional nature of theatre and drama was replaced by a worldly and professional outlook. Amateur actors who had participated in great civic pageants every few years were no longer needed, but professionals who were available on a continuing basis were in demand. No longer used to glorify God and teach Church dogma, drama and theatre had to justify themselves on other grounds. Deprived of

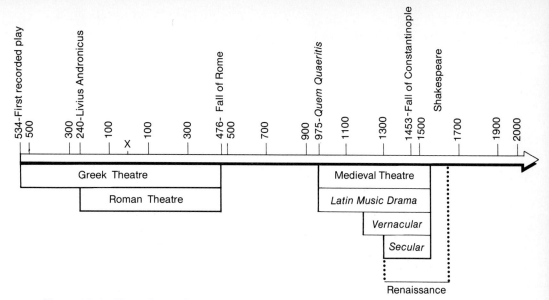

Figure 12-8. **Time Line.** It is important to recognize that Latin music drama continued to be performed even after the vernacular religious plays and the secular medieval plays commenced and that all of these medieval forms overlapped many plays of the Renaissance, including Shakespeare's.

financial subsidy, theatre became a commercial venture. With religious plays forbidden, secular plays were needed if audiences long accustomed to dramatic entertainments were to be satisfied, and so potential playwrights turned to classical plays and stories for inspiration and sources.

The Golden Ages in England and Spain

BACKGROUND

Beginning around 1300, new ideas, social organizations, attitudes, and discoveries were peeking through the medieval order of Europe. For the next two hundred years, these new ideas gradually took hold and, in country after country, heralded the arrival of the *Renaissance* (literally, "rebirth"). For reasons of politics, religion, geography, and even accident, the Renaissance did not reach all countries simultaneously, nor did it manifest itself identically in every place, but by the beginning of the sixteenth century, its power throughout western Europe was evident, and it had revolutionized many former attitudes and practices of Europe.

For hundreds of years, the Church at Rome had defined the social and political realities of the Western world, working closely with secular princes to thwart all encroachments on their shared power and wealth. But when internal strife and external politics caused the removal of the papacy to

257

Avignon, France, in 1305, both the legitimacy and the power of the Church as a world leader became increasingly suspect. In keeping with the doctrine of Apocalyptism, people of the early Middle Ages had supposed that within a few years the present, temporal world would be destroyed in a holocaust, that the unrighteous would be purged, and that the righteous, now purified, would be transported to a world of bliss. But by 1300, a growing suspicion had surfaced that the Last Judgment was not so imminent as had first been supposed. As the immediacy of the hereafter receded, an awareness of the joys of this life increased, and so new secular and temporal interests joined earlier divine and eternal concerns. A love of God and His ways, long the basis of human behavior, was joined by a newfound admiration for humankind, whose worth, intelligence, and beauty began to be celebrated.

Alongside this concern for people and their earthly lives (an attitude called *humanism*) emerged important new philosophical positions. The older theology, a complete system of thought based on divine revelation, gave way to competing philosophical systems that stressed *secularism* (that is, they advocated ethical conduct as an end in itself rather than as a prerequisite to heaven, and they argued for logical systems of thought capable of existence independent of divine revelation).

Nor was science immune to a reexamination of previously held assumptions. The church-supported cosmology of the Egyptian philosopher Ptolemy, which placed the Earth at the center of the universe, and the human, God's favorite creation, at the center of the Earth, was assaulted and finally toppled by another view (supported in the Renaissance by Copernicus) that pictured a sun-centered universe in which human beings were relegated to life on a relatively minor planet, clearly no longer at the center of things. Nor was the Church so united as before. As its wealth accumulated and its allegiance to the noble classes solidified, its worldly interests came into ever greater conflict with its spiritual pronouncements. Unable to reform its practices from within and unwilling to remain a party to its abuses, some Christians (like Martin Luther, fl. 1546) protested against the Church at Rome and launched what came to be called the *Reformation*.

In sum, although God, His Church, and His theology remained the central fact of human life in the Renaissance, they were no longer absolute and unquestioned. Humanism and secularism were competing with them for acceptance. But the emergence of new ideas and attitudes was only part of the phenomenon. Vital, too, were factors that encouraged the widespread dissemination of the new spirit. Two elements in particular were critical: the growth of trade and the arrival of the printing press in Italy.

As long as the basis of wealth and social structures was agricultural activity on an essentially self-contained manor, the exchange of goods and ideas was limited. But, by 1300, shipping and trade were joining agriculture as important means of livelihood. Towns grew and overshadowed the manors, and commerce increasingly involved coinage as well as barter. Trade, both national and international, permitted and even encouraged a flow of ideas as well as of goods, an effortless exchange not possible as long as self-contained

Figure 12-9. **Renaissance.** Renewed interest in Greece and Rome focused attention again on Classical plays. Here, a late fifteenth-century painting. Notice that the lower half of the picture depicts a medieval city while the upper half appears to show a circular theatre (*Theatrum*), of the sort presumably used for revivals of Terence's (*Tere-tius*) plays. Masked performers (*Ioculatores*) appear to perform while a man (*Calliopius*) reads from a text.

agricultural units dominated the economic life of Europe. At the center of most of the various trade routes of the fourteenth century were the several city-states of Italy, which soon became the focus of a blossoming commerce of ideas, skills, and products. When Constantinople fell to the Turks in 1453, many scholars and artists came to Italy from the Middle and Far East, bringing with them their knowledge and their books. Thus, plays and treatises from ancient Greece and Rome, rescued from endangered libraries arrived in Italy, where their study and interpretation began almost at once.

The introduction of the Gutenberg printing press to Italy at about the same time (1467) allowed the rapid reproduction of documents arriving from the East as well as of the interpretations and imitations of these documents. Certainly, the printing press allowed a veritable explosion of accessible information, so much so that, by 1500, numerous academies in the city-states of Italy were devoted to the study and production of Roman plays. Shortly thereafter, Italians began writing their own plays in imitation of the Roman models.

Patronage of the arts during the Renaissance was a major and acknowledged source of prestige, and because the nobles' courts engaged in rivalries over which was to become the cultural center, painters, musicians, sculptors, architects, and writers flourished.

The appearance and effects of the Renaissance were markedly different in northern and southern Europe. The impact of the northern Renaissance on the medieval theatre in England brought about a golden age of theatre, including the plays of William Shakespeare.

THEATRE IN ENGLAND (1550–1650)

THE AGE OF SHAKESPEARE.   The reign of Elizabeth I (r. 1558–1603) brought greatness to the country. With her ascent to the throne, England achieved the political and religious stability that permitted its arts and literature to thrive. When, in an attempt to mute religious controversies, the queen outlawed all religious drama, she opened the way for the rapid development of a secular tradition of plays and playgoing. When the queen finally agreed to the execution of Mary Stuart (1587), her chief rival for the throne and the center of Catholic assaults on the church and throne, Elizabeth's political situation was secured, and the domination of Anglican Protestants within the Church of England was affirmed. The English navy defeated the Spanish Armada in 1588 and established itself as ruler of the seas and leader among the trading nations. England, for the first time in generations, was at peace at home and abroad and was filled with a national confidence and lust for life seldom paralleled in history.

Added to the general well-being of the nation was the vigor of the court, the schools, and the universities, where scholars were remaking Italian humanism and classical documents with an eye to English needs and preferences. In particular, four university students (called the *University Wits*) were applying classical scholarship to the needs of the English public stage and laying the foundations for the vigorous theatre to come: Robert Green, Thomas Kyd, John Lyly, and Christopher Marlowe developed elegant prose and blank verse, romantic comedies, and complex protagonists. These University Wits brought the erudition of humanistic scholarship to the English stage.

ELIZABETHAN THEATRES.   By 1580, London had two different kinds of theatre: the outdoor, or "public," playhouse, and the indoor, or "private," playhouse. The precise appearance of these theatres cannot be known, but some general features can be deduced from a careful reading of the extant plays in the light of information gleaned from a contemporary building contract for the Fortune (public) Theatre, a contemporary sketch of the Swan (public) Theatre, a contemporary drawing of the Cockpit at Court (private) Theatre, and from various accounts taken from contemporary diaries, letters, and financial records (particularly those of Philip Henslowe).

Public Theatres. The outdoor, public theatres (of which nine were built between 1576 and 1642) consisted of a round or polygonal, roofed, multi-leveled auditorium that surrounded an open *yard,* into which jutted a platform raised to a height of four to six feet. The entire yard (or *pit*) and part of the stage platform were unroofed. The audience, probably numbering as many

Figure 12-10. **English Public Theatre, Exterior.** By enlarging a detail of a contemporary map, we can see the exteriors of the bearbaiting arena, the Rose Theatre, and Shakespeare's Globe Theatre, all of which have similar shapes and display flags.

as 2,500, surrounded the playing area on three sides, some standing in the pit, and others seated in the *galleries* or the still more exclusive *lords' rooms*.

The actors worked on the raised stage and apparently awaited cues and changed costumes in the *tiring house*, located at the rear of the platform. Covering part of the stage was a roof (called the *heavens*) that was supported by columns resting on the stage and apparently decorated on its underside with pictures of stars, planets, and signs of the zodiac. From the heavens flew in gods and properties as needed by the action.

The stage floor was pierced with *traps*, through which devils, spirits, and other characters could appear and disappear. Connecting the tiring house with the stage were at least two doors, which often represented widely divergent locations (as, for example, when one led to the fields of France and the other to the shores of England). Atop the tiring house, a flag flew on days of performance, and at a level just below, in an area called the *hut*,

261

were probably housed the various pieces of equipment and machinery needed for special effects. A *musicians' gallery* was apparently located just below the hut, at the third level above the stage.

Other points are less certain. The plays clearly required two playing levels, an upper and a lower, and some sort of *discovery space*, a place where objects and characters could be hidden from view and discovered at the appropriate time. Most scholars agree that the discovery space was located between the two doors, but some conceive of it as a permanent architectural part of the theatre, whereas others conceive of it as a portable unit to be added or deleted as required; some picture the discovery space as a recessed alcove (a kind of miniproscenium theatre), whereas others see it as a pavilion that jutted out into the stage. Obviously, any decision about the conformation of the space at stage level had implications for the upper level as well. Obviously, too, the degree of permanence of the discovery space would radically affect the general appearance of the theatre. The whole problem has been made thornier by the absence of such a space in the Swan sketch and by the appalling problems with sight lines that any sort of discovery space seemed likely to introduce. Because the available evidence will not permit the issues to be resolved, ideas about the appearance of Shakespeare's playhouse must remain tentative.

Private Theatres. About the indoor, or private, playhouses, even less is known. They were roofed, smaller, and therefore more expensive to attend than the public playhouses. Despite their name, they were open to anyone caring to pay. Initially, the private theatres attracted the most fashionable audiences of London: they came to see erudite plays performed by troupes of boy actors. By 1610, however, as the popularity of children's troupes waned, the adult troupes that performed in the public theatres in the summer took over the private houses for their winter performances. The fact is significant because it indicates that the arrangement of the stage spaces in the theatres was very similar.

STAGING. Elaborate scenery, frequently shifted, was impossible in the Elizabethan theatres; various small properties suggested the specific (sometimes simultaneous) locations. Costuming was far more important than scenery to the visual excitement of the performance. Contemporary accounts spoke of luscious fabrics in rich colors. Although fanciful characters like devils, angels, sprites, and allegorical figures appeared in garments designed and made especially for the theatre, most roles were played in Elizabethan garments, regardless of their historic reality. Occasionally, different periods, countries, or races were signified by the emblematic addition of a drapery or a turban, but historical accuracy was never a goal of the costume. Most actors wore contemporary dress that differed from that of the audience only by being more elegant. The similarity of dress between actors and spectators doubtless served to heighten the sense of a shared theatrical experience, as did the relative proximity of the audience to the stage and the constancy of the lighting (stage and auditorium were equally visible, the plays' being performed during daylight). Clearly, the underlying conventions of this staging were medieval.

Figure 12-11. **English Public Theatre, Interior.** This sketch is a re-drawing of the famous historical depiction of the Swan theatre. The labels, translated here from the Latin of the original drawing, leave many questions unanswered: Who are the people in the "actors house"? What is under the stage?

ACTORS AND ACTING. By the time of Shakespeare, English actors had attained a satisfactory level of financial and social stability, in part because the Master of Revels, a member of the royal household, licensed acting troupes and guaranteed those licensed the right to play unhampered by threats of arrest for vagabondage, and in part because most troupes were at least nominally attached to the house of a noble above the rank of baron. Although few actors became truly wealthy, most were well paid by the standards of the day, and some (like Shakespeare) were able to retire in style and live like gentlemen.

The troupes themselves were organized as democratic, self-governing units (sharing companies) whose members shared expenses, profits, and responsibilities for production. A very few members owned a part of the theatre building itself; these were called *householders*. The most valuable members of the company held a whole share in the costumes, properties, and other company possessions; lesser members owned only half or quarter shares, with

Figure 12-12. **Elizabethan Actors.** A noted comic actor of Shakespeare's time, Tarleton, and several actors in the popular play of the day, *The Spanish Tragedy*. Both reveal details of costumes, properties, and, incidentally, musical instruments during Shakespeare's era.

their influence and income reduced accordingly. In addition, each company hired some actors and stagehands (*hirelings*), who worked for a salary rather than for a share of the profits. All members were male, the roles of women being taken by men or young boys, many of whom were apprenticed to leading actors in the troupe. Among the actors, most specialized in certain kinds of roles (e.g., clowns, women, or heroes), and some were widely admired in Shakespeare's day: Richard Tarleton, William Kemp, and Robert Armin as clowns, and Richard Burbage and Edward Alleyn as tragedians.

The precise style of acting is unclear, but vocal power and flexibility were clearly prized. Plays of the period offered ample opportunity to display breath control and verbal dexterity in the monologues, soliloquies, complicated figures of speech, and symmetrical and extended phrases. On the other hand, oratorical and rhetorical techniques did not seem to have overpowered the actors' search for naturalness. Contemporary accounts, including lines from Shakespeare's *Hamlet*, spoke of an acting style capable of moving actors and audiences alike. The goal was apparently a convincing representation of a character in action performed by an actor with a well-tuned vocal instrument.

By Shakespeare's day as well, the importance of drama and theatre had been argued and demonstrated by leading literary figures. In response to attacks on the theatre as an instrument of the devil, a temptation designed to lure people from useful work, both Thomas Lodge and Sir Phillip Sydney had countered that drama was a most effective way of providing moral instruction and encouraging worthwhile actions in ordinary people, and this defense succeeded in pacifying many of the theatre's critics, at least for a while.

By the time Shakespeare arrived in London (c. 1590) to begin his career, then, England was a proud and growing nation whose power was only beginning to be recognized. Its seat of government, London, had permanent native theatres, educated playwrights, trained and experienced actors, and a legitimacy derived from its supposedly exalted purpose.

SHAKESPEARE. William Shakespeare (1564–1616) was the greatest playwright of the English-speaking world and one of the greatest dramatists of Western civilization. Between 1590 and 1613, a period now acknowledged as the Golden Age of English Drama, Shakespeare wrote thirty-eight plays, which for convenience are customarily divided into three types: the history plays (those treating *English* history), like *Henry IV* (Parts 1 and 2), *Henry V, Henry VI* (Parts 1, 2, and 3), *Henry VIII, Richard II*, and *Richard III*; the tragedies, like *Romeo and Juliet, Julius Caesar, Hamlet, King Lear, Othello,*

Figure 12-13. **Shakespeare Around the World.** For the past two hundred years, Shakespeare's plays have been performed throughout the world. Shown here is a German actor as Shylock (left) and American actors in *Richard III* (right), both from the nineteenth century.

Macbeth, and *Antony and Cleopatra*; and the comedies, ranging from popular romantic works like *Love's Labor's Lost*, *As You Like It*, *Twelfth Night*, *Much Ado About Nothing*, and *A Midsummer Night's Dream*, to the darker tragi-comedies like *All's Well That Ends Well* and *Measure for Measure*.

Features that tended to recur throughout his plays and those of his contemporaries include the following:

1. Shakespeare generally adopted an *early point of attack*; that is, he began his plays near the beginning of the story, with the result that the audience sees the story develop onstage rather than learning about it secondhand, through messengers or reporters.

2. Shakespeare customarily developed several lines of action ("subplots"). Early in his plays, the various lines appear to be separate and independent, but as the play moves toward its resolution, the several lines gradually merge so that by the play's end, the unity of the various lines is evident.

3. Shakespeare filled his plays with a large number and variety of incidents. The mixing of tears and laughter is not uncommon, nor is the close juxta-position of tender scenes of love with brawling scenes of confrontation.

4. Shakespeare ranged freely in time and place, allowing his actions to unfold across several months and in several locales.

5. Shakespeare used an unusually large number and range of characters. Casts of thirty are common, and among the characters can be found kings and gravediggers, pedants and clowns, old people and youths, city dwellers and rustics, rich people and poor ones.

6. The language in the plays is infinitely varied. Within the same play are found passages of exquisite lyricism, elegant figures of speech, ribald slang, witty aphorisms, and pedestrian prose, all carefully chosen to enhance the play's dramatic action.

In sum, the art of Shakespeare was an expansive one that filled a very large dramatic canvas with portraits of a wide cross-section of humanity engaged in acts ranging from the heroic to the mundane. The texture of the plays is rich, detailed, and allusive.

OTHER DRAMATISTS. With Shakespeare's death in 1616 came a decline in the quality, if not the quantity, of drama. Although many of the playwrights were esteemed in their own day (most notably Ben Jonson, John Fletcher, Francis Beaumont, John Webster, and John Ford), none has achieved the modern admiration accorded Shakespeare. Thus, the golden age of English theatre was already in decline after 1616.

THE COURT MASQUE. By invitation only, some individuals formed a courtly audience for plays and spectacles staged in royal and noble houses. Although both Henry VIII (Elizabeth's father) and Elizabeth had staged theatrical entertainments from time to time, it was the Stuart kings who followed them, James I (r. 1603–1625) and Charles I (r. 1625–1642), who perfected the splendid court *masques*. Stuart masques were allegorical stories designed to compliment a particular individual or occasion. Their texts were little more than pretexts for the elaborate scenic displays and lavish costumes that characterized the presentations. Although the major roles and all of the comic or villainous characters were portrayed by professional actors, the courtiers themselves performed the heart of the masques, three spectacular dances. Great sums of money ensured the splendor of the entertainments; a single masque, *The Triumph of Love*, for example, cost a staggering 21,000 pounds at a time when the average *annual* wage for a skilled worker was about 25 pounds.

Although many leading dramatists wrote masques, Ben Jonson and William Davenant were the most significant. Jonson, perhaps the leading playwright of the period excluding Shakespeare, became annoyed that the text assumed such a clearly secondary position to the scenery, and so he stopped writing masques in 1631, leaving Davenant as the primary author of the courtly entertainment thereafter. The star of the masques, however, was neither Jonson nor Davenant but the scenic designer Inigo Jones. An Englishman by birth, Jones studied design at the court of Florence in Italy, where he learned the newest techniques of stage painting, rigging, and design. He introduced many of these into the English court when, in 1605, he staged his first masque for James I. *By the end of his career, Jones had introduced into the English courts* (but *not* into the theatres) *all the major elements of Italianae staging then developed* (see pp. 278–279).

Stuart masques, then, have a significance that exceeds the number of persons who saw them. First, they were using Italianate systems of staging during the first half of the seventeenth century, at a time when the English public and private theatres still relied on scenic practices that were essentially medieval. Second, the close association of the masques with the monarchy, added to the Puritans' displeasure at their expense, were major factors in the Puritans' decision to outlaw the theatre when they seized power.

THE CIVIL WAR.   In 1642, a civil war broke out between the Monarchists (those wishing to keep Charles I on the throne and, implicitly, Roman Catholic influence strong within the Church of England) and the Puritans (those who wished to purify the Church of England of all its Romish practices and, therefore, to remove Charles I from power). The Puritans deposed Charles, seized power, formed a government—and closed the theatres. It took a second civil war, however, to put Oliver Cromwell in power and to bring stability to the war-torn island.

Cromwell put an end for a time to legitimate theatre in England, but, as music was not banned, William Davenant produced operas during the period, and, in these productions he introduced the Italianate system to the general public. Also, the bribery of petty officials apparently made it possible to produce plays occasionally, for contemporary records of arrests and repeated legal sanctions suggest continued, if reduced, theatrical activity between 1642 and 1660.

On Cromwell's death, no acceptable successor could be found, and so Parliament finally called Charles II, son of Charles I, from France, where he had lived in exile. For the period of the Interregnum (the period "between kings," 1642–1660), the English theatres were closed.

Aery Spirit   *Seugn Scolton*   *A Brother of the Rosicros.*

Figure 12-14. **Masque.** Staged in noble houses throughout Western Europe, masques were very expensive. Their expense and their close association with the monarchy contributed to the Puritans' growing hostility to the theatre in England. Here, costume designs by Inigo Jones.

When the theatres reopened in 1660 with the restoration of the monarchy, both the drama and the staging traditions were very different, indeed.

THE SPANISH GOLDEN AGE (c. 1550–c. 1650)

In the sixteenth and early seventeenth centuries, Spain vied with England for supremacy on the seas and in the New World. With a strong navy and a strong monarch, Spain sought to subdue England, first through marriage (to Mary or Elizabeth) and, failing that, through war on the seas (the Spanish Armada). Unsuccessful on both counts, Spain shortly thereafter withdrew from the mainstream of Europe to pursue its own God-centered view of life, government, and society. But during the early years of the seventeenth century, Spain had a strong and developing theatre.

Medieval religious theatre saw the rise of the Corpus Christi play in the 1540s; at almost the same time, Spanish professional actors began organizing as sharing companies and traveling to major towns, where they performed on temporary (booth) stages in whatever locations seemed suitable. Traditional religious plays, comedies and farces, school and university plays, and even court *entremeses* (similar to English interludes and Italian *intermezzi*) formed their repertory.

These companies differed from the English companies, however, in their use of women as actors. Exactly when women first appeared on the Spanish stage is unclear, but they were certainly there by the time of the first two permanent theatres in Madrid: the Corral del Cruz (1580) and the Corral del Principe (1584). Thereafter, some actors were able to settle in the city, touring only when the permanent theatres were closed.

THEATRE BUILDINGS.   Spanish theatres of the Golden Age shared several features with the public theatres of Elizabethan England:

1. They were outdoors.
2. A five- or six-foot-high platform jutted out in front of a background pierced by entrances.
3. On the stage platform were two columns holding up a roof that covered part of the acting area.
4. There was a raised, secondary acting area.
5. An audience area existed slightly below and in front of the stage, with additional audience areas provided by galleries above and around it.
6. Flying machines and stage traps were available, probably remnants of the medieval stage magic.

Spanish theatres, however, had some features not encountered in England. The permanent Spanish theatres were set up in *corrales* (yards in the center of blocks of houses), over which an awning stretched as protection against the elements. Some of the audience stood in the central courtyard (*patio*) or sat on covered benches (*gradas*) along the sides. Opposite the stage at the second level was a gallery (*cazuela*) set aside for women, who were segregated from the men in the audience. The *cazuela* had its own entrance to the street, which was guarded by police. Along the side houses were windows covered with grills (*aposentos*) through which people could watch the play. Above the *cazuela* were two additional galleries, the second level divided into boxes, and the third (*tertulia*) holding the cheapest seats. The stage itself was somewhat smaller than the Globe's and had a back curtain that, when opened, revealed an additional acting area (an "inner below").

STAGING CONVENTIONS.   Spanish scenery and costuming conventions were similar to those in England, although larger scenic pieces were probably common. Large properties (e.g., a fountain, a tomb, or a ship's rigging) were sometimes set behind the curtain. Costumes were emblematic, with a mixture of contemporary garments and special dress and no attempt at unified "design."

PLAYS AND PLAYWRIGHTS.   The Spanish Golden Age produced thousands of plays, including secular tragicomedies (*comedias*), plays on religious subjects (*autos sacramentales*), cloak-and-sword plays (*capa y espada*), and farces. The earliest important playwright, Lope de Rueda, specialized in

Figure 12-15. Spanish Carro. An historical sketch of a Spanish *carro* (like the English pageant wagon) drawn up to a stage. Notice that the *carro* holds some sort of scenic unit. (*Courtesy of the Archivero de Villa, Ayuntamiento de Madrid.*)

Figure 12-16. **Spanish Theatre.** A speculative reconstruction of the Corral del Príncipe, Madrid. The numbers show: 1. the machine space over the stage; 2. the backstage area; 3. the curtained discovery space; 4. the stage; 5. the *patio*, with benches near the stage; 6. the sloping roof over the lowest rank of loges, with the grilled windows (*aposentos*) in the wall above; 7. the exterior street wall, showing one of several entrances. *(Reconstruction by Kenneth M. Cameron.)*

farces and religious plays. Lope de Vega may have originated the cape-and-sword plays, swashbucklers that subsequently influenced both English and French dramatists. The author of over five hundred works, Lope de Vega is now best known for his *Fuenteovejuna*, a play that still finds occasional contemporary production. Tirso de Molina is remembered for his Don Juan play, *The Trickster of Seville*. The best-known Spanish playwright of the Golden Age, however, was Pedro Calderón de la Barca, whose *Life Is a Dream* epitomized the poetry and intellect of his best works. Calderón stopped writing for the stage around 1640; the theatres were closed shortly thereafter for a time of royal mourning (1644–1649). When they reopened, the Golden Age of Spanish theatre had passed, although the theatres remained in use into the eighteenth century.

Illusionistic Theatres I: Neoclassicism and Italianate Staging

Theatre in Italy (1550–1750)

The Renaissance in Italy, unlike that in England and Spain, revolutionized theatre and drama. In their efforts to recapture the practices of Greece and Rome, Italian artists set theatres in Europe on a new path—a path toward *illusionism*. Theatre was henceforth to seek an illusion of real life.

Three contributions of the Italians were to have far-reaching effects: (1) the Neoclassical ideal in playwriting and criticism; (2) the Italianate system of staging and architecture; and (3) the popular theatre known as *commedia dell'arte*.

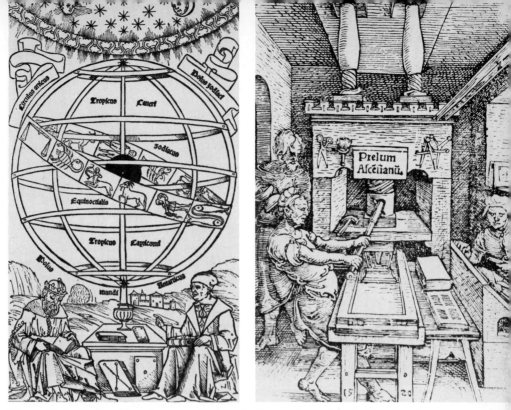

Figure 13-1. **Italian Renaissance.** Two major innovations of the Italian Renaissance: a major reconceptualization of the nature of the universe, and the coming of the printing press. (The frontispiece to Ptolemy, 1496, and a handpress of the sixteenth century.)

NEOCLASSICISM

Neoclassicism literally means "new classicism," but in fact it was based far more heavily on Rome than on Greece. Neoclassicism, as first developed by the Italians and later adopted throughout most of western Europe, rested on five major points: (1) verisimilitude, with its offspring decorum; (2) purity of genres; (3) the "three unities"; (4) the five-act form; and (5) the twofold purpose: to teach and to please.

VERISIMILITUDE. Central to Neoclassical doctrine was a complex concept called *verisimilitude*—literally, "truth seeming." But the meaning of *verisimilitude* is more involved than its facile definition might suggest, for serious artists of all ages have aimed to tell the "truth." Because the characteristics of art throughout the ages have changed, it is probably safe to conclude that the arts differed from age to age because the truth that the artists saw and sought to depict had changed. Thus, the critical problem for a student of Neoclassicism is to understand what "truth" meant to the Neoclassicist.

Truth for the Neoclassicist resided in the essential, the general, the typical, and the class rather than in the particular, the individual, or the unique. To get at truth, a Neoclassical artist had to cut away all that was temporary or accidental in favor of those qualities that were fundamental and unchanging. To be true meant to be *usually* true, *generally* accurate, *typically* the case. The humanness of one person, for example, rested in those essential qualities that he or she shared with all other people, regardless of the historical accident of place, century, or nationality of birth. Individual differences were not important because they were not essential to humanness. Such a view of truth placed a premium on classification and categorization, and *verisimilitude* had a meaning very different from that ascribed to it by our own age's view of the importance of individuality and uniqueness.

Neoclassical truth implied other matters as well. Verisimilitude in drama required the elimination of events that could not reasonably be expected to happen in real life. Although an exception was made when ancient stories or myths incorporating supernatural events were dramatized, even then the dramatist was expected to minimize the importance of such events, perhaps by putting the action offstage. Because in real life people generally talk to one another rather than to themselves, monologues and soliloquies were customarily abandoned in favor of dialogue between major characters and their *confidants*.

DECORUM. The tendency of people to behave in certain ways based on age, social rank, occupation, gender, and so forth could be observed; therefore, characters in drama were expected to display proper *decorum* (that is, they were to embody the traits normally held by members of their class) or, if they did not, to suffer ridicule or punishment for their deviations.

MORALITY. Finally, because it was believed that God ruled the world in accord with a divine plan and that He was a good God, verisimilitude required that dramatic actions be organized in such a way that good was rewarded and evil punished, in keeping with eternal truth. Although in daily life good occasionally went unrewarded and evil unpunished, such observable events were believed to be aberrational and therefore to be unsuitable subjects for drama.

PURITY OF GENRES. From the concept of *verisimilitude* came another bulwark of Neoclassicism, *purity of genres*. In the drama, this meant that the two major forms, tragedy and comedy, must not be mixed. The injunction against mixing did not mean merely that funny scenes were improper for tragedy or that unhappy endings were inappropriate for comedy. Both tragedy and comedy were far more rigidly defined than today, and the rule against mixing the forms meant that no element belonging to the one should appear in the other. For example, tragedy was to depict people of high station involved in affairs of state; its language was to be elevated and poetic; its endings were to be unhappy. Comedy, on the other hand, was to display persons of the lower and middle classes embroiled in domestic difficulties and intrigues. Its language was always less elevated, and often prosaic, and its endings were happy. Purity of genres meant, then, that a prose tragedy or a domestic tragedy could not exist—both were a contradiction in terms.

It also meant that kings and queens did not appear in comedies, nor were affairs of state suitable subjects for the comic author.

THE UNITIES.   Finally, based on verisimilitude and on current interpretations of ancient commentators, the Neoclassical notion of the "three unities" (time, place, and action) developed. Although Aristotle had argued cogently for plays with a unified action, Neoclassical theorists were more concerned that their plays unfold within a reasonable time and a limited place so that verisimilitude would not be strained. No audience would believe, the Neoclassical argument went, that months had passed or oceans had been crossed while the audience sat in the same place for a few hours. Although theorists varied in the strictness of their requirements for unity (some argued for a single room, others allowed a single town; some required that the playing time of the drama equal the actual time elapsed, others permitted a twenty-four-hour time period), most Italian theorists accepted some version of the three unities after about 1570.

FIVE-ACT PLAY.   By then, as well, Neoclassicists had adopted the *five-act play form* as standard for drama, a norm probably derived from the theories of Horace and the practices of Seneca.

PURPOSES OF DRAMA.   Finally, the Neoclassicists sought a justification for drama and theatre and found it in their ability to teach moral precepts while entertaining and delighting an audience. *To teach* and *to please* were defined as the *dual purposes of drama,* and playwrights desiring critical acclaim took care that their plays did both. The idea of a drama's existing only for its own sake or as an expression of an individual artist was not accepted by major Renaissance theorists.

After about 1570, Neoclassical ideas became the standard for Italian dramas. By 1600, Neoclassical standards were being accepted in other parts of Europe, where they remained dominant for the next two hundred years among educated and courtly audiences. Neoclassicism's propriety and concentration may account for its lack of appeal to many people, who sought more spectacle than the three unities permitted. Thus, despite the acceptance of Neoclassicism as an ideal, its tenets were undercut in a variety of ways.

ITALIANATE STAGING

Italianate staging, like Neoclassicism, developed as an amalgam of ideas and techniques from classical Rome (and to a lesser extent from ancient Greece) and contemporary Italy.

VITRUVIUS.   In 1486, Vitruvius's work on Roman architecture was printed. The dissemination of *De Architectura* was so rapid that by 1500 its major points had been accepted as authoritative, and a number of contemporary Italian interpretations of it had been undertaken.

Figure 13-2. **Italianate Staging.** Serlio's interpretation of Vitruvius's written descriptions, showing a tragic, a comic, and a satyric scene. Featuring forced, single-point perspective with a sloping stage and built-up architectural details, the sets could not be changed. *(Courtesy of the Bowling Green State University Library.)*

PERSPECTIVE. Although his books dealt with architecture and scenery, Vitruvius provided no illustrations of his ideal theatre, and so the Italians translated his words and ideas in light of contemporary practices in art and architecture, most notably the current fascination with *linear perspective.* Although known to the ancients, perspective, when it was rediscovered by the Italians around 1500, caused an artistic revolution. Artists struggled to master the intricacies of the "new" technique, and uninitiated spectators hailed its ability to trick the senses of if by magic.

SERLIO.   Soon the potential of perspective painting for scenic decoration was recognized, and, in 1545, Sebastiano Serlio (1475–1554) published the second book of his seven-volume *Dell' Architeitura*, which became the most authoritative interpretation of Vitruvius to date. Serlio's work established the guidelines for theatrical architects and designers for the next hundred years.

Serlio's interpretation of Vitruvius's Roman theatre, however erroneous, set a model for permanent theatres built in Rome during the Renaissance. Vitruvius was obviously describing the outdoor, circular Roman theatre that he knew. Wealthy Italians, on the other hand, were accustomed to plays produced in banqueting halls in the homes of the wealthy. When the first permanent theatres were envisioned, therefore, the task was to fit the classical theatre as described by Vitruvius into the rectangular spaces familiar to the Italians and, in some way, to accommodate the result to the current fashion for linear perspective. An early solution was the Teatro Olimpico, whose five doors corresponded roughly to Vitruvius's description of five stage openings, except that now each door had a vista in forced perspective. A later theatre used a permanent proscenium arch that protected the illusion of perspective and featured a series of additional arches farther back on the stage, each increasing the sense of depth and heightening the illusion.

In scenic display as well as in theatrical architecture, Serlio's interpretation of Vitruvius set the standard. From Vitruvius's scant descriptions of tragic, comic, and satyric scenes, Serlio elaborated each into detailed directions, with illustrations drawn in perspective. A brief comparison of Vitruvius and Serlio as they described one setting will suggest the differences.

Of the satyric scene, Vitruvius said, "Satyric scenes are decorated with trees, caverns, mountains, and other rustic objects delineated in landscaped style." Of the same scenes, Serlio (as translated into English in 1611) amplified, "The Satiricall Scenes are to Represent Satirs, wherein you must place all those things that be rude and rusticall." He then went on to quote Vitruvius as calling for "Trees, Rootes, Herbs, Hils, and Flowers, and with some countrey houses. . . . And for that in our dayes these things were made in Winter, where there were but fewe greene Trees, Herbs, and Flowres to be found; then you must make these things of Silke, which will be more commendable than the naturall things themselves."

In the remainder of the book, Serlio provided such tips on stagecraft as the proper use of colored lights, the production of fire effects, the building of fanciful costumes, and the use of pasteboard figures on a perspective stage. After its printing in 1545, Serlio's account, a blending of the classical descriptions of Vitruvius with current Italian scenic practices, swept western Europe and became the basis of what was called the *Italianate system* of staging.

ITALIANATE SCENERY.   With certain modest modifications related to the particular country and the specific date, Italianate settings shared these features throughout the sixteenth, seventeenth, and early eighteenth centuries:

1. The scenery was painted in single-point perspective, calculated from a seat toward the back of the orchestra (usually reserved for the most important noble associated with the theatre).
2. The scenery consisted of a series of wings (paired *flats*, i.e., wooden frames covered with fabric) positioned at each side of the stage, with each pair placed relatively closer to the center line of the stage than the one in front of it, so that the apparent distance increased. The setting culminated at the back of the stage in a single backdrop painted in perspective (or alternately, a shutter formed when a set of wings was shoved together and then painted in perspective).
3. The scenery was placed behind the proscenium arch and thus behind the actors, forming a background against which they played, rather than an environment for the action.
4. The stage was raked, or slanted, to increase the sense of depth by forcing the perspective. Sometimes, the front part of the stage, where the actors performed, was flat and only the portion of the stage behind the proscenium arch was raked; at other times, the rake began at the front of the platform and continued uninterrupted to the back wall.
5. Overhead machinery and theatrical rigging were hidden from view by a series of *borders* (fabric, framed or unframed) arranged to enhance perspective.

Figure 13-3. **Proscenium Theater with Perspective Setting.** An actor of the sixteenth century addressing his audience, with forced, single-point perspective suggesting a sense of distance toward the back of the stage.

6. A proscenium arch (or several) framed the whole picture, thereby protecting the illusion created by the perspective painting.

CHANGEABLE SCENERY.   Having developed this basic system for decorating the stage, Italian artists set about almost at once to perfect it. Specifically, they investigated ways of shifting scenery in order to permit a rapid change of place. Experimentation soon revealed that quick changes required the replacement of all three-dimensional details with two-dimensional, painted settings, as well as the replacement of *angle wings* (two flats hinged together) by flat wings. By the 1640s, the methods of scenic change were well developed and were summarized in two influential works, one by Niccolo Sabattini and another by Joseph Furttenbach. But the real breakthrough came in 1645, when Giacomo Torelli (1608–1678) astonished the theatrical world with his invention of a new mechanism for changing scenery: the *chariot-and-pole system.* The name derived from the small wagons (or chariots) that ran on tracks beneath the stage and carried on them a long pole that extended from the chariots through slits in the stage floor up to a height sufficient to provide a sturdy support for scenic pieces, which were attached to the poles at stage level. The idea was a simple one: as the chariots moved on their tracks toward the center of the stage, a piece of scenery came into view; as the chariot moved off to the side, a piece of scenery disappeared. By devising an elaborate system of ropes and pulleys, Torelli succeeded in rigging everything together so that the turn of a single winch could produce a complete change of setting. By coordinating such changes with the machinery used to produce special effects, like flying, trapping, wave making, thunder, lightning, and explosions, he was able to achieve a truly magical effect. Such tricks earned Torelli the name of the "Great Wizard."

A contradiction clearly existed between the ideals of drama, where Neoclassicism called for the unities of time, place, and action and an avoidance of supernatural events, and the ideals of scenic display, whose Italianate artists stressed increasingly elaborate splendors involving multiple scenes, instant transformations, and a variety of spectacular effects. In Italy, as elsewhere, the tension was resolved by producing dramas simply and by expending imagination and money for the production of lavish operas, dances, and *intermezzi* (courtly entertainments typically given between the acts of a play). By the mid-seventeenth century, the Italian opera had become the most popular form of dramatic entertainment in Italy. As Italian opera was exported to France, Germany, and the rest of Europe, so were many of Italy's latest scenic techniques.

COMMEDIA DELL'ARTE

Neoclassical dramas and elaborately staged operas were primarily the entertainment of the noble, the wealthy, and the erudite. Among the common folk, another, very different kind of dramatic entertainment was flourishing: the *commedia dell'arte* ("professional playing"). Although neither the origins nor the sources of *commedia* are well understood, its major characteristics were well established by 1550, and Italian troupes of *commedia* players were touring western Europe by 1600.

Commedia players worked from a basic story outline *(scenario)* within which they improvised much of their dialogue and action. Each actor in the troupe played the same character in almost every scenario and therefore wore the same costume and mask, reused the same bits of comic business *(lazzi)*, and even repeated some of the same dialogue from scenario to scenario. Most troupes had ten or twelve members, each of whom assumed the role of one of the stock characters. Each troupe had one or two sets of young lovers *(innamorati)* and a host of masked comic characters, the most common of which were Capitano (the captain), Pantalone (the merchant), Dottore (the doctor), and the several *zanni* (servants) like Arlecchino (Harlequin), Brighella, Scaramuccio, and Pulcinello.

Organized as sharing companies, such troupes toured constantly as they tried to scratch out a living in the theatre, without the protection or the financial support of noble houses. Although the influence of *commedia* extended throughout Europe, its ephemeral nature militated against its leaving a lasting record (especially scripts), and so today this popular Italian comedy is a phenomenon whose excitement and vigor cannot be recaptured.

Despite Italy's unquestioned leadership in dramatic theory and scenic display and in spite of its unique popular comedy, Italian theatre and drama did not attain lasting international prominence. By 1750, except for opera Italy was no longer a world leader in theatre. Both England and France had outstripped their teacher and had attained an international reputation by the end of the seventeenth century, and both achieved a lasting acclaim never given the Italians, from whom they drew.

Figure 13-4. **Design by Torelli.** Torelli combined some of the elaborate special effects developed during the middle ages (like this stage glory) with the Renaissance's interest in perspective to produce scenery noted for its visual excitement.

Figure 13-5. **Commedia dell'Arte Characters.** Scaramuccio, the boastful Capitano (shown here as Cap. Zerbino), together with tricksters like Scapino and Fricasso, typically were masked players; the young lovers usually played without masks.

Scapino.   Cap. Zerbino.

Scaramucia.   Fricasso.

Theatre in France (1550–1750)

The ideas and practices of the Italian Renaissance reached and affected French courts and universities early. However, France, unlike England, failed to achieve political and religious stability in the sixteenth century, and so the development of a vigorous public theatre was delayed.

Not until about 1600 did a popular playwright, Alexandre Hardy (c. 1572–1632), emerge to challenge improvised French farces performed by itinerant actors as the mainstay of French popular theatre. And not until 1625 did the first acting troupe establish itself permanently in Paris at the Hôtel de Bourgogne, a theatre built almost seventy-five years earlier by a religious

Figure 13-6. **French Farce.** France had a popular, partly improvised theatre—shown here at the Hôtel de Bourgogne in Paris—not unlike Italy's *commedia dell'arte*. Some of these leading farce actors joined Molière after about 1660. (*From Loliée*, La Comédie Française.)

fraternity devoted to the production of religious plays in Paris (before they were outlawed in 1548). Thus, at a time when English theatre had already enjoyed the vigor and excellence of Shakespeare, the French public theatre was merely at the brink of its golden age.

CORNEILLE AND *LE CID*

Political stability arrived in Paris following the ascent of Louis XIII to the throne (r. 1610–1643), and the French public theatre began its climb to greatness. A number of educated men started to write for the theatre, among them Pierre Corneille (1606–1684), whose play *Le Cid* (produced in 1636) marked a turning point in French drama. Based on a Spanish play that depicted a welter of events strewn through several locations and many years, *Le Cid* was rewritten by Corneille to bring it into closer accord with the Neoclassical ideal. Thus, the six acts of the Spanish piece were reduced to five, the several years compressed into a single day, and the numerous locales squeezed into a single town. Still, the play departed from Neoclassical tragedy; for example, it had a happy ending, and its numerous incidents strained verisimilitude. Cardinal Richelieu, long a promoter of Italian culture, resolved to use the play as a test case in his efforts to bring France closer in line with Italian practices. He therefore submitted the play for evaluation to the recently formed French Academy, a prestigious literary society charged with maintaining the purity of French language and literature. The verdict of the academy was clear. It praised *Le Cid* wherever it conformed to Neoclassical precepts and condemned it wherever it strayed from them. French playwrights, including Corneille, were quick to conclude that critical acclaim would rest on strict adherence to the principles of Neoclassicism. And so, after 1636, Neoclassicism dominated French drama for over one hundred years.

TORELLI AND ITALIANATE STAGING

In 1641, Cardinal Richelieu opened the first Italianate theatre in France, the Palais-Cardinal. His successor, Cardinal Mazarin, who shared Richelieu's taste for Italian opera and perspective decor, brought Giacomo Torelli to Paris in 1645. Already famous in Italy, Torelli installed his chariot-and-pole systems in the Palais-Royal (formerly the Palais-Cardinal, but renamed when Louis XIV appropriated it on Richelieu's death) and in the newly remodeled Petit Bourbon. Torelli's early productions marked the acceptance of all major Italianate scenic conventions in the French theatre. Henceforth, the Neo-classical plays, with their stark and simple settings, competed with lavish operas, ballets, and *machine plays* (plays written particularly for the display of scenic marvels) for the attention of Parisian audiences.

Between 1660 and 1700 under Louis XIV, France attained a glory equal

Figure 13-7. **Italianate Theater in France.** The king and Cardinal Richelieu shown seated in chairs placed where the single-point perspective is most effective; other courtiers stood or sat in two long galleries along the side of the Palais-Cardinal.

to that of Shakespeare's England. The period was characterized by four major traits:

1. The continuing strength of Neoclassicism as the dramatic ideal.
2. The continued acceptance of Italianate staging conventions.
3. The emergence of three master playwrights: Pierre Corneille, Jean Racine (1639–1699), and Jean Baptiste Poquelin, or Molière (1622–1673).
4. The presence of five permanent acting troupes in Paris.

MAJOR DRAMATISTS

RACINE.   Although Pierre Corneille wrote important plays until after 1675, his fame was eclipsed by that of Jean Racine. Born three years after the first production of *Le Cid*, Racine was raised by Jansenists, a Catholic sect with an overriding preoccupation with sin and guilt, concerns that permeated Racine's major plays. Educated in the Greek and Roman classics, Racine based his only comedy, *The Litigants*, on Aristophanes' comedy *The Wasps*, and his most esteemed tragedy, *Phèdre*, on Euripides' *Hippolytus*.

Phèdre, one of the finest tragedies ever written, was a model of Neoclassicism. Because the play's major conflicts occur within the character of Phèdre, the Neoclassical requirements for unity were easily accommodated; and, because Phèdre's passion leads to her downfall, Neoclassical commitment to the punishment of evil was amply satisfied. *Phèdre*, unlike *Le Cid*, was Neoclassical through and through, and its achievement in plot, character, and diction placed it clearly among the masterpieces of dramatic literature. In short, France accomplished what England did not: lasting and popular drama based on Neoclassical theory.

MOLIÈRE.   At about the same time, French comedy found its genius in the actor-dramatist Molière. At about the time that theatres were closing in England, Molière was leaving home to form a traveling theatrical troupe in France. By 1660, he was head of the troupe, wrote most of its plays, and had firmly established it at court as a favorite of Louis XIV. Perhaps the greatest comic writer of all times, Molière used his own experiences as an actor as well as his knowledge of Roman comedies, Italian *commedia*, and indigenous French farces to develop comedies that ridiculed social and moral pretentiousness. Molière's comedy typically depicts characters made ludicrous by their deviations from decorum. Although his dialogue is often clever, verbal elegance and wit for their own sake do not form the core of his plays; instead the comedies depend heavily on farcical business (like *commedia's lazzi*) and visual gags for their power. Of his more than twenty plays, the best known are probably *The Doctor in Spite of Himself* (1666), *The School for Wives* (1662), *Tartuffe* (1669), *The Miser* (1668), and *The Imaginary Invalid* (1673). While acting the leading role in *The Imaginary Invalid*, Molière was seized by convulsions and died a few hours later, denied last

Figure 13-8. **Molière: Actor and Playwright.** A true "man of the theatre," Molière both acted with and managed an acting troupe before he gained his reputation as a playwright.

rites by the church because of his life as an actor and granted Christian burial only through the direct intervention of Louis XIV.

ACTORS AND ACTING

Obviously, the life of French actors was not easy. Some troupes were granted royal subsidies, and Louis XIII had tried to improve their reputation and social acceptability by royal edict. Nonetheless, French actors were denied civic and religious rights throughout most of the seventeenth and eighteenth centuries, a situation that led many actors to adopt pseudonyms in order to spare their families anguish and reproach. Forced to tour continuously until 1625, only the most talented actors were gradually able to settle in Paris as members of a permanent troupe. By 1660, there were five such troupes in Paris: the players at the Hôtel de Bourgogne; those at the Théâtre Marais (a tennis court converted into an Italianate theatre, as was a common continental practice); Molière's troupe at the Palais-Royal; a *commedia* troupe from Italy, which alternated with Molière at the same theatre; and at court, the opera, music, and dance troupe headed by Jean-Baptiste Lully (1632–1687). All were sharing companies, and all maintained a full complement of actresses. France had women in its acting companies at least fifty years before England. Unlike England, however, France had no householders, no actors who owned parts of the theatre building.

Figure 13-9. **Molière's Comedies.**
Molière often poked fun at social pretension, such as the silliness of renouncing social manners in *The Misanthrope* and the foolishness of avarice in *The Miser*, contemporaneous frontispieces of which are shown here.

With Molière's death came the amalgamation of his troupe with those of the Bourgogne and the Marais to form the new Comédie Française, which became France's national theatre. Membership in this sharing company was fixed; therefore, new members could not be elected until others had retired or died. Because of its financial rewards, including a substantial pension for retired members, the list of applicants was long. Many never made it, but those who did held a monopoly on the legal performance of tragedies and comedies for the Parisian public.

Lully's troupe likewise held a monopoly on the production of musical entertainments and spectacles, and the *commedia* troupe (after a brief banishment for a political indiscretion) had exclusive performance rights to comic operas. Members of these three troupes were expected to continue the traditions already established, not to initiate new techniques. The result was a highly polished but quite tradition-bound style of production.

THE EIGHTEENTH CENTURY

Around 1700 in France, a new conservatism was noticeable in both theatre and drama. Louis XIV had grown old and cautious. Dramatists, perhaps intimidated by the genius of Corneille, Racine, and Molière, strove by and large to copy their style. A modest shift toward morality and sentimentality occurred. In tragedy, for example, Voltaire (1694–1778) sought to loosen the bonds of Neoclassicism by introducing some Shakespearean features to the French stage, particularly more spectacle and a greater range of permissible subjects, but his efforts before 1750 were largely frustrated. In comedy, Pierre Claude Nivelle de La Chaussée (1692–1754) pitted virtuous heroes against numerous obstacles that they finally overcame in a burst of energy and good humor. The audience was moved to tears by the expressed sentiments of the sympathetic characters and by the rewards heaped on them for their virtuous behavior. Such *sentimental* and *tearful comedies* were a far cry from Molière's works, where the frailty and stubbornness of the characters provoked hearty laughter from spectators of all social classes.

SCENIC INNOVATIONS.   Scenic displays in the opera and the ballet, although perhaps more sumptuous than before, changed little in basic concept. Two innovations, however, did make their way to France from Italy by the first half of the eighteenth century. The first, *angle perspective*, meant that scenic artists relegated vistas to the sides, and the actors could work closer to the scenery at center stage without violating the perspective. The second, a *changed scale*, meant that only the lower portions of the scenery were portrayed. With the tops no longer visible, the scenery seemed to disappear into the overhead spaces and out of sight, thereby multiplying the apparent size of the setting and producing a sense of vastness and monumentality that dwarfed the individual actors playing before it.

Figure 13-10. **Angle Perspective and Monumentality.** Two major innovations in scenic design, in large part the work of the famous Bibiena family, came from Italy during the eighteenth century. *(Courtesy of The New York Public Library.)*

STAGING PRACTICES.   Acting was still applauded to the degree that it was oratorically interesting and vocally sound. Costumes, in keeping with the Neoclassical view that time and place were relatively unimportant, consisted of the most splendid contemporary outfits that the actors could afford, the lavishness of the costume always being a more accurate index to the wealth of the actor than to the character being impersonated.

In sum, the French theatre for the first half of the eighteenth century recalled its past glories when the genius of Corneille, Racine, Molière, and Torelli had established it as the leader of the civilized world. Changes from seventeenth-century practices were few and infrequent. When made, they were almost always in the direction of elaborating Neoclassical dramas and Italianate staging. Thus, by 1750, French theatre was tradition-bound, highly conventionalized, and perhaps out of touch with the lives of everyday French citizens. In a short one hundred years (1650–1750), the theatre had moved from a vigorous and forward-looking activity to a depressed and backward-gazing one.

NEW FORMS OF DRAMA.   With no outlet for the talents of the many actors and writers who were denied access to the Comédie Française, and with only limited satisfaction from the erudite plays of Neoclassicism, some French men and women worked in illegal theatres, that is, theatres other than the Comédie Française and the Opéra. Joining jugglers, dancers, and similar entertainers who had long appeared at French fairs, theatrical troupes began to form and play just outside the law, practicing all manner of stratagems to avoid open conflict with the monopolies held by the licensed troupes. From the experiments of these illegitimate theatres (which before 1800 moved to the Parisian "boulevards") developed the forerunners of comic opera and melodrama, forms that flourished in the great Romantic theatre of the next century.

The English Restoration to c. 1750

When the English monarchy was restored in 1660, theatre was reinstated almost immediately. Until new permanent theatres could be built, companies used whatever spaces were available (spaces left over from pre-Commonwealth days or tennis courts remodeled for theatrical productions). English theatre was organized as a monopoly in which only two troupes were licensed, originally those of William Davenant and Thomas Killigrew (1612–1683). Although these monopolies were often challenged and although they changed hands and specific regulations from time to time, they were continuously reaffirmed, most strongly in the *Licensing Act of 1737*, which allowed only two legitimate theatres in London, at Drury Lane and at Covent Garden, and at the same time forbade the presentation of any play not previously licensed by the Lord Chamberlain. Throughout the period, therefore, only two "legitimate" theatres played.

WOMEN ON STAGE

Probably the most revolutionary change to occur at the Restoration was the introduction of women on the stage and into the acting companies. Their presence seems to have encouraged, fairly or not, the reputation of frivolity and even libertinism that early pervaded the Restoration playhouse. Actresses after about 1661 assumed all female roles except those of witches and comic old women (roles that continued to be played by men).

RESTORATION DRAMA

Many plays written during the age of Shakespeare continued to be produced (usually in severely adapted versions), but the new plays, both comic and serious, were closer to continental Neoclassicism than to Shakespeare, and both became increasingly sentimental as the eighteenth century wore on.

COMEDY OF MANNERS.   Most famous today are the Restoration "comedies of manners," plays whose witty dialogue and sophisticated sexual behavior reflect the highly artificial, mannered, and aristocratic society of the day. The heroes and heroines are "virtuous" if they succeed in capturing and satisfying a lover or in cuckolding a husband and avoiding detection. "Honor" depends not on integrity but on reputation, and "wit," the ability to express ideas in a clever and apt way, is prized above all. The admirable characters in the plays are those who can operate successfully within the intricate social sphere; the foolish and laughable are those whose lack of wit or upbringing denies them access to social elegance. In short, the comedies depict the mores and conventions of a courtly society where elegance of phrase and the *appearance*

Figure 13-11. **Restoration Comedy of Manners.** The most enduring dramas of the English Restoration were the witty and titillating comedies by Congreve, Etherege, and Wycherley. Shown here in an eighteenth-century production is Congreve's *The Way of the World.*

of propriety were more highly prized than lofty morals and sincere feelings. Among the most famous authors of Restoration comedies were William Congreve (1670–1729); George Etherege (c. 1634–1691); and William Wycherley (1640–1715).

HEROIC AND NEOCLASSICAL TRAGEDY.   "Heroic" tragedies present the inevitable conflict between love and duty. In a world far removed from that of the Restoration comedies, tragic heroes are flawless and heroines chaste. The dialogue is bombastic and replete with "heroic couplets," two-line units of rhymed iambic pentameter (probably an attempt to reproduce in English the verse form of French Neoclassicists, the twelve-syllabled Alexandrine). The idealization and formality of this kind of tragedy make it unusually susceptible to parody, and so burlesques of it soon appeared.

Original

> *So, two kind Turtles, when a storm is nigh,*
> *Look up; and see it gath'ring in the skie:*
> *Each calls his Mate to shelter in the Groves,*
> *Leaving in murmures, their unfinish'd Loves.*
> *Perch'd on some dropping Branch they sit alone,*
> *And Cooe, and harken to each others moan.*

from The Conquest of Granada by John Dryden

Burlesque

> *So Boar and Sow, when any storm is nigh,*
> *Sniff up, and smell it gath'ring in the sky;*
> *Boar beckons Sow to trot in Chestnut Groves,*
> *And there to consummate their unfinish'd Loves;*
> *Pensive in mud they wallow all alone,*
> *And snore and gruntle to each others moan.*

from The Rehearsal by George Villiers, 2nd Duke of Buckingham

Succumbing both to the onslaught of burlesque and to the changing tastes of audiences, heroic tragedies declined in public favor, their place being filled by Neoclassical tragedies like John Dryden's *All for Love* (1677), a rewriting of Shakespeare's *Antony and Cleopatra* that brought it closer to the principles of Neoclassicism.

EIGHTEENTH-CENTURY ENGLISH DRAMA TO 1750

The eighteenth century brought a change of values. Absolute monarchs were giving way to constitutional governments, and the rights of leadership were coming to include not only landed aristocrats but also merchants from the cities. With these changes, values grew steadily more conservative, middle-class, moralistic, and, eventually, *sentimental*.

Sentimentalism asserted the basic goodness of each individual. This doctrine contrasted with the previous, Neoclassical, view that human existence was a continuing struggle between good and evil. According to the sentimentalist, evil came about through corruption; it was not part of human nature at birth. Sentimentalism thus implied that, although people might not be perfect, they were perfectible. Literature should therefore show virtuous people acting virtuously in their daily lives. Heroic behavior and ethical perfection need not be restricted to some idealized world of pastoral poetry or exotic tragedy. Sentimentalism affected both comedies and serious dramas in England (as in France).

COMEDY.   The amoral tone of Restoration comedies had become offensive to many. In its place came the view that drama should teach morality. One result was that comedies became more sentimental. At first, the change was merely in the plays' endings: young lovers philandered and cuckolded throughout four acts of the play but, in the fifth, repented and declared their intention to lead a moral and upright life henceforth. By the 1730s, heroes and heroines were becoming the virtuous embodiments of middle-class values, struggling cheerfully against adversity until, at the end, their courage and persistence were rewarded. Prized especially were characters able to express their insights into human goodness in pithy statements (which came to be called *sentiments*). Thus, the label *sentimental hero* or *heroine* implied not only those who embodied virtues and who recognized such virtue in others but also those whose speech was rich in sentiments. The audiences of the day experienced "a pleasure too exquisite for laughter," and so the terms *tearful comedy* and *sentimental comedy* predominated in the comic literature by the middle of the eighteenth century.

SERIOUS DRAMA.   George Lillo's *The London Merchant* (1731) was a major break with the Neoclassical ideal. In *The London Merchant,* a middle-class hero is led astray by love and is ultimately punished. Although teaching morality by showing the punishment of evil (the play was done in London for years to educate apprentices in proper working attitudes), the "tragedy" is nonetheless a far cry from strict Neoclassicism because it is written in prose, features a middle-class hero, and deals with affairs of the heart and the marketplace, rather than affairs of state.

NEW FORMS OF DRAMA.   Neoclassical plays did not satisfy the English taste for scenic splendor and spectacular effects. Thus, opera and a number of so-called minor forms developed to provide outlets for visual display. Native English opera was gradually replaced in public esteem by spectacular Italian operas, whose popularity soared in the eighteenth century. But burlesques, ballad operas, and most of all *pantomimes* also grew in public favor. English pantomimes typically combined elements of *commedia dell'arte,* farce, mythology, and contemporary satire with elaborate scenes of spectacle to produce a short *afterpiece,* that is, something to be performed after the evening's play. Often, the dialogue was merely an excuse for major scenes of transformation, in which Harlequin, by a wave of his magic wand, changed all places and people into new and dazzling locales and characters. Because new scenery was often commissioned for pantomimes, many innovations in the design and execution of settings in England can be credited to pantomimic displays.

THEATRE BUILDINGS

The auditorium of the Restoration playhouse was divided into box, pit, and gallery. In England, as in France, certain favored audience members sat on the stage itself. The stage, although still jutting out into the pit, now had a proscenium arch and a raked stage behind it, where grooves were installed to facilitate scene changes. Most of the acting took place on the *forestage*. Most of the scenery, on the other hand, was located behind the proscenium. Initially, the forestage was as large as the stage behind the proscenium, probably an attempt to synthesize earlier Elizabethan practice with currently fashionable Italian practice. As the period wore on, however, the size of the forestage decreased and the stage space behind the proscenium increased, so that, by 1750, little difference existed between English and French or Italian stages. Between 1660 and 1750, both the stage and the auditorium increased in size as the composition of the audience and the repertory of the plays changed. The Restoration theatres seated about 650, whereas, by 1750, Covent Garden could accommodate about 1,500.

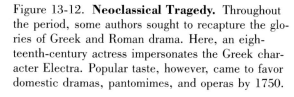

Figure 13-12. **Neoclassical Tragedy.** Throughout the period, some authors sought to recapture the glories of Greek and Roman drama. Here, an eighteenth-century actress impersonates the Greek character Electra. Popular taste, however, came to favor domestic dramas, pantomimes, and operas by 1750.

Figure 13-13. **Restoration Playhouse.** Behind the proscenium arch can be seen a rather typical Italian setting, with wings, a shutter, and borders in single-point perspective. In front of the proscenium is a deep forestage with two doors and a space for onstage seating. *(Courtesy of Richard Leacroft. First published in* Theatre Notebook.*)*

SCENERY

Scenic practices, too, were Italianate. Wings, borders, and shutters were standard. A group of stock sets appropriate for each form of drama (comedy, tragedy, or pastoral) allowed the theatres to provide scenery for most Neo-classical plays. When the theatres required new settings, which was seldom except for pantomimes, they simply commissioned them from painters of the day. Because lighting was still by candles, audience and actors were equally illuminated, although by the early eighteenth century some modest attempts were being made to dim and color lights. Costuming continued to be the major source of visual excitement, and most actors wore an elaborate and sumptuous version of contemporary fashion.

ACTORS AND ACTING

The earlier tendency of actors to specialize in certain kinds of roles became gradually more rigid until, by 1750, clearly defined *lines of business* emerged. New actors or actresses were hired as *utility players*, and gained their experience by playing a great number of small and varied roles. They then declared a specialty in a specific kind of role: a walking lady or gentleman (third line); a specialist in low comedy, or stage eccentric (second line); or a hero or heroine (first line). Once committed to a particular line of business, actors did not stray far from it, regardless of age. (Shakespeare's Juliet, for example, was often played by women in their fifties because they were "first-line" players). Along with lines of business came a practice known as *possession of parts*, an agreement that an actor who played a role in the company possessed that role for as long as he or she remained in the company. Both practices obviously encouraged conservatism in acting and placed a premium on tradition rather than innovation. The tradition perpetuated depended heavily on vocal power and versatility and on formality and elegance rather than "truth to life." For example, some actors apparently intoned or chanted the poetic and lyrical passages of tragedies, much as the recitative of opera is delivered today, and many actors played for *points*, expecting to receive applause for passages particularly well delivered (in which case, the actor might repeat the passage).

Although some acting troupes continued to be organized as sharing ventures, some performers by the early eighteenth century preferred a fixed salary that they could augment by benefit performances. For "benefits," the actor or the group of actors received all of the profits from the evening, a sum that occasionally equaled or exceeded a year's salary.

The most famous actors and actresses of this period included Thomas Betterton (c. 1635–1710), whose portrayal of Shakespearean heroes was unrivaled at the time; Nell Gwyn (1650–1687), whose success in "breeches roles" made her almost as famous as her position as an official mistress of the king; Colley Cibber (1671–1757), noted for his portrayal of fops; Anne Oldfield (1683–1730), the first actress to be buried at Westminster Abbey; James Quin (1693–1766), whose oratorical and formal style epitomized the "old school" of Neoclassical acting; and Charles Macklin (1699–1797), whose prosaic readings and "natural style" anticipated the end of the old and the beginning of a new English style of acting.

AMERICAN PROFESSIONAL THEATRE

Many English actors and actresses found themselves squeezed out of the profitable theatres of London by the stringent enforcement of the Licensing Act of 1737. Some sought a living in the English provinces; but one group, headed by William and Lewis Hallam, chose to go to America, instead. In 1752, the troupe arrived in Virginia and, after building a theatre, opened with Shakespeare's *Merchant of Venice*. This group (although reorganized and enlarged after the death of Lewis Hallam and renamed The American Company in recognition of America's break with England) toured the towns of the East Coast with almost no competition until the 1790s. Its repertory, acting styles, and production conventions were English, with appropriate adjustments made for the needs of almost constant touring.

Illusionistic Theatres II: Romanticism and Realism

Romanticism

BACKGROUND

After 1750, the decline of Neoclassicism was rapid and pronounced. Sentimental views gained strength and joined with new views on the sources of beauty, the function of art, the nature of truth. Artists and theorists in increasing numbers reacted against the rules of Neoclassicism. When the various strands of these new ideas coalesced into something resembling a system of views, it was called *Romanticism*.

Romanticism took many forms. Its extraordinary diversity caused one critic to suggest that we should always speak of Romanti*cisms*, to remind ourselves constantly of its plural, shifting nature. Certainly, Romanticism as practiced

295

by English poets like Keats and Shelley was very different from that of French playwrights like Dumas or German philosophers like Kant.

In spite of its complexity, Romanticism, as it peaked through western Europe and America between 1789 and 1843, seemed to share some basic views that can be summarized.

First, Romanticism was marked by a profound interest in nature, which took many forms. In gardening, for example, Romantics sought a "natural" look that included gnarled trees, jagged rocks, and tangled greenery rather than the previously preferred formal gardens with carefully pruned trees and symmetrical arrays of flowers and bushes. In behavior, natural feelings (instincts) were accepted as more reliable guides to proper behavior than was educated opinion. The Romantics' *distrust of reason* sprang from the view that reason was a product of civilization and education and thus corruptible; instinct was the product of nature and thus reliable.

The celebration of nature led to a glorification of natural people, *noble savages* whom civilization had left alone in a natural state, such as American Indians, African blacks, and South Sea Islanders. Within contemporary society, the *common people*, especially rural peasants, were most admired because they were least affected by such artificial aspects of civilization as class and etiquette.

The desire to return to nature led to *primitivism*, a belief in the superiority of a simple and unsophisticated way of life, a life close to nature. With primitivism came a desire to study old civilizations, particularly those of ancient Egypt, Greece, and the Middle Ages (thus, *antiquarianism* and *medievalism*). For the Romantics, history was a process of decline or decay, not one of progress and improvement.

Second, the Romantics believed intensely (if erratically) in human equality. Civilization had created a number of artificial and social structures to divide people into classes, and so implied that some people were better than others. Romantics braced against such an assumption. The age was thus one of revolutions: the American Revolution (1776); the French Revolution (1791); the Napoleonic Wars (1798–1815); the Europe-wide revolutions of 1830 and 1848; and the American Civil War (1865). Antislavery societies flourished; women's rights organizations formed. Most of the political turmoils during the period can be explained as a continuing struggle between those attempting to maintain the status quo (monarchy or slavery or white male suffrage) and those striving to change society in the direction of more individual freedom and more democratic processes.

Third, Romanticism placed a premium on detail, for in the particular example rested the pathway to truth. The specific, the unique, and the particular were important because the study of any single detail could lead to a better understanding of the universe, all parts of which were related. The details (and so the study) of history and geography were important because they led to an understanding of the characteristics that separated one age from other times and places. To establish uniqueness was to affirm identity.

Fourth, the Romantics believed that truth must always be sought but that

Figure 14-1. **Noble Savage.** Romantic artists tended to glorify groups like American Indians and African blacks. Here, America's first major actor, Edwin Forrest, plays one of his most famous roles, the Indian Chief Metamora.

its attainment in this life was unlikely. Artists and philosophers were the people most likely to have insights into truth; but their insights were both curse and blessing because most people were unable or unwilling to see the truth. To be an artist, then, was to be out of step with society; thus, the Romantic view of the *artist as misunderstood genius.* To strive for perfection was an obligation, but to achieve it was an impossibility. The constant yearning for unattainable truth lent a *melancholy* cast to life, a trait that marked much Romantic art.

Fifth, art for the Romantics served an exalted purpose. In this world, tensions exist between the physical and the spiritual, the material and the ideal. The role of art was to lead people to perceive the underlying unity of existence, to eliminate the apparent conflict: the purpose of art was "to make man whole again." Although the artist could perceive unity amid apparent disunity, he or she might be unable to share that truth, for its perception was based on *insight* and *genius,* rather than on intellect and craft. Art could therefore not be taught; it was not subject to rules. If Romantic artists searched for truth in the myriad details of external nature, they found it often within themselves. Thus, *subjectivity* and *introspection* became hallmarks of Romantic art.

Sixth, criticism, according to the Romantics, was subjective and personal. The worth of a picture or a poem could not be determined by its social utility or its adherence to a set of external criteria. Rather, its merit lay in its ability to stimulate feeling and understanding in the spectator. In a revolutionary

I. R. Cruikshank, Del.   White, Sculpt.

Ant. She's mine—approach and die!
Paul. Thine! miscreant, tremble!
   [*Music.—they fight a decided combat—*ANTOINE *strikes* ROSEN-
FORD *a violent blow.*

ACT II. SCENE 2.

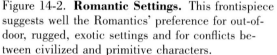

Figure 14-2. **Romantic Settings.** This frontispiece suggests well the Romantics' preference for out-of-door, rugged, exotic settings and for conflicts between civilized and primitive characters.

leap, Romantic criticism moved the basis of judgment of a work of art from the work to the perceiver of the work. An obvious effect was to democratize art, by making one person's opinion of art as good as another's.

The effect of Romanticism on theatre (and the other arts) was significant, if erratic. In general, Romantic art took as its setting the remote and exotic, either past civilizations (especially Greece and the Middle Ages) or primitive societies. Tales of children, commoners, rustics, and savages unfolded against detailed backgrounds of forests, caves, dungeons, pastures, and jungles. In plays, the appeal was more often to the spectators' emotions than to their intellects, and visually interesting episodes predominated over verbally satisfying ones. Special effects involving wild animals, natural disasters, shipwrecks, and snowstorms prefigured the disaster movies of today. While aristocrats flocked to the opera and the ballet (both arts reached new heights of popularity and excellence during the early nineteenth century), the middle and lower classes virtually took over the theatre.

PLAYS IN THE THEATRE (1750–1850)

Revivals of Shakespeare were a mainstay of the Romantic theatre, which produced them in new theatrical settings designed to illustrate the locales mentioned in the dramatic texts and to stress the plays' exotic qualities. Some Neoclassical works remained in the repertory, but mostly new plays written to flaunt Neoclassical conventions prevailed.

SERIOUS DRAMA.   During the Romantic period, a recognizable cleavage appeared between those serious plays deemed critically important and those considered merely popular. Among the critically important works can be found plays ranging from domestic tragedies to philosophical inquiries. Among the serious plays for the popular theatre, only melodramas mattered.

The earliest of the plays deemed critically important were sentimental plays that dealt with the everyday problems of the middle class. In France, Denis Diderot proposed recognition of a new kind of play, which he termed the *drame* (a serious play treating domestic matters), and he provided a model for it in his play *The Illegitimate Son* (1757). In Germany, Gotthold Ephraim Lessing translated Diderot's works and added his own pleas for domestic dramas, providing Germany's first successful one when he wrote *Miss Sara Sampson* (1755). In England, after an early surge of interest in George Lillo's *The London Merchant* (1731), only sporadic and largely unsuccessful plays of the sort appeared. Although some serious domestic plays (*drames*) continued well into the nineteenth century, their place was largely taken over by the ubiquitous melodrama, whose appeal continued to spread, engulfing most other forms of serious drama by the middle of the nineteenth century.

Germany produced major philosophical dramas. Following the publication of Lessing's *Nathan the Wise* (1779) and a surge of dramatic experiments under a group of writers called the *Storm and Stress* (fl. 1770–1790), two authors emerged as significant: Johann Wolfgang von Goethe (1749–1832) and Friedrich Schiller (1759–1805).

GOETHE.   Goethe had early embraced many doctrines of the Storm and Stress movement and, under their influence, had written *Goetz von Berlichin-*

Figure 14-3. **Shakespearean Revivals.** Now staged in proscenium theatres and in illusionistic, painted settings, Shakespeare's plays reached new heights of popularity during the Romantic Age. *(Courtesy of the Department of Rare Books and Special Collections of The University of Rochester Libraries.)*

gen (1773), a piece that required over six hours to perform and more than fifty separate scenes to contain its sprawling action. Later, Goethe sought to perfect an alternate style of production that would capture the patterns undergirding everyday life. His final work, *Faust*, in two parts (1808 and 1831), told the story of the human search for truth and fulfillment and came to epitomize for many the Romantic dilemma. Never intended for the stage, the work is an episodic presentation of a philosophical point of view and an acknowledged literary (as opposed to theatrical) masterpiece.

SCHILLER. Schiller, like Goethe, began as a Storm and Stress writer but later joined Goethe in seeking a new style of production that would create a distance between the spectators and the stage and thereby present them with a glimpse of the ideal world. Of Schiller's many works, the best known now are *The Robbers* (1782), whose immediate success created a vogue for other "Robin Hood" plays, and *William Tell* (1804), a celebration of individual worth and democratic government.

Less philosophical but considerably more stageworthy were French Romantic plays like *Hernani* by Victor Hugo (1802–1885). Its first production in 1830 caused a riot in the theatre. At issue was the question of whether to permit certain attitudes and practices of the Romantic authors (long accepted and popular in the commercial theatres of the boulevards) to invade and presumably sully the theatrical life of the Comédie Française. *Hernani* was written in elevated and poetic language; it portrayed rulers and nobles involved in the affairs of state and was cast in a traditional five-act form. But the play incorporated some features of Romanticism to which traditionalists objected. Common people were shown in conflict with a ruler, scenes of violence and death were portrayed on the stage, and moments of humor were tucked into an otherwise turgid story. The battle of *Hernani*, fought both in the pit of the Comédie Française and the literary circles of Paris, was resolved in favor of the Romantics, and so 1830 is the date now given for the acceptance of Romanticism into the mainstream of France's theatrical life (several years after it had been accepted in England, Germany, and America). The failure of another Romantic play by Victor Hugo in 1843 marked the end of self-conscious French Romanticism, making it one of the shortest dramatic movements in history.

Perhaps because the English found in Shakespeare the traits they most prized, English Romantics produced no new serious dramas of consequence. Although English Romantic poets and novelists (Coleridge, Wordsworth, Keats, Shelley, Byron, and Scott) all wrote plays, most were closet dramas (some intentionally, others by default), and none contributed significantly to the English or American theatre.

MELODRAMA.   The most popular form of drama during the Romantic age was *melodrama*. Although not new (such plays have probably existed in all ages), melodrama attained new stature and significance in the theatre of the late eighteenth century and the nineteenth century.

Melodrama means literally "music drama," a name derived from the ex-

Figure 14-4. **Romantic Melodrama.**
Stock characters—hero, heroine, villain, and comic sidekick—were staples of nineteenth-century melodrama.

tensive use of music within the plays. Much like popular television and movies of today, nineteenth-century melodramas used *emotional music* to provide the proper mood and background for the action and to underscore moments of suspense and surprise. Music was also often used to identify characters for the audience. Such music, called *signature music,* was played when a character was about to enter or leave or to perform some astounding feat.

Melodrama presented a highly simplified moral universe in which good and evil were clearly defined and obviously embodied in easily recognizable stock characters. A physically attractive hero and heroine (often in love) possessed a kindness and virtue that were as unmistakable as they were unblemished. These characters, along with their friends and servants, represented the forces of good. Propelling the action of the play was a villain, whose physical appearance as well as behavior captured the essential attributes of evil. The remaining characters were most often friends or sidekicks of the three defining characters and almost always included at least one comic (relief) character. The villain initiated the action of the melodrama by posing a threat to the hero or the heroine; he or she escaped, and the villain posed another threat; he or she again escaped; and so on. The episodic play thus progressed by a series of threats and escapes, each reversal becoming more extreme than the last, until the final incident, when the hero or heroine might move from almost certain death to a happy marriage in a matter of minutes.

Finally, many melodramas depended heavily on an array of special effects—fires, explosions, drownings, earthquakes—both as threats to the sympathetic characters during the action of the play and as a means of obtaining the downfall of the villain in the final scenes. As well, many melodramas developed around the use of various animals: most common were *equestrian dramas* (horses), and *canine melodramas* (dogs). The interest of the Romantic writers in sea stories gave rise to *nautical melodramas.*

Between 1750 and 1850, two writers of melodrama were especially important: Kotzebue and Pixerecourt.

KOTZEBUE. The German playwright August Friedrich von Kotzebue (1761–1819) wrote over two hundred plays, many translated into English and French and performed throughout the world. Kotzebue was particularly successful with his *domestic melodramas,* which featured errant but repentant wives and upright but forgiving husbands. His plays titillated audiences without offending them and introduced potentially controversial views without seeming to attack the audience's standards of propriety. Most of all, Kotzebue took the lives of common people and gave them dignity by treating them seriously. From about 1780 until his death, Kotzebue was acknowledged as the most popular playwright in the world.

PIXÉRÉCOURT. Réné Charles Guilbert de Pixérécourt (1773–1844) was the French author of more than one hundred plays. He set a fashion for canine melodramas and disaster melodramas, which might require a flood to sweep through the stage, uprooting a tree and bearing the heroine away on a board, or might use a volcanic eruption to foil the villain. Because the physical requirements were often so demanding, Pixérécourt insisted on directing his own plays in order to ensure their success. Pixérécourt, therefore, figured prominently in the history of French directors as well as of French playwrights.

Although some critics have scoffed at melodrama, its popularity and persistence argue that attention should be paid to it. In the nineteenth century, it was revered by many, and unquestionably it attracted to the theatre a mass audience new to the art of the stage. This audience of middle- and lower-class patrons cheered and laughed and wept openly and enthusiastically at the exploits of the heroes and heroines, and their support made theatre the major form of entertainment for over one hundred years.

COMEDY.   During the Romantic period, at least three different types of comedies competed for public favor: sentimental comedy, "laughing" comedy, and the "well-made play."

Probably closest in tone to the early romantic ideas of innate human goodness were the *sentimental comedies*, those written to appeal to the audience's sense of virtue rather than to its sense of humor. Although most contained some laughable situations and an occasionally funny character, the plays' primary appeal depended on their depiction of the successful struggles of virtuous characters whose laudable goals ensured their ultimate success.

Like melodrama, sentimental comedy has been scorned and largely ignored

Figure 14-5. **Romantic Melodrama.** Exciting special effects often included the most recent inventions. Shown here is a scene from one of America's most popular melodramas, showing the newly developed train. (*From Stanley Appelbaum,* Advertising Woodcuts from The Nineteenth Century Stage. *New York: Dover, 1977.*)

in modern times. But in its own day, its popularity and importance were unquestionable. Leading writers of sentimental comedy were the Frenchman Diderot (1713–1784) and the German Lessing (1729–1781). Sentimental comedies' popularity eroded after about 1800 as that of melodrama increased.

Some argued strongly for abandoning sentimental comedy and returning to "laughing" comedy. Three authors in particular were associated with its increasing reputation: Beaumarchais (Pierre Augustin Caron, 1732–1799); Oliver Goldsmith (c. 1730–1774); and Richard Brinsley Sheridan (1751–1816). Beaumarchais's reputation rests now principally on *The Barber of Seville* (1775) and *The Marriage of Figaro* (1783), both laughing comedies that develop by means of intrigue while poking fun at aspects of French society. Goldsmith's most popular comedy, *She Stoops to Conquer* (1773), depicts the laughable consequences of mistaken identity and benign trickery that temporarily keep two pairs of young lovers separated. Its popularity continues even today, and the play remains in the active repertory of many English and American companies. Sheridan's *The Rivals* (1775) and *The School for Scandal* (1777) were especially prized for their witty dialogue and colorful portraits of engaging characters. It is a testament to the strength of the doctrine of sentimentalism that both of Sheridan's plays use its techniques even while objecting to its principles. Laughing comedy's importance was eclipsed after 1830 by the growing popularity of the "well-made play."

The most popular comic writer of the hundred years between 1750 and 1850 was undoubtedly Eugène Scribe (1791–1861), a Frenchman who wrote more than three hundred plays for the Parisian theatres. Their translation into German and English and their frequent production in those countries and in America throughout the nineteenth century caused French comedy to set the standard for the world by mid-century.

Scribe's techniques (like careful preparation and meticulous networks of relationships) were designed to give the appearance of an action tightly unified by cause and effect when, in fact, the plays were built around multiple lines of action that unfolded by chance and coincidence. The phrase *well-made play* was used first as a compliment to describe the particular kind of play that Scribe perfected, but because later scholars deplored the superficiality of his works, the term became one of derision during the twentieth century. But Scribe and the well-made play exerted considerable influence on later writers, both among commercial authors (most importantly Victorien Sardou, 1831–1908) and among the later realists like Alexandre Dumas *fils* (1824–1895) and Henrik Ibsen (1825–1906). The well-made plays of Scribe and others dominated the stages of western Europe and America during the nineteenth century and, with melodrama, were probably the mainstay of that theatre.

POPULAR ENTERTAINMENTS.   Other kinds of entertainments also continued to be popular. Specialty acts featured jugglers, singers, tumblers, magicians, and others. Pantomimes increased in length as their popularity grew until they provided a whole evening's fare. Short musical revues or brief

Figure 14-6. **Romantic Melodrama.** Spectacular scenes of fire, smoke, water, and rescue were staples of the melodramas of the nineteenth and early twentieth century. *(From Appelbaum,* Advertising Woodcuts.*)*

topical skits using music and verse (*vaudevilles*) appealed to the politically minded. Comic operas, whose sentimental stories were set to original music, provided entertainment for those who liked music but found opera perplexing or dull. Parodies, burlesques, circus entertainments, and water shows appealed to popular audiences.

PRACTICES OF THE THEATRES (1750–1850)

The major trends in the theatre between 1750 and 1850 were the following:

1. The middle and lower classes came into the theatres in increasing numbers.
2. The number and the seating capacity of theatres increased.
3. The size and complexity of stages and support areas increased (although the size of the forestage decreased).
4. The number, accuracy, and consistency of visual details (scenery, properties, and costumes) increased, as emphasis shifted from the aural to the visual aspects of production.

THEATRE SIZE. Because theatre was the form of entertainment preferred by vast numbers of people and because Romantic plays stressed spectacle, new theatres built and those remodeled between 1750 and 1850 featured ever-larger auditoriums and ever-more-sophisticated stages and support

Figure 14-7. **Enlarged Theatre Buildings.** As the lower classes streamed into the cities and into the theatres, new theatres were built and old ones enlarged, often to include as many as five balconies.

areas. For example, London's Covent Garden Theatre seated fewer than 1,500 people in the 1730s but could accommodate 3,000 by 1793. The Drury Lane Theatre seated only 650 in 1700 but had a capacity of 3,600 during the early years of the nineteenth century. In America, the original Chestnut Street Theatre of Philadelphia (opened in 1794) was built to house 1,200 but was soon enlarged to accommodate more than 2,000. In France, all the major theatres were enlarged and modernized between 1750 and 1800, with particular attention given to improving sight lines, increasing seating capacity, and creating greater potential for staging spectacles. Between 1775 and 1800, more than thirty permanent theatres were built in Germany, most of which incorporated elaborate machinery to permit rapid and simultaneous changes of setting; by 1850, the number had grown to sixty-five.

AUDIENCE ARRANGEMENT. The standard configuration for the audience area was box, pit, and gallery, with boxes originally the most prized and expensive seats. As *seeing* the spectacular effects gradually became more important than *hearing* the vocal displays of the actors, the advantage shifted to the pit (later called the *orchestra*); and so box seats gave way to orchestra seats as the most favored and expensive in the theatre. The cheapest seats were always those of the upper balconies (in large theatres, there might be as many as five levels). Called the *gods*, the audience in the upper galleries were primarily working-class people who were noted for their bad manners at theatrical performances.

SCENERY.   About 1760, spectators were no longer permitted to sit on the stages in England and France, for onstage spectators clearly destroyed the illusion of reality and took up spaces now needed for scenery and acting areas. By the 1770s, with the spectators gone from the stage, designers were free to create a complete stage picture. Phillippe Jacques de Loutherbourg (1740–1812), England's leading designer, began to reproduce familiar English locations on the stage and thus created a vogue for "local color" settings. In France, the scenery at the boulevard theatres depicted examples of French local color as well as "authentic" reproductions of places in the Orient, the Americas, Russia, and so on.

Scenery consisted of a combination of wings, drops (large pieces of fabric suspended from above the stage and extending to the floor), borders, and ground rows (cut-away flats adapted to stand free on the stage floor), the overall arrangement being called *wing-and-drop scenery.* All scenic pieces were carefully painted to achieve the illusion of reality, and some were cut away (in the shape of leaves at their edges, for example) or layered (in gauzes or other fabrics) to enhance the illusion still more. Because many plays of the Romantic period were set out of doors, the borders often consisted of a combination of sky, clouds, and leaves, while the flats and drops were forests, trees, grasses, rocks, and similar natural scenes. For plays set in medieval

Figure 14-8. **Wing and Drop.** In addition to the wings, drop, and borders, notice the stage trap in which the "drowning man" appears, the cut-away leaves in the sky border, the ground rows down left, and the three-dimensional lock gate.

castles, tombs, or dungeons, all flats, drops, and borders might be painted to resemble large stones.

Whenever required by the play's action, three-dimensional details were included; for example, a bridge would be built if characters had to walk on it. But most of the scenery was two-dimensional, with all the details painted on it.

LIGHTING.   The scene was lit by candles or oil lamps (or, after 1830, in some theatres, by gas) placed at the front of the stage as *footlights* and behind the several sets of wings. In no case was the illumination very high, and so both scenery and actors were only dimly visible.

SPECIAL EFFECTS.   The basic settings were enlivened by an enormous variety of special equipment and effects. Characters and objects flew about by means of elaborate systems of ropes and pulleys; they disappeared and appeared magically through various traps in the floor and, less often, through rotating wall panels. Fountains and waterfalls gushed and flowed by means of specially installed water systems. Moving panoramas and dioramas permitted designers to achieve the illusion of travel onstage. By unwinding a large painted cloth from one giant spool onto another, the landscape behind an onstage boat or carriage could be made to unroll and the vehicle would seem to move. When, late in the nineteenth century, such panoramas were combined with treadmills, even horse races and chariot races could be staged. Volcanic eruptions, fires, thunder, lightning, rainstorms, explosions—all were a part of the theatre's spectacle, and all were popular with mass audiences.

The use of scenery and special effects appeared to be governed by three overriding and interrelated assumptions:

1. The stage picture should present the illusion of reality (thus the name *pictorial illusionism* was used to describe the scenery during the period).
2. Many details should be included in order to particularize the settings.
3. Because time and place were important, historical and geographical accuracy of detail was appropriate.

Although there was a considerable gap between these goals and their realization, designers moved steadily in the direction of their ideals from about 1750 to 1850.

ANTIQUARIANISM.   Celebration of the remote and great attention to accurate details increasingly won public acclaim and so became increasingly practiced by theatrical managers during the nineteenth century. For example, William Charles Macready (1793–1873) managed London's two leading theatres during the 1830s and 1840s and was the first director who *consistently* sought historical accuracy in both scenery and costumes. By 1850, even in

America, whose theatre was late in getting under way, *antiquarianism* had made its mark, and historical accuracy in theatrical settings and costumes was, if not achieved, at least approached.

THEATRE COMPANIES.   Some troupes, like the Comédie Française, continued to operate as sharing companies, but most performers now worked for a fixed salary that was supplemented by the gate receipts of one or more "benefit" performances.

For a time, the *stock company* dominated, that is, a group of actors who stayed together over a period of years, performing appropriate roles in a variety of plays and each contributing to the reputation of the company as a whole. After about 1830, however, perhaps as a consequence of the Romantics' growing attachment to the idea of "individual genius," and most certainly because of improved transportation networks (particularly the expanding system of railroads), the company system gradually declined. In its place came the "starring system," which meant that leading performers moved from stock company to stock company, where they played the plum parts, supported by resident players. The starring system, although exceedingly popular with audiences, caused numerous problems for the acting profession. One French actress, for example, demanded and received a salary equal to that of her country's prime minister, leaving little for her fellow artists.

In time, there was a rage for child stars, who played not only Shakespearean roles like King Lear and Hamlet but also the heroes in various melodramas of the day, where they single-handedly foiled the villains. The public also relished "breeches roles," that is, women playing men's roles in men's clothing; perhaps the attraction was that the breeches revealed the actress's body far more than current fashion permitted and therefore provided a bit of titillation quite separate from the play's dramatic offerings.

Figure 14-9. **Antiquarianism.** Historically accurate details of setting and costume were sought not only in new plays but also in Shakespearean revivals, like the design for a Shakespearean production shown here.

MASTER BURKE AS HAMLET.

Figure 14-10. **Child Stars.** For a time, children's playing of Shakespeare's major characters was a rage. Shown here is one such child star in the role of Hamlet.

ACTING STYLE.   Acting style changed between 1750 and 1850, presenting alternate versions of "truth in acting." At one extreme was the formal (or "classical") and at the other pole the natural (or "romantic").

FORMAL ACTING. Formal acting predominated from the beginning of the period until about 1815, although its various expressions were quite diverse. The emphasis seemed to be on vocal power and on dignified, restrained interpretations of character. Such performers typically excelled in tragic roles, where poetic diction encouraged a declamatory or oratorical delivery. Perhaps the most extreme example of an accepted actor performing in this tradition was the English James Quin (1693–1766).

David Garrick (1717–1779), on the other hand, was admired for his "easy and familiar, yet forcible style of speaking and acting." Acknowledged as the greatest English actor of the last half of the eighteenth century, Garrick was, however, far from our conception of natural; for example, he persisted in playing Shakespeare's Macbeth in the dress of a military officer of the eighteenth century, complete with a tail wig, and in drawing attention to himself (to the detriment of the acting company) by "the restless abundance of his action and his gestures."

By the 1790s, the leading formal actors in England were a brother and sister, John Phillip Kemble (1757–1823) and Sarah Kemble Siddons (1755–1831), who were applauded for the stateliness, grandeur, and dignity of their performances. Every country had its classical actors: in America, Thomas A. Cooper (1776–1849); in France, Talma (1763–1826); in Germany, Emil Devrient (1803–1872). And in every country, the same general patterns of changing taste were observable.

Figure 14-11. **Romantic Acting.** The Romantic actor Edmund Kean as Hamlet, a favorite role of many Romantic actors, perhaps because of its emphasis on self-searching and melancholy.

ROMANTIC ACTING. A revolution in English acting appears to have occurred when Edmund Kean (1787–1833) made his London debut in 1814. Kean abandoned dignity and intellect in favor of flamboyance and passion. To see Kean act "was to read Shakespeare by flashes of lightning." Apparently, passionate outbursts and novel interpretations marked the actors labeled "natural" or "romantic" during the period. Other important performers in this tradition were the English/American, Junius Brutus Booth (1796–1852) and the French Frédérick Lemaître (1800–1876).

Scarcely had Romantic acting seized the imagination of the public, however, when it, too, began to appear artificial. It was gradually replaced by yet another "natural" style after 1850, a style that came to be called *realistic* acting.

SUMMARY

The profound changes that can be seen between 1750 and 1850 were the result of changes in what audiences would accept as "real" or "true."

In 1750, generalized scenery and costumes formed a sparse background for the actors. Audiences, still largely upper class, were unperturbed by lack of detail or by its inaccuracy, for they thrilled to the verbal displays of excellently trained and elegantly attired actors. They sought and found their artistic truth in the formal, generalized portraits of an upper- or middle-class hero that formed the basis of most of the new plays.

In 1850, carefully painted settings and historically accurate costumes provided a richly detailed background. The audiences, now mostly middle and lower class, sought lavish spectacle, complete with elaborate special effects. They expected reasonably authentic sets and costumes and appreciated actors who could grip the emotions. Such audiences sought and found artistic truth in the detailed representations of individual people and places.

Post-Romanticism: Richard Wagner and the Bayreuth Theatre

Although Richard Wagner (1813–1883) is most often associated with the fields of music and opera, he was an important theorist and practitioner of the theatre as well. Two contributions in particular assured Wagner his place in the history of theatre: (1) his call for a unified work of art and (2) his development of a classless theatre.

Wagner argued that the artist should be a mythmaker who presents an ideal world to the spectators, providing them with a communal experience that highlights for them their shared culture. The best drama, according to Wagner, was one that combined music and poetry to achieve a total art, one that fused the emotional with the intellectual.

For Wagner, the experience of the audience was the critical factor in planning and shaping a work of art. He sought a stage production so compelling that spectators would be drawn in and would believe in and empathize with the world behind the proscenium arch. Indeed, for Wagner, the success of a production was measured primarily by its ability to capture the emotions of the audience and to transport them to a new sense of shared purpose.

MASTER ARTWORK

To achieve the ideal production, one capable of entrancing an audience, Wagner proclaimed the need for a "master artwork," or "united artwork," by which he meant a work in which all elements of the drama and of theatrical production were carefully synthesized into a unified whole. Such unity could be achieved only, according to Wagner, when a single person, a supreme artist, controlled every aspect of the production. Indeed, it was Wagner's concept of the master artist, the single controlling force behind a work of art, that did much to establish the role of the director as the central artist in the theatre, a view dominating many practices of the modern theatre.

CLASSLESS THEATRE

Wagner was able to build a theatre that would allow him to put some of his theories into practice. Opened in 1876, the Bayreuth Festspielhaus included features that helped Wagner establish his ideal world of the stage. Rather

Figure 14-12. **Wagnerian Production.** Wagner relied heavily on staging techniques common in the Romantic theatre. Above, the effect as seen by the audience; below, the staging techniques used backstage to accomplish it.

than one proscenium arch, the theatre at Bayreuth had several; the orchestra pit, customarily in full view of the audience, at Bayreuth extended partway under the stage and was entirely hidden from the sight of the audience. Steam jets installed at the front of the stage permitted special effects like fog and mist to help establish the mood of the production and to mask the changes in scenery. Such unusual architectural features were joined by certain new practices—like darkening the auditorium during the drama and forbidding the musicians to tune their instruments in the pit—to separate the real world of the audience (in the auditorium) from the ideal world of the drama (on the stage). This separation of the two worlds Wagner referred to as the "mystic chasm."

Unusual as some of these features were, they were less innovative and influential than changes that Wagner introduced into the auditorium at Bayreuth. Whether because of a desire to democratize the theatre or because of the increasing importance of seeing (rather than hearing) a play, Wagner eliminated the box, pit, and gallery in favor of a new "classless" theatre in which every seat had an equally good view of the stage and each ticket cost

Figure 14-13. **Wagner's Bayreuth Theatre.** Continental seating produced a "classless theatre" that other theatres later adopted in preference to the box, pit, and gallery arrangement.

the same amount of money. The seats at Bayreuth were arranged in the shape of a fan, with the shorter rows closer to the stage and with entrances at the end of each row. This kind of arrangement came to be called *continental seating*, and some version of it was widely adopted as new theatres were constructed during the twentieth century.

Although, in fact, Wagner's productions seldom strayed far from the sort of illusionism common during the last years of the nineteenth century, his theories and architectural innovations placed him outside the mainstream of his day and made him a precursor of later experimenters.

Realism

After Romanticism, the split between drama considered worthy of serious attention and that considered merely entertaining persisted. From 1850 through the 1950s, the significant drama and staging were in a style called *realism*. The commercial theatre and drama, a conservative force, lagged decades behind but finally embraced a diluted and trivialized realism by the end of World War I.

BACKGROUND

By the 1850s, certain problems that had grown out of society's shifting bases of wealth and its developing industrialization were becoming clear. The products of industry were being distributed unevenly, and the gap between those who did the work and those who reaped the profits was widening, a development that led Karl Marx (1818–1883) to propose an alternative method of social and economic organization for society. Urban poverty was on the rise and, with it, urban crime. Political instability gave way to political repression, which, in turn, fanned latent dissatisfactions that demanded immediate correction.

At roughly this same time, science offered new theories that threatened to undermine previously accepted views of humanness. Charles Darwin (1809–1882) proposed that human beings had evolved from simpler forms of life and that they were not a separate, special act of creation. He therefore seemed to suggest that people were more like animals than like angels and that their capacity was limited by environmental forces. Gregor Mendel (1822–1884), through his work with corn, showed that certain traits were passed from generation to generation in statistically predictable ways. From there, it was only a short step to the conclusion that people, like plants and other animals, were defined by their genes and that they were neither free agents nor special creatures. Sigmund Freud (1856–1939) proposed that people's behavior was not at base rational and so their motives were not understandable, even to themselves. His emphasis on subconscious desires and repressed responses hinted that people were trapped into patterns of behavior by forces (often sexual and aggressive) that they neither controlled nor understood. One result of such developments in science was to dislodge humankind from the philosophic pedestal on which it had rested since the Middle Ages.

Finally, revolutionary technological advances had the effects of changing both the way people lived and the way they saw the world. Impressive changes in transportation (steamboats, railroads, automobiles, and airplanes) and communication (telegraph, telephone, radio, and television) speeded up the flow of information, goods, and people. Improved vaccines, antibiotics, and surgical techniques slowed down death rates. Science and technology seemed to ensure eventual answers even to complex questions. History, therefore, seemed to be progressing inexorably toward a better world.

Realism—and its more extreme relative, *naturalism*—arose in part as responses to these new social and philosophical conditions. Realists and naturalists were *materialists:* they believed that truth resided in the material objects observable in the physical, external world. They were also *objectivists:* they believed that truth could be discovered through the application of scientific observation and could be replicated by a series of objective observers.

According to the realists and the naturalists, the function of art, like that of science, was the betterment of humankind, and so the method of the artist should be that of the scientist. Because truth resided in material objects, art, to be true, had to depict the material, tangible world. Because problems could be solved only through application of the scientific method, dramatists

Figure 14-14. **Urbanization and Industrialization.** Appalling problems occasioned by the factory system were becoming all too apparent by the middle of the nineteenth century.

Figure 14-15. **Materialism and Objectivism.** If truth resides in objects that can be seen and touched, then artists wishing to tell the truth will include numerous objects in their settings, as in this production from the late nineteenth century.

should emulate scientists and strive to become objective observers of the social milieu. Plays should be set in contemporary times and places, for only they could be observed firsthand by the playwright. As the highest purpose of art was the betterment of humanity, the subject of plays should be contemporary life and its problems.

While sharing with realists a belief in the efficacy of science as a solver of problems and in the role of drama in the improvement of society, the naturalists differed in their definition of what problems most needed attention and their hope for the future. The naturalists stressed the problems of the poor and tended to be pessimistic about the possible solution of these problems. According to the naturalists, people were victims, not actors in life. Their destiny was *controlled* by factors like heredity and environment, factors over which they had little, if any, influence. Because the naturalists attempted to give the impression that their plays were an actual record of life, the dramas often appeared formless and unstructured, traits that gave rise to the phrase "a slice of life" to describe some naturalists' plays.

LEADING FIGURES IN REALISM AND NATURALISM

GEORG II, DUKE OF SAXE-MEININGEN. One of the first important contributors to the realistic staging *of prerealistic drama* was Georg II, Duke of Saxe-Meiningen (fl. 1870s–1880s). In some ways, the duke was merely perfecting and popularizing ideals of staging promulgated much earlier; nonetheless, it was he who influenced the later, important realists.

Saxe-Meiningen objected to many practices of the theatrical mainstream

Figure 14-16. **The Duke of Saxe-Meiningen as Director.** An early modern director, the duke took great care with his crowd scenes so that they would appear real, as in this scene from *Julius Caesar*. (See the same scene in Figures 8-5, 8-6, and 8-9.)

because they resulted in productions that lacked unity (internal consistency) and that seemed artificial and unreal. For the duke, the art of the theatre was the art of providing the *illusion of reality;* he therefore sought methods of production that would lead to "an intensified reality and [would] give remote events . . . the quality of actuality, of being lived for the first time." To this end, the duke stressed *lifelike acting;* accurate scenery, costumes, and properties; and unity.

ACTING. In Saxe-Meiningen's group, there were no stars. Each member of the company was eligible to play any role; and each member, if not cast as a major character, was required to play in crowd scenes, something a star of the old sort would never have done. Moreover, each actor in a crowd scene was given lines and actions that were carefully rehearsed. To make the crowds seem real, the duke divided his actors into several groups, each led by an experienced actor. To increase a sense of realism in crowd scenes, the actors were to avoid parallel lines on stage, to make crosses on the stage diagonally rather than parallel with the curtain line, to keep one foot off the ground whenever possible (by placing it on a step or by kneeling on one knee), and to be aware of each neighbor's stance so that it would not be repeated. *Variety* within a crowd led to its seeming reality. All actors were told to look at one another rather than at the audience, to react to what was said and done onstage, and to behave naturally (even if it meant delivering a line while not facing the audience).

STAGING. The Duke believed that all elements of a production required coordination. The setting must be an integral part of the play, and so he encouraged his actors to move *within* the setting rather than merely playing in front of it (as was currently fashionable). If actors were to move within an environment, the scenic details had to be three-dimensional rather than painted, and so actual objects were used in the settings. Simultaneously, the duke strove to provide several levels (e.g., rocks, steps, and platforms), so that the scenic design would not stop abruptly at the stage floor. In these ways, he did much to popularize the use of real, three-dimensional details.

Historical accuracy in both scenery and costumes was important. Georg II designed and supervised every aspect of the physical production. To increase accuracy in the selection of details, he divided each century into thirds and even differentiated among various national groups within each period. To increase accuracy of construction, he used authentic fabrics instead of the cheaper substitutes often resorted to in the commercial houses of the day; many items were made in his own shops. Moreover, he required all actors, from the most to the least important, to wear the costumes that were designed for them, regardless of the current fashions, and to acquaint themselves with the postures and stances peculiar to the period. Even the makeup was designed according to existing portraits of the time.

Beginning in 1874 (eight years after the duke took over the theatre), the Meiningen plays began touring western Europe and Russia. From then until its last tour in 1890, the troupe gave more than 2,800 performances in thirty-six cities. From these performances came the group's international reputation and its influence on people like André Antoine and Konstantin Stanislavski.

ANDRÉ ANTOINE AND THE THÉÂTRE-LIBRE.   André Antoine (1853–1943) abhorred the commercial theatres of Paris, disapproved of the way actors were trained at the Paris Conservatoire (France's leading school for actors), objected to the scenic practices of the major theatres, and decried the flimsiness of contemporary popular drama. What was needed, Antoine concluded, was a theatre where new and controversial plays could gain carefully mounted and realistically acted productions. Thus, when an amateur group to which he belonged balked at producing a daring new play, Antoine undertook the production himself and, spurred by early success, became the full-time director of his own new theatre in 1887. He named it the Théâtre-Libre (Free Theatre) and described it as nothing less than "a machine of war, poised for the conquest of Paris."

THE "FOURTH WALL." Antoine believed with the naturalists that environment determined, or at least heavily influenced, human behavior. Stage setting was therefore very important. For this reason, Antoine took great care to make his stage settings as believable and as much like real life as possible. He designed a room, placing the furniture and accessories in it, only then deciding which "wall" of the room was to be removed so that the audience could see in. Antoine depended heavily on actual, three-dimensional objects rather than their painted substitutes. For one play, he brought real sides of

Figure 14-17. **Antoine: Naturalism.** Antoine popularized an approach to theatre called naturalism, which stressed the problems of the underclass displayed in settings filled with three-dimensional (rather than painted) objects.

beef on his stage; for another, real trees and birds' nests; and for another, a real student's actual room furnishings. The attention that he paid to realistic detail and his reliance on actual objects led to his being called by many the father of naturalistic staging. Jean Julien, a contemporary of Antoine's, seemed to sum up the goal of Antoine: "The front of the stage must be a fourth wall, transparent for the public, opaque for the player."

ACTING. Antoine believed that actors should appear to be real people, not actors in a play. Unfortunately, actors trained at the Paris Conservatoire could not portray real life on stage because they had been trained to use their voices in special theatrical ways, to align their bodies in unlifelike poses, and to play to their audiences directly. Antoine wanted his actors to say their lines naturally, just as one might engage in a conversation with friends and, at the same time, to move about the furniture and accessories just as in real life. Sincerity and conviction were the qualities he sought, and so he advised his actors to ignore the audience and to speak to one another in conversational tones—in short, to try to *be*, rather than to *act*, the characters in the play. Perhaps for these reasons, Antoine often used amateur actors in his theatre, actors who had not received conventional training for the commercial theatre and who were therefore more receptive to the experimental, new style of naturalistic acting.

PLAYS. Although Antoine produced a wide range of plays while at the Théâtre-Libre, he seemed most comfortable with plays in the realistic and naturalistic styles. Although many such plays had been written before Antoine opened his theatre, few had escaped the censors. Because Antoine organized his theatre as a subscription house, he was able to bypass the threats of censorship. Consequently, he was able to introduce to Parisians a wide range of French and foreign authors whose works were considered too scandalous for production in the major theatres of the day. Plays by Émile Zola, Leo Tolstoy, August Strindberg, Henrik Ibsen, and Gerhart Hauptmann were produced by Antoine even while they were forbidden productions elsewhere.

The major contributions of Antoine and the Théâtre-Libre (1887–1896) were (1) to popularize acting techniques leading toward naturalness on stage; (2) to gain acceptance for scenic practices now known as "fourth-wall realism," with all that implies about scenic detail and literal objects; (3) to introduce a new generation of playwrights (both French and foreign) to the theatregoing public of Paris; and (4) to establish a model for a censor-free theatre.

The most significant experimental theatre of its day, the Théâtre-Libre gave rise to a number of similar theatres throughout the world. Called the *independent theatre movement*, this blossoming of small, independent theatres in several countries almost simultaneously gave the impetus to an ultimate acceptance of realism as the mainstream of the commercial theatre, an acceptance completed by early in the twentieth century.

KONSTANTIN STANISLAVSKI AND THE MOSCOW ART THEATRE. When the Meiningen company toured Russia in 1885 and again in 1890, its impact was strong indeed, for the German troupe was presenting a kind of ensemble acting and quality of visual detail not previously witnessed in Russia.

Two men, Konstantin Stanislavski (1863–1938) and Vladimir Nemirovich-Danchenko (1858–1943) saw the Meiningen company and were impressed. They decided to establish a new kind of theatre in Moscow, an experimental theatre whose goals were (1) to remain free of the demands of commercialism; (2) to avoid overemphasis on the scenic elements of production; and (3) to

Figure 14-18. **Antoine: New Playwrights.** Antoine introduced many important new playwrights to France, including Maxim Gorky, whose naturalistic masterpiece *The Lower Depths* is shown here in a Parisian production.

Figure 14-19. **Chekhov at the Moscow Art Theatre.** In addition to revolutionizing the training of actors, Stanislavski also introduced the plays of Chekhov, in which he often acted. Here, *Uncle Vanya. (From Oliver Sayler,* The Moscow Art Theatre Series of Russian Plays. *New York: Brentano's, 1923.)*

reflect the inner truth of the play. For this theatre, Nemirovich-Danchenko was to select the plays and handle the administration, while Stanislavski was to serve as the production director.

From its opening in 1898, the Moscow Art Theatre was known for its careful realistic-naturalistic productions. During its early years, the greatest attention was given to the accuracy of historical detail in all areas of the physical production, but, within ten years, Stanislavski's interest moved from a largely external realism toward finding an inner truth for actors. External realism from this time on became, for Stanislavski, merely a key to opening the inner reality of the plays, and he strove to develop techniques that would help the actors achieve an inner truth.

By 1917, he had developed, from personal experience and observation of others, his major ideas for training actors, ideas that he codified in a series of books that have since been translated into more than twenty languages (the dates are for the American editions): *My Life in Art* (1924), *An Actor Prepares* (1936), *Building a Character* (1949), and *Creating a Role* (1961). Together, these books represent what has come to be called the Stanislavski "system" of actor training, although Stanislavski himself neither insisted that his was the only way to train actors nor that his methods should be studied and mastered by everyone.

Although today Stanislavski's reputation rests largely on his contributions to actors' training, he was in his own time considered an innovative director. During the early years of the Moscow Art Theatre, Stanislavski worked in a rather autocratic fashion, planning each detail of his actors' vocal inflections, gestures, movements, and so on. But as his interest in the problems of the actor grew, and as his actors became more skillful, he abandoned his dogmatic approach and became more of an interpreter and helpmate to the actors. His ideal became for the director and the actors to grow together in their understanding of the play; therefore, he no longer appeared at rehearsals with a detailed production book containing minute directions for the actors. Only after the group had grasped the psychology of the roles and the complex interrelationships (often a three-month process) did the actors begin to work on the stage. Beginning with very small units in the play and moving gradually to acts and finally to the whole play, the actors and the director built a performance, a process often requiring six months or longer.

It was probably this careful attention to psychological detail that permitted Stanislavski's company to succeed with the plays of Anton Chekhov where others before had failed. On the other hand, it should be clear that such rehearsal procedures are seldom possible in commercial ventures.

What began in 1898 as an experiment in external realism and was by 1906 an experiment in psychological realism had become an established tradition in Russia by the time of the Russian Revolution (1917). Because a number of Russians trained in "the system" left their country after the revolution, the teachings of Stanislavski came to the attention of the outside world. Mikhail Chekhov and Vera Kommissarzhevsky worked in Europe and the United States and brought their own versions of "the system" with them. Richard Boleslavsky and Maria Ouspenskaya came to the United States and led the American Laboratory Theatre, where they had as students Harold Clurman, Lee Strasberg, and Stella Adler, founders of the Group Theatre, America's major propagators of Stanislavski's system of actor training (although by their time somewhat altered and renamed the "Method").

Figure 14-20. *The Three Sisters* **at the Moscow Art Theatre.** Stanislavski's emphasis on the inner reality of characters made him Russia's first successful interpreter of Chekhov's plays. *(From Sayler, Series.)*

Figure 14-21. **Box Set.** Realistic and naturalistic staging tended to abandon the old wing and drop in favor of the new box set, a stage "room," built of flats, with the audience looking through what would be its fourth wall.

THEATRE BUILDINGS

Theatres that were built for realistic plays or those remodeled to improve their spaces for realistic productions tended to be intimate proscenium houses without apron or proscenium doors. Because the scenic requirements were relatively simple, few provided elaborate machinery for shifting scenery. The prized seats were in the orchestra. The auditoriums often abandoned box, pit, and gallery arrangements in favor of some modification of Wagner's seating plan. The audiences consisted primarily of the middle classes, perhaps because it was most often their problems that were being addressed. The availability of electricity for theatrical lighting after the 1880s had two major results. It made the control and therefore the artistic manipulation of lighting possible, and it extended the life expectancy of theatre buildings by reducing the number of theatre fires, a plague of theatres during the first half of the century.

STAGING

As staged, realistic and naturalistic plays shared many traits. Both set their plays in the contemporary world; both included numerous details; both relied on three-dimensional objects rather than their painted representations; and both adopted conventions of acting that focused the actors' attention onstage and discouraged them from moving in front of the arch or openly acknowledging the audience (which now sat in a darkened auditorium). Both abandoned wing-and-drop scenery in favor of a *box set*, a stage "room" built of flats but with one wall missing so that the audience could look through it.

Although agreeing on these basic conventions, the two styles often looked quite different onstage, mostly because their dramatic subjects and characters differed. The realists, who treated problems of the middle class, set their plays in well-appointed living rooms with standard furnishings (e.g., lamps, ashtrays, portraits) and costumed their characters as the prosperous people they were. The naturalists, dealing with the problems of the poor and down-trodden, set their plays in places like hovels, factories, and bars and costumed their characters in the rags of poverty.

REALISTIC DRAMA

Realism in the drama began tentatively and cautiously. Although French writers like Alexandre Dumas *fils* and Eugène Scribe presaged realism, it was the Norwegian Henrik Ibsen (1828–1906) who brought the several philosophical and artistic strands into successful dramatic shape and launched realism as the major artistic movement.

IBSEN. With plays like *A Doll's House* (1879), *Ghosts* (1881), and *Hedda Gabler* (1890), Ibsen broke with the sentimentalized problem plays of earlier days and assumed his controversial role as the attacker of society's values. Structurally, his plays were fairly traditional: they told a story and moved logically from event to event just as well-made plays had done for years. But their content was shocking: when individuals came into conflict with society, they were no longer assumed to be guilty and society blameless. Indeed, social customs and traditional morality were exposed by Ibsen as a tangle of inconsistencies and irrelevancies. The problems addressed were customarily those of the middle and managerial classes. Questions like the proper role of women, the ethics of euthanasia, the morality of business and war, and the economics of religion formed the basis of serious probings into social behavior. Theatrical producers throughout the world who believed that drama

Figure 14-22. **Realism: Ibsen.** The famous Italian actress Eleanora Duse appears here in Ibsen's *Rosmersholm*, in a box setting typical of the time.

should be involved in the social issues of the day applauded the Norwegian dramatist, and soon other artists began to translate, produce, and, later, emulate his plays.

SHAW.   In England, George Bernard Shaw (1856–1950) became one of Ibsen's most vocal and influential supporters. A prolific writer and a (Fabian) socialist, Shaw delighted in puncturing time-honored assumptions about human behavior and exposing various forms of social posturing. In an early play, *Arms and the Man* (1894), he spoofed romantic notions of love and war and satirized the then-popular comic form, the well-made play. Later, he turned to consider contemporary social situations in plays like *Major Barbara* (1905), *The Doctor's Dilemma* (1906), *Getting Married* (1908), and *Heartbreak House* (1914–1919). Unlike many realists, Shaw always retained his sense of humor; he almost always wrote comedies, and their popularity did much to ensure the final acceptance of realistic drama in England before the close of World War I.

CHEKHOV.   In Russia, realism took a still different turn. Anton Chekhov (1860–1904) scored his first success in 1898 when *The Seagull* was produced at the Moscow Art Theatre. Within seven years, he had contributed *The Three Sisters* (1900), *Uncle Vanya* (1889), and *The Cherry Orchard* (1902) to the growing literature of the realistic style. Chekhov's plays differed from those of Ibsen and Shaw in their tendency toward poetic expression and symbolic meanings. Chekhov's manipulation of language, with careful rhythms, measured pauses, deliberate banalities, and artful repetitions, produced a sense of reality based on compelling psychological truths as well as a degree of music and allusion uncommon in prose dramas. His incorporation of symbols into the texts (often the plays' titles bear clues) served to extend the plays' significance beyond the drab daily lives of the central characters. Chekhov took for his study the daily lives of people trapped in social situations. In some ways, he foretold the Russian Revolution by depicting the isolation of the aristocracy and its inevitable extinction. In another sense, he portrayed the loneliness and the comic desperation of all people who continue to hope while living in a hopeless situation, who persist in believing that help will come when none, in fact, is to be had.

NATURALISTIC DRAMA

Among the most successful playwrights in the naturalistic style were August Strindberg (1849–1912), Gerhart Hauptmann (1862–1946), Émile Zola (1849–1902), and Maxim Gorky (1868–1936).

PROBLEMS WITH REALISM

Even before realism became the mainstream of theatrical life in Europe and America, some writers and theorists had begun to chafe under its limitations. Four questions in particular were the focus of discussion and concern:

1. *How can realistic drama be kept interesting?*

Before realism, most serious dramatists had depicted characters who were considerably removed from everyday experience—princes, kings, demigods—who participated in events that were out of the ordinary: a war, a national crisis, a cosmic struggle. The plays were set in faraway times and places, environments that were, in themselves, often mysterious and compelling. When confronting a crisis, these exalted characters burst into passages of extreme lyricism in which the full resources of the language (rhythm, rhyme, and metaphor) were marshaled to produce heights of emotional intensity.

But realistic drama, by definition, portrayed ordinary people involved in mundane situations. Their language necessarily resembled everyday conversation and their clothing reflected their middle- or lower-class status. What then, made them interesting? Audience pleasure seemed to depend largely on the factor of *recognition* alone. Although this factor is a very potent one, it was being asked to carry the entire weight of provoking and maintaining interest, a burden that proved too heavy for many dramas.

2. *How can realistic drama be made significant?*

Traditionally, in serious drama, playwrights depicted serious actions that were of consequence to a large range of people—a nation or even a world. But realistic dramas typically dealt with working men and women as they lived out rather humdrum lives. If no more was at stake than the happiness of a single individual or a small family, who beyond their immediate friends would find it significant?

Some realistic dramatists increased the significance of their plays' actions by having the protagonist represent something bigger, something more gen-

Figure 14-23. **Naturalism.** Although similar to realism, naturalism stressed the problems of the social underclass, setting the plays in sordid surroundings. Here, Maxim Gorky's *The Lower Depths* in Moscow. Compare with the French production in Figure 14-18.

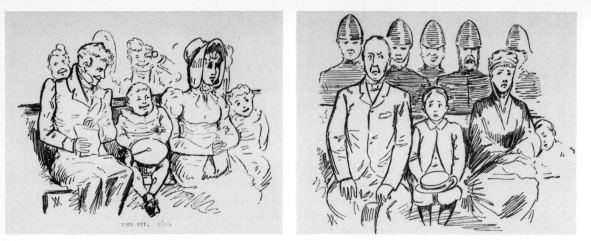

Figure 14-24. **Changing Audiences.** A cartoonist contrasts a happy and relaxed family attending the theatre around 1800 (left) with the same family in 1880 (right), calling attention not only to the repression associated with the age of Queen Victoria but also to the increasing passivity of theatre audiences in the late nineteenth century.

eral. Willy Loman in *Death of a Salesman*, for example, was made to stand for all salesmen, or all working men. Such a solution, however, pulled against the very philosophical assumptions on which realism was based. Perhaps more seriously, abstractions are often undramatic. Poetry and the novel, where the reader can return time and again to study and consider the text, are usually better media for abstractions and symbolizations than are plays, where the living presence of the actors encourages specificity and where the basis of the form is action rather than idea or word.

3. *What is the role of the audience in a realistic theatre?*

Even though the stage in realistic drama was a close reproduction of the real world and the actors a duplication of everyday people, the separation of the audience from the dramatic action in "fourth-wall realism" (as signified by the presence of a proscenium arch) was greater than ever before. The conventions of the style required the audience to sit in a darkened auditorium and to watch silently as a separate world unfolded behind the proscenium arch. The actors, for their part, behaved as if the audience were not there, turning their backs and mumbling lines in an attempt to reproduce the inarticulateness of everyday conversations. The result was a world on the stage quite separate from the real world where the audience sat. It is ironic that realistic drama and staging, which had seemed to bring the world of the stage closer to that of the audience, ended by separating them to a degree unparalleled in the history of the theatre.

4. *How can the theatrical event be kept probable (or believable)?*

All playwrights, of course, must construct plays that are probable, or believable, if they are to capture the interest and the commitment of an audience. But only the realist additionally required that the world in the play resemble, on a one-to-one basis, the world outside: the theatrical scenery was to be a photographic likeness of the outside world, and the actors were to be the embodiment of everyday people. To produce the familiar and to

make it believable proved too demanding a chore for many realistic playwrights.

Because of these problems, a variety of alternatives to realistic plays and
staging were being proposed and tested by the 1890s.

The Commercial Mainstream

1850–1900

Commercial houses in France, England, and America during the last half of
the nineteenth century featured plays of the sort popularized by the Romantic
theatre. The most popular of them ran for dozens, even hundreds, of nights
and played to audiences of all social classes and artistic tastes.

REVIVALS.   Shakespeare's plays were produced often and were given elaborate settings designed to reproduce faithfully the illusion of specific locales
mentioned in the text. "Illustrating" Shakespeare became popular, and so
The Merchant of Venice used real water for onstage canals, and *Romeo and
Juliet* reproduced in detail the historical Juliet's tomb. Countless plays from
the first half of the nineteenth century and a few from the eighteenth were
also revived. Most popular, of course, were the spectacular melodramas,

Figure 14-25. **Illustrating Shakespeare.** Continuing interest in antiquarianism
led to productions that sought to recapture with complete accuracy the details of
the past, as in this production of *The Merchant of Venice.*

which thrilled audiences by their elaborate special effects and exotic costumes.

COMEDIES.   The most popular playwright of the period was probably the Frenchman Victorien Sardou (1831–1908), who is best remembered for well-made plays like *A Scrap of Paper* (1860). Although less well known today, Sardou's historical spectacles set in exotic locales were applauded by contemporaries for the lavishness of their costumes and scenery and the correctness of their many details. For the famous actress Sarah Bernhardt (1844–1923), virtually a cult figure of the age, Sardou wrote plays like *La Tosca* (1887), from which Giacomo Puccini's opera was derived. Although seldom produced today, Sardou's plays swept the stages of America and England as well as those of France during the last half of the nineteenth century. Their hold on the commercial theatre caused George Bernard Shaw to denounce English theatre of his day as mere "Sardoodledom."

Two of Sardou's compatriots were particularly successful authors of farce. Eugène Labiche (1815–1888), with *The Italian Straw Hat* (1851), and George Feydeau (1862–1921), with *A Flea in Her Ear* (1907), set the style for plays based on a highly complicated set of adventures unfolding at rapid-fire pace amidst rooms with many doors, through which a variety of odd characters bustled on their way to and from ever greater misadventures. Because these plays often dealt with amorous misunderstandings, they were the forerunners of the still popular "French bedroom farce."

Figure 14-26. **Boucicault's *The Octoroon.*** Clearly a melodrama, but one that included consideration of a contemporary social problem: American slavery.

MELODRAMA.   Among the most important popular writers of serious drama was the Irish-American Dion Boucicault (1822–1890). Specializing in melodramas, Boucicault fused sentimentality with sensationalism, letting the stories unfold against a background rich in local color. He captured large audiences on two continents with works like *The Corsican Brothers* (1852), *The Poor of New York* (1857), and *The Octoroon* (1859). The popularity of his plays gave Boucicault a degree of financial security virtually unknown at the time. He demanded and received a percentage of receipts for each performance of his plays, thus instituting the practice of *paying royalties to playwrights*. By 1886, an international copyright agreement had been instituted, in part because of Boucicault's influence.

Although none was so well known as Boucicault, a number of other dramatists of the time thrilled audiences with plays that featured heroes tied to railroad tracks, heroines trapped in burning buildings, onstage eruptions of volcanoes, chariot races, and other spectacular effects.

Probably the most popular play in the world during this period was an American melodrama called *Uncle Tom's Cabin* (1852), based on the novel by Harriet Beecher Stowe. A highly romanticized view of slavery in the Old South, the play included scenes of slaves escaping across the ice-clogged Ohio River (hotly pursued by dogs and slave traders), little Eva being carried to heaven by angels amidst the weeping of her family and friends, and Uncle Tom being cruelly beaten by that villain of villains, Simon Legree. The success of the play was unprecedented. By 1879, there were twelve different Tom companies (theatre groups producing no plays except *Uncle Tom's Cabin*) crisscrossing America. By 1899, there were between four hundred and five hundred such companies, with some actors making a life's work of "Tomming," never acting in—or even seeing—another play. Various versions played in Germany, France, and England, and twelve different American versions were in print in 1900. The play's popularity remained strong through World War I, when more than a dozen companies still traveled about performing only this one play.

MUSICAL ENTERTAINMENTS.   Although operettas like those of Jacques Offenbach (1819–1889) were popular, they were eclipsed by the work of two Englishmen, William S. Gilbert (1836–1911) and Arthur Sullivan (1842–1900), whose *H.M.S. Pinafore* (1878), *The Pirates of Penzance* (1879), *The Mikado* (1885), and *The Gondoliers* (1889), among others, remain popular to this day.

In America, burlesque (and its cousin, vaudeville) were quite popular. Originally little more than parodies and variety acts, both were well established in the American theatre during the first half of the century. Burlesque became overwhelmingly a male entertainment after Lydia Thompson's "British Blondes" took America by storm in 1869. Increasingly thereafter, the popularity of burlesque depended on a combination of spectacles, song, dance, and female legs. Soon after World War I, "striptease" was added, and burlesque moved still further to the outskirts of respectability. Vaudeville,

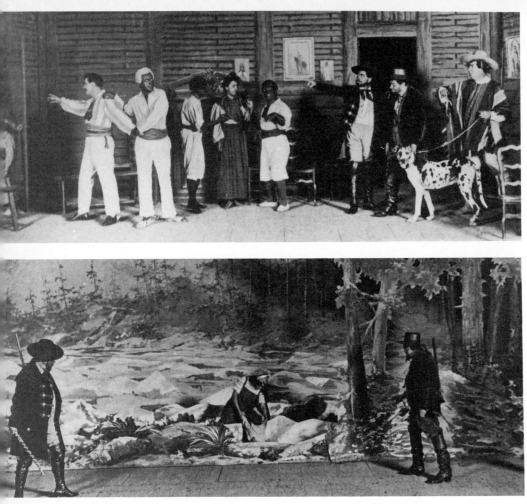

Figure 14-27. **Uncle Tom's Cabin.** Some actors made their entire careers in performances of this single play. Because the black slaves were almost always performed by white actors in black face, however, *Uncle Tom's Cabin* did not help promote the careers of black performers in this country. Here, a French production. *(From* Le Théâtre.)

on the other hand, flourished as a family entertainment, some of its stars moving to radio and the movies in the 1930s.

THEATRICAL STARS. The pleasure of theatregoers, however, was not entirely bound up with the plays themselves, for the period was one of theatrical stars of the highest rank. Many leading actors traveled from city to city to play starring roles with resident stock companies; others traveled with their entire productions (cast, costumes, and scenery) across continents to satisfy audiences who thronged to the theatres to see the latest star. France, in addition to Sarah Bernhardt, produced Benoît Constant Coquelin (1841–1909). England's most famous actor was Henry Irving (1838–1905), whose performances as Mathias in a now-forgotten melodrama named *The Bells* (1871) spanned thirty-four years and eight hundred performances. That, together with his Shakespearean successes, led to his being knighted, the first English actor to be so honored. In America, the leading actors were Joseph Jefferson (1829–1905), whose fame rested primarily on his portrayal of the title role in *Rip Van Winkle;* Edwin Booth (1833–1893), regarded by his contemporaries as Shakespeare's finest interpreter but probably remembered today by more people as the brother of President Lincoln's assassin; and James O'Neill (1847–1920), who made an acting career in *The Count of Monte Cristo* (1883) and fathered America's highly regarded native dramatist Eugene O'Neill.

COMMERCIAL PRODUCERS.   During this period, too, the financial organization behind commercial production began to change. The *actor-managers* (stars who also funded and administered their own productions) like Irving gradually gave way to the modern *producer,* a person not an actor—and eventually not a theatre artist at all—who undertook finance and organization. In America, early producers were Augustin Daly (1836–1899), also a playwright and director; and David Belasco (1854–1931), a playwright and director famous for his meticulous (and well-advertised) commercial realism.

1900–1960

Perhaps by 1900, but certainly by the end of World War I (1918), realism in the drama and in theatrical production had been widely accepted in the commercial houses of France, England, and America. By the 1920s, the Parisian boulevard theatres regularly played serious pieces dealing with social

Figure 14-28. **David Belasco as Producer.** Businessmen like Augustin Daly and David Belasco emerged as producers at the turn of the century. Here, Belasco's production of his own *The Girl of the Golden West,* a clear example of commercial realism. *(Courtesy of the Theatre Collection of the New York Public Library.)*

problems, and audiences no longer found them controversial. The commercial theatres in London found both Ibsen and Shaw palatable and played realistic dramas as well as sophisticated domestic comedies by authors like Noel Coward (1899–1973) and Somerset Maugham (1874–1965).

THE UNITED STATES IN THE 1920S.   Broadway was booming. Between 200 and 275 new productions a year were not unusual. The cost of a production was as low as $2,000 for some of the simple pieces and seldom more than $10,000, even for elaborate realistic plays. New theatres were being built to keep up with the demand as audiences flocked to attend. For an average price of three dollars, a patron could buy the best seat in the house. The long run was an established theatrical fact. Inevitably, with the enormous vitality and the great number of original plays, many were trivial and some were downright awful (such plays were called *turkeys*, because weak shows were customarily scheduled to open on Thanksgiving Day in the hopes of improving their ticket sales). But many of the plays were memorable; some are still staged today.

George S. Kaufman (1889–1961), a master of the wisecrack, wrote (both alone and with a variety of collaborators, the most constant of whom was Moss Hart) a series of zany comedies like *You Can't Take It with You* and *The Man Who Came to Dinner.* Several sentimentalized versions of urban life and gangsterland formed the basis of popular melodramas of the decade like *The Front Page* and *Broadway.*

The Ziegfeld Follies was enormously popular with audiences; this entertainment featured songs, dances, and variety acts and enjoyed the services of the nation's favorite composer, Irving Berlin. But musical comedy took on a new shape after Jerome Kern and Oscar Hammerstein produced *Showboat* (1927) and demonstrated that musicals in which music was well integrated with the characters and the story were even more appealing than old-fashioned variety acts.

The Theatre Guild (founded in 1919) was the most dynamic producing organization of the decade. Early in its career, it attacked the provincialism of American theatre by importing a series of foreign works by important and controversial new authors: Tolstoy's *The Power of Darkness* (1920), Strindberg's *The Dance of Death* (1920), Ibsen's *Peer Gynt* (1923), and a large number of plays by G. B. Shaw. By the mid-1920s, American playwrights were competing with the foreigners as authors of serious realistic drama, and so the Guild produced new plays by Elmer Rice, Sidney Howard, S. N. Behrman, and most of all Eugene O'Neill (1888–1953). Between March 1924 and January 1925, five of his plays were appearing in New York: *Welded, All God's Chillun Got Wings, Desire Under the Elms, The Fountain,* and *The Great God Brown.* By the end of the decade, his plays were producing profits in excess of those awarded to many pieces of commercial fluff. In the short period between 1926 and 1928, the Guild produced fourteen plays, thereby leading Broadway into one of its most exultant periods and establishing serious realistic drama as an accepted part of the Broadway theatre.

Figure 14-29. **Significant Commercial Theatre.** Important foreign playwrights to reach America's commercial theatre included George Bernard Shaw, whose *Mrs. Warren's Profession* is shown here in a production at the University of Wyoming. *(Directed by Gladys Crane, scenery by Don Seay, and costumes by Lee Hodgson.)*

After 1930, the Guild's influence waned as its finances became more precarious, and, in an attempt to improve its balance sheet, it moved closer to the practices of other commercial producers, finally becoming scarcely distinguishable from them.

THE UNITED STATES IN THE 1930S. The Group Theatre, after its founding in 1931, became a militant voice for anticommercial theatres in New York. The Group focused attention on various social causes, particularly those relevant to poor and downtrodden classes, and flirted with government displeasure for their presumably leftist leanings. More important, the Group popularized an American version of Stanislavski's acting techniques (called the "Method") and established a visual style for American plays that came to be called *selective* (or *simplified*) *realism*. When it produced Clifford Odets's play *Waiting for Lefty* (1935), the Group stunned audiences, launched the career of Odets, and heralded the arrival of "relevant" social drama in New York.

Other serious dramatists were at work, as well. Elmer Rice received a Pulitzer Prize for his naturalistic portrayal of urban life in *Street Scene* (1929). Maxwell Anderson contributed a variety of successful plays: some, like *Elizabeth the Queen*, were experiments with verse drama in a pseudo-Shakespearean style; and in *Winterset* (1936), Anderson even tried to write a modern verse tragedy about young people caught up in urban gangs and street crime. Challenging Anderson as leading authors of the period were Robert Sherwood (1896–1955) and Lillian Hellman (1905–1984). Sherwood's early success, *The Petrified Forest* (1935), was followed closely by *Idiot's Delight*, which

335

won a Pulitzer prize in 1936. Lillian Hellman burst on the scene in 1934 with *The Children's Hour,* a play with allusions to lesbianism in a girl's school, and then cemented her initial success with *The Little Foxes* (1939) and *Watch on the Rhine* (1941), a warning about Nazi Germany.

Musicals were in their heyday, with composers like Cole Porter (1891–1964) and George Gershwin (1898–1937). Porter's long career peaked with his score for *Kiss Me, Kate* (1948), a musical based loosely on Shakespeare's *The Taming of the Shrew,* but, as early as 1920, he had been contributing tunes to America's musical theater like "Let's Do It," "What Is This Thing Called Love?" "Night and Day," and "Begin the Beguine." His biggest hit during the 1930s was the score for *Anything Goes* (1934), starring Ethel Merman. With a very different but equally substantial talent, Gershwin wrote songs for a variety of musicals before he finally hit his stride with *Of Thee I Sing* (1931), a stinging satire of American politics for which his music captured the lethal and jeering quality of the book by George S. Kaufman and Morrie Ryskind. Gershwin is best remembered for his *Porgy and Bess* (1935), an American classic that has played in theatres and opera houses all over the world. People still hum "Summertime," "I Got Plenty o' Nuttin'," and "It Ain't Necessarily So." Gershwin's fame, of course, is not limited to his Broadway credits. His pioneering work in modern music with pieces like "Rhapsody in Blue" and "An American in Paris" speeded the acceptance of American jazz as a legitimate musical form.

But perhaps the most exciting development in the American theatre of the 1930s was also the least characteristic. In 1935, the federal government launched the Federal Theatre Project, a program designed to assist the vast number of theatre artists who had been thrown out of work by the worsening Depression. Part of the program's excitement was its national character, for the Federal Theatre established units in many states—California as well as New York, North Carolina as well as Michigan—and revitalized a sagging industry by introducing both new forms and new artists to the American scene. In New York, for example, the first "living newspaper," a kind of staged documentary, dealt with society's most pressing problems: housing, farm prices, and war. Not surprisingly, when anti-Communism became the cry of government, living newspapers were denounced as Communist plots. In 1939, by failing to provide appropriations, the government closed its first far-reaching experiment in the support of the arts. But before its demise, the Federal Theatre had spawned a number of new artists and theatres, most notably Orson Welles (1915–1985), John Houseman (b. 1902), and the Mercury Theatre.

Quite different from the strident Federal Theatre was the benign voice of a new playwright who devised a simple drama of life in small-town USA. With *Our Town* (1938), Thornton Wilder (1897–1975) affirmed human greatness at a time when America was recovering from a depression and listening to the sounds from Europe of an impending second world war. Requiring no scenery and few properties, the play quickly became a mainstay of high school, community, and college theatres across the land. Also in 1938, Wilder

Figure 14-30. *The Matchmaker* **Made Musical.** Thornton Wilder's comedy, *The Matchmaker*, was made into the popular musical *Hello, Dolly!*, shown here in a production at the University of Maryland. *(Directed by Ronald O'Leary.)*

wrote *The Merchant of Yonkers*, which failed in its original production but enjoyed a successful revival as *The Matchmaker* (1954) and then, set to music, as *Hello, Dolly!* (1964), one of America's most popular and enduring musicals.

Despite the many excellent playwrights of the 1930s, the American commercial theatre was in trouble by the end of the decade. The Depression had made money scarce at the same time that other forms of entertainment began to compete for the public's entertainment dollar. Spectator sports and movies (particularly after Al Jolson talked in *The Jazz Singer* in 1927) demanded an increasing share of the shrinking dollar at the same time that theatrical unions were exercising new muscle and demanding better wages from a theatre less able than before to provide them. And the nation was moving toward involvement in a second disastrous world war.

THE UNITED STATES IN THE 1940S AND 1950S. During the war (1941–1945), Broadway artists supported the war effort, revived earlier successes, and occasionally produced a successful new show like Mary Chase's *Harvey*, a charming look at an aging man and his (imagined) six-foot-tall rabbit, and Garson Kanin's *Born Yesterday*, with Judy Holliday as the dumb blond girlfriend of a war profiteer. The decade's most exciting event, however, was the first performance of the musical *Oklahoma!* (1943), which lifted audiences from the ugly realities of a foreign war and returned them to a happier time

Figure 14-31. **Tennessee Williams.**
One of the most important American
playrights since World War II,
Tennessee Williams often wrote memory
plays like *The Glass Menagerie. (Murray State University. Directed by Mark Malinauskas.)*

in rural America. The musical, by Richard Rogers and Oscar Hammerstein II, was brilliantly choreographed by Agnes de Mille, with the result that ballet and dance became an integral part of musicals for the next several decades. Rodgers and Hammerstein, encouraged by the success of *Oklahoma!,* followed with, among others, *Carousel* (1945) and *South Pacific* (1947), musical plays that still form part of our repertory.

The war years launched the careers of two major American playwrights whose works were to dominate the stage for the next decade and to firmly establish American realism and simplified staging as the styles of the 1940s and 1950s. Tennessee Williams (1914–1983) won the Drama Critics Circle Award for his first major Broadway production, *The Glass Menagerie* (1945), a wistful memory play vaguely reminiscent of the impressionists and Chekhov. In 1947, *A Streetcar Named Desire* reached Broadway and Williams was hailed as a writer of the first rank; and Marlon Brando was propelled to stardom for his portrayal of the inarticulate and slovenly Stanley Kowalski, a success that popularized the "Method" as America's contribution to the acting of realistic and naturalistic plays. Elia Kazan's reputation as a director of great subtlety and sensitivity was assured, and "selective realism" was established as the model of designers for years to come. For this play, Williams received both the Pulitzer Prize and the Drama Critics Circle Award.

The Off-Broadway movement is usually dated from 1952, when Williams's *Summer and Smoke* gained critical acclaim in a production at Circle in the Square, the first major hit in a theatre located below Forty-second Street in thirty years. Although some critics consider Williams's subsequent plays inferior to his earlier efforts, many are memorable pieces that continue to find production around the country, among them *Cat on a Hot Tin Roof* (1954), *Sweet Bird of Youth* (1959), and *The Night of the Iguana* (1961).

Just as Williams's realism differed from that first introduced in Europe in the late nineteenth century, so, too, did Arthur Miller's, but in another direction. *All My Sons* (1947) told of an American businessman who knowingly sold inferior products for America's war effort in order to turn a profit. Despite the Drama Critics Circle Award, the play was banned in occupied Europe after the war and was denounced by some as a smear on the American business community. Miller was under suspicion, therefore, when he wrote *Death of a Salesman* (1947), an acknowledged American masterpiece. In this play, realistic scenes are interspersed with remembered scenes as seen through the eyes and ears of the disordered protagonist, Willy Loman. *Death of a Salesman*, as directed by Elia Kazan and designed by Jo Mielziner, won both a Pulitzer Prize and the Drama Critics Circle Award and further promoted the conventions of American realism. Although Miller continued to write

Figure 14-32. **Arthur Miller.** Miller's most famous works are *Death of a Salesman* and *The Crucible*, the latter shown here in a production at Essex Community College. *(Photo by Norman McCullough.)*

important American plays, some critics feel that he never again attained his early accomplishments with plays like *The Crucible* (1953), perhaps a response to Senator Joseph McCarthy's witch hunt for Communists in American society; *A View from the Bridge* (1955); *After the Fall* (1964); and *The Price* (1968).

Although the successes of Williams and Miller tended to obscure the works of other promising writers, plays like *Picnic* and *Come Back, Little Sheba* and *Bus Stop* (all by William Inge) and *The Member of the Wedding* (by Carson McCullers) and musicals like *Finian's Rainbow* and *Brigadoon* were also popular.

But during the 1940s and 1950s, despite the advent of Williams and Miller, the Broadway theatre appeared to be in serious trouble. Its death was often predicted—and not without justification. Whereas, in 1930–1931, there had been 187 new productions, by 1940–1941 there were only 72. Theatres were being abandoned, torn down, or converted into movie houses; some were even being used for girlie shows. The block around Times Square degenerated into an atmosphere more reminiscent of a carnival or a sex bazaar than of the center of the American theatre. Many legitimate theatres were permanently dark. Theatre real estate had been made unprofitable by the soaring costs of land in Manhattan and by the strict fire codes that had been imposed. Just when it appeared that things could not get worse, television for the first time covered a presidential convention and clearly established itself as an important national entertainment industry (1948). Clearly, the theatrical mainstream was in trouble.

Apparently the death of the American theatre was greatly exaggerated, however, for by the mid-1960s, Broadway's vitality and strength were clearly on the upsurge.

The Avant-garde: 1890s–1960

The years between 1890 and 1960 saw a proliferation of *isms:* neoromanticism, formalism, symbolism, impressionism, expressionism, constructivism, futurism, absurdism, and so on. Each strove to address and solve one or more of the problems inherent in realism. As each developed, grew, and declined, the mainstream of realism shifted slightly to accommodate various attributes of the competing styles. As a result, although realism remained the mainstream of theatre from about 1900 through 1960, it shifted perceptibly throughout that period as it incorporated first one and then another new approach to playwriting or staging.

Impressionism

Impressionism (fl. 1890s) was a style that sought to capture and reproduce the fleeting moments of awareness that were believed to constitute the essence of human existence. By reproducing faithfully these fleeting glimpses, art could provide insights into the truth that lay underneath the external world. Probably the playwright who wrote most successfully in the style was Maurice Maeterlinck (1862–1949). In short plays like *The Intruder* (1890) and *The Interior* (1894) and in longer plays like *Pelléas and Mélisande* (1892) and *The Blue Bird* (1908), Maeterlinck presented a world far removed from that of mundane reality. Introspection and subjectivity permeate the plays, which are typically moody and mysterious works hinting at a life controlled by unseen and inexplicable forces manipulating passive and often perplexed characters. The actions seem hazy, distant, out of focus; indeed, in the theatre, the plays were often played behind gauzes (*scrims*) or clouds of fog and moved between patches of light, dark, and shadow.

For impressionists like Maeterlinck, a play aimed to convey intuitions about a truth more profound than the tangible, objective, external world of the realists. Through symbols, it alluded to a significance beyond the immediate, and through its language and stories it aspired to arouse interest by its exoticism.

Impressionism in the drama was not of lasting importance, perhaps because its emphasis on internal states and spiritual glimpses was better suited to the page than to the stage. Some of its techniques, however, were appealing and

Figure 15-1. **Impressionism.** Among the earliest reactions against realism were the impressionistic plays of Maeterlinck, whose *The Blue Bird* is shown here in a London production. *(From* Le Théâtre.*)*

so were adopted by realists like Ibsen (in his later plays), Chekhov, and, more recently, Tennessee Williams.

Symbolism

The impressionists were closely allied with the symbolists, of whom the most famous were the theatrical practitioners Adolphe Appia (1862–1928) and Gordon Craig (1872–1966). Appia believed that artistic unity was the fundamental goal of theatrical production and that lighting was the element best able to fuse all other elements into an artistic whole. Like music, its auditory counterpart, light was capable of continual change to reflect shifting moods and emotions within the play. Like music, too, light could be orchestrated by variations in its direction, intensity, and color to produce a rhythm designed to underscore the dramatic action. Because he found an aesthetic contradiction between the three-dimensional actor and the two-dimensional floor set at right angles to the two-dimensional painted scenes still popular in his day, Appia sought ways to provide the stage floor and scenery with mass so that the actor could better blend with them. He solved the problem in part by devising three-dimensional settings composed of series of steps, ramps, and platforms, among which the living actor could comfortably move.

Figure 15-2. **Symbolism.** Appia's design for Wagner's *Parsifal* reveals the designer's interest in the effects of mass, light, and shadow. *(From Oskar Fischel, Das Moderne Buhnenbild. Berlin: Verlag Ernst Wasmuth A.-G., 1923.)*

Like Appia, Craig opposed scenic illusions and favored instead a simple visual statement that eliminated inessential details and avoided photographic reproductions of specific places. His emphasis was on the manipulation of line and mass to achieve, first, a unity of design and, ultimately, a unity for the total production. Although Craig placed less emphasis on the importance of the actor and the text than Appia, they agreed on the importance of the visual elements of the production. Perhaps it would not be an injustice to designate Appia as the formulator of the theories that Craig later popularized. The theories of Appia and Craig gained a secure foothold in theatrical practice following World War I.

Expressionism

Whereas impressionism sought to present echoes of a transitory and mysterious truth, *expressionism* (fl. 1910s–1930s) usually focused on political and social questions. If impressionism produced a dreamlike vision, expressionism created a stage world closer to the nightmare. The plays were often didactic and cautioned the world against the impending cataclysms to be caused by uncontrolled industrialism, rampant impersonalization, and other threats posed by the modern industrial state. Seldom did the plays tell a simple story; more often, they developed as episodic examinations or demonstrations of a central thesis. They customarily unfolded in a world of bizarre and garish colors, jagged angles, and oddly proportioned objects (perhaps because they were often told through the mind of the protagonist, whose mental vision was distorted). Actors, often dressed identically, moved in mechanical or puppetlike ways and often spoke in disconnected or telegraphic conversations. They bore names of types rather than people: The Mother, The Son, The Cipher, and so on. Conventional ideas of time and space collapsed; in their place were elastic units where years could fly by as seconds crept and adjacent objects appeared as if seen through the opposite ends of a telescope.

Expressionism as a movement was most developed in Germany. Its two leading playwrights were Georg Kaiser (1878–1945), whose best-known plays are *From Morn to Midnight* (1916) and the *Gas* trilogy, and Ernst Toller (1893–1939), whose best-known works are *Man and the Masses* (1921) and *Hurrah, We Live* (1927).

Expressionistic plays are seldom produced today outside university theatres, but their influence has been substantial for three reasons. First, many of the techniques were adapted and used by the growing film industry. Second, some expressionistic techniques were adapted to the needs of important playwrights in the realistic mainstream, notably (in America) Arthur Miller, Eugene O'Neill, and Edward Albee. Third, German expressionism was an early influence on Erwin Piscator and Bertolt Brecht, whose "epic theatre"

Figure 15-3. **Expressionism.** A nightmare world of trapped humanity is seen here in Toller's *Man and the Masses. (From* The Theatre.*)*

became a major force in European and American theatres during the 1940s, 1950s, and 1960s. Staging devices popularized by expressionism (and constructivism), although softened, continue to influence designers in contemporary theatre and film down to the present day.

Constructivism

In Russia, the practices of Vsevolod Myerhold (1874–1940) paralleled many of those associated with the German expressionists. Although early in his career Myerhold directed experimental works for Stanislavski, during the 1920s he devoted himself to developing a theatrical art suitable for the machine age. He relied on two major techniques: *biomechanics* and *constructivism. Biomechanics* referred to a training system and performance style for actors: they were to be well-trained "machines" for carrying out the assignments given them, and so they needed rigorous physical training in ballet, gymnastics, circus techniques, and so on. *Constructivism* referred to Myerhold's conclusions that scenery should not attempt to represent any particular place but that it should provide a "machine" on which actors could perform. In practice, Myerhold's sets were often elaborate combinations of platforms, steps, ramps, wheels, and trapezes. The goal of both biomechanics and

Figure 15-4. **Constructivism.** Popularized in Russia by Myerhold, constructivist settings were conceived as machines on which actors could work rather than as representations of specific places. *(From* Theatre Arts.*)*

constructivism was to undercut the realist's emphasis on internal motivation for actors and literal representation in scenery and costumes and to retheatricalize the theatre.

Absurdism

Just after World War II, several new playwrights caused a temporary flurry of excitement. Not comprising a self-conscious movement, these playwrights were nonetheless grouped together and given the name *absurdists* by a contemporary scholar, Martin Esslin. *Absurdism* (fl. 1940s and 1950s) was itself a blend of earlier abortive experiments of the French avant-garde. With *dadaism* (fl. 1920s), it shared an emphasis on life's meaninglessness and art's irrelevancy and a commitment to irrationality and nihilism as appropriate responses to life and living. With *surrealism* (fl. 1920s), it viewed the source of insight as a person's subconscious mind. Most important, with *existentialism* (fl. 1930s and 1940s), it sought an answer to the plaguing question: What does it mean to exist and to be? Jean-Paul Sartre (1905–1980), a philosopher turned playwright and a major advocate of existentialism, sought to establish a code of life based on a consistent atheism, where the absence of absolute moral laws left human beings adrift in a world without order or purpose: each person must define his or her own value system and then act accordingly.

Absurdism stressed that the world was unreasonable, illogical, incongruous, and out of harmony. The word *absurd*, then, meant not *rediculous* but *without meaning.* According to the absurdists, the only order in life was what a person constructed; the only moral systems were those that the individual defined. To incorporate these views into dramatic form, the absurdists abandoned telling a story in favor of communicating an experience; they abandoned a dramatic unity based on causality and replaced it with one whose source, and indeed whose very presence, was not always clear to the uninitiated. The plays were often constructed as a circle (ending just where they began, after displaying a series of unrelated incidents) and as the intensification of a single event (ending just where they had begun but in the midst of more people or more objects). Usually, the puzzling quality of the plays came from the devaluation of language as a carrier of meaning: in the plays, *what happens* on stage often transcends and contradicts *what is said* there. The tonal and rhythmic dimensions of words are often more important to the play than is their literal sense. The absurdists, unlike their most important predecessors, the existentialists, did not discuss and argue about the meaninglessness of life; they simply presented it concretely onstage, using actors to participate in apparently senseless non sequiturs amidst what seemed, on the surface, to be inarticulate and incomprehensible exchanges of dialogue.

Although absurdists like Samuel Beckett (b. 1906), Eugène Ionesco (b. 1912), and Edward Albee (b. 1928) were exceedingly popular for a time, few of their plays find contemporary production outside the educational theatre—Beckett's *Waiting for Godot* (1953) and Albee's *Who's Afraid of Virginia Woolf?* are obvious exceptions. Still, many of the techniques popularized by absurdists appear in the works of contemporary playwrights.

Figure 15-5. **Surrealism.** A precursor of Absurdism, surrealism denied the truth of surface reality and sought instead insights from within. Here, *The Breasts of Teiresias* obviously intends the audience to know it is watching theatre, not life. (*From Huntley Carter,* The New Spirit in the European Theatre, 1914-1924. *London: Benn, 1925.*)

Brecht and Artaud

Although all of the styles described here have had an impact on today's theatre, the theories and practices of Bertolt Brecht and Antonin Artaud have probably been more influential than any others. These two theorists operated from quite different sets of assumptions about the nature of theatre and the purpose of art, but they shared a disdain for realism with all of its trappings. Although it may be a falsification, at least in part, it may be useful to regard Brecht as developing from the expressionistic German traditions and Artaud from the impressionistic and surrealistic traditions of the French theatre. Together, their theories can help account for much of the experimentation during the 1960s and 1970s.

BERTOLT BRECHT AND EPIC THEATRE

Bertolt Brecht (1898–1956) believed that theatre should educate *citizens* (participants in a political system) in how to bring about socially responsible change. He saw theatre as a way of making a controversial topic easier to consider. His commitment to a socially responsive theatre doubtless came, in part, from his being both Jewish and leftist at a time when Hitler was rising to power in Germany.

Traditional theatres, whether those of Wagner or Saxe-Meiningen, sought

Figure 15-6. **Brecht and Epic Theatre.** Costumed actors playing the gods in Brecht's *The Good Woman of Setzuan*. Compare with the original design in the color insert. *(Designs by Dennis Parker, USAA.)*

an illusion that allowed the members of the audience to believe in and identify with the onstage actions. In such theatres, Brecht observed, audiences reached a state of self-oblivion: "Looking around, one discovers more or less motionless bodies in a curious state . . . they have their eyes open, but they don't look, they stare . . . they stare at the stage as if spellbound." As Brecht was a Marxist and viewed theatre as an instrument for change, he objected to a theatre that mesmerized its audiences and made them passive. Brecht therefore strove to redefine the relationship between the theatre, its audience, and the society at large. He proposed that if he jarred audiences periodically out of their identification with the action, he would succeed in shaking their complacency and in forcing them to think about what they saw onstage. He sought, therefore, alternately to engage and estrange his audiences, a technique he called *Verfremdungseffekt* (usually translated as the *alienation effect* or, simply, the *A-effect*).

To achieve alienation required artists to work in new ways. Actors were encouraged to hold themselves distant from their roles by speaking the stage directions out loud during the rehearsal process, to think of their characters in the third person rather than in the first person, and to use the past tense rather than the present tense when talking of their work. Such procedures made an actor a commentator rather than an impersonator, an evaluator of the action as well as a demonstrator of it.

Brecht urged lighting designers to expose the instruments to remind the spectators that they were in a theatre and that the illumination was coming from a high-wattage lamp rather than from the sun. If a set was to represent a town, it should look like a town that had been built for the theatre; it should not be built with the goal of "fooling" the audience into accepting it as a real town. Theatrical elements should be juxtaposed in unexpected ways so that each could make an independent contribution and comment on the ideas of the play. Thus, if the set was to make one point, the costumes should make a different one; a grisly story of war and atrocity might be set to a lively tune with a lilting melody; the seeming incongruity would force the audience to consider the apparent conflict of elements and to draw conclusions about the absurdity of war. In short, Brecht proposed that each artist make an independent contribution to the production and to the didactic purpose of the script and that each element be used not to create an atmosphere that encouraged the audience to identify with the action (as in traditional theatre) but to reinforce the didactic purpose of the drama.

Brecht was a playwright as well as a theorist and a director. His plays typically consisted of a series of short episodes connected by songs, narratives, placards, or similar devices. The purpose was to engage the interest and belief of the audience (within each episode) and then to break the spell by forcing the spectator to think about and evaluate the meaning and implications of the episodes (by manipulating various materials between them). Brecht once described the way a play should work in this way: "Individual events must be tied together in such a way that the knots are strikingly noticeable; the events must not follow upon one another imperceptibly, but rather one must be able to pass judgment in the midst of them." Among his most successful and best-known plays are *The Threepenny Opera* (1928), *Mother Courage and Her Children* (1938), *Galileo* (1938–1939), *The Good Woman of Setzuan* (1938–1939), and *The Caucasian Chalk Circle* (1944–1945).

The whole complex of techniques of staging and playwriting used by Brecht came to be called *epic theatre*, a term he adopted to distinguish his theater from traditional drama of the sort described by Aristotle in his *Poetics* and from unified theatre of the kind advocated by Wagner. The name *epic*, too, captured many of the qualities that Brecht prized: the mixing of narrative and dramatic episodes, the telescoping of time and place, and the spanning of years and countries on a consequent grand scale (similar to that achieved in epic poetry.).

Although Brecht was not the first to use either these techniques or the term *epic* (Erwin Piscator, 1893–1966, had been active in the same kind of experimentation several years earlier), Brecht popularized the term and the practices through his own plays, his theoretical writings (particularly the "Little Organon for the Theater," 1948), and his productions at the Berliner Ensemble, after 1954 East Germany's most prestigious theatre.

ANTONIN ARTAUD AND THE THEATRE OF CRUELTY

Antonin Artaud (1895–1948) fit the stereotype of the misunderstood and tormented artist. A visionary rather than a practical man, Artaud was an influential theorist immediately following World War II; by the 1960s, he was virtually a cult hero among the theatrical avant-garde in Europe and the United States.

Although Artaud was an actor, a director, a playwright, a poet, and a screenwriter, it was as a theorist that he made his greatest impact. *The Theater and Its Double*, a compilation of Artaud's major essays, was published in France in 1938 but was not translated into English until the late 1950s. Because Artaud believed that important ideas came not from logical reasoning or rational thinking but from intuition, experience, and feelings, he developed his major ideas and positions by poetic rather than prosaic techniques, by means of images and metaphors rather than through traditional argument or discursive prose. For this reason, many people have found the book difficult to read and understand. Nonetheless, Artaud's major points seem clear enough, particularly if the reader attends to the major metaphors that appear: the theatre as *plague*, as *double*, and as *cruelty*.

First, Artaud called for theatre to return to its rightful place as a great force in humanity, a force for putting people back in touch with the intensity of living. Comparing theatre to a plague, Artaud attributed to both the power to release conflicts, to disengage powers, and to liberate possibilities: "It appears that by means of the plague, a gigantic abscess, as much moral as social, has been collectively drained; and that like the plague, the theatre has been created to drain abscesses collectively." He declared that theatre

Figure 15-7. **Brecht and Artaud.** Peter Weiss's *The Persecution and Assassination of Marat as Performed by the Inmates of Charenton Under the Direction of the Marquis de Sade* combined elements of both Brecht and Artaud, as is clear in this production at the University of South Carolina. *(Directed by Richard Jennings.)*

caused people to confront themselves honestly, letting fall their individual masks and confessing their social hypocrisies.

Second, Western theatre had lost its magic and its vibrance and had become merely a pale imitation, a *double*, of the true theatre (that is, the Eastern theatre). In order to regain its power, the Western theatre must reject logical demonstrations and causal actions and instead seize and impel its spectators toward truth, forcing them to apprehend meaning through the whole of their bodies. To this end, Artaud proposed "a theatre in which violent physical images crush and hypnotize the sensibility . . . as by a whirlwind of higher forces."

Third, Artaud wanted to remove the script from the center of his theatre, for he believed that words, grammatical structure, and syntactical patterns were insufficient carriers of meaning. Truth came instead from spiritual signs whose meaning emerged intuitively and "with enough violence to make useless any translation into logical discursive language." Artaud wished to substitute gestures, signs, symbols, rhythms, and sounds for ordinary language; he advocated "a superabundance of impression, each richer than the next." He was convinced that theatre was neither logical, nor paraphrasable, nor rational; it was intuitive, primitive, magical, and potentially powerful.

Fourth, the audience was central to the theatre. Artaud dismissed notions of art as a kind of personal therapy for the artist. Theatre was good only when it profoundly moved its audiences, when it returned them to the subconscious energies that lay under the veneer of civilization and civilized behavior. Whereas Brecht wished to cause an audience to *think* about a social or political issue, Artaud wanted to move an audience to *feel* or *experience* a spiritual awakening, to participate in something that might be called a *communion* in its real sense of a *coming together.*

Fifth, Artaud called for a *theatre of cruelty,* a theatre that showed the "terrible and necessary cruelty which things can exercise against us. We are not free. And the sky can still fall on our heads. And the theatre has been created to teach us that first of all." Cruelty, then, was primarily psychic rather than physical.

To achieve his theatre of cruelty, Artaud developed a number of techniques seldom used in commercial productions. Because he wanted to bombard the senses with various stimuli in order to cause the whole organism (not merely the mind) to be moved, he experimented with ways of manipulating light and sound: in both, he adopted the abrupt, the discordant, the sudden, the shrill, the garish. Lights changed colors quickly, alternated intensity violently; sound was loud, sudden, often amplified. Scenery was subservient to the other elements of production, with the audiences placed in an environment created by actors, lights, sound, and the space for the production (Artaud preferred barns, factories, and the like to conventional theatres). The actors were encouraged to use their bodies and their voices to provide scenery, sounds, and visual effects and not to be bound by notions of psychological realism and character analysis. Actors were to address the senses of the spectators, not merely their minds.

Artaud's theories, in many forms and with many distortions, were appropriated and applied after 1950 by theatre artists, makers of movies, and especially modern rock music stars. Whatever one may think of his pronouncements, it is clear that, although long in coming, their acceptance has been widespread.

CHAPTER 16

Contemporary Theatre in America: 1960s–1980s

Background

The period opened with the 1960 election of the young, handsome, and wealthy John Kennedy, an event that promised an era of idealism moderated by sophistication. It continued in the 1980s with the old, handsome, and wealthy Ronald Reagan, in an era of idealism marked anew by sophistication. In between were chaos, turmoil, and shame.

The press called Kennedy's Washington *Camelot*, an allusion to both the medieval land of chivalry and to the Broadway musical *Camelot*, which enjoyed enormous popularity during the Kennedy years. Kennedy's assassination in 1963 stunned the nation and marked the end of Camelot. Political and social upheavals culminated in a wave of assassinations: of Robert Kennedy, of Martin Luther King, Jr., and of several members of the Black

Panthers. Peaceful efforts toward civil and human rights turned impatient, then strident, and finally lethal, with school buses overturned and burned in cities like Boston and Louisville and with students killed by authorities at places like Kent State University and South Carolina State College. The Vietnam war began optimistically enough when a speedy victory seemed certain, but, dragging on, it sapped the will and strength of the country, caused many to question the role of the United States as international policeman, and led many citizens into acts of civil disobedience. The country's youth attacked the presumed hypocrisy of the over-thirty generation and rejected many traditional values in such areas as loyalty, patriotism, marriage, motherhood, and the family. Adopting odd modes of dress and hair style, many openly advocated increased sexual freedom, the legalization of other drugs (alcohol being already legal in most states), and an end to the military draft.

Lyndon Johnson, who succeeded Kennedy, failed to survive the civil unrest and the growing unpopularity of the war in Vietnam, and he declined to seek reelection in 1968.

Richard Nixon's election was heralded by many as the nation's return to sanity and stability. Nixon wound the war down, and, in 1972, he was reelected by an impressive margin. He resigned in disgrace in 1974, however, because of alleged abuses of power in the notorious Watergate affair. Again shocked, the American public sheltered under the quiet leadership of Gerald Ford, a man not elected to any executive post but appointed by Nixon when his elected vice-president resigned because of alleged criminal acts.

The 1970s ended somewhat tentatively under the administration of a quiet born-again Christian from Georgia, Jimmy Carter, whose presidency (1976–1980) was plagued by inflation and a humiliating hostage affair in Iran. The public rejected Carter's bid for reelection. It seemed anxious for a stronger, more optimistic, perhaps less soul-searching leader.

Figure 16-1. **Social Turmoil.** The controversial war in Vietnam provided the subject of several plays, among the most successful David Rabe's *Streamers*, seen here in production at the University of South Carolina. *(Directed by James A. Patterson.)*

Figure 16-2. **Affirming America.** By the late 1970s, the social turmoil had largely subsided, replaced by feelings of indulgence well captured in musicals like *Follies*, by Stephen Sondheim, here in production at the University of Arizona. *(Directed by Robert C. Burroughs.)*

In 1980, Ronald Reagan was elected and quickly moved to slow inflation and to raise feelings of national pride. Despite setbacks in the Middle East and repeated scandals within his administration, he retained an enormous personal popularity and was reelected overwhelmingly in 1984.

As mysteriously as it had surfaced, the social and political turmoil had subsided by 1980, leaving behind a rather self-satisfied society. By the mid-1980s, business was flourishing; social elegance had resurfaced; and pride in America had become a national slogan. To be sure, there were some ominous signs: The military was rebuilding; the number of homeless was increasing; the controversy over abortion was holding steady; the AIDS crisis was growing; the Middle East and Central America were threatening to explode. But the American public seemed confident that a new and happier time had arrived with Reagan's presidency.

Theatre

If anything can be said to characterize the theatre of this period, it was its eclecticism, that is, its use of many diverse styles for its own needs. Its theatre buildings were variously shaped, variously funded, and variously located (see pp. 88–105).

The theatre closely reflected society's major shifts. The commercial theatre of Broadway and Off-Broadway struggled with its continuing financial problems. During the civil turmoil of the 1960s and early 1970s, a strong non-commercial flourished, offering an alternative to mainstream culture. The home of the avant-garde was mostly Off-Off Broadway, where, in the late 1950s, Joe Cino opened his coffeehouse (Caffe Cino) to poetry readings and dramatic productions. Soon others followed suit, most notably Ellen Stewart at La Mama ETC (Experimental Theatre Club), probably the period's most successful producer of nontraditional theatre works and the winner of several Obies for sustained achievement in the noncommercial theatre. As the social convulsions subsided, the avant-garde withered away, so that by the late 1970s and the 1980s only its vestiges were visible.

Non-Mainstream Theatre in the United States, 1960–present

POLITICAL THEATRES

The 1960s saw a quickened interest in theatre as a weapon for political battles. The goal was to shake people from their complacency and to convert them from passive observers into active participants in a social revolution. Theatre groups with this goal moved out of buildings and into the streets, the fields, and even the elevators of office buildings. The terms *street theatre* and *guerrilla theatre* were coined to describe those productions that were brought directly to people wherever they congregated, for those labels stressed the supposed similarity of such groups to guerrilla fighters, with all that term implies about a small cadre of well-trained, mobile, elite soldiers for the revolution.

INDIVIDUAL COMPANIES.   THE LIVING THEATRE.   Probably the most famous and certainly the most controversial of the several political groups of the 1960s was the Living Theatre, founded by Judith Malina and Julian Beck.

After a somewhat tentative beginning in 1947, the group achieved recognition by the late 1950s as one of the most important experimental Off-Broadway theatres. During this early period, the group performed rather traditional, if often somewhat angry and bitter, works, including Jack Gelber's *The Connection* (1959) and Kenneth Brown's *The Brig* (1963), as well as works by Luigi Pirandello, Bertolt Brecht, and William Carlos Williams.

Problems with tax collectors and local police, however, encouraged the troupe to tour Europe in 1964. By the time they returned in 1968, they had a different identity, a changed working method, and new stature: the Living Theatre of the late 1960s was a theatrical commune devoted to the production of revolutionary drama. Their international reputation rested primarily on three works: *Frankenstein* (1965), *Antigone* (1967), and *Paradise Now* (1968), each a strong call for revolution and benevolent anarchy.

As the group toured the United States with these plays, critical responses were predictably varied. One critic dubbed *Paradise Now* "a full scale disaster"; another dismissed it as "a fraud." The group itself was characterized as "a platform for anarchy and nothing more." But Eric Bentley, a respected critic, said that the troupe had to be reckoned with: "The Living Theatre

Figure 16-3. **Political Theatre.** Various political issues brought people into the streets with performances intended to provoke social change. Here, a street theatre in Columbia, South Carolina, promoting nuclear disarmament.

represents the most resolute attempt during the past twenty years to create a theatre which would be a radical alternative to Broadway and Off-Broadway."

The group left the country again in 1969 and entered another phase. In a formal declaration, the group announced its division into four cells, each to be centered in a different city and focusing on a distinct revolutionary concern: political, environmental, cultural, and spiritual. Although the collective remained active and deeply committed to promoting revolution, by the mid-1970s its impact on the American theatre was clearly waning.

PETER SCHUMANN AND THE BREAD AND PUPPET THEATRE. Founded in 1961, Schumann's theatre called for a rejection of violence and capitalism in favor of love and community. Its name came from two of its major traits: bread was usually passed about the audience as a part of the performance, and puppets of all sizes told stories based on fairy tales, legends, and myths aimed at recapturing simple human values in a complex world. Playing outdoors in found spaces and using common, often found, materials for costumes and properties, the Bread and Puppet toured widely, taking theatre to people wherever they might be. In 1978, the company was awarded its second Obie, this one for sustained achievement in the American theatre.

THE SAN FRANCISCO MIME TROUPE. From its founding in 1959 until 1966, the company used mostly the techniques of silent mime or *commedia dell'arte*. Beginning in the mid-1960s, however, the group got swept up in political activism and soon thereafter reorganized itself as a collective devoted to social change. Thereafter, the group largely abandoned traditional plays in favor of pieces devised around subjects like racism, sexism, militarism, and capitalism: "We are committed to change, not art." Playing mostly outdoors, in parks, squares, and playgrounds, the company developed a highly visual production style marked by broad, nonrepresentational acting; paratheatrical elements, including puppets and dance; and a strong emphasis on music. The group earned Obies in 1968 and 1973.

EL TEATRO CAMPESINO. El Teatro Campesino, under the leadership of Luis Valdez, was founded in 1965 at the height of labor disputes among the

357

Figure 16-4. **Bread and Puppet Theatre.** In a colorfully painted truck and bus, actors and their large puppets travel widely to perform for audiences gathered out of doors. *(Courtesy of Evelyn Beck.)*

farm owners, the powerful Teamsters Union, and a rival union of Chicanos headed by César Chavez. El Teatro Campesino successfully promoted the bid of Chavez by entering the labor camps, organizing the workers, and satirizing the competing Teamsters Union and the wealthy farm owners.

The primary weapons were the *actos*, short, slapstick skits, about fifteen minutes long, punctuated with songs and cries for action. Because both actors and audiences often spoke only Spanish or English, the *actos* used few words and much action. Signs and masks helped the workers follow the story. For example, in a favorite *acto*, a grower entered, wearing a sign reading "Smiling Jack." As he began to spew platitudes about his love of the Mexican-American worker, other signs began to appear near him: "Liar," "Gringo," "Jackass," and finally "Strike." In this way, the *acto* not only illustrated the problem the worker faced with hypocritical growers but also suggested a solution to the problem: organize a strike. The strikebreaker was often a target of the *actos*. One began, "After God had finished the rattlesnake, the toad and the vampire, he had some awful substance left over with which he made the Strikebreaker."

Within a few years, El Teatro Campesino had extended its political activity to other areas of Chicano life. *Actos* began to treat the Vietnam war, cultural identity, drugs, and Chicano history as well as farm labor problems. In 1970, however, during a demonstration in Los Angeles, riots led to a death, and Luis Valdez, stunned, took stock and changed the direction of El Teatro.

Shortly thereafter, El Teatro Campesino became El Centro Campesino, a religious commune devoted to revitalizing Chicano culture. The commune's theatrical performances became considerably more benign than before, with *mitos* (mythic stories seeking to recapture the roots of Chicano culture) replacing the militant *actos*.

By the 1980s, Valdez had moved the group even closer to mainstream American culture—and mainstream theatre, producing plays in commercial theatres on the West Coast and in New York.

POLITICAL THEATRE MOVEMENTS. BLACK THEATRE. Although black performers in America date from well before the Civil War, and black theatre companies were firmly established within black communities by the end of the nineteenth century, their performers and plays seldom reached America's commercial theatres until midway in this century.

Before the 1960s, most *commercial* plays featuring black characters had been written by whites, who often shamelessly stereotyped blacks and placed them in inferior social positions, where they were patronized by wealthier, wittier, and more powerful white characters. Paul Green's *In Abraham's Bosom* (1926), Carson McCullers's *The Member of the Wedding* (1950), and Marc Connelly's *Green Pastures* (1930), although sensitive and thoughtful treatments of black characters by white playwrights, nonetheless displayed many of the common stereotypes.

Public images died hard, but they did die. The French playwright Jean Genet, in *The Blacks* (1959), reversed the traditions of the minstrel show and used black actors in white face to display the abuses of power. Although many American blacks rejected the play's thesis—that blacks will come to power only by adopting the tactics of their white oppressors—few failed to realize that the play represented a turning point in the portrayal of black people. In 1959, too, Lorraine Hansberry's *A Raisin in the Sun* appeared, an early portrait of black family life in which the peculiar tensions between women and men were sympathetically and sensitively sketched. When she won the Pulitzer Prize for drama, she became the first black woman so honored, and her play is now considered an American classic.

With the racial turmoil of the 1960s and the early 1970s, blacks turned in large numbers to the arts as a way of demanding change and repairing their ruptured society. A black critic explained:

> *Black Art is the aesthetic and spiritual sister of the Black Power concept. As such, it envisions an art that speaks directly to the needs and aspirations of Black America. . . . Theatre exists in direct relationship to the audience it claims to serve. The decadence and inanity of the contemporary American Theatre is an accurate reflection of the state of American society.*

The black theatre movement is said to date from 1964 and the production of LeRoi Jones's first two plays, *The Toilet* and *Dutchman*, both of which presented a chilling picture of racial barriers, human hatred, and the sense-less suffering that results from racism. Thereafter, the stereotypical stage Negro was increasingly replaced by more honest, if often less agreeable, black characters. Throughout the 1960s and the early 1970s, Jones (now known by his Muslim name, Imamu Amiri Baraka) remained the most militant and best known black playwright, with works like *Slave Ship* (1967) and *The Death of Malcolm X* (1965).

Alongside such antiwhite and separatist works, however, were plays de-picting the politics and economics of life within the black community. Ron Milner's *Who's Got his Own* (1966) presented a strong black woman struggling to teach her son to love and respect his father; Douglas Turner Ward's *Day of Absence* (1967) poked fun at whites as they were outwitted by cleverer blacks, whose disappearance for a single day led to the collapse of the white social structure; Alice Childress's *Mojo* (1970) suggested that black men and women could work out their differences and exist happily as equals if they loved and respected one another.

By the mid-1970s, black authors felt free to criticize other blacks. Ntozake Shange's *For Colored Girls Who Have Considered Suicide/When the Rainbow Is Enuf* (1976) explored the double oppression of being black and female and

Figure 16-5a. **Black Theatre.** The Federal Theatre Project contributed important plays and artists to black theatre in this country. Here, *Prelude to Spring + 50* from the Federal Theatre, produced by Afro-American Arts Institute, Indiana University. *(Directed by Winona Fletcher. Photograph courtesy of The Herald Tele-phone, Bloomington, Indiana.)*

Figure 16-5b. **Black Theatre.** As interest in the African heritage of Black Americans grows, increasing numbers of African plays are finding production in the United States. Here, a Nigerian play, Femi Osofisan's *Farewell to a Cannibal Rage*, in production at Stanford University. *(Directed by Sandra Richards; costumes and scenery by John B. Wilson, lighting and photo by Alexander Stewart.)*

presented a most unflattering portrait of black males, some of whom were portrayed as brutalizing black women as they themselves had been previously brutalized. Originally staged in a black theatre, this powerful "choreopoem" eventually moved to Broadway, where it captivated audiences and earned the coveted Tony Award. With the success of *Colored Girls*, it became clear that plays once considered suitable only for black audiences could be successful in the mainstream of America's commercial theatre.

A few of the major authors and their best-known works can serve to indicate the robust state of black theatre: Ed Bullins, *The Electronic Nigger* (1968); Lonne Elder III, *Ceremonies in Dark Old Men* (1968); Charles Gordone, *No Place to Be Somebody* (1969); Adrienne Kennedy, *The Owl Answers* (1969); Joseph Walker, *The River Niger* (1972); Charles Fuller, *A Soldier's Story* (1981); and August Wilson, *Fences* (1987).

Among the major theatres dedicated to producing black plays for primarily black audiences were the Negro Ensemble Company, the New Lafayette Theatre, and Spirit House (all in the New York area) and the Watts Writers Workshop, the Performing Arts Society of Los Angeles, and the Inner City Cultural Center (in the Los Angeles and San Francisco areas). Black theatres, like black plays, served their audiences in very different ways, some favoring political statements, others avoiding polemical works altogether. In Los Angeles, for example, while one theatre specialized in revolutionary pieces, another, across town, was producing a "black version" of *Death of a Salesman.*

361

Figure 16-6. **Black Theatre.** Plays from the European repertory form an important part of the production programs of many historically black colleges and universities. Ibsen's *Hedda Gabler,* produced at South Carolina State College. *(Directed by H. D. Flowers, II. Photo by Danny Overcash.)*

Both believed they were serving the particular needs of their specific audiences.

With new plays and special theatres came calls for a new criticism. Some black critics took the position that their audiences saw and understood art in ways different from whites. Traditional aesthetics were at best irrelevant and at worst corrupting. Those black artists and critics sought an aesthetic that was moral and corrective, one that supported plays that, in a direct and immediate way, affected the lives of black theatregoers. A black critic explained, "The question for the black critic today is not how beautiful a melody, a play, a poem, or a novel is, but how much more beautiful [that] poem, melody, or play [has] made the life of a single black man." This attack on the accepted canon of Western drama raised issues that were still being debated in the 1980s.

Predictably, perhaps, many works by black artists were indistinguishable from the typical commercial fare so roundly criticized just a few years earlier. *The Wiz* (a musical based on the *Wizard of Oz*), *Bubbling Brown Sugar,* and *Dreamgirls,* except for black casts, were standard commercial fare. But they were attracting large audiences of blacks and whites and receiving acclaim from established reviewers.

WOMEN'S THEATRE. If black theatre and drama were products of the social upheavals of the 1950s and the 1960s, women's theatres were clearly a phenomenon of the 1970s. From the formation of the first groups in 1969, increasing numbers of people, mostly female, banded together into theatrical units that aimed to promote the goals of feminism, the careers of women artists, or both. By the mid-1970s, more than forty such groups were flourishing; by 1980, more than a hundred such groups had formed. Unlike black theatres, which were usually found in urban settings and amid high concentrations of blacks, women's theatres sprang up in places as diverse as New York City and Greenville, South Carolina.

The theatres ranged in size from those depending on one or two unpaid and inexperienced volunteers to organizations of professionals numbering into the hundreds. Budgets, too, varied widely, with some groups existing on a shoestring and the good wishes of friends and others displaying a financial statement in the hundreds of thousands of dollars. Organization, repertory, working methods, and artistic excellence were highly diversified, but the groups all shared the conviction that women had been subjected to unfair discrimination based on their gender and that theatre could serve in some way to correct the resulting inequities.

Like the black theatres, the women's theatres attempted to serve different audiences and to serve them in different ways. Some groups, like the Women's

Figure 16-7. **Women's Theatre.** In *The Club*, women actors play members of a men's club in order to make points about sexism in society. (*The University of South Carolina. Directed by James A. Patterson.*)

Interart in New York City and the Los Angeles Feminist Theatre, existed primarily to provide employment for women artists. Such groups, seeing that women had inadequate opportunities to display their crafts, served as a showcase for the works of women playwrights, designers, and directors. Because their goal was to display women's art in the most favorable light possible, artistic excellence was a primary goal of each production. Critical acceptance by the theatrical mainstream was the ultimate measure of success. But other groups, like the now-defunct It's All Right to Be Woman Theatre (also in New York), believed the problems of women to be so deeply rooted in the society that only a major social upheaval could bring about their correction. Such groups were revolutionary and tended to adopt tactics designed to taunt, shock, or shame a lethargic society into corrective action. These groups cared not at all for the approval of the established critics, because they believed that traditional theatre was a male-dominated, and hence oppressive, institution.

Two techniques in particular came to be associated with revolutionary women's theatres: a preference for collective or communal organization and the use of improvised performance material, much of it uncommonly personal. Like guerrilla theatres, many feminist groups replaced the traditional theatrical hierarchy (a director leading a team of actors, designers, and technicians) with a leaderless group working together and with the audience to create a theatrical experience. The idea seemed to be that hierarchy suggests competition, and competitiveness is a masculine trait; collectivity, on the other hand, involves cooperation, a quality to be prized in the new social order.

Perhaps this view accounts as well for the groups' frequent preference for scripts that were cooperatively developed through improvisations. The actors, occasionally aided by their audiences, were encouraged to dip into their own experiences of being women in today's society and, from these shared personal experiences, to improvise dramatic presentations. Apparently such efforts, although naive, were capable of provoking audiences to awareness and action, for, in several instances, women reported changed lives as a result of encounters with a feminist production.

Although many women's theatres relied on guerrilla events and improvised presentations, others simply sought more new plays by women. During the 1970s, three feminist playwrights attracted special attention: Megan Terry, Myrna Lamb, and Martha Boesing.

Terry first came to national prominence as a member of the Open Theatre (see p. 368). In addition to a strong antiwar stance, best seen in her play *Viet Rock*, Terry took the position that stereotyping by gender, although pervasive, was wrong. Out of this conviction grew four of her best-known works: *Calm Down Mother* (1966), written specifically for women of the Open Theatre; *Keep Tightly Closed in a Cool Dry Place* (1967); *In the Gloaming, Oh My Darling* (1966); and *Approaching Simone* (1970). Terry moved from New York to the Omaha (Nebraska) Magic Theatre, where she serves as resident playwright.

The first production of Lamb's play *The Mod Donna* (1970) is said to mark

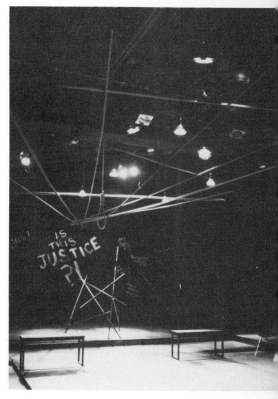

Figure 16-8. **Women's Theatre.** In Martha Boesing's *Antigone Too*, a chorus of historical women who have engaged in civil disobedience form the chorus against which the familiar Greek story is retold. *(University of Maryland. Directed by Bobbie Ausubel.)*

the beginning of the feminist theatre movement. Produced by Joseph Papp at the New York Shakespeare Festival's Public Theatre, the play's bizarre style—episodes reminiscent of soap opera, interrupted by commercials and alternated with choral poetry—puzzled audiences, and its attacks on the traditional roles of women and on the family polarized viewers. Conservatives saw it as an attack on American values; feminists considered it an exposé of their oppression. Other well-known plays by Lamb include *Scyklon Z* (1969) and *Crab Quadrille* (1976).

Boesing served from 1974 to 1984 as resident playwright for At the Foot of the Mountain, a feminist theatre in Minneapolis, Minnesota. One of several feminist playwrights who chose to work outside New York and in a feminist context, Boesing combined political activism and playwriting, seeing them as inseparable. Her most often produced works include *Raped!* (1974), *The Web* (1982), and *Antigone Too* (1984).

Women's plays have recently begun to find production in the commercial theatre in increasing numbers. Among the best known of such works are Gretchen Cryer's *I'm Getting My Act Together and Taking It on the Road* (1978), Marsha Norman's *'Night Mother* (1983), Wendy Wasserstein's *Uncommon Women* (1977), Beth Henley's *Crimes of the Heart* (1981), Maria Irene Fornes's *Fefu and Her Friends* (1978), and, from England, Caryl Churchill's *Cloud Nine* (1981), *Top Girls* (1982), and *Serious Money* (1987).

The number of plays by and about women that have achieved commercial success since the mid-1970s may signal a new trend that bears watching.

EXPERIMENTAL THEATRES

Calls to change society were accompanied by calls to change the art of the theatre, at least as practiced by the traditional, commercial theatres of New

Figure 16-9. **Women's Theatre.** In *Cloud Nine*, a white actor plays a black servant (shown with feather fan), a doll represents a daughter, and a male actor plays the colonial's wife (here holding book). *(The University of Iowa. Directed by Judith Lyons.)*

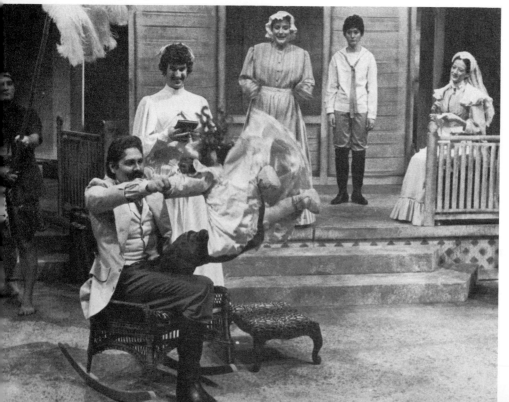

York's Broadway, London's West End, and Paris's boulevards. Experimental theatres did not share a common vision of what the new theatre ought to become; therefore, not only were the groups numerous, they were also diverse, adopting different working methods, selecting different kinds of plays, arranging themselves in various performing spaces, and formulating a welter of theoretical and critical positions.

Although their emphases varied, most groups seemed interested in exploring, through their work, some version of the following issues:

1. *What is the nature of theatre?* How does theatre differ from other performing arts? From the electronic media? From life?

2. *What are the appropriate audience and setting for theatre?* What is the proper role of the audience in the theatrical event? Is theatre an activity or a place? Are some arrangements of actors and audience better than others? Should there be limits on the size of an audience? How are spectators different from performers?

3. *What structures can best organize theatre for production?* In a collaborative art such as theatre, is it best for all participants to work together as equals, or should there be a single guiding vision? Should there be a hierarchy of artists, or should a collective effort be substituted? To produce the best art, should artists live as well as work together?

4. *What is the appropriate relationship between the written script and the live performance?* Is a written script necessary? Is a script really a text, or is it a pretext? How heavily should the script depend on language? By what means does the script—and then the performance—best affect spectators: Should it address its appeals to the head, the heart, or the viscera? And in what proportions?

Like the political groups, the experimental theatres thrived during the 1960s and 1970s. But, also like the political groups, the experimental theatres lost their vigor thereafter. Although some continued into the 1980s, their most innovative work dated from the earlier decades. After that period, they became largely an echo of themselves.

JERZY GROTOWSKI AND THE POLISH LABORATORY THEATRE.   Formed in 1959 in Wroclaw (Breslau), Poland, the Polish Laboratory Theatre did not appear in an English-speaking country until 1968, and its American influence is normally dated from that performance. Through his performances and his book (*Towards a Poor Theatre*), Grotowski became associated with four major ideas:

1. A poor theatre, one where all external trappings (scenery, lighting, and costumes) were stripped away, leaving only the actor and the audience as essential to the theatre.
2. A holy theatre, one capable of portraying humanity's suffering, its ethical plights, its search for meaning, and its moral imperatives.

3. Pure actors, stripped of all protective devices (by a process Grotowski called the *via negativa*), so that they may enter into a genuine communion with the audience.

4. Audiences that, as one of the two essential elements of the theatre, are treated with great respect by a limitation of their size and a careful arrangement of their experiences.

After 1973, Grotowski became increasingly interested in breaking down the usual distinctions between performer and spectator. To this end, he experimented with a variety of "paratheatrical" (theatrelike or theatre-related) activities in which the traditional separation was eliminated.

JOSEPH CHAIKIN AND THE OPEN THEATRE.   Formed in 1963 as an alternative to the "closed theatre" of Broadway, Chaikin's Open Theatre wished to explore the nature of theatre, the nature of acting, and the relationship between theatre and other aesthetic forms, especially narrative. Its emphasis was on the process of preparation, not on the performance itself. Indeed, public performance was incidental.

To build an ensemble, the actors engaged in theatre games and improvisations designed to build trust and to increase group awareness. Playwrights, who were also members of the ensemble, developed texts from the improvisations of the group. Although such plays varied, many shared some combination of these characteristics:

1. A unity achieved through exploring a central idea or theme rather than through telling a story.
2. A free and often disconnected treatment of time and place.
3. The use of *transformations*, a technique in which actors played several characters without corresponding changes in costume or makeup, and without clear transitions in the dialogue.
4. A reliance on the actors to provide their own environment by "becoming" the setting and the sounds (for example, an actor plays a sheep in the field, another a snake on a tree, and several become the sirens of ambulances), transforming into other characters and objects as needed.

The success of two of the Open Theatre's plays, *Viet Rock* (Megan Terry, 1966) and *America Hurrah* (Jean Claude Van Itallie, 1966) led to the group's dissolution. Chaikin explained, "For us there was no impetus left to do anything else, to do any research. . . . We had been processed as a 'success.' " Rather than redefinining the group, Chaikin decided to disband it while its original goals were still more or less intact.

ROBERT WILSON AND THE BYRD HOFFMAN SCHOOL OF BYRDS.   Regarded by New York critics as one of the most original minds working in theatre today, Robert Wilson has largely abandoned written, narrative texts

Figure 16-10. **Experimental Theatre: Chaikin.** Developed with the Open Theatre, Jean Claude van Itallie's *America Hurrah!* quickly became a favorite of colleges and universities. Here, *Interview*, produced by Elmira College. *(Directed by Jack Jenkins. Design by Peter Lach.)*

in favor of a "theatre of images." He is heavily influenced by practices in contemporary music, dance, sculpture, painting, and cinema and is dependent on his collaborator, Christopher Knowles, whose autistic world apparently provides materials for Wilson's artistic creations. Wilson's work is noted especially for its treatment of time, space, and sound.

Wilson's interest is in the moment, when time is often slowed down, speeded up, or repeated, so that the audience experiences an abundance of visual and aural images from which to construct a personal reality. Theatrical and real time are wholly elastic, allowing a languid exploration of a moment in order to arrive at a kind of "artistic boredom," which operates as a guiding aesthetic principle in the works. The audience is to experience the static instant of time rather than to understand the implications of its flow.

Language and music often surround the audience, recorded sounds coming from loudspeakers throughout the auditorium and mixing with live sounds emanating from the stage. Words are used not for their meaning but for their sounds; therefore, alogical sentences are often rearranged and repeated at differing rates of speed. The speech may be uninflected; the music may be atonal; and noise may contribute to the general "aural junk sculpture" said to characterize the performances. The seemingly endless repetitions of non-denotative sounds contribute to the trancelike, incantatory quality that defines Wilson's work.

Perhaps because Wilson is himself a painter, his interest in the stage as a space of visual images is strong. The tableau is a major unit, from which and into which actors form and dissolve into pictorial and sculptural groups, often in conjunction with other images provided by slides and films. Again, repetition and reiteration serve to multiply sensory impressions and to produce what one critic called "a frigid picture of an inner landscape."

Among Wilson's most famous works are *Deafman Glance* (1971), *Einstein on the Beach* (1976, music by Philip Glass), and *Civil Wars* (1984).

RICHARD FOREMAN AND THE ONTOLOGICAL-HYSTERIC THEATRE.
Richard Foreman seeks a theatre in which a master artist controls all ele-

ments. He therefore conceives the work, writes the text, designs and supervises the building of the costumes and sets, records the sound track, and directs the (usually untrained) actors. His control continues through the performances, because he personally manipulates the tape and slide presentations that structure his scripts, thus dictating the pace of both action and dialogue. For Foreman, performance is simply "a continuation of [the] writing process."

Conceiving of theatre as more a visual than a storytelling art, Foreman uses techniques normally associated with painting and film. Actors are assigned stage positions on the basis of spatial needs rather than psychology. Moving from tableau to tableau, often in a single plane and facing the audience in the manner of a photograph, the actors produce the effect of a slow-motion or stop-action film, where a series of individual pictures unroll slowly before the eyes of the theatregoer. Foreman uses filmic techniques like off-screen narration and scene titles. He often disconnects sound and picture, as, for example, by having the play's dialogue taped to be played over loudspeakers, leaving the live actors largely mute.

Finally, he strives to create an art that compels through the accumulation of details rather than through their rigid selection. He wants each viewer to

Figure 16-11. **Experimental Theatres: Wilson.** Sylvie Guillem (2nd from left and Patrick Dupond (center) in *Le Martyre de Saint Sebastien*, Robert Wilson's first full-length ballet set to the music of Claude Debussy. *(Photo Credit: Rodolphe Torette.)*

Figure 16-12. **Broadway:** *Hair.* The production of *Hair* in 1967 marked a turning point in Broadway theatre; thereafter, nudity and scatology were increasingly accepted in theatre. *(Photograph by Martha Swope.)*

create some personal meaning from the multiple images, to engage in an act of creation rather than of reception.

Founded in 1968, Foreman's theatre has twenty or so works to its credit, among them *Sophie* (1973) and *Rhoda in Potatoland,* for which he won a special Obie in 1976.

MABOU MINES.   Often grouped with Wilson's and Foreman's is the work of Mabou Mines, the most important artists of which are Lee Breuer and JoAnne Akalaitis. Mabou Mines shares the others' interest in sound, space, and time and so shares many of their painterly and filmic techniques. They differ in several important ways, however. Mabou Mines (1) tends to work collaboratively, creating scripts that tell something resembling stories; (2) incorporates both the floor and the back wall as its performance space, a radical departure that, in turn, (3) causes the audience to reorder its customary angle of perception to include actors who relate horizontally as well as vertically to the floor.

Carrying its nontraditional work even into the recording of scripts, Mabou Mines published *Red Horse Animation* (1970) in the form of a comic book, which used both picture and caption to "tell" the production. In 1975, the group won a special Obie for the quality of its work, and Lee Breuer won Obies for his *Shaggy Dog Animation* (1978) and *A Prelude to Death in Venice* (1980).

CHARLES LUDLAM AND THE RIDICULOUS THEATRICAL COMPANY. Since its founding in 1967, this startlingly different theatre has been noted for its outrageous, highly theatrical, high-camp productions.

As playwright, the late Charles Ludlam sought verbal richness and allusiveness through "cultural recyclings," a technique that involved taking snippets of dialogue, characters, and events from an array of sources. For example, for his *Camille* (1973), in which Ludlam played the consumptive heroine, he plundered freely from Dumas's play, Verdi's opera (*La Traviata*), and Garbo's filmed version. Obviously, this theatre's appeal is to a culturally and theatrically literate audience that can take delight in the creative manipulation of historical sources.

As director, Ludlam moved with breakneck pacing, visual slapstick, and verbal non sequiturs to create a mad world, a picture of reality that bordered on the anarchic. For a ridiculous opera based loosely on Wagner's *Ring* cycle, for example, Ludlam transformed the original Valkyries into lesbian motorcyclists, and Valhalla into New York's Lincoln Center. Unexpected and shocking titles (*Turds in Hell*) combined with outlandish jokes ("I don't think of myself as castrated; I think of myself as extremely well circumcised") added to the ambiguous sexuality so firmly associated with this company.

With more than twenty years' work and as many plays to his credit, Ludlam received Obies in 1970, 1973, 1975, and 1977. He had a small but devoted following at his death in 1987, and his company continues to produce.

Post-modern Theory and Criticism

Radical changes in dramatic text and theatrical performances have called for equally radical changes in thinking about them. Several new approaches to literary and theatrical criticism have therefore emerged (e.g., phenomenology, structuralism, deconstructionism, and semiotics), but none has been widely accepted. All have attempted to grapple more directly than has been usual in traditional criticism with the problems of "reading" a performance (as distinct from reading a text), and all seem to be as concerned with the perceptions of the audience as with the structure of the text.

Commercial Theatre in the United States (1960–Present)

MUSICALS

Despite the rising costs of production, musicals continue to dominate the Broadway theatre. During the 1960s, the most successful musicals had an air of optimism: *Camelot* (1960), *Hello, Dolly!* (1964), *Fiddler on the Roof* (1964), *The Man of La Mancha* (1965), and *Mame* (1966) on Broadway; and

Off-Broadway *The Fantasticks* (1960), *You're a Good Man, Charlie Brown* (1967), and *Jacques Brel Is Alive and Well and Living in Paris* (1968).

The Broadway production of *Hair* (1967) marked a turning point. Produced first Off-Broadway by Joseph Papp, *Hair* portrayed a group of impoverished but affable hippies as they lived and loved together against a background of drug use, civil disobedience, and the military draft. The show's popularity led to the acceptance in the mainstream theatre of practices formerly taboo: irreverence, four-letter words, and nudity, to cite the most obvious.

The musicals of the 1970s brought fame to Stephen Sondheim, whose *Follies* (1970), *A Little Night Music* (1972), *Pacific Overtures* (1975), and *Sweeney Todd* (1978) all won major awards. *A Chorus Line* (1975) epitomized the 1970s as *Hair* had the 1960s. Moved to Broadway after a successful run at Papp's Public Theatre, *A Chorus Line* told of the lives and hardships of dancers auditioning for a Broadway show. Really little more than a loosely knit series of personally revealing monologues, *A Chorus Line* dazzled audi-

Figure 16-13. **Broadway: *Cats.*** Typical of today's Broadway plays, *Cats* is a musical comedy heavily dependent on spectacle; it was imported from London, where it proved it could be a commercial success. (© *1982 Martha Swope.*)

Figure 16-14. **Serious Plays: David Mamet.** *Sexual Perversity in Chicago*, shown here in production at the University of Iowa Theatres. *(Directed by James Finney.)*

ences through the energy of its dance and touched them with the intimacy of its revelations. Somewhere between a revue and a play, *A Chorus Line* accelerated Broadway's love affair with dance and spawned such imitations as *Dancin'* and *The American Dance Machine*. It also solidified the importance of choreographer-directors like Bob Fosse, Michael Bennett, and Tommy Tune. Indeed, by the late 1970s, with the notable exception of Hal Prince, every major director of musicals on Broadway was also a choreographer.

The 1980s echoed the 1970s, with Sondheim's *Sunday in the Park with George* winning both a Pulitzer Prize and a New York Drama Critics Award at mid-decade. Two imports from England (*Cats* and *Evita*), an adaptation from France (*La Cage Aux Folles*), and a rejuvenated old movie (*42nd Street*) joined *Dreamgirls* as the prize-winning musicals early in the decade.

SERIOUS PLAYS

Few significant serious pieces emerged either on or Off-Broadway. Some American playwrights from the 1950s continued writing (Lillian Hellman, Tennessee Williams, and Arthur Miller), but none achieved the acclaim formerly given their work. During the 1960s, Edward Albee won critical acclaim for plays like *Who's Afraid of Virginia Woolf?* (1962), *Tiny Alice* (1963), and *A Delicate Balance* (1966), but critics found less merit in his later plays.

During the 1970s and 1980s, critical attention shifted to David Rabe, David Mamet, and Sam Shepard. In plays like *Sticks and Bones* (1971), *The Basic Training of Pavlo Hummel* (1973), and *Streamers* (1977), David Rabe tried to make sense of America's military experiences. David Mamet attracted attention with *A Life in the Theatre* (1977), *Sexual Perversity in Chicago* (1977), and *Glengarry Glen Ross*, for which, in 1984, he was awarded both a Pulitzer Prize and a New York Drama Critics Award. In plays like *Tooth of Crime* (1972), *Suicide in B Flat* (1976), *Buried Child* (1978, for which he won a Pulitzer) and *Lie of the Mind* (1985, for which he won the New York Drama Critics Award), Sam Shepard treated the effects of American popular culture on art and social structure.

Several other American playwrights have shown promise (for example, Lanford Wilson, Charles Fuller, Marsha Norman, and Ntozake Shange), but their final impact cannot yet be assessed.

Despite some promising native playwrights, the American theatre would have been seriously impoverished had it not been for the continuing British imports. In the 1960s and 1970s, the work of British directors like Peter Brook (*Marat/Sade*, 1964; *A Midsummer Night's Dream*, 1970) joined the plays of dramatists like Harold Pinter (*The Birthday Party*, 1961; *The Homecoming*, 1967; *Old Times*, 1971; and *No Man's Land*, 1975) as significant additions to the American Theatre. More recently, works of Caryl Churchill (*Cloud Nine*) and Michael Frayne (*Noises Off*) have attracted American audiences. But during the 1981–1982 season, *The Life and Adventures of Nicholas Nickleby* (a dramatization of the novel by Charles Dickens) became the theatrical event against which all others were to be subsequently judged.

Figure 16-15. **Comedy: Neil Simon.** Phenomenally successful with American audiences for more than twenty years. Here the largely autobiographical *Brighton Beach Memoirs. (The University of South Carolina. Directed by James A. Patterson.)*

With $100 tickets and five-plus hours in the theatre, this importation easily ranked as the cultural event of the decade.

COMEDY

In comedy, American drama fared better, primarily because of Neil Simon, a playwright who has been phenomenally successful with audiences. Major plays from the 1960s (*Barefoot in the Park, The Odd Couple, Plaza Suite*) established his reputation as the master gag writer of the theatre. During the 1970s, that reputation was solidified with works like *Last of the Red Hot Lovers, The Prisoner of Second Avenue,* and *California Suite.* In the 1980s, Simon produced semiautobiographical plays that were acclaimed by audiences and reviewers alike: *Brighton Beach Memoirs, Biloxi Blues,* and *Broadway Bound.*

Although no one else has come close to Simon's success in comedy, other comic writers have kept commercial comedy a moneymaker. These authors and titles may suggest the ephemeral quality of much commercial comedy: in the 1960s, Jean Kerr (*Mary, Mary*) and Robert Anderson (*You Know I Can't Hear You When the Water's Running*); in the 1970s, Bob Randall (*Six Rms Riv Vu*) and Donald Coburn (*Gin Game*); and in the 1980s, Christopher Durang (*Beyond Therapy*), Beth Henley (*Crimes of the Heart*), and Wendy Wasserstein (*Uncommon Women and Others*).

Non-Western Theatre

It is possible to give only a brief survey of theatres outside the European tradition. The focus of this book has been the self-aware narrative theatre derived from that of ancient Greece and now the dominant theatre of Europe (including the Soviet Union), North America, and Central and South America. That theatre is now also important in most of the places to be discussed in this chapter, where a Western theatre form often exists alongside a non-Western (for them, traditional) theatre of quite different type.

International mass communication and high-speed, cheap transportation have made international cross-influences important factors in contemporary art. Cultural influence tends to follow political and economic influence. The present world position of the United States has given American culture great importance in non-Western cultures: McDonald's hamburgers appear in Tokyo, Coca-Cola cans alongside roads in central Africa. With these come films and television and, with them, ideas of impersonation and dramatization and theory different from indigenous ideas. The result is sometimes a mixture.

It is not always possible, therefore, to identify purely non-Western forms in non-Western cultures: cross-influence has already had its effect. Nor is it any longer possible, especially in former colonial areas (especially Africa), to say what—if any—theatre existed before the Western idea of theatre arrived.

"Ritual"

Africa, along with pre-Columbian North America, Southeast Asia, and parts of the Pacific, raises the unanswerable question of whether or not certain social and religious forms can be considered as theatre. Generally, these forms are lumped under the word *ritual*, although they include widely different activities in vastly different cultures.

Those "rituals" of non-Western cultures that are most often suggested as forms of theatre share certain common elements:

- Communal binding of all those present, so that the identifying characteristic is not "art" but "community."
- Overlap or eradication of lines between audience and performers.
- Purpose—to heal, to honor, to mourn—very different from the purpose usually given Western theatre (to instruct, to entertain, to make money).

In addition, such "ritual" events have characteristics that make them formally very different from theatre as we have defined it:

- Indifference to an established (theatre) space.
- Diffused focus; an event may take place over several miles of countryside, without audience or with audience unable to see any but flashes of the event.
- Lack of visual clues to locale or anything resembling scenery.

Some Western theatre people, however, have been drawn to such "rituals" because of their incorporation of elements sometimes found in Western theatre:

- Masks.
- Costumes.
- Dance and music.
- "Text," although not written text; rather, an orally transmitted, sometimes improvised one.

Figure 17-1. **Mask.** Many social activities, including "ritual" and theatre, use masks. This one is from West Africa.

Paratheatrical Forms

Other than these still-debated "rituals," traditional non-Western forms that are related to theatre and that have received much attention from Western theatre scholars include:

- Storytelling, often with music (or at least drumming) and mime; for example, the *griot* of West Africa and the *meddah* of Turkey.
- Cultural transmission—the passing on of knowledge in cultures without writing. This varies enormously, from simple but expert pantomime of birds and animals (Botswana Bushmen) to elaborate instruction in traditions through pantomime, song, and dance.
- Dance, often with narrative and elaborate theatrical effects, especially costumes and masks—for example, the elaborate temple dances of Southeast Asia.
- Puppet theatre—for example, the Karagoz shadow puppets of Turkey and the large Bunraku puppets of Japan.

Neither "ritual" nor these other forms are discussed here as kinds of theatre, although elements of them appear clearly in several non-Western theatres.

Africa

Africa is a huge and diverse continent. Its precolonial cultures were many and varied, and they persist as both tribal heritages and individual languages.

379

Figure 17-2. **African Drama.** Chris Nwamuo's *The Prisoners* at the Nigerian Universities Theatre Arts Festival, 1986.

The modern boundaries of Africa are often the boundaries of convenience set up by European colonizers. The colonial period, although relatively short, changed Africa radically; when new African nations became independent in the late 1950s and 1960s, they had to cope with the conflicting realities of old and new, of tribalism and colonialism, of Western and non-Western. By and large, they have done this well, but not without struggle and not without failures. The continent continues to have enormous economic difficulties, particularly as its populations increase and its need for industrialized goods grows. Conditions in many of these countries have not been conducive to the creation of theatre.

For our purposes, Africa can be considered in five geographical areas:

- North Africa, which is considered here with the Islamic world.
- Central Africa, whose theatre has not been a major art.
- West Africa, particularly Ghana and Nigeria.
- East Africa, particularly Kenya.
- South Africa.

The colonial influence on these last three areas was primarily British, with an important French presence in parts of West Africa. Many contemporary theatre artists, therefore, have theatrical or educational experience in Europe, and many are attuned to English or French as the language of criticism, and often of drama.

As well, the universities have commonly become theatre centers. If not specifically Western, the universities are nonetheless modern institutions with structures like those of the industrial nations' universities, which they often emulate. They frequently have departments of drama and grant advanced drama degrees. Thus, even while being the main force in encouraging a native theatre, the universities exist in a Western environment. The African universities most important to the growth of theatre have been the University of Ibadan (Nigeria), the University of Ghana, the University of Dar es Salaam (Tanzania), Makerere University (Uganda), and the University of Nairobi (Kenya).

WEST AFRICA

GHANA.   A native theatre form, concert party theatre, emerged in the 1920s. (*Concert party* is itself a British term.) It was narrative vaudeville, sometimes funny but sometimes serious, dealing mostly in subjects from domestic life. The leading figure was Ishmael Johnson, called the first professional actor in Africa. Efua Sutherland, one of Ghana's outstanding dramatists and theatre artists, has said that "Concert Party Theatre is the only fully evolved indigenous form of theatre. . . . It enjoys a countrywide appeal."

In the 1950s, the Ghana Drama Studio (Accra) was founded by Efua Sutherland. There, she produced new Ghanaian plays, including her own *Foriwa* (1967). Ama Ata Aidoo (also a woman) is the author of *Anowa* (1970) and other plays. Both dramatists, as well as others in Ghana's theatre, have had close connections with the University of Ghana. More recently, playwrights like J. C. de Graft (*Muntu,* 1976) and Asiedu Yirenkyi have gained notice.

NIGERIA.   Nigeria is a very large nation with dense population centers and many universities. Out of one of its dominant languages, Yoruba, has come a traditional masked performance, the Alarinjo, on which the "father figure" of Nigerian theatre (as one Nigerian critic has called him), Hubert Ogunde, drew. Creator of a native concert party form, Ogunde wrote and produced many plays (*Yoruba Ronu,* 1964) for his own traveling troupe and was a seminal figure in an indigenous form, Yoruba opera. Rich in music, Yoruba opera is performed by touring companies that are able to create with Yoruba audiences some of the communal feeling of ritual. In part, this communality is possible because of the plays' use of traditional stories and moral ideas. Other important Yoruba-opera actor-dramatists have been Kola Ogunmola and Duro Lapido, the latter the head of the Duro Lapido National Theatre.

Unquestionably, however, the most important figure in Nigerian theatre has been Wole Soyinka, winner of the Nobel Prize for Literature in 1986. Soyinka's first play was produced while he was at the Royal Court Theatre in London; his later plays, like *The Trials of Brother Jero* (1964), have gained international acclaim and have (as with many African theatre people) got him

Figure 17-3. **African Theatre.** Femi Osofisan's *The Chattering and the Song*, with Irene Orubo and Jimi Solanke, produced at the Arts Theatre, the University of Ibadan. *(Directed by the author. Sheila Walker Jeyifous photo.)*

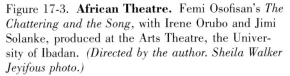

into trouble with the government during periods of stress. Nigeria continues to have an active theatre scene, with theatre training at several universities; such activity has encouraged newer playwrights like Femi Osofisan. (See Figure 17-3.)

EAST AFRICA

KENYA. Markedly different from West Africa, the East African nation of Kenya is distinct in both culture and language. Masks, for example, are virtually unknown in Kenya; the dominant language, Kiswahili, is not spoken west of the Zaire border.

The outstanding theatre figure of Kenya is Ngugi Wa Thiongo. Ngugi's plays and novels were concerned in the 1960s with the problems of independence and freedom from Western influence and, in some cases, with much earlier historical conflicts of his Kikuyu people (the education crisis of the 1920s, for example). However, plays like *I Will Marry When I Want* (written with Ngugi wa Mirii, 1980) have powerful implications for postindependence Kenya. As a result, Ngugi has had difficulty performing in recent years: his theatre company at the Kamiri Cultural Centre was forbidden to play in 1982, and he was for several years in detention outside Nairobi, the capital. He has left the country.

Elsewhere in East Africa, Tanzania has tried to encourage the growth of

Kiswahili theatre, and Uganda saw the beginnings of a native theatre, but political events—particularly the waves of violence in Uganda from the late 1970s on—have muted the importance of theatre.

CHARACTERISTICS OF EAST AND WEST AFRICAN THEATRE

Distinct as they are in language, East and West African theatre share certain characteristics. Their common colonial history and strong efforts at pan-African awareness have, perhaps, tended to bring them together despite obstacles.

The theatres have in common:

- Frequent connections with the universities, especially cultural centers and departments of African studies.
- Use of (mostly) amateur performers.
- Openness to various kinds of theatre space.
- A developing body of indigenous theory and criticism.

As well, certain qualities are common to their dramas:

- Extensive use of nonrealistic elements, especially music and dance.
- Extensive use of recognizable cultural elements: proverbs, drumming, cultural symbols, gestures, history.
- Didacticism.
- Openness to dramatic symbolism, including symbolic character.
- Looseness of structure and largeness of cast, idea, and scope.
- Use of both African and Western languages—typically English or French, a regional language (Yoruba, Hausa, or Kiswahili), and sometimes a tribal one.

These African plays are not as well known as they should be in the United States, perhaps precisely because of their most typical elements, which make them very different from Western commercial realism.

SOUTH AFRICA

South Africa remains a colonial nation in that power is vested in its white minority. As a result, its most visible art is colonial, and theatre is Western theatre in the white areas of the cities.

A playwright of great international importance has appeared in this ambivalent situation: Athol Fugard. Widely produced in Europe and the United States, Fugard is the author of plays that accept the current Western idea of drama as their base. Usually realistic, these plays have made powerful

Figure 17-4. **South African Theatre.** Thelma Pooe in Matsemala Manaka's *Children of Asazi*, directed by the author. Part of *Woza Afrika*, a festival of South African theatre first presented in the United States at Lincoln Center for the Performing Arts, New York. *(Photo courtesy of the New Playwrights Theatre, Washington, D.C.)*

presentations of the South African racial crisis on the world's stages—for example, the 1982 success of *'Master Harold'* . . . *and the Boys.*

In the black townships of South Africa, it appears that a theatre that is less clearly Western has come into being. Censorship in South Africa mutes our awareness of this theatre, but appearances like Woza Afrika's in the United States in 1986 and 1987 show that an indigenous drama and theatre are vigorous.

The Islamic World

With the appearance of the prophet Muhammad in the late sixth century A.D., a new religion, Islam, spread rapidly from the Arabian peninsula: north into the Near East; west along all of Mediterranean Africa and down the East African coast; and east into India and Southeast Asia. For complex reasons, the world of Islam was hostile to theatre (although not to storytelling, puppetry, and dance). As well, it drastically limited the public life of women, including their appearance on the stage.

Islamic peoples developed a highly sophisticated literature, especially in Persian and Arabic, along with other arts; theatre, however, was largely ignored until the nineteenth century. Turkey was an exception.

TURKEY

The Seljuk Turks were Islamic but not Arabic. They conquered what was left of the Byzantine Empire, taking Constantinople in 1453. They thus became the last heirs of what was left of Rome—and perhaps of Rome's theatre.

The Seljuk rule was fairly tolerant and allowed residence by foreign enclaves, including Jews and Christians. Occupying parts of modern Rumania, Bulgaria, and Greece, as well as Turkey, the Seljuks maintained contacts with both Europe and the East. Their successors, the Ottoman Turks, founded a new empire that, in turn, weakened until, following their alliance with Germany during World War I, they were replaced by a republic under Kemal Attaturk. The new government brought about the emancipation of women, then the founding of a state theatre and conservatory in the 1930s, led by Muhsin Ertugrul. Contemporary Turkey has professional theatre companies that perform Western and Turkish plays, and Turkey has a vigorous film industry.

TRADITIONAL TURKISH THEATRE. Turkey also had a popular, traditional theatre that has now effectively disappeared. A popular comic form called *orta oyunu* persisted into the twentieth century. Although its origins are not known, scholars suggest that it may be a continuation of Byzantine mime, taken over by the Seljuk Turks after their conquest of Constantinople. Some similarities to Italian *commedia dell'arte*—comic regional types, improvisation, stock costumes and characters—suggest influence but may be the result of a common root or may be coincidence.

Orta oyunu was performed by traveling troupes that included actors, dancers, and musicians; at the end of the nineteenth century, there were said to be as many as five hundred such performers. At the head of each troupe was the actor who played Pisekar, the central figure; opposite him was the actor who played Kavuklu, his comic foil. Women's roles were played by men. The tone was populist, sometimes rowdy. Playing usually in the open without scenery, the *orta oyunu* actors relied on mimicry, comic exaggeration, and theatrical use of the body. Important characteristics of this form of theatre were

- Freedom from established theatre spaces.
- Popularity of subject and language.
- Lack of scenery, except for an all-purpose cloth enclosure or tent.
- Continuity of characters over many years.

NONTRADITIONAL ISLAMIC THEATRE

A nontraditional theatre is known in Islamic countries, particularly since the late nineteenth century. Generally, such theatre has been the result of Western influence or of imitation of the West. The development of an Islamic theatre apparently came about because of European domination of certain Islamic

Figure 17-5. **Turkish Theatre.** M. Engin Erim's *Butun Menekseler Annem Kokar*, at the Turkish State Theatres, Ankara. *(Directed by Semih Sergen. Courtesy of the Turkish Culture and Tourism Office, Washington, D.C.)*

areas: France in Lebanon; Great Britain in Egypt, Syria, and what is now Jordan; and Italy in Somalia. Following European example, young dramatists began to write and produce plays in Damascus and Cairo, and Cairo became the center for a theatre heavily dependent on music. An important figure early in the twentieth century was the actor-manager Hijazi.

A few women had appeared on the infant Islamic stage—most of them Christians and Jews—but after World War I, a liberal movement in Islam loosened some restrictions. In Cairo, a government-funded theatre was set up in 1948.

Modern Egyptian drama has been dominated by three people: Twfiq Al-Hakim, a pioneering intellectual playwright who showed the influence of both French and English drama; Nu'man 'Ashour, who first used spoken Egyptian, rather than classical literary Arabic, on the stage in plays like *The People Downstairs*; and Rashad Rushdy, called by one critic "the bedrock of the tragic form" for plays like *Egypt, My Love*.

Nonetheless, theatre in Islamic countries cannot yet be called vigorous, although film flourishes, especially in Egypt. Particularly since the rise of Islamic fundamentalism in the 1970s and the economic hardships of the same period, theatre has had the status of a minor, and perhaps a threatened, art. An Arab Theatre Foundation was created in 1985.

The East

Major traditional theatres have appeared in a number of cultures of the Orient. The cultures themselves have often been conservative and religious, with the result that arts—including theatre—have often been preserved centuries after their initial creative energies were gone. Elites within the cultures have often prized these arts, seeing in their preservation an expression of their own continuity. As a result, the modern nations that have emerged from these ancient cultures now typically display a dual theatrical sensibility: one track is re-creative and backward-looking, displaying the sensibility of a museum; the other is creative and forward-looking, displaying the sensibility of Western art.

Neither track is "better" than the other. Appreciation of the traditional theatres has changed; like great works of painting or sculpture, they are preserved for their beauty, even though their languages may no longer be the languages of discourse and their styles may be almost foreign. In many cases, experienced audiences for some of these traditional theatres follow performances with annotated scripts open before them, as some seasoned Western lovers of music follow orchestral concerts and operas.

As one Western scholar has pointed out, traditional Eastern theatre is an art of the "invisible world"—the world of religion, often a religion of demons, spirits, and multiple divinities. Generally, these Eastern traditional theatres are profoundly nonrealistic and share certain common elements:

- Highly stylized, dancelike movement.
- Nonrealistic makeup or masks.
- Non-Western dramatic form, meaning that they are not based on Aristotelian ideas of action, unity, and the interrelated parts of the play.
- Acting styles far removed from Western ideas of impersonation, often with radically different uses of the voice (so that Westerners have called some forms "operas"), for which years of rigorous training are required.

Despite similarities, however, traditional Eastern forms are so different from each other that one looks as foreign to an Easterner from another culture as it does to a Westerner.

Figure 17-6. **Eastern Theatre.** A modern performance of Japanese Kabuki. A scene from *Shibaraku*, a Kabuki classic. *(Courtesy of the Japan Information and Cultural Center, Washington, D.C.)*

The theatres that we shall consider come from three modern nations: India, Japan, and China.

INDIA

The multilingual culture of India was already old when Alexander the Great reached the Indus River in 27 B.C. The huge Indian subcontinent stretched from the icy Himalayas to the tropical Indian Ocean coast, broken politically into many units. Dominated early by pantheistic Hinduism, India saw a major shift to Islam in the north after the twelfth century. Europeans began to set up trading enclaves in the sixteenth century, and England began the period of the "British Raj" at the end of the eighteenth, dominating the entire subcontinent from the mid-nineteenth through the mid-twentieth centuries. Independent again after World War II, the subcontinent is now made up of the nations of India, Pakistan, and Bangladesh.

It is the modern state of India that maintains an important tradition of theatre, as well as a minor modern theatre and a world-famous film industry centered in Bombay, Calcutta, and Madras.

SANSKRIT THEATRE. Sanskrit was the spoken and written language of India, then of its ruling and intellectual classes, until a thousand or so years ago. It was the language of an important treatise on the theatre, the *Natyasastra*, and of the drama.

THE *NATYASASTRA*. Probably derived from oral tradition and ascribed to the "mythical" authority Bharata, the *Natyasastra* was a long treatise on theatre and drama, analogous to Aristotle's *Poetics*, probably written down between 200 B.C. and A.D. 200. Its basic assumptions were those of Hinduism: a universe of unity expressed through multiplicity, therefore aesthetically an art of multiple forms—dance, song, and poetry—unified through total performance into a form that would induce in the receptive audience a state of understanding—*rasa*. The *Natyasastra* is a valuable source of theatrical evidence, revealing an ancient India of touring professional acting companies that included both men and women; of permanent theatres built of wood and stone, with elevated stages and close connections to temples; and of rigid caste limits, restricting this kind of theatre to the high and elitist Brahmin caste.

THE DRAMA. Sanskrit drama included at least a thousand plays in the period A.D. 200–800. Of these, the plays of Kalidasa are best known in the West, and his *Sakuntala,* which reached Europe in the early nineteenth century, is the most often seen. In seven "acts," it follows a highly romantic love action between a king and the modest Sakuntala and includes the intercession of gods, a curse, and a ring that is lost and then found in the belly of a fish. Like much of Sanskrit drama, it took as its source the *Mahabharata,* which, with the *Ramayana,* is the great source work of Hindu culture. *Sakuntala* is a play of many scenes, places, and moods, unified not by action but by *rasa,* the state of perception and emotion (in this case, love) induced in the audience.

POPULAR OFFSHOOTS OF SANSKRIT THEATRE: KUTTIYATAM. Sanskrit, already the language of a small elite, became archaic after about 800; popular languages took its place. In many places in India, Sanskrit theatre absorbed or was absorbed into other forms; the results were highly varied. The most important extant form is *Kuttiyatam*, still performed in the state of Kerala, in southern India. It is characterized by:

- Inclusion of part or all of a traditional Sanskrit play.
- Interpretation of and comment on the Sanskrit by a popular figure, the Vidusaka, who can be satirical, comic, and parodic.
- Performance by family troupes of the *Chakyar* lineage, traceable to the tenth century in Kerala; these actors undergo years of rigorous training.
- Creation of an indigenous theatre architectural type, the *kuttambalam*, which has a square, raised stage with a pillar-supported roof; a rear wall with two doors and two copper drums (for rhythmic accompaniment); and an audience area surrounding the stage on three sides. The *kuttambalam* is built close to a temple so that the actors perform facing the deity.

Kuttiyatam performances go on for several, sometimes many, days. Like Sanskrit theatre, they include totally integrated dance, poetry, music, story,

Figure 17-7. **Eastern Theatre.** Kathakali, an Indian form. *(Courtesy of The Asia Society, New York. Photo, Clifford R. Jones.)*

and impersonation. Although aesthetically based in the *Natyasastra*, Kutti-yatam violates Sanskrit purity (its clowning has been called obscene, for example) but offers the possibility of adaptation and change, which pure Sanskrit drama did not.

NON-SANSKRIT THEATRE: KATHAKALI. Because of the great importance of movement, especially highly controlled and traditional movement, most Indian theatre has close affinities with dance. Certain forms are often called *dance drama* or *dance theatre* because the dance element is so important. Because they include story and impersonation, some of these forms can be included here; of them, a spectacular example is *Kathakali*, which, like Kuttiyatam, had its origins in Kerala.

Kathakali, like many Indian dramatic types, uses stories from the *Ramayana* and the *Mahabharata*; these are sung by one group of performers while others dance to the accompaniment of loud, fast drumming. No raised stage is used and there is no theatre structure: performers work outdoors on a flat earth square about sixteen feet on a side. The only light is an oil fire. There is no scenery. While the singers recite the text and the drummers pound, the dancers, in astonishing makeup and elaborate but almost abstract costumes, mime, sign, and dance, impersonating characters with intricate hand symbols, facial expressions, and body movements.

Most spectacular of Kathakali elements is the makeup, which can take all day to apply. The entire face is colored, then decorated with lines and planes of other intense colors. False "beards" of rice paste are built up; the eyes are reddened by the insertion of a special seed. In this theatre of the demonic and the divine, such utterly nonrealistic makeup is essential.

All Kathakali performers are male, and the dancers' training takes many years.

NONTRADITIONAL THEATRE. British residents of India built Western theatres as early as the eighteenth century and began to perform Western plays, to which some Indians were invited. In the nineteenth century, Western theatre became one of the foci of antitraditionalism, and a Western style of Indian drama emerged. The most influential among those who bridged classical and modern Indian styles was Rabindranath Tagore (1861–1941), India's first Nobel laureate. Tagore's ideal of a native drama that would provide a modern fusion of poetry, music, and movement, however, has not been realized. The popular modern Indian form is film, not theatre, and outside cities like Calcutta and Bombay, professional secular theatre does not flourish. The Indian theatrical tradition is religious; the modern state—with its capacity for funding the arts—is secular. The gulf between the two is great.

JAPAN

Japan, situated on a chain of islands in the Pacific Ocean off the Asian mainland, developed early under Chinese influence and then, after about the fourteenth century A.D., rejected China and its ways. From then until the middle of the nineteenth century, Japan turned inward, deliberately turning its back on the outside, particularly the West, except for minor trading contacts. However, in the 1850s an American fleet "opened" Japan, and thereafter a pronounced political and cultural shift led to the rapid development of one of the world's great modern nations. Despite its defeat and heavy losses in World War II, Japan at the close of the twentieth century is a major technological and industrial power.

Several forces created traditional Japanese theatre: a feudal society with an emperor nominally at its top; a warrior ethic that made the samurai warrior a model and placed the military ruler at the actual head of state from the sixteenth through the mid-nineteenth centuries; and religion, including native Shinto ("the way of the gods"), Chinese Confucianism, and, above all, a form of Indian Buddhism, Zen.

Dance was probably fundamental to all Japanese theatre. Important dramatic theatre developed from or alongside it, incorporating movement forms that demanded special training. Like Indian theatre, then, Japan created an important dance form (Bugaku) and dramatic forms that were nonrealistic, preserved more or less in their ancient forms for hundreds of years.

Two of these forms are of particular interest.

NOH.   Noh has been called "the oldest major theatre art . . . still regularly performed." Poetic and austere, it is a theatrical expression of Zen Buddhism. Its originators were a father and son, Kanami (1333–1384) and Zeami (1363–1444), both professional actors attached to a temple. They wrote most of the

Figure 17-8. **Eastern Theatre.** Japanese *Noh. (Courtesy of the Japan Information and Cultural Center, Washington, D.C.)*

more than two hundred extant Noh plays, creating a body of work with certain rigid characteristics:

- A three-part structure of *jo*, *ha*, and *kyu*.
- A form based on the interaction of two characters—the *waki*, as it were an accidental confidant, and the *shite*, the protagonist—with a chorus.
- Classification of plays into five subject categories: god, man, woman, insanity, and demon.

Traditionally, a Noh performance took all day and consisted of five plays—one from each category, in the above order—and an introductory dance, the *okina*, which used an ancient Sanskrit (Indian) text. All five plays have the same active shape:

- *Jo:* the *waki* introduces himself and "travels" (to chorus accompaniment) to a destination symbolized by a pillar on the stage; the *shite* enters, and *waki* and *shite* engage in question and answer to reveal the *shite*'s reason for being at that place and his or her concern.
- *Ha:* the *shite* dances; the dance is related (as expression, narrative, or symbol) to the *shite*'s concern.
- *Kyu:* the *shite* appears in a new self called forth by the first two sections—for example, a possessing demon or a ghost. Resolution comes from this confrontation with hidden reality.

Noh plots are simple; their abundant exposition seems natural to a form that is concerned not with events but with the effects of past events. The protagonists are usually tormented figures—dishonored warriors, crazed women, guilty priests—whose appearance in the *kyu* section in a different form is, to a Westerner, a kind of exorcism. Profoundly influenced by Zen Buddhism, however, Noh's ideology is intuitive, not rational, and its goal is an understanding reached by a mental leap from appearance to reality.

Modern Noh performances rarely include five plays because of the plays' length and difficulty. The style and staging, however, remain largely unchanged:

- A small, raised stage, with all entrances made along a raised passage (*hashigakari*) at one side; at the rear is a wall with a pine tree painted on it.
- Onstage musicians (three percussionists and flute) and chorus, soberly costumed and unmasked.
- Male performers, with the male voice undisguised for female roles.
- A very deliberate tempo.
- Masks for certain characters.
- Elaborate and beautiful costumes, but no scenery, and rare, often symbolic properties.

Figure 17-9. **Eastern Theatre.** Japanese *kyogen*, a comic form associated with the *Noh*. From an 1895 painting by the American artist John La Farge.

Noh had an important offshoot: Kyogen.

KYOGEN. Of later (fifteenth-century) creation but based in much earlier forms, Kyogen is a comic drama performed between Noh dramas. It seems a contradiction, for it mocks the very austerity and aristocratic spirituality that make Noh what it is. The reason usually given is that Kyogen was written by commoners at a period when commoners attended Noh performances; Kyogen expressed their attitudes. Kyogen is very funny, dealing in the universals of comedy. Its most typical character is a comic servant who serves a feudal lord and is, of course, smarter than he. Kyogen used the Noh stage but no orchestra or chorus.

KABUKI.   Although it owes some characteristics to Noh, the far more robust and spectacular form of Kabuki, which appeared in the seventeenth century, quickly established itself as a different and far more popular form. Early censorship actually strengthened the form, leading to much more active and diverse texts (when music and dance were temporarily suppressed) and much more carefully defined acting (when first women, then young men, were banned from the stage).

In its developed form, Kabuki's principal characteristics are:

- Long, fully developed actions in multiact structures.
- Multiplicity of characters and scenes.
- Illusionism, with direct imitation of contemporary (seventeenth-century) life.

The Kabuki also developed its own theatre and style, which included:

- A large raised stage with a raised walkway to it, the *hanamichi*, through the audience (originally, there were two such walkways and a connecting walkway at the rear).
- Spectacular scenery, including the revolving stage, introduced c. 1750 (the first in the world); trap doors; and a front curtain.
- Elaborate but fundamentally illusionistic makeup.
- Complex, beautiful costumes, including the spectacular feature called *hikinuki*—costumes so constructed that at a gesture they completely change, literally turning themselves inside out to reveal, for example, a man in armor where a woman had stood.
- All-male companies, with the art of the female impersonator carried to great detail; as a result, Kabuki became above all an actor's, rather than a playwright's, art. Great Kabuki actors have been declared national treasures, like great paintings or great buildings.

Kabuki stories were drawn from many sources and were often heroic and "romantic." Whereas Noh is a theatre of resignation and withdrawal from the world, Kabuki is a theatre of confrontation and an embracing of the world.

NONTRADITIONAL JAPANESE THEATRE.   The abrupt influx of Western ideas in the nineteenth century corresponded roughly with the rise of dramatic realism in the West. The result was the somewhat exotic blossoming of several imitations of Western theatre, some of them not very well understood by their practitioners. Two important trends appeared before the end of the century:

- "Political" theatre—the use of a more or less realistic style for partisan plays as Japan encountered party politics.
- Shimpa—a melodramatic, popular form neither Eastern nor Western, using elements of both, including women in female roles.

In addition, a modern theatre that kept pace with theatrical changes in the West emerged after the turn of the century. Although not widely popular, it introduced major Western forms and encouraged a Japanese acting style distinct from Kabuki.

Until the 1930s, leftist and proletarian theatres were important; however, censorship under the war governments of the 1930s and 1940s virtually ended modern drama for that period. After World War II, the American occupation government imposed a new kind of censorship—this one prejudicial to Kabuki and traditional forms—and modern theatres began to appear again. A new Japanese play, Junji Kinoshita's *Twilight Crane* (1950), has been called "a milestone in the history of modern Japanese playwriting"; it successfully fused Japanese art with modern concerns and was widely produced.

Recent nontraditional hits have emphasized plays as diverse as a musical version of *Gone with the Wind* and the plays of Shakespeare. Japan's large

Figure 17-10. **Eastern Theatre.** Nineteenth-century Japanese *kabuki*, from a British publication.

cities now have professional nontraditional troupes, but theatre is not a truly popular art; like India, Japan is in love with film.

CHINA

Like India's, China's is an ancient culture that developed in a region of diverse geography and languages. Nonetheless, while Europe was struggling to create order after the collapse of Rome, China was already a stable empire whose central administration effectively governed a vast area. Invaders changed the governors but not the institutions of government, and, until the early twentieth century, Chinese society and Chinese culture existed self-sufficiently, exerting influence on Japan and Southeast Asia.

Central to Chinese society were reverence for the past ("ancestor worship") and Confucianism, a moral system based in ideas of stability and family. Social order was strongly marked. Literacy was limited to a small group. Trade and the amassing of wealth were despised. Paradoxically, then, a popular theatre developed whose actors were social outcasts and whose patrons were often wealthy merchants.

The last imperial government of China fell in 1906. Thereafter, more or less stable, more or less democratic governments held on until the Japanese invasion in 1937 and World War II, when much of the country was overrun. In 1949, a Communist government under Mao Zedong (old style, Mao Tse-tung) took over. The Cultural Revolution of 1966–1976 saw much traditional Chinese culture attacked. Since Mao's death in 1976, Chinese life has been liberalized.

A civilization of many languages and many geographical areas produces

Figure 17-11. **Eastern Theatre.** Beijing (Chinese) opera. The great actor Mei Lan Fang in a woman's role. (*Courtesy of* China Pictorial *and the Embassy of the People's Republic of China.*)

many kinds of theatre. One scholar estimates that more than three hundred regional styles of Chinese theatre exist. Nonetheless, they are represented by—and to some extent are being absorbed by—one of them.

CHINESE OPERA. The Western designation of Chinese theatre as "opera" suggests one of its major characteristics: reliance on song and musical accompaniment. Chinese music is very different from Western music, and the style of production is very different from that of Western opera, but the name persists. Significantly, too, it accurately reflects the minor role of dance in Chinese theatre.

Early precursors included a form of theatre known as early as the ninth century A.D., for which a palace theatre school, the Pear Garden, was established. In the fourteenth-century Yuan dynasty, China's most important dramas were written. Yuan drama included:

- Performance by both men and women.
- Multiact dramatic structure, with one major song per act.
- Division of characters into four types: man, woman, and two types of clowns.
- Reliance on classical novels and history for stories and characters.

A great play of the Yuan period, still performed, was Gao Ming's *The Lute Song* (c. 1360). Hundreds of other plays were written, produced by traveling troupes of actors in temporary theatres throughout southern China.

Classical Chinese theatre as it is now understood—called *Beijing opera* after the city where it appeared (formerly called Peking)—developed in the nineteenth century on the foundation of Yuan and other forms. It is typified by:

- Multiact dramas.
- All male actors.
- Song and music virtually throughout.
- Division of characters into four major types: male, female, painted face, and clown (*painted face* referring to those using elaborate makeup, e.g., demons and warriors).
- A reliance on traditional sources for stories and characters.

Although the tradition of itinerant actors continued (troupes rarely stayed at the same theatre more than a few days, even in big cities), permanent theatres were built. Beijing opera in the nineteenth century became an enormously popular form. Leading actors moved from one theatre to another in the way that Western opera stars move; the repertory was generally so well known that without rehearsal, they could step into a part in any theatre. The performances themselves relied on centuries-old conventions, on stages all of the same type. Outstanding elements included:

- A raised, pillared stage with an audience on three sides.
- No scenery, entrances left and right, and restriction of large properties to chairs and tables (which could be used as walls, mountains, and so on).
- An acting style removed from reality, the result of up to twenty years of rigorous training in every gesture and slightest facial movement.
- An onstage orchestra and property man.
- Symbols and signs—for example, carrying a whip symbolized riding, and running with small flags symbolized wind.
- Almost unbelievable acrobatics—used, for example, in battle scenes.

Western accounts of nineteenth-century Beijing opera performances described remarkable noise—laughing, talking, and socializing; the orchestra tuning its instruments; actors in a scene but not active drinking tea or blowing noses—but these descriptions may have reflected a corrupt, late stage. However, authorities agree that Beijing opera, like Kabuki, was an actor's art: audiences came to see the great actor only at his great moments. By the late nineteenth century, the rest was a social event. For those great moments, however, there was quiet, and adulation afterward.

One name stands out in later Beijing opera: Mei Lan Fang (1894–1943). A superb actor of women's roles, he toured extensively in the West, restored some classical elements to Beijing opera, and was a force for the preservation of the form through World War II. His memoirs are an important record of actor training and theatre history.

Figure 17-12. **Eastern Theatre.** Facial makeup for roles in Beijing opera. A *jing* actor makes up before a performance. *(Courtesy of China Pictorial, and the Embassy of the People's Republic of China.)*

NONTRADITIONAL CHINESE THEATRE. The fall of the last dynasty loosened antitraditional feelings; antitraditionalists turned West. *Uncle Tom's Cabin* was one of the first non-Chinese plays produced (1911). Others followed, bringing disturbing innovations: popular, rather than classical, language; non-Confucian social and moral questions; all-spoken (not sung) drama; and, after 1924, actresses in female roles. The first coeducational theatre school was created in 1930. A new drama emerged, typified by Ts'ao Yu's *Thunderstorm* and his play of World War II, *Metamorphosis*, which encountered difficulties with both the Communists and the anti-Communists.

With the Communist rise to power in 1949, Chinese theatre went into a period of change, some of it under Russian influence (evident in the introduction of classical ballet, for example). It was wrenched from any illusion of stability by the Cultural Revolution in 1966. Led by Jiang Qing, wife of Mao Zedong (and herself a former minor actress), an attack was launched on traditional theatre, and a new drama of revolutionary heroism was preached. A model opera, *Taking Tiger Mountain by Strategy*, was produced, incorporating conventions of Beijing opera but relentless in its revolutionary emphasis. The Cultural Revolution ended with Mao Zedung's death in 1976 and the arrest of Jiang Qing and the Gang of Four.

Contemporary Chinese theatre includes traditional Beijing opera and modern theatre, as well as resurgent regional theatre forms. In addition, the Republic of China (Taiwan) preserves some traditional forms, and opera companies exist in the Chinese communities of Western cities like San Francisco.

Afterpiece

As even so short a glance at theatres of the nonWestern worlds as this one shows, the theatre is a most complex art. Each theatre is an expression and a reflection of its culture, and those cultures are themselves internally varied and immensely different from each other. Whether we look at the variations of Chinese opera, the local differences among Indian forms, or the richness of the many African types, we find more kinds of theatre than that one word can ever, it would seem, hope to cover.

When, then, we add these to the richness of our own theatre—classical tragedy, *commedia dell'arte*, musicals, avant-gardism—we are at first overcome by the sheer size of theatre as an institution. If, on top of this, we consider the many ways we have considered the subject—as history; as creative art; as critical object; as human study—we understand, at least, why theatre is the most comprehensive and the most human of the arts—the one most like human experience itself.

We said at the beginning of this book that a healthy art had variety and complexity. This enormous vigor makes it difficult but rewarding to study. We have said in many ways that theatre performance is temporary, that theatre happens only as we watch, a trait that makes it challenging to try to analyze. Such study and such analysis, we believe, make theatre a rewarding subject for continued study for many, for lifelong creative work for some.

Neither study of theatre nor work in it has any end but a personal decision to end. There is no last act, no final curtain. Further work beyond this introductory level, whether as scholar or artist, should be undertaken with what (we hope) has been this book's underlying point: that the greatest of world arts, however approached, is the source of great and lifelong enjoyment.

Glossary

(Discussion will be found on the page or pages indicated, where appropriate.)

A-Effect. See *Alienation*. (349)

Absurdism. A style of drama popularized in France after World War II that viewed human existence as meaningless and treated language as an inadequate means of communication. Major authors include Samuel Beckett and Eugène Ionesco. (346–347)

Academy. A group formed to further a specific artistic or literary end; for example, the French Academy and the rhetorical academies of the Renaissance. (282–283)

Action. According to Aristotle, a causally linked sequence of events, with beginning, middle, and end; the proper and best way to unify a play. More popularly, the single and unified human process of which a drama is the imitation. To some modern critics, an interaction (between dramatic protagonist and others).

Actor-Manager. A starring actor who is head and nominal artistic director of a company; for example, Sir Henry Irving in the late nineteenth century in England. (333)

Actors Equity. See *Unions*. (93)

Actos. Very short, politically significant playlets. Term associated with Chicano theater, particularly the work of El Teatro Campesino. (358–359)

Aesthetics. Study of the nature of beauty.

Agit Prop. Short for *agitation propaganda*. A kind of political drama popular in the 1920s and 1930s in America. Phrase subsequently used to describe all didactic drama whose social stance was unusually militant.

Alienation. Customary, but perhaps misleading, translation of the German *verfremdung*, "to make strange." Term now almost always associated with Bertolt Brecht's epic theatre, which aims to distance the spectator from the play's action in order to force conscious consideration of the political and social issues raised by the play. Shortened often to A-effect. (349)

Angle Perspective. Multipoint perspective; results when several vanishing points are located away from the center of the stage so that vistas appear toward the wings. (287)

Angle Wing. Wings consisting of two parts hinged together, one rectangular flat placed parallel with the proscenium arch and one (called the return) placed at an angle to it in order to increase the sense of distance. (On a raked stage, the return is not a rectangle but a trapezoid.) (279)

Antiquarianism. The study of the details of past civilizations, often with a view to reproducing historically accurate settings onstage. Movement was popular toward the end of the eighteenth century and is viewed as a precursor to Romanticism. (308–309)

Apron. That part of a stage that extends in front of the proscenium arch. (90)

Arena Theatre. A theatre in which the audience completely surrounds the playing area. Also called *theatre in the round*. (90)

Atellan Farce. A short, rustic, improvised, and often bawdy play especially popular in Rome during the first centuries B.C. and A.D. Possibly the forerunner of the *commedia dell'arte* (see entry). (234)

Audition. A session at which a theatre artist, usually an actor, displays his or her craft in order to secure a job. (149)

Autos Sacramentales. Vernacular religious plays of sixteenth- and seventeenth-century Spain. (270)

Ballad Opera. A "minor" form of musical drama especially popular during the eighteenth and nineteenth centuries in England and featuring political satire interlarded with familiar tunes for which new and topical lyrics were devised; for example, John Gay's *The Beggar's Opera*. (291)

Beat. A rhythmic unit in a play; defined variously by different actors and directors. (186)

Benefit. A performance, the profit of which is set aside for a particular actor, company member, or cause. In the eighteenth and nineteenth centuries, a primary means of supplementing an actor's annual salary. Now, any performance done for charity. (94)

Biomechanics. The concept and the complex of techniques devised by Vsevolod Meyerhold to train actors so that their bodies could be as responsive as a machine. (345)

Blocking. Stage movement for actors, given in rehearsal (usually) by the director. (175–183)

Body Language. Communicable emotional states understood from posture and other conscious and unconscious use of the body. See also *Gesture*. (137)

Book. 1. The spoken text of a play or musical; early musicals with stories and dialogue were called *book musicals*; 2. Several flats hinged together and folded together form a *book of flats*; 3. To *book* a production is to schedule a performance of it.

Border. Curtain, or less often flats or cutouts, suspended at intervals behind the proscenium arch to mask the overhead rigging. Particularly important in Italianate settings. (278)

Boulevard. Historically the permanent home of the old traveling-fair theatres of eighteenth-century Paris and later of the illegitimate houses where melodrama and comic opera flourished during the nineteenth century. Now refers to the district of the commercial theatres in Paris and means roughly what the word *Broadway* implies in the United States.

Box. Historically the favored, and most expensive, seats in a theater. Made by sectioning off parts of a gallery, boxes were spacious and outfitted with armed chairs, in contrast to the crowded galleries, whose seats consisted of backless benches, and to the pit, where originally no seats were provided. (88)

Box Set. Interior setting represented by flats forming three sides (the fourth wall being the proscenium line); first used around 1830 and common after 1850. (324)

Breeches Role. Role in which an actress portrays a male character and dresses as a man, presumably adding sexual titillation to dramatic interest. (309)

Broadway. In popular parlance, that area of New York City on and adjacent to the street named Broadway where the commercial theatre of America is concentrated. (91–94)

Bugaku. Traditional Japanese dance form. (391)

Bunraku. Traditional Japanese puppet theatre using half-life-size dolls manipulated by puppeteers visible to the audience. (379)

Burlesque. In eighteenth- and nineteenth-century theatre, a form of "minor" drama popular in England and featuring satire and parody. In America of the late nineteenth century and the twentieth century, a kind of entertainment originally dependent on a series of variety acts but later including elements of female display (including striptease) in its major offerings. After moving to the fringes of respectability by the 1940s, burlesque disappeared in the United States by the late 1950s.

Business. Activity performed by actor(s) at given points in a performance; for example, the *business* of lighting a cigarette or cooking a meal. See also *Lines of business*.

Byplay. Business that takes place alongside the primary action and that is slightly different from it; for example, in *Tartuffe*, Orgon's behavior under the table while Tartuffe is trying to seduce Orgon's wife.

Catharsis. Aristotle cited as the end cause of tragedy "the arousal and catharsis of such emotions [pity and fear]," a statement popularly understood to mean that tragedy "purges" fear and pity from the audience; but alternative interpretations suggest that tragedy arouses and satisfies such emotions within its own structure and characters. Highly controversial and elusive concept.

Causality. Belief that human events have causes (and therefore consequences); as a result, events are seen as joined in a chain of cause and effect.

Centering. Actor's term for localization of human energy source in the body, usually in the abdomen. (134)

Character. One of Aristotle's six parts of a play, the material of plot and the formal cause of thought; an agent (participant, doer) in the play whose qualities and traits arise from ethical deliberation. In popular parlance, the agents or "people" in the play. (53–56)

Chariot and Pole. An elaborate system for changing elements of the scenery simultaneously. Devised by Giacomo Torelli in the seventeenth century, the system involved scenery attached to poles that rose through slits in the stage floor from chariots that ran on tracks in the basement and depended on an intricate system of interlocking ropes, pulleys, wheels, and windlasses for their simultaneous movement. (279)

Chorus. In Greek drama of the fifth century B.C., a group of men (number uncertain) who sang, chanted, spoke, and moved, usually in unison, and who, with the actors (three in tragedy and five in comedy), performed the plays. In the Renaissance, a single character named *Chorus* who provided information and commentary about the action in some tragedies. In modern times, the groups that sing and/or dance in musical comedies, operettas, ballets, and operas.

City Dionysia. The major religious festival devoted to the worship of the god Dionysus in Athens. The first records of tragedy appeared at this festival in 534 B.C., and so it is called the home of tragedy. See also *Festivals*. (219)

Classical. Specifically refers to that period of Greek drama and theatre from 534 B.C. to 336 B.C. (the advent of the Hellenistic period). Loosely used now to refer to Greek and Roman drama and theatre in general (a period dating roughly from the sixth century B.C. through the sixth century A.D., about twelve hundred years.)

Climax. The highest point of plot excitement for the audience. (50)

Cloak and Sword Play (*capa y espada*). Romantic Spanish plays of love and dueling—swashbucklers. (270)

Closet drama. Plays written to be read, not performed. (47)

Comedy. A kind (genre) of drama variously discussed in terms of its having a happy ending, dealing with the material, mundane world, dealing with the low and middle classes, dealing with myths of rebirth and social regeneration, and so on.

Comedy of Manners. Refers most often to seventeenth- and eighteenth-century comedies whose focus is the proper social behavior of a single class. (289)

Comic Opera. A "minor" form of musical drama popular first in the eighteenth century and characterized then by sentimental stories set to original music. Later used to mean an opera in which some parts were spoken (in contrast to "grand opera," where everything was sung). (288)

Commedia dell'Arte. Italian popular comedy of the fifteenth through seventeenth centuries. Featured performances improvised from scenarios by a set of stock characters and repeated from play to play and troupe to troupe. See also *Lazzi.* (279–281)

Community Theatre. Theatre performed by and for members of a given community, especially a city or town. Usually amateur, with sometimes professional directors, designers, and business staff. (101–102)

Complication. Ascending or tying action. That part of the plot in which the action is growing tenser and more intricate up to the point of crisis (turning point), after which the action unties and resolves in a section called the *denouement* (see entry). (52)

Composition. Arrangement of visual elements for aesthetic effect. (180)

Confidant. In drama, a character to whom another leading character gives private information. (56)

Confraternity. In France, a religious brotherhood, many of which sponsored or produced plays during the Middle Ages. One, the Confraternity of the Passion, held a monopoly on play production in Paris into the 1570s. (249)

Constructivism. A nonrealistic style of scenic design associated with Vsevolod Meyerhold and marked by its view that a good set is a machine for doing plays, not a representation of familiar locales. Incorporated simple machines on stage and often revealed the method of its own construction. (345–346)

Continental Seating. First devised by Wagner in the late nineteenth century for his theatre at Bayreuth; eschews a central aisle in favor of entrances and exits at the end of each aisle. (315)

Convention. A way of doing things agreed on by a (usually unstated) contract between audience and artists; for example, characters' singing their most important feelings and emotions is a *convention* of musical comedy. (35–36)

Corpus Christi. A spring festival established in the fourteenth century in honor of the Christian Eucharist at which medieval cycle plays and cosmic dramas (see entry) were often performed. Also see *Festivals.* (269)

Corrales. Spanish theatres of the late middle ages, sited in open courtyards among houses. (269)

Cosmic Drama. Long dramatic presentations popular in the Middle Ages that depicted religious events from the Creation to the Last Judgment. Short plays were combined until the total presentation could last several days or weeks and occasionally a month or more. See also *Cycle play.* (255)

Court Theatre. A theatre located at the court of a nobleman. After the Renaissance, Italianate theatre, whose perspective was drawn with the vanishing points established from the chair of the theatre where the ruler sat, making his the best seat in the house. (218)

Crisis. Decisive moment at the high point of a rising action. (52)

Criticism. The careful, systematic, and imaginative study and evaluation of works of drama and theatre (or any other form of art). (208–209)

Cue. Immediate stimulus for a line, an action, or an effect.

Cycle Play. Medieval (especially English) dramas covering the "cycle" of history from the creation of the world to doomsday. See also *Cosmic drama*. (255)

Decision. In Aristotelian criticism, the most highly characterizing trait of a dramatic agent; the trait that translates idea into action and thus, in Aristotelian terms, unites with plot (in the sense here of action). See also *Plot* and *Action*. (62)

Declamation. A style of verbal delivery that emphasizes beauty of sound, speech, and rhetorical meaning rather than the realistic imitation of everyday speaking.

Decorum. In Neoclassical theory, the behavior of a dramatic character in keeping with his or her social status, age, sex, and occupation; based on the requirements of *verisimilitude* (see entry). (274)

Denouement. That part of the plot that follows the crisis (turning point) and that includes the untangling or resolving of the play's complications. (52)

Determinism. Philosophical stance undergirding Naturalistic drama that asserts that human behavior and destiny are determined by factors, especially heredity and environment, largely beyond human control.

Deus ex Machina. Literally, "the god from the machine," a reference to a deity who flew in at the conclusion of some Greek tragedies (particularly those of Euripides) to assure the play's appropriate outcome. Popularly, any ending of a play that is obviously contrived. (223)

Deuteragonist. In classical Greece, the second actor. (223)

Diaphragm. Large muscle, located atop the abdominal cavity, that forces air into and out of the lungs and thus figures prominently in the proper production of sound. (138)

Diction. In Aristotle, one of the six parts of a play; also called language; the formal cause of music, the material of thought; the words of a play. Popularly the proper and clear formation of the play's words. (50)

Didacticism. "Teaching." In the theatre, plays are didactic when they emphasize ideological content rather than artistic form.

Dimmer. Instrument for controlling the intensity of light by manipulating the amount of electricity that reaches individual lamps. (202)

Dionysia. A Greek religious festival in honor of the god Dionysus. The City Dionysia and the Rural Dionysia both included drama as a part of the celebration, but the city festival was clearly the dominant one of the two. See also *Festivals*. (219)

Diorama. Distant scene viewed through a cutout or other opening in scenery. Also, a three-dimensional arrangement of figures and painted scenes. (308)

Dithyramb. A hymn of praise, often to the god Dionysus, performed by a chorus of men or boys; a regular part of the religious festival of Athens after 509 B.C. (215)

Discovery Space. Permanent or temporary space in the Elizabethan (Shakespearean) playhouse that permitted actors and locales to be hidden from view and then "discovered" (or revealed) when needed. Location, appearance, and even invariable existence of the space are hotly disputed. (262)

Domestic Tragedy. A serious play dealing with domestic problems of the middle or lower classes. In the eighteenth century, a reaction against "regular" or Neoclassical tragedy. See also *Purity of genres*. (291)

Double. 1. To play more than one role. 2. *The Theatre and Its Double*, an influential book by Antonin Artaud, calls the Western theatre merely a shadow or *double* of the (to him) true and vital Eastern theatre.

Downstage. That part of the stage closest to the front. In early Italianate theatres, the stage floor was raked (slanted) up from the front to the back; therefore to move forward on the stage was literally to move "down the stage." (178)

Drama. 1. In the eighteenth century, a serious play (*drame*, in France) that dealt with domestic issues and thus failed to conform to the standard Neoclassical definition of tragedy. 2. Any serious play that is not a tragedy. 3. The literary component of performance, the *play*—often contrasted with the *theatre*.

Dramaturgy. Practice and study of creation of plays for the theatre; the work of the dramaturg. (209–210)

Dress Rehearsal. A final rehearsal in which all visual elements of production, including costumes, are used. Typically a rehearsal that strives to duplicate, insofar as possible, an actual performance. (187)

Drop. Backdrop. Large curtain, usually of painted canvas, hung at the rear of the stage to provide literal and visual closure for the stage setting. (278)

Dual-Issue Ending. Double ending. Ending of a play when good is rewarded *and* evil is punished. Associated with melodrama particularly. (302)

Eclectic(ism). Gathering of materials from many sources; popularly a mixture of styles and methods. In twentieth-century theatre, the idea that each play calls forth its own production style.

Educational Theatre. Theatre by and (in part) for students in an elementary, secondary, or collegiate setting. (99–101)

Eccyclema. In classical Greece, a machine used to thrust objects or people (often dead) from inside the scene house and into view of the audience. Probably some sort of wheeled platform that rolled or rotated through the *skene's* central door. (223)

Ensemble. A performing group. Also, a group acting method that emphasizes unity and consistency of performances.

Environmental Theater. 1. Theatre whose performance is the audience's environment, so that the performance surrounds some or all of the audience and the line between performance space and audience space breaks down. 2. Theatre done in nontraditional space.

Epic Theatre. Term originated by Erwin Piscator and popularized by Brecht to describe a theatre where the audience response is objective, not subjective, and where such narrative devices as film projections, titles, and storytelling are used. See also *Alienation*. (348–350)

Epilogue. A short scene that comes at the conclusion of the main line(s) of action.

Episodic plot. Plot whose incidents are connected by idea or metaphor or character, not by cause and effect. (51)

Existentialism. A philosophical system that lies at the root of absurdism (see entry) whose basic assumptions are the absence of transcendental values, the isolation of humans and their acts, and the lack of causality in the universe. (346)

Experimental Theatre. Any theatre whose methods or goals depart markedly from the mainstream of its day; thus, in the eighteenth century, Romanticism was experimental; in the heyday of American Realism, Absurdism was experimental.

Exposition. Necessary information about prior events, or a part of a play given over to communicating such information; because it is a "telling" and not an enacting of narrative, it is usually nondramatic. (51)

Expressionism. A style of theatre popular in Europe after World War I and typified by symbolic presentation of meaning, often as viewed from the standpoint of the main character; distortions of time, space, and proportion are common. (344–345)

Façade Stage. One that puts the actors in front of a neutral (non-representational) surface. (222)

Farce. Form of comedy "stuffed" with laughs that arise not from verbal wit or humane profundity but (usually) mechanics: business, mix-ups, mistaken identities, etc. (163)

Festivals. In Greece, religious worship took place in private and at major public festivals. In and around Athens, there were four festivals devoted to the god Dionysus. At three of these, records of drama appeared during the fifth century B.C. At the festival of no other gods can such records be found. See *City Dionysia*, *Rural Dionysia*, and *Lenaia*. During the Middle Ages, there were Christian festivals at which dramas were often produced. See also *Corpus Christi*.

Flat. A structure upon which scenery is painted, consisting of a wooden frame and canvas covering; usually of a size to be carried by one or two persons for shifting. Used in both Italianate staging and box sets (see entries).

Floodlights. Broad-beam stage instruments that "flood" a large area with light. (202)

Flying. Method of handling scenery for quick shifting by raising it out of sight over the stage with one of various systems of ropes, pulleys, counterweights, machines, and so on. Also, the illusion of flight in actors and properties through the use of concealed wires and the same system of ropes and pulleys.

Focus. The point or object that draws the eye of the audience to the stage picture. (180)

Followspot. Powerful, hard-edged lighting instrument mounted so that an operator can "follow" action with the light. (202)

Footlights. Light sources arranged along the front of a stage (between actors and audience) to throw light upward from stage level to eliminate shadows from harsh overhead lighting. Rarely used with modern lighting systems, but standard equipment with candle, oil, gas, and early electrical systems (c. 1650–1920). (202)

Forestage. That part of the stage in front of the scenery, especially in Renaissance stages, using a slanted floor for forced perspective in the scenic area. See also *Apron.* (278)

Formalism. 1. Strict adherence to established ways (forms) of doing things. 2. In scenic design, use of nonrepresentational shapes and forms as the design base. 3. In criticism, attention to matters of dramatic form and structure as distinct from philosophical and sociological issues, etc.

Functionalism. Aesthetic or artistic method that focuses on the function of objects (scenery, for example) instead of on prettiness.

Gallery. The highest audience areas in nineteenth-century theatres (box, pit, and gallery), hence, the cheapest seats; the balconies. (306)

Genre. In dramatic criticism, a category of plays: comedy, tragedy, melodrama, farce. Popularly, any category. (61–63)

Gesture. In one sense, any human act that conveys meaning (i.e., a speech is a gesture). In a more limited sense, a planned physical movement that conveys meaning, like waving a hand or pointing a finger.

Given Circumstances. In Stanislavskian vocabulary, those aspects of character that are beyond the character's or actor's control: age, sex, state of health, and so on. (146)

Glory. In medieval and Renaissance art, a cloud or sunburst in which divinities appeared. In the theatre of those periods, a flown platform made to look like a cloud or sunburst. (251)

Gradas. Covered bleacher-style seats at ground level in the Spanish *corrales* (which see). (270)

Graeco-Roman. That period in Greece and Greek lands when Roman domination had arrived, usually dated from C. 100 B.C. to the fall of the Western Roman Empire, C. A.D. 550. In theatre architecture, those Greek theatres that were remodeled to bring them in closer accord with the Roman ideals of beauty. (Not to be confused with Roman theatres built in Greek lands.) (232)

Griot. West African storyteller. (379)

Groove. A shallow channel in the stage floor in which a flat rode, for quick scene changes; a bank of several grooves would allow one flat to be pulled aside while another was pushed on in its place, seemingly in the same plane. (292)

Ground Plan. The "map" of the playing area for a scene, with doors, furniture, walls, and so on indicated to scale. (169–170)

Ground Row. A piece of scenery at stage level, often used to hide stage-level machinery or lights or to increase the sense of distance. (307)

Guerrilla Theatre. Didactic political theatre done in nontheatrical spaces — streets, factories, subways — without previous announcement; hit-and-run performances like guerrilla attacks. (356)

Guilds. Religious and, sometimes, trade or professional organizations in the Middle Ages that became the producers of civic medieval theatre. (249–250)

Hamartia. Aristotle's concept of error or failure of judgment by the tragic hero (sometimes translated inaccurately as "tragic flaw.") (231)

Hanamichi. In the Japanese Kabuki theatre, a walkway through the audience used by actors to get to and from the stage. (394)

Happy Idea. The basic premise on which a particular Greek old comedy was based. For example, the *happy idea* in *Lysistrata* is that women can prevent war by withholding sex. (282)

Hashigakari. In the Japanese Noh theatre, a walkway at the side of the stage for the actors' entrances and exits. (392)

Heavens. 1. Area above the stage: in the Elizabethan theatre, the underside of the roof that extended over the stage. 2. In the nineteenth century, the highest gallery. (261)

Hellenistic. 1. That period of Greek history dating from the coming of Alexander the Great (C. 100 B.C.). 2. In theatre architecture, those Greek theatres built during the Hellenistic period. (229–231)

Hero, Heroine. 1. A figure embodying a culture's most valued qualities (for example, Achilles in *The Iliad*) and hence the central figure in a heroic tragedy. 2. Popularly the leading character in a play or, more precisely, the leading male character in a play. 3. In melodrama, the male character who loves the heroine. See also *Protagonist*.

Heroic. Of or relating to a hero; by extension, exalted. *Heroic* couplets are two lines of rhyming iambic pentameter, probably an English attempt to reproduce the French Alexandrine, the approved verse for Neoclassical tragedy. *Heroic acting* stressed the vocal and physical grandeur of the actor. *Heroic tragedy*, popular during the seventeenth and eighteenth centuries, customarily treated the conflict between love and duty and was written in heroic couplets.

High Comedy. Comedy of intellect and language, usually emphasizing upper-class characters and concerns. See also *Comedy*.

Hireling. In professional companies of the Renaissance and after, an actor or technician hired by the shareholders to work for a set wage at a set task. (264)

Hikinuki. In Japanese Kabuki performance, the sudden transformation of a costume into a completely different one. (394)

Householder. Member of a professional company who owns a share of the theatre building itself. (263)

Humanism. That philosophy that believes that people should be at the center of their own deepest concerns. (258)

Idea. In Aristotelian criticism, the moral expression of character through language; more generally, the intellectual statement of the *meaning* (see entry) of a play or a performance. (56–58)

Identification. Audience attitude in which the audience member believes that important elements of himself are to be found in a dramatic character; the audience "identifies" with the character. A suspect theory. (75)

Illusion of the First Time. An expression used by an English critic (late nineteenth century) to describe the effect of good realistic acting: that is, the event seems to be happening for the first time *to the character.* (152)

Illusionism. Scenic practices (with analogs in acting, directing, and other theatre arts) that rely on a belief in the theatrical imitation of the real world. (307–308)

Imagination. In acting, inventive faculty of the actor. (See also *Instrument.*) More generally, that faculty of mind or feeling, usually thought to be nonlinear, imagistic, metaphorical, and playful.

Impressionism. A style of art that sought truth in the fleeting moments of consciousness. Prevalent in the drama and theatre of the 1890s, Impressionism was noted for its moody and mysterious quality. (242–243)

Improvisation. Acting technique or exercise emphasizing immediacy of response and invention rather than rehearsed behavior. (141–142)

Instrument. The actor's physical self. See also *Imagination.*

Interlude. A kind of dramatic fare performed between other events, as between the courses of a banquet. Important during the Middle Ages and the Renaissance and connected with the rise of the professional actor. (256)

Intermezzi. Italian entertainments usually given at courts and presented between other forms of entertainment. See *Interlude.* (269)

Interregnum. "Between the kings"—that period of English history (1642–1660) after Charles I was removed from the throne and before Charles II was restored; with a Puritan government in power, theatres were closed. (267)

Italianate Staging. A kind of staging developed during the Renaissance in Italy and marked by a proscenium arch and perspective scenery arranged in wing and drop. (275–279)

Kuttambalam. Theatre type used by an Indian *Kuttiyattam* (which see): square, roofed stage with audience on three sides. (389)

Kuttiyattam. Indian theatrical form, derived from Sanskrit drama. (389–390)

Kyogen. Japanese theatre form: comic interludes between parts of a Noh performance. (392–393)

Laughing Comedy. Specifically, comedy dating from the late eighteenth century and intended to restore the comic (laughing) spirit to the comedies of the age—in contrast to the then-popular sentimental or tearful comedies (See entry). (304)

Lazzi. Stock bits of business designed to provoke a particular response, usually laughter, from the audience. Associated particularly with the *commedia dell'arte* and the French farce of the seventeenth century. (280)

Lenaia. One of three major Athenian religious festivals devoted to the public worship of the god Dionysus at which drama was recorded. The home of comedy. See also *Festivals.* (219)

Lines of Business. A range of roles in which an actor would specialize for the major part of his or her acting career. Particularly important during the seventeenth and eighteenth centuries. (293)

Liturgical. Associated with the liturgy of the church; in drama, the kinds of plays that were done inside churches as part of the religious services and thus were performed in Latin, by the clergy, and were usually chanted or sung rather than spoken. (246–247)

Low Comedy. A kind of comedy that depends for its humor primarily on situation, visual gags, or obscenity. See also *Comedy.*

Ludi. 1. In Rome, festivals or *ludi* were given for public worship of a variety of gods and on various public occasions like military victories and the funerals of government officials. As drama was often included as a part of the festivals, they are important in a history of Roman theatre. 2. Early medieval term for plays.

Mansion. The particularized setting in the medieval theatre that, together with the *platea*, or generalized playing space, constituted the major staging elements of that theatre. Several mansions were placed around or adjacent to the *platea* at once — thus "simultaneous staging." See also *Platea.* (248)

Masque. Spectacular theatrical form, especially of the Renaissance and the Neoclassical periods, usually associated with *court theatres* (see entry) or special events. Emphasis was put on costumes and effects, with much music and dancing; amateur actors frequently performed. For example, Ben Jonson's many court masques. (266–267)

Master Artwork. *Gesamtkunstwerk.* Both team and concept popularized by Richard Wagner, who argued that such a work would be the artistic fusion of all major artistic elements, including music, into a single work under the artistic supervision of a single master artist. (312)

Meaning. Intellectual content suggested or inspired by a play or a performance. All plays have meaning, however trivial, and most plays and performances have several meanings. Best thought of as "range of meaning" or "world of meaning." (168–169)

Master of Secrets. That craftsman/artist of the medieval theatre charged with the execution of special effects in the dramas. (251)

Mechane. Machine, or *machina.* In classical Greece, a crane by means of which actors and objects could be flown into the playing area (orchestra). (223)

Medieval. That period of world history dating roughly from the fall of the Western Roman Empire (C. A.D. 550) to the fall of Constantinople and the beginning of the Renaissance (C. 1450). In drama, the period between 975, the first record of drama in the church, and C. 1550, when religious drama was outlawed in many countries throughout Europe. (244)

Melodrama. Literally "music drama." A kind of drama associated with a simplified moral universe, a set of stock characters (hero, heroine, villain, comic relief), rapid turns in the dramatic action, and a dual-issue ending. Leading form of drama throughout the nineteenth century. (62–63)

Method. The American version of Stanislavski's "system" of actor training. (146–148)

Middle Comedy. That transitional kind of Greek comedy dating from C. 404 B.C., the defeat of Athens by Sparta, and 336 B.C., the begining of the Hellenistic age. Less topical than Greek old comedy, middle comedy dealt more with domestic issues and everyday life of the Athenian middle class. (228)

Mime. 1. A kind of drama dating at least from the sixth century B.C. in Greece in which *unmasked* actors of both sexes portrayed often bawdy and obscene stories. The first *professional* performers appeared in the mime. In Greece, the form was never permitted in the religious festivals, but in Rome, it became the most popular kind of drama after the first century A.D. 2. Form of silent modern theatre.

Miracle Plays. Medieval plays treating the lives of saints. (254)

Monopoly. Legal control or exclusive domination of a theatrical locale; the courts of both France and England in the late seventeenth century, for example, granted licenses to a limited number of theatres that thus gained *monopolies.* (286, 288)

Morality Plays. Allegorical medieval plays, like *Everyman,* that depict the eternal struggle between good and evil that transpires in this world, using characters like Vice, Virtue, Wisdom, and so on. (258)

Motivation. In Stanislavskian vocabulary, the dramatic justification for an action or a set of behaviors onstage. (146)

Music. One of Aristotle's six parts of a play: the material for diction. Popularly, the kind of art form having harmony and rhythm. (60–61)

Musical. An American musical comedy, a form traceable to the mid-nineteenth century and now typified by a spoken text or *book* (see entry) with songs and (usually) dances and a singing-dancing chorus.

Mysteries. Medieval plays treating events based on the Bible or the Apocrypha and performed singly or in combination to produce the so-called cycle or cosmic dramas (see entries). (254)

Myth. Story with a religious or magical base, featuring a myth hero who typifies important features of the culture, for example, the myth of Oedipus (ancient Greece) or the myth of Skunniwundi (American Indian). In a less precise sense, some critics speak of the myth behind or imbedded in a work of narrative art and even of a dream, that is, the culturally important pattern that can be found there.

Naturalism. A style of theatre and drama most popular from C. 1880 to 1900 that dealt with the sordid problems of the middle and lower classes in settings remarkable for the number and accuracy of details. Practitioners included Émile Zola, André Antoine, and Maksim Gorky. See also *Determinism*. (316)

Natyasastra. Ancient Indian (Sanskrit) work on theatre aesthetics. (388)

Neoclassical. A style of drama and theatre from the Italian Renaissance based loosely on interpretations of Aristotle and Horace. Major tenets were: verisimilitude, decorum, purity of genres (see all of these entries), the five-act form, and the twofold purpose of drama: to teach and to please. (272–275)

Neoromanticism. Literally, "new Romanticism." A style of theatre and drama of the late nineteenth century that sought to recapture the idealism and exoticism of early nineteenth-century Romanticism. A reaction against the pessimism and sordidness of the Realists and the Naturalists. (341)

New Comedy. That form of Greek comedy dating from the Hellenistic and Graeco-Roman periods and treating the domestic complications of the Athenian middle class. A major source for Roman comedy. (230)

Noble Savage. A manifestation of *primitivism* (see entry) that depicted a romanticized view of primitive people and led to an artistic presentation of American Indians, African slaves, and so on as major figures in art. (296)

Obie. Awards given annually to performers, playwrights, designers, and productions that made significant contributions to the Off-Broadway theatre scene. Name comes from the first letters of Off-Broadway.

Objective. In Stanislavskian vocabulary, a character's goal within a beat or scene; the goal of a motivation (149)

Old Comedy. That form of Greek comedy written during the Classical period (see entry) and featuring topical political and social commentary set in highly predictable structural and metrical patterns. (228)

Off-Broadway. Popularly, those small, originally experimental but now often quite commercial theatres that are located outside the Times Square/Broadway area. Theatres with a seating capacity of fewer than three hundred that are authorized to pay lower wages and fees than are the larger, Broadway houses. (95–96)

Off-Off-Broadway. Popularly, the very small nontraditional theatres located in churches, coffee houses, and so on that fall considerably out of the commercial mainstream. Theatres with highly limited seating capacities that may be granted exemptions from a wide variety of union regulations and scales. (96–97)

Orchestra. 1. That area of the Greek and Roman theatre that lay between the audience area and the scene house. 2. Originally the circular space where actors and chorus danced and performed plays; later a half circle that was used as a seating space for important people and only occasionally as a performance area. 3. In modern times, the prized seating area on the ground level of a theatre and adjacent to the stage.

Organic. Suggesting growth from a definable beginning; developing naturally.

Orta Oyunu. Traditional Turkish comic theatre form. (385)

Pacing. Apparent rate of performance; partly a matter of speed with which the performance goes forward, but also related to intensity of action and complication and the artistic ways (actor's intensity, for example) that the action is realized. (181)

Pageant. In the medieval period, a movable stage, a wagon on which plays were mounted and performed in parts of England, Spain, and occasionally Continental Europe. By extension, the plays performed on such wagons. (253)

Pantomime. In the Roman theatre, a dance/story performed by a single actor with the accompaniment of a small group of musicians, particularly during the Christian era. 2. In the eighteenth and nineteenth centuries, a "minor" form of entertainment marked by elaborate spectacle and often featuring *commedia* characters and a scene of magical transformation.

Paratheatrical. Related to or parallel to the theatrical. Used to refer to activities tangential to theatre: circus, parades, and so on. (379)

Patio. Ground-level audience area in the Spanish *corrales* (which see). (269)

Performing Arts. Those arts that depend on a live performer in the presence of a live audience, for example, theatre, dance, opera, musical concerts. (5)

Performance Criticism. Objective analysis and explanation of performance (rather than of, for example, drama alone). (207–208)

Performance Theory. Objective description of the nature of performance (rather than of, for example, drama alone). (207–208)

Periaktoi. Stage machines in use by the Hellenistic period in Greece. An early method of scene changing that consisted of a triangle extended in space and mounted on a central pivot so that when the pivot was rotated, three different scenes could be shown to an audience. (241)

Period Movement. Actors' movements imitative or suggestive of the way people moved, or are thought to have moved, in another historical period. (194–195)

Perspective. Simulation of visual distance by the manipulation of size of objects. (276)

Phallus. Simulation of the male sex organ. In Greek old comedy and satyr plays, phalluses were enlarged and otherwise made prominent for purposes of comic effect. (224)

Phonetic. Relating to the human voice and human speech; symbolizing (in letters or pictures, for example) precise human sounds, as in the phonetic alphabet. (139)

Pictorialism. Directorial use of the proscenium stage's potential for creating pictures, for both aesthetic and ideological ends. (176–180)

Picturization. Directorial creation of stage groupings ("pictures") that show or symbolize relationships or meanings; storytelling through stage pictures. (179–180)

Pit. 1. Area of the audience on the ground floor and adjacent to the stage. Historically an inexpensive area because originally no seats were provided there and later only backless benches were used. By the end of the nineteenth century, a preferred seating area (now called the orchestra section). 2. Now refers often to the area reserved for members of the orchestra playing for opera, ballet, and musical comedy.

Platea. The unlocalized playing area in the medieval theatre. See also *Mansion*. (248)

Plot. 1. In Aristotle, one of the six parts of a play and the most important of the six; the formal cause of character; the soul of tragedy; the architectonic part of a play. 2. Popularly the story of a play, a novel, and so on. (50–53)

Political Theatre. The kind of theatre devoted to achieving political and social rather than artistic goals. (103–104)

Poor Theatre. Phrase popularized by Jerzy Grotowski and referring to the kind of theatrical production that is stripped of all (to him) inessential elements (scenery, costuming, lighting, etc.) and focuses only on the relationship between actor and audience. (367–368)

Possession of Parts. During the seventeenth and especially the eighteenth centuries, the practice of leaving a role with an actor throughout a career. Under the system, a sixty-year-old woman playing Juliet in Shakespeare's tragedy was not unheard of. (294)

Presentational. Style of performance and design that lays emphasis on *presenting* a theatrical event to an audience. Contrasts with representational (see entry) which stresses the reproduction of life on stage for an audience that merely looks on.

Preview. Public performance given prior to the official opening of a play, often to test the audience's response. (187)

Primitivism. Interest in life and societies of primitive people; associated in particular with the Romantic movement of the late eighteenth and early nineteenth centuries. (296)

Private Theatre. In Elizabethan and Stuart England, indoor theatres that were open to the public but were expensive because of their relatively limited seating capacity. Located on monastic lands, these theatres were outside the jurisdiction of the city of London. Initially they housed children's troupes, but later the regular adult troupes used them as a winter home. (262)

Probability. In drama, the internally closed system that allows each event in a play to seem likely and believable for that play (for example, the appearance of God in a medieval cycle play). (328)

Prologue. In Greek drama, that part of the play that precedes the entrance of the chorus. In other periods, a short introductory speech delivered by an actor, either in or out of character, to set the scene, warm up the audience, defend the play, or entertain.

Properties. Objects used on stage — furniture, cigarettes, dishware.

Proscenium (Theatre). Theatre building in which the audience area is set off from the acting area by a proscenium arch that frames the stage, protects the perspective, masks the backstage area, etc. The audience views the onstage action from one side only. (88)

Protagonist. In Greek theatre, the first (or major) actor, the one who competed for the prize in acting. Later, the leading character in any play (the "hero"). (225)

Psychological Realism. A kind of theatre that relies on a view of human behavior as defined by late nineteenth-century and twentieth-century psychology.

Purity of Genres. Neoclassical tenet that elements of tragedy and those of comedy could not be mixed. The injunction was not merely against including funny scenes in tragedy but also against treating domestic issues or writing in prose, these elements being of the nature of comedy. (274–275)

Raisonneur. In drama, a character who speaks for the author. (56)

Raked Stage. Stage slanted up from front to back to enhance the perspective. Stages began their rakes either at the front of the apron or at the proscenium line. (278)

Rasa. Important element of Sanskrit aesthetic theory — the inducing of an appropriate emotion in the audience. (388)

Realism. The style of drama and theatre dating from the late nineteenth and early twentieth centuries that strove to reproduce on stage the details of everyday life with a view to improving the human and social condition. (315–317)

Regional Theatre. Theatre outside New York City in the United States and Canada; term usually restricted to professional, nontouring companies. (97–98)

Rehearsal. The practicing of plays, either whole or in part, in order to improve their performance. (149–150)

Renaissance. Literally, "rebirth"; refers to a renewed interest in the learning and culture of ancient Greece and Rome. Beginning in Italy, the Renaissance spread throughout Western Europe from C. 1450 to C. 1650. (257–260)

Repertory. A set group of performance pieces done by a company is its repertory. Also, the practice in such a company of alternating pieces so that they are done *in repertory*. Loosely, a resident professional theatre company in the United States, called a *repertory theatre*.

Representational. A style of performance and design that lays emphasis on re-creating onstage aspects of daily life; the audience members are thought of as passive onlookers. Contrasts with *presentational* (see entry), a style that stresses *presenting* an event *for an audience*.

Restoration. The period of English history that dates from 1660, when King Charles II was restored to the throne. (288)

Reviewer. A person who views an artistic event and then writes his/her descriptive evaluation of it for immediate publication. (210–211)

Rhythm. Regular and measurable repetition. (180–183)

Rigging. The combination of ropes, lines, pulleys, pipes, and so on that permit the manipulation of scenic units backstage.

Ritual. Any oft-repeated act that has a specific goal. *Ritual theory*: a theory that asserts that drama derived from religious rituals (in Greece, for example, religious rituals devoted to the worship of the god Dionysus). (378–379, 215)

Roman. A period in theatre and drama dating from C. 364 B.C. to C. A.D. 550 and customarily subdivided into the Republican period (C. 364 B.C.–C. 27 B.C.) and the Empire (C. 27 B.C.–C. A.D. 550).

Romanticism. A style of theatre and drama dating from C. 1790 to C. 1850 and marked by an interest in the exotic, the subjective, the emotional, and the individual. Began in part as a reaction against the strictures of Neoclassicism; grew out of the eighteenth century's sentimentalism (see entry). (295–298)

Royalties. Payments made to authors (and their representatives) for permission to reproduce, in text or in performance, their artistic products (plays, designs, etc.). (117)

Run-Through. A kind of rehearsal in which the actors perform long sections of the play (or the whole play) without interruption, usually for the purpose of improving the sense of continuity, shaping the whole, and so on. (186–187)

Rural Dionysia. One of three Athenian festivals devoted to the public worship of the god Dionysus at which drama appeared. See also *Festivals*. (219)

Satyr Play. A short, rustic, and often obscene play included in the Dionysian festivals of Greece at the conclusion of the tragedies. (228–229)

Scaffold. In medieval staging in England, the localizing structure in or near the *platea*. See also *Mansion*. (253)

Scenario. In general, the prose description of a play's story. In the *commedia dell'arte*, the written outlines of plot and characters from which the actors improvised the particular actions of performance. (280)

Scrim. Mesh used in scenery; becomes transparent when lighted from behind, opaque when lighted from the front; useful for transformations, misty effects, and so forth. (342)

Script. Play text. See also *Text* and *Book*.

Secularism. Belief in the validity and importance of life and things on earth. Often contrasted with spiritualism, other-worldliness, or religiosity. The Renaissance period was marked by a rising *secularism.* (258)

Sense Memory. Recall of a sensory response — smell, taste, sound — with both its cause and the actor's reaction; important to the creation of a character's behavior in some theories of acting. (141)

Sententiae. Pithy, short statements about the human condition. Associated with the tragedies of Seneca and with those of his successors in the Renaissance. (235)

Sentimentalism. Prevalent during the eighteenth century, sentimentalism assumed the innate goodness of humanity and attributed evil to faulty instruction or bad example. A precursor of the Romanticism of the nineteenth century. (290–291)

Sentimental Comedy. A kind of comedy particularly popular during the eighteenth century in which people's virtues rather than their foibles were stressed. The audience were expected to experience something "too exquisite for laughter." Virtuous characters expressed themselves in pious "sentiments." (303–304)

Shareholder. Member of a sharing company who owned a part of the company's stocks of costumes, scenery, properties, and so on. Sharing companies were the usual organization of troupes from the Renaissance until the eighteenth century (and beyond), when some actors began to prefer fixed salaries to shares. (263)

Shimpa. Modern Japanese theatre form of mixed genres and origins. (394)

Shite. In Noh theatre, the protagonist. (392)

Shutter. Large flat, paired with another of the same kind, to close off the back of the scene in Italianate staging; an alternative to a backdrop; sometimes used for units at the sides. When pierced with a cutout, it became a "relieve" and showed a *diorama* (see entry). (278)

Sight Lines. Extreme limits of the audience's vision, drawn from the farthest and/or highest seat on each side through the proscenium arch or scenery obtruding farthest onstage. Anything beyond the sight lines cannot be seen by some members of the audience. (88)

Signature Music. Music associated with certain characters or certain types of characters, particularly in the melodramas of the nineteenth century. Stage directions indicate "Mary's music," "Jim's music," and so on. (302)

Simultaneous Staging. The practice, particularly during the Middle Ages, of representing several locations on the stage at one time. In medieval staging, several *mansions* (see entry), representing particular places, were arranged around a *platea,* or generalized playing space.

Skene. The scene house in the Greek theatre. Its appearance can first be documented with the first performance of the *Oresteia* in 458 B.C. Its exact appearance from that time until the first stone theatre came into existence (probably in the late fourth century B.C.) is uncertain. (222)

Slice of Life. Critical notion closely associated with Naturalism and used to describe plays that avoided the trappings of Romanticism and the obvious contrivance of well-made plays in favor of a seemingly literal reproduction of daily life on the stage. (317)

Soliloquy. An intensely emotional passage, often lyric, delivered by a person onstage alone.

Spectacle. One of Aristotle's six parts of a play, the part of least interest to the poet but of most importance in differentiating the dramatic form from the narrative and the epic. In everyday parlance, all visual elements of production and, by extension, particular plays, scenes, or events in which visual elements predominate. (61, 68–70)

Spine. In Stanislavskian vocabulary, the consistent line that connects all elements of a character through a play. See *Through line*. (148)

Stage Left. The left half of the stage as defined by someone standing onstage facing the audience. (178)

Stage Right. The right half of the stage as defined by someone standing onstage facing the audience. (178)

Star. Dominant actor or actress whose name and presence draw an audience. (332)

Star System. Company organization in which minor characters are played by actors for the season, while central roles are taken by stars (see entry) brought in for one production; still common in opera, sometimes seen in summer theatres. (332–333)

Stock Company. Theatre company in which actors play standardized roles and (originally) owned shares of stock in the company. (309)

Storm and Stress. *Sturm und Drang;* a theatrical movement in Germany during the 1770s and 1780s that was marked by its militant experimentation with dramatic form, theatrical style, and social statement. (299)

Story. Narrative; coherent sequence of incidents; "what happens." A general, non-technical term that should not be confused with *plot*. (71–73)

Street Theatre. Theatre, often political, that takes place outside traditional theatre spaces and without traditional theatrical trappings. (356)

Style. 1. Distinctive combination of elements. 2. In Aristotelean terms, the way in which the manner is joined to the means. 3. Particulars of surface, as distinguished from substance. 4. "The way a thing is done" in a time and place. (37–40)

Subtext. In Stanislavskian vocabulary, action "between the lines," implied but not stated in the text. (164)

Superobjective. In Stanislavskian vocabulary, the "life goal" of the character.

Surrealism. A style popular immediately following World War I that rejected every-day logic in favor of a free expression of the subconscious (or dream) state. (346)

Symbolism. A style of theatre and drama popular during the 1890s and the early twentieth century that stressed the importance of subjectivity and spirituality and sought its effects through the use of symbol, legend, myth, and mood. (343–344)

Technical Rehearsal. Rehearsal devoted to the practice and perfection of the various technical elements of the show (lighting, sound, flying, trapping, and so on.) (187)

Tendencies. In Stanislavskian vocabulary, aspects of an actor's performance that digress from the *through line* (see entry). (149)

Text. The written record of a play, including dialogue and stage directions; a play-script.

Theatre of Cruelty. Phrase popularized by Antonin Artaud to describe a kind of theatre that touched the basic precivilized elements of people through disrupting normal "civilized" expectations about appearance, practice, sound, and so forth. (352)

Three Unities. In Neoclassical (Western) dramatic theory, the unities of time, place, and action. (275)

Through Line. In Stanislavskian vocabulary, a consistent element of character running through a scene or a play. (148)

Thrust Stage. Dominant kind of staging during Shakespeare's time in England that is being revived in many contemporary theatres. Also called *three-quarter round* because the audience surrounds the action on three sides as the stage juts into the audience area. (88–89)

Timing. Actor's sense of tempo and rhythm. (180–182)

Tiring House. The building from which the Elizabethan platform, or thrust, stage extended. A place where the actors attired themselves. (261)

Tony. Annual awards made by the directors of the American Theatre Wing in memory of Antoinette Perry to recognize outstanding contributions to the current New York theatrical season.

Tragedy. In popular parlance, any serious play, usually including an unhappy ending. According to Aristotle, "an imitation of a worthy or illustrious and perfect action, possessing magnitude, in pleasing language, using separately the several species of imitation in its parts, by men acting, and not through narration, through pity and fear effecting a catharsis of such passion." At this point in theatrical history, almost indefinable.

Transformation. 1. Technique popularized in the 1960s whereby an actor portrayed several characters without any changes in costume, makeup, or mask, relying instead on changing voice and body attitudes in full view of the audience. 2. In medieval and Renaissance theatre, seemingly magical changes of men into beasts, women into salt, and so on.

Trap. Unit in stage floor for appearances and disappearances; varies from a simple door to complex machines for raising and lowering while moving forward, backward, and sideways. (308)

Tritagonist. The third actor in Greek tragedies. Typically played a series of minor and bit parts. (225)

Trope. An interpolation in a liturgical text. The medieval drama is believed to have been derived from medieval troping. (247)

Union. An alliance of persons formed to secure material benefits and better working conditions. Major theatrical unions are USAA (United Scenic Artists of America, for designers); Equity (Actors Equity Association, for actors); IATSE (International Alliance of Theatrical Stage Employees, for theatre technicians). (93)

Unity. Cohesion or consistency. When applied to a text, it refers to the method of organizing: unity of plot, unity of character, unity of action. When applied to design, it refers to how well all the visual elements fit together to achieve an artistic whole.

Upstage. The sections of the stage closest to the back wall. Comes from a time when stages were raked, or slanted, from the front to the back, so that upstage meant quite literally walking *up* the stage toward the back wall. (178)

Unit Set. A single setting on which all scenes may be played. (197)

Vaudeville. 1. In America in the nineteenth and twentieth centuries, vaudeville was popular family entertainment featuring a collection of variety acts, skits, short plays, and song-and-dance routines. 2. In France in the eighteenth and nineteenth centuries, *vaudeville* referred to *comédie-en-vaudeville*, short satiric pieces, often topical, that were interspersed with new lyrics set to familiar tunes and sprinkled with rhyming couplets *(vaudevilles)*. The form in France is roughly equivalent to the *ballad opera* (see entry) in England.

Verisimilitude. Central concept in Neoclassical theory and criticism. Literal meaning is "truth-seemingness," but used historically, at a time when *truth* referred to the general, typical, categorical truth. Not to be confused with "realism." (273–274)

Via Negativa. "The negative path." Popularized by Jerzy Grotowski in actor training; the necessity to strip away all disguises, masks, or protections of the performer so that he may begin work at a very basic and truthful level. (368)

Vidusaka. Ironic commentator in Indian *kuttiyattam* (which see). (389)

Villain. Character in melodrama who opposes the forces of good (represented by the hero and the heroine) and who, at the play's end, is punished for his evil ways. Typically the villain propels the action of a melodrama. (302)

Vocal Folds. Tissue in the throat over which air passes to make sound; incorrectly called *vocal cords*. (137)

Wagon. Wheeled platform that moves on and off a stage, particularly a proscenium stage; also, in medieval theatre, a movable scenic unit and playing area, or pageant (which see). (88, 253)

Waki. In Noh theatre, the second character, usually a confidant. (392)

Well-Made Play. A play written by or in the manner of Eugène Scribe and marked by careful preparation, seeming cause-and-effect organization of action, announced entrances and exits, and heavy reliance on external objects or characters to provide apparent connections among diverse lines of action. Now often used as a term of derision. (304)

Wings. 1. Scenic pieces *(flats)* placed parallel to the stage front, or nearly so, on each side of the stage; combined with overhead units for "wing-and-border" settings. 2. The offstage area beyond the side units of scenery — "in the wings." (From which is derived *wing space*, the amount of room offstage at the sides.) (278, 188)

Yoruba opera. Nigerian theatrical form. (381)

Zanni. In *commedia dell'arte*, the group of comic servants that includes Arlecchino, Trufaldino, etc. (280)

Index

Note: Pages in *italics* refer to illustrations.